AF693189

AI for Sustainable and Resilient Systems Engineering

by

ant

Table of Contents

Chapter 1: The Evolving Landscape of Infrastructure Systems

Infrastructure, the foundational backbone of modern society, is facing an unprecedented confluence of challenges. These systems, ranging from intricate transportation networks and robust energy grids to vital water supply and sanitation systems, are not merely physical structures but are complex, interconnected ecosystems that underpin economic activity, public health, and daily life. However, the very success and longevity of these systems have brought them to a critical juncture. Many of our most vital infrastructure networks are aging, having been constructed during periods of different demographic and technological realities. This aging presents a dual threat: increasing susceptibility to failure due to wear and tear, and a reduced capacity to meet the escalating demands of a rapidly evolving world.

The pressure on these aging systems is compounded by several powerful global trends. Foremost among these is the relentless march of urbanization. As populations continue to migrate from rural areas to cities, urban centers are experiencing an explosion in demand for services that these same aging infrastructures are expected to provide. This includes not only more housing but also greater capacity for transportation, energy, water, and waste management. The strain on existing networks becomes immense, often pushing them beyond their designed operational limits. This burgeoning demand necessitates not just maintenance but significant upgrades and expansion, a proposition that is both financially and logistically challenging. The sheer scale of population growth, both globally and within burgeoning megacities, means that the infrastructure deficit is not static; it is a dynamic and ever-widening gap that requires constant attention and innovative solutions.

Compounding these issues is the undeniable and increasingly disruptive force of climate change. The once predictable patterns of weather are giving way to greater volatility and extremity. Infrastructure systems, designed with historical climate data in mind, are now proving vulnerable to a new generation of environmental stressors. Extreme weather events – intensifying hurricanes, more frequent and severe floods, prolonged droughts, and extreme heatwaves – pose direct threats to the physical integrity and operational continuity of our infrastructure. Bridges can be undermined by floodwaters, power grids can be crippled by storms, water systems can be strained by drought, and heatwaves can buckle roads and compromise the performance of critical equipment. These events not only cause immediate damage and service disruption but also necessitate costly repairs and long-term adaptation strategies. The resilience of infrastructure is no longer a theoretical consideration but a pressing necessity, requiring a fundamental re-evaluation of design standards and operational protocols.

Beyond the direct impacts of aging and climate change, there is a growing imperative for resource efficiency. In an era of finite natural resources and heightened environmental consciousness, the way infrastructure is designed, built, and operated must become significantly more sustainable. Traditional linear models of resource consumption – take, make, dispose – are no longer tenable. Infrastructure projects are significant consumers of energy and materials, and their operational phases can generate substantial waste and emissions. The challenge lies in transitioning to a more circular economy, where resources are conserved, waste is minimized, and environmental footprints are reduced. This includes everything from selecting sustainable construction materials and optimizing energy usage in buildings and transport to improving water conservation and developing efficient waste management systems. The demand for greater efficiency is driven not only by environmental concerns but also by economic realities, as efficient systems often translate to lower operational costs and reduced resource dependence.

These multifaceted challenges – aging assets, escalating demand from urbanization, the disruptive impacts of climate change, and the urgent need for resource efficiency – collectively render traditional engineering approaches increasingly insufficient. The complexity, interconnectedness, and dynamic nature of modern infrastructure problems often exceed the capabilities of conventional design, analysis, and management techniques. Many of these issues involve non-linear relationships, feedback loops, and unpredictable external factors that are difficult to model using static, deterministic methods. For example, simply building a wider road might induce more traffic, or increasing the capacity of a water treatment plant might not solve underlying issues of leakage in the distribution network. The interconnectedness means that a failure or inefficiency in one system can have cascading effects on others. A power outage can cripple traffic signals, water pumps, and communication networks, illustrating how siloed approaches to infrastructure management are no longer viable.

Consequently, there is an undeniable and urgent imperative for innovation across all facets of infrastructure: in its design, its operation, and its maintenance. This innovation must move beyond incremental improvements and embrace transformative technologies and methodologies. The future of infrastructure hinges on our ability to develop systems that are not only functional and robust but also adaptable, resilient, and sustainable. This requires a paradigm shift in how we think about infrastructure – viewing it not as static assets but as dynamic, intelligent, and interconnected systems that can learn, adapt, and self-optimize. This evolving perspective calls for engineers to equip themselves with new tools and approaches, moving beyond traditional civil engineering principles to incorporate elements of systems thinking, data science, and advanced computational methods.

The drivers for this evolution are clear and compelling. The growing global population, projected to reach nearly 10 billion by 2050, will continue to place immense pressure on urban infrastructure. Furthermore, the increasing awareness of environmental limits and the tangible impacts of climate change demand a more responsible and sustainable approach to development. Coupled with rapid advancements in digital technologies, these pressures create fertile ground for the application of novel solutions. Among these, Artificial Intelligence (AI) stands out as a particularly promising and transformative technology. AI offers the potential to analyze complex datasets, identify subtle patterns, make accurate predictions, and automate decision-making processes at a scale and speed that were previously unimaginable. Its ability to learn from data and adapt to changing conditions makes it ideally suited to address the dynamic and complex challenges facing modern infrastructure systems. This book is dedicated to exploring how these advanced technologies, particularly AI, can be harnessed to meet the evolving demands and overcome the significant hurdles in designing, operating, and maintaining the critical infrastructure of the 21st century and beyond.

The concept of sustainability, when applied to the realm of infrastructure, transcends simple notions of environmental protection or long-term operational efficiency. It demands a holistic, integrated approach that balances three interdependent pillars: environmental stewardship, social equity, and economic viability. This "triple bottom line" provides a robust framework for evaluating infrastructure projects not just by their immediate functionality, but by their enduring impact on the planet, its people, and the prosperity of future generations. Without a clear understanding and rigorous application of these interconnected principles, efforts to modernize and enhance infrastructure risk falling short of their ultimate goals, potentially exacerbating existing problems or creating new ones.

The environmental dimension of infrastructure sustainability is perhaps the most immediately apparent. It centers on minimizing the ecological footprint associated with the entire lifecycle of an infrastructure asset, from its conception and construction through its operation, maintenance, and eventual decommissioning. This involves a deep consideration of resource consumption, waste generation, and pollution. A critical tool in this assessment is the concept of the carbon footprint, which quantifies the total greenhouse gas emissions attributable to an infrastructure project. This includes emissions from the extraction and processing of raw materials, the manufacturing of components, transportation of materials and labor to the site, construction activities, energy consumed during operation, and end-of-life disposal or recycling. Infrastructure projects are notoriously material- and energy-intensive, making their carbon footprint a significant factor in global emissions targets. Reducing this footprint necessitates a shift towards low-carbon materials, energy-efficient design, and the integration of renewable energy sources into infrastructure operations. For instance, the choice between traditional concrete and novel, lower-carbon alternatives for bridge construction, or the integration of solar panels on public buildings and transport hubs, are tangible examples of environmental considerations in action.

Beyond direct carbon emissions, a comprehensive environmental assessment requires a lifecycle perspective, often formalized through Material Lifecycle Assessments (MLAs). MLAs meticulously track the environmental impacts of materials from "cradle to grave" or, increasingly, "cradle to cradle" in a circular economy model. This includes evaluating resource depletion, water usage, land use change, habitat disruption, and the generation of hazardous waste at each stage. For example, the production of steel, a ubiquitous construction material, is energy-intensive and can generate significant air and water pollution. Understanding these impacts allows for informed choices, such as prioritizing recycled steel, exploring alternative structural materials, or designing for disassembly and reuse at the end of an asset's life. Similarly, the construction and operation of water infrastructure, such as dams and treatment plants, have profound implications for local ecosystems, affecting water flow, aquatic life, and riparian habitats. Sustainable infrastructure aims to mitigate these impacts through careful site selection, the use of nature-based solutions where appropriate, and efficient water management practices. Water usage efficiency is paramount, particularly in regions facing water scarcity, and includes minimizing leaks in distribution networks, promoting water-reusing technologies, and designing facilities that require less potable water for their operation. The overall ecological impact extends to biodiversity, and sustainable infrastructure strives to minimize habitat fragmentation, protect endangered species, and, where possible, enhance ecological value through green infrastructure initiatives.

The social pillar of sustainability focuses on the impact of infrastructure on communities and individuals. It emphasizes equity, accessibility, safety, and the overall well-being of the populace. This means ensuring that infrastructure serves all segments of society, not just privileged groups, and that its benefits are distributed fairly. For example, transportation networks should provide accessible and affordable options for people of all incomes and abilities, connecting them to employment, education, and essential services. This involves considering not just the physical presence of infrastructure but also its social implications, such as displacement of communities during construction or the impact of noise and pollution on nearby residents. Equitable service provision is a cornerstone of social sustainability. This means that access to clean water, reliable energy, safe sanitation, and efficient transportation should not be a luxury but a fundamental right, available to all, regardless of socioeconomic status or geographic location. When infrastructure development prioritizes certain areas or demographics over others, it can exacerbate existing social inequalities. Therefore, social impact assessments are crucial, involving community engagement and participation to ensure that infrastructure projects align with the needs and aspirations of the people they are intended to serve. Furthermore, the safety of infrastructure is a non-negotiable social imperative. This includes designing and maintaining structures to withstand natural hazards and ensuring that operational systems are secure against failures or malicious intent, thereby protecting public safety and confidence. The long-term viability of infrastructure also has a significant social dimension; an asset that rapidly becomes obsolete or unaffordable to maintain can lead to social disruption and the abandonment of communities.

The economic pillar of sustainability is concerned with the financial viability and long-term economic benefits of infrastructure systems. It goes beyond initial construction costs to consider the total cost of ownership, including operation, maintenance, repair, and eventual disposal or repurposing. An economically sustainable infrastructure project should generate a positive return on investment, not necessarily in purely financial terms, but also in terms of broader economic benefits such as job creation, increased productivity, and enhanced economic competitiveness. This requires efficient resource allocation, robust financial planning, and innovative funding models. The concept of resilience, both environmental and economic, is also critical here. Infrastructure must be designed to withstand shocks, whether from extreme weather events, economic downturns, or technological disruptions, with minimal disruption to economic activity. This often involves investing in adaptive capacity and redundancy. The long-term viability of infrastructure hinges on its ability to remain functional and relevant over extended periods. This means anticipating future demand, incorporating flexibility into designs, and adopting maintenance strategies that prevent premature obsolescence. For instance, a transportation system designed with future technological advancements, like autonomous vehicles or increased demand for public transit, in mind will be more economically viable in the long run than one built solely for current needs. Furthermore, the economic sustainability of infrastructure is deeply intertwined with its environmental and social performance. Resource-efficient infrastructure often leads to lower operational costs, while equitable service provision can foster a more stable and productive workforce, contributing to overall economic growth. A critical aspect of economic sustainability is the efficient use of capital. Large-scale infrastructure projects represent significant public and private investment. Ensuring that these investments are made wisely, prioritizing projects that offer the greatest long-term value and deliver on sustainability objectives, is paramount. This involves rigorous cost-benefit analyses that incorporate environmental and social externalities, moving beyond narrow financial metrics to a more comprehensive assessment of value.

The integration of these three pillars – environmental, social, and economic – is essential for defining true sustainability in infrastructure. An infrastructure system that is environmentally sound but socially inequitable or economically unviable is not sustainable in the long run. Conversely, a project that focuses solely on economic returns without considering its environmental impact or social consequences risks creating significant long-term liabilities. The pursuit of sustainability in infrastructure, therefore, necessitates a paradigm shift from traditional, siloed approaches to a more integrated, systems-based thinking. This involves interdisciplinary collaboration, innovative financing mechanisms, and a commitment to continuous improvement and adaptation. As we explore the role of advanced technologies like Artificial Intelligence (AI) in infrastructure, it is this comprehensive definition of sustainability that must guide our evaluation. AI-driven solutions hold immense promise for optimizing performance, enhancing resilience, and reducing the environmental footprint of infrastructure. However, their ultimate success will be measured not only by their technological sophistication but by their ability to contribute to a more environmentally responsible, socially equitable, and economically sound infrastructure for generations to come. Without this foundational understanding of sustainability, the application of AI, or any other advanced technology, risks being a technically impressive but ultimately incomplete solution to the complex challenges facing our built environment. The goal is not merely to build more, but to build better – to create infrastructure that endures, serves, and enhances the well-being of both people and the planet.

The challenge of defining and implementing infrastructure sustainability is further complicated by the sheer scale and complexity of modern infrastructure systems. These are not isolated components but intricate networks that interact and depend on each other. A robust energy grid is essential for powering transportation systems and water treatment plants; reliable water supply is critical for industrial processes and public health; and effective communication networks underpin the management of all other critical infrastructure. Therefore, sustainability must be considered at the system level, acknowledging these interdependencies. For example, a decision to transition to electric vehicles, while reducing tailpipe emissions, places increased demand on the electricity grid. A sustainable approach would simultaneously address the grid's capacity, its reliance on renewable energy sources, and the environmental impact of battery production and disposal. Similarly, investing solely in new road construction without considering the environmental and social impacts of increased vehicle traffic, or the potential for promoting more sustainable modes of transport, represents a fragmented approach to sustainability.

Moreover, the concept of "long-term viability" in infrastructure sustainability extends beyond mere physical durability. It encompasses adaptability to changing societal needs, technological advancements, and evolving environmental conditions. Infrastructure designed today must be capable of serving future generations, who may have different mobility patterns, energy requirements, and climate exposures. This necessitates a degree of foresight and flexibility in design and planning. Infrastructure assets often have lifespans of decades, if not centuries. Decisions made today about materials, design standards, and operational philosophies will have ramifications for generations to come. Therefore, a truly sustainable approach must be forward-looking, anticipating future challenges and opportunities. This might involve designing structures that can be easily upgraded or repurposed, or implementing flexible operational systems that can adapt to fluctuating demand or new technologies. For instance, a building designed with modular components and adaptable internal layouts is more likely to remain relevant and useful over time than a rigidly constructed edifice.

The principle of minimal environmental degradation is a direct consequence of the ecological focus. It implies a proactive effort to prevent harm to natural systems, rather than simply mitigating damage after it occurs. This includes conserving biodiversity, protecting natural resources like soil and water, and minimizing pollution of air, land, and water. It also involves embracing restorative practices, aiming to leave natural environments in a better state than they were found. Green infrastructure, for example, which uses natural systems and processes to provide infrastructure services – such as permeable pavements to manage stormwater runoff, or urban forests to improve air quality and reduce the urban heat island effect – exemplifies this commitment to working with, rather than against, nature. This approach not only reduces environmental impact but can also provide co-benefits, such as enhanced aesthetic value and improved public health outcomes.

Equitable service provision, as highlighted earlier, is fundamental to the social dimension. It demands that the benefits of infrastructure be shared broadly across society and that no community is left behind. This requires careful consideration of accessibility for all demographic groups, including the elderly, people with disabilities, and low-income populations. It also means ensuring that essential services are affordable and reliable for everyone. The digital divide, for instance, is a growing concern in the context of increasingly digitized infrastructure services. Ensuring equitable access to high-speed internet and digital literacy training is becoming an essential component of social sustainability in the digital age. When infrastructure development leads to gentrification or displacement of existing communities, it undermines social sustainability, even if the new infrastructure is technically advanced and environmentally sound. Therefore, robust community engagement, fair compensation for displaced individuals, and the provision of alternative housing and services are critical considerations.

Ultimately, the journey towards sustainable infrastructure is an ongoing process of learning, adaptation, and innovation. It requires a commitment to data collection and analysis to monitor performance against sustainability indicators, and a willingness to adjust strategies and adopt new approaches as knowledge and circumstances evolve. The very definition of sustainability itself is dynamic, evolving with our understanding of the planet's limits and the needs of society. Therefore, the pursuit of sustainable infrastructure is not a destination, but a continuous journey toward creating built environments that are not only functional and resilient but also ethically responsible and environmentally regenerative, laying the groundwork for a thriving future for all.

Infrastructure resilience stands as a cornerstone for ensuring the continuous functioning of essential services in an era marked by escalating unpredictability. It is not merely about the ability of an infrastructure system to endure a single event, but rather its inherent capacity to withstand, adapt to, and recover from a wide spectrum of disruptions. This multifaceted concept is critical for safeguarding communities, economies, and the very fabric of modern society against an increasingly volatile global landscape. At its core, resilience refers to the system's ability to maintain essential functions during and immediately after a disruptive event, and to quickly restore full operational capacity with minimal degradation of service. This involves a proactive and integrated approach to design, operation, and maintenance, anticipating potential failures rather than merely reacting to them.

The spectrum of threats that infrastructure systems must contend with is broad and ever-evolving. These can be broadly categorized into acute shocks and chronic stresses. Shocks are typically sudden, intense events that can overwhelm a system's capacity. Natural disasters represent a significant category of shocks, including events such as earthquakes that can shake foundations and disrupt underground utilities, floods that can inundate critical facilities and damage power lines, hurricanes and typhoons that bring high winds and storm surges, wildfires that threaten power grids and communication lines, and extreme temperature events like heatwaves or severe cold snaps that can strain energy systems and compromise material integrity. Beyond natural phenomena, technological failures can also act as sudden shocks. These might include catastrophic equipment malfunctions, widespread power outages due to grid instability, or failures in communication networks that cripple the coordinated operation of other systems. The increasing reliance on digital technologies also exposes infrastructure to sophisticated cyberattacks, which can disrupt operations, compromise data, or even lead to physical damage by manipulating control systems. Societal disruptions, such as labor strikes, civil unrest, or pandemics, can also exert significant pressure on infrastructure by impeding maintenance, disrupting supply chains, or altering demand patterns.

Chronic stresses, in contrast to acute shocks, are persistent, long-term pressures that gradually degrade infrastructure performance and capacity. These can include aging infrastructure that is nearing the end of its design life and requires more frequent repairs and replacements, inadequate funding for maintenance and upgrades, changing environmental conditions such as rising sea levels or increased frequency of extreme weather events, economic shifts that affect demand for services or the availability of resources, and evolving regulatory requirements. While individual stresses might not cause immediate system failure, their cumulative effect can significantly weaken an infrastructure system, making it more vulnerable to shocks and slower to recover when disruptions occur. For instance, an aging water distribution network might be more prone to leaks (a chronic stress), and when combined with a severe drought (another chronic stress), it can lead to significant water shortages that are exacerbated by a sudden pump failure (a shock).

Measuring the resilience of infrastructure is a complex undertaking, requiring a nuanced understanding of various performance indicators. One key metric is
recovery time, which quantifies the duration it takes for an infrastructure system to return to its pre-disruption level of functionality or a predefined acceptable operational state. A highly resilient system will have a short recovery time, minimizing the period of service interruption. **Robustness** refers to the system's ability to withstand a given level of stress or shock without experiencing catastrophic failure. A robust system can absorb a certain amount of impact while continuing to operate, albeit potentially at a reduced capacity. This is often achieved through built-in redundancies and strong structural integrity. **Adaptability** is the capacity of the system to adjust its configuration or operational strategies in response to changing conditions or ongoing disruptions. This might involve rerouting power, implementing temporary traffic management solutions, or shifting to alternative communication channels. An adaptable system can maintain essential functions even when its standard operating procedures are compromised. **Redundancy** is a critical design principle for enhancing resilience. It involves having backup systems or alternative pathways that can take over if a primary component fails. This can manifest as multiple power sources for critical facilities, redundant communication links, or parallel transportation routes. While redundancy can increase initial costs and complexity, it significantly improves the system's ability to absorb shocks and maintain continuity.

The interconnectedness of modern infrastructure systems presents a formidable challenge to resilience planning. Critical infrastructure sectors are deeply intertwined, and a failure in one can trigger a cascade of failures across others. This phenomenon, known as a **cascading failure**, can amplify the impact of an initial disruption far beyond the directly affected sector. For example, a widespread power outage (a failure in the energy sector) can cripple transportation systems reliant on electric signaling and control, disrupt communication networks that depend on powered infrastructure, halt water and wastewater treatment plants, and impede the functioning of healthcare facilities that require electricity for life support systems and medical equipment. Similarly, a cyberattack on a financial system could disrupt the ability to fund emergency response efforts or pay for essential supplies, affecting multiple sectors. The breakdown of a major transportation artery due to a natural disaster can disrupt the delivery of fuel to power plants, the supply of food and medicine to communities, and the movement of emergency personnel and equipment. Understanding these interdependencies is crucial for developing effective resilience strategies. It necessitates a holistic, systems-thinking approach that considers not just the individual components of an infrastructure network, but also their dynamic interactions and potential failure modes.

To illustrate the concept of cascading failures, consider the impact of a severe earthquake on a metropolitan region. An earthquake might directly damage buildings, bridges, and utility lines, representing the initial shock. This damage can lead to power outages as electrical substations fail or transmission lines are severed. The loss of power would then disrupt water pumping stations, leading to a loss of water pressure and potentially compromised water quality, affecting both residential use and firefighting capabilities. Communication networks, reliant on powered infrastructure, would likely experience outages or severe degradation, hindering emergency response coordination and public information dissemination. Transportation networks, with damaged roads, bridges, and rail lines, would become impassable, impeding the movement of people, goods, and emergency services. The failure of these interconnected systems amplifies the initial impact, turning a localized event into a widespread crisis that impacts public health, economic activity, and social order.

The concept of redundancy is often implemented to prevent or mitigate such cascading failures. In the energy sector, this might involve maintaining sufficient reserve generation capacity or establishing interconnections with neighboring grids to import power during local outages. For communication networks, it could mean deploying diverse routing technologies and having multiple fiber optic cable paths. In transportation, it could involve developing alternative routes or investing in flexible public transit options that can be scaled up or rerouted. The principle of modularity also plays a role; designing systems in discrete, interconnected modules allows for easier isolation and repair of damaged sections without bringing the entire system down.

The challenges of ensuring infrastructure resilience are compounded by the dynamic nature of risks. Climate change, for instance, is altering the frequency and intensity of extreme weather events, making historical data less reliable for predictive modeling. The rapid pace of technological advancement, while offering new solutions, also introduces new vulnerabilities, such as those associated with artificial intelligence, the Internet of Things, and sophisticated cyber threats. Moreover, demographic shifts, urbanization, and economic globalization create new patterns of demand and exposure that infrastructure must be able to accommodate.

Therefore, building resilient infrastructure is not a one-time fix but an ongoing process of assessment, adaptation, and investment. It requires continuous monitoring of system performance, regular risk assessments to identify emerging threats, and strategic investments in upgrades, maintenance, and new technologies. It also demands a shift in mindset from a focus on simply building for efficiency and capacity to one that prioritizes the ability to withstand and recover from disruption. This includes fostering a culture of preparedness within infrastructure operators, developing robust emergency response plans, and engaging with communities to build their own resilience capacities. Ultimately, resilient infrastructure is a fundamental enabler of a secure, prosperous, and sustainable future in a world that is increasingly defined by its unpredictability.

The advent of sophisticated sensing technologies, embedded systems, and the pervasive connectivity of the Internet of Things (IoT) have transformed infrastructure systems from static physical assets into dynamic, data-generating ecosystems. This burgeoning stream of information represents an unprecedented opportunity for optimizing performance, enhancing reliability, and proactively managing the complex challenges inherent in operating and maintaining these vital networks. Understanding the multifaceted nature of this data is the foundational step in unlocking its full potential for infrastructure management.

At its core, infrastructure generates a diverse array of data types, each offering a unique perspective on the system's health, operational status, and environmental context.
Sensor readings form a primary category, capturing real-time environmental and operational parameters. In transportation networks, this includes data from traffic sensors, such as vehicle counts, speed, and occupancy, as well as GPS data from individual vehicles providing insights into travel times and route adherence. For energy grids, sensors monitor voltage, current, frequency, temperature, and fault indicators across substations, transmission lines, and generation facilities. Water and wastewater systems deploy sensors to track flow rates, pressure levels, water quality parameters (like pH, turbidity, and chemical concentrations), and the operational status of pumps and valves.

Structural health monitoring systems in bridges and buildings utilize strain gauges, accelerometers, and displacement sensors to detect subtle changes indicative of material fatigue or structural compromise. Environmental sensors deployed along coastlines or riverbanks provide critical data on water levels, wave height, and wind speed, crucial for flood and storm surge prediction. Even the physical movement of goods in logistics and supply chains is increasingly tracked through RFID tags, GPS locators, and telematics devices.

Beyond immediate environmental and operational metrics, **operational logs** provide a historical record of system behavior. These logs detail events, commands executed, system responses, and any anomalies or alarms triggered during operation. For an electrical substation, this might include records of circuit breaker operations, transformer tap changes, and protective relay activations. For a traffic management system, it could log signal timings, pedestrian crossing activations, and incident detection events. Communication networks generate logs detailing connection attempts, data transfer rates, error messages, and network congestion points. These logs are invaluable for diagnosing past issues, understanding system load patterns, and identifying recurring operational inefficiencies.

Maintenance records represent another critical data source, offering a historical perspective on the upkeep and repair of infrastructure assets. This includes scheduled maintenance activities, unscheduled repairs, component replacements, inspection reports, and diagnostic findings. Detailed records of pump overhauls in a water treatment plant, tunnel inspections for a transit system, or paving schedules for roads all contribute to a comprehensive understanding of an asset's lifecycle and its maintenance history. This data is fundamental for evaluating the effectiveness of maintenance strategies, predicting future maintenance needs, and optimizing resource allocation. It also helps in understanding the relationship between maintenance actions and subsequent system performance and reliability.

Geographical Information Systems (GIS) data provides the spatial context for all other data types. This includes detailed maps of infrastructure networks, asset locations, property boundaries, elevation data, land use information, and demographic data. GIS layers can integrate sensor readings to visualize real-time conditions across a network, overlay maintenance records onto specific assets, or model the potential impact of extreme weather events on vulnerable infrastructure. For instance, a GIS platform can illustrate how a flood warning relates to the elevation of critical wastewater pump stations or how a power outage impacts specific residential areas. The combination of geospatial data with operational and sensor data allows for sophisticated spatial analysis, enabling better planning, risk assessment, and emergency response coordination.

Furthermore,
asset management databases consolidate information about individual infrastructure components, including their specifications, installation dates, warranty information, inspection history, and replacement costs. This data supports long-term capital planning, replacement strategies, and financial forecasting. Data from **customer interactions**, such as service outage reports, billing inquiries, or feedback forms, can also provide indirect insights into infrastructure performance and public perception. Finally, **external data sources**, including weather forecasts, seismic activity reports, traffic volumes from third-party providers, and socio-economic indicators, can be integrated to enrich the understanding of operational context and potential external impacts on infrastructure.

The sheer volume, velocity, and variety of data generated by these disparate sources, however, present significant challenges in its acquisition, quality assurance, and overall management.

Data silos represent a pervasive problem, where data is collected and stored by different departments, agencies, or even individual systems, often in incompatible formats and isolated from each other. This fragmentation hinders a holistic view of the infrastructure and makes cross-system analysis extremely difficult. For example, traffic data might be managed by a transportation department, while energy consumption data is held by a utility company, and neither system easily shares information, making it challenging to analyze the energy impact of traffic congestion or vice versa.

Data quality is another critical concern. Sensor malfunctions, calibration drift, transmission errors, or human input mistakes can lead to inaccurate or incomplete data. **Missing values** are common, arising from sensor failures, network outages, or incomplete data entry. How these missing values are handled—whether by imputation, interpolation, or simply exclusion—can significantly impact the reliability of any subsequent analysis. **Data noise**, which refers to random fluctuations or errors in the data, can obscure underlying trends and patterns. Distinguishing between genuine operational fluctuations and noisy data requires sophisticated filtering and cleaning techniques. The sheer scale of the data, often referred to as **big data**, also poses challenges in terms of storage, processing, and real-time analysis. Traditional data management techniques may be insufficient to handle terabytes or petabytes of data efficiently.

The aggregation and management of diverse data types require robust **data governance** frameworks. This involves establishing clear policies and procedures for data collection, storage, access, security, and lifecycle management. It includes defining data ownership, ensuring data privacy and compliance with regulations, and establishing standards for data quality and interoperability. Effective data governance ensures that data is treated as a valuable organizational asset, managed systematically, and leveraged effectively. This involves defining data dictionaries, metadata standards, and data lineage tracking to understand the origin and transformations applied to data. Implementing a federated data model or a data lake architecture can help break down silos by creating a centralized repository that can ingest and process data from various sources in its raw or semi-processed form, while maintaining necessary access controls and security protocols.

The challenges of data acquisition, quality, and management are not merely technical hurdles; they have direct implications for the effectiveness of infrastructure management decisions. If data is siloed, decision-makers may lack crucial context. If data is of poor quality, decisions based upon it can lead to suboptimal outcomes, wasted resources, or even catastrophic failures. For instance, inaccurate sensor readings from a bridge could lead to unnecessary closures or, more dangerously, a failure to detect a critical structural weakness, with potentially devastating consequences. Inadequate maintenance records might result in essential repairs being overlooked, leading to premature asset failure and higher long-term costs.

Recognizing these challenges, the industry is increasingly turning to advanced analytical techniques, particularly
big data analytics, to extract meaningful insights from the vast ocean of infrastructure data. Big data analytics encompasses a range of methodologies and tools designed to process and analyze large, complex datasets, uncovering hidden patterns, correlations, and trends that would be impossible to discern through traditional means. This is not simply about collecting more data, but about developing the capacity to understand and utilize it effectively.

The application of big data analytics to infrastructure management offers transformative potential across several key areas.
Predictive maintenance stands out as a prime example. By analyzing historical sensor data, operational logs, and maintenance records,

algorithms can identify subtle patterns that precede equipment failure. For instance, an unusual vibration signature from a pump motor, a slight increase in operating temperature, or a deviation in power consumption, when analyzed in aggregate and over time, can signal an impending breakdown days, weeks, or even months in advance. This allows maintenance teams to schedule repairs proactively during planned outages or at a time that minimizes disruption, rather than reacting to a sudden failure which can lead to costly emergency repairs, extended downtime, and significant service interruptions. For a railway network, predicting the failure of a signaling component can prevent a major disruption to train schedules. For an energy utility, predicting transformer failure can avert widespread power outages during peak demand.

Performance optimization is another significant benefit. By analyzing real-time traffic flows, energy consumption patterns, or water distribution pressures, infrastructure operators can dynamically adjust system parameters to improve efficiency and service delivery. Smart traffic lights can respond to real-time traffic volume, optimizing signal timing to reduce congestion and travel times. Variable speed limits on highways can be adjusted based on real-time traffic density and weather conditions to enhance safety and flow. In energy grids, sophisticated analytics can optimize power generation and distribution in real-time, responding to fluctuations in demand and renewable energy supply, thereby reducing energy waste and improving grid stability. Water utilities can use analytics to detect leaks in the distribution network by comparing water input with metered output, identifying anomalies that indicate water loss.

Risk assessment and resilience planning are significantly enhanced by big data analytics. By integrating data on asset condition, historical failure rates, environmental conditions (including climate change projections), and potential threat scenarios (such as cyberattacks or extreme weather events), operators can develop more accurate risk models. This allows for the identification of the most vulnerable assets and the prioritization of investments in mitigation and adaptation strategies. For example, analytics can help identify which sections of a coastal levee system are most susceptible to rising sea levels and increased storm intensity, guiding reinforcement efforts. Understanding interdependencies between different infrastructure systems through data analysis is also crucial for anticipating cascading failures and developing comprehensive emergency response plans.

Operational efficiency and resource allocation can be streamlined. By analyzing historical data on labor, materials, and equipment usage for maintenance and repair activities, managers can optimize scheduling, workforce deployment, and inventory management. This leads to reduced operational costs and improved productivity. For a public transit system, analyzing ridership data across different routes and times can inform decisions about service frequency and fleet deployment, ensuring resources are allocated where demand is highest.

The transition to a data-driven approach to infrastructure management necessitates a strategic focus on
data governance. This goes beyond simply storing data; it involves establishing a clear framework for how data is collected, managed, accessed, and utilized throughout its lifecycle. A robust data governance strategy ensures data integrity, security, and compliance with relevant regulations. It defines roles and responsibilities for data stewardship, establishes data quality standards, and promotes data interoperability across different systems. This is particularly important in sectors with critical infrastructure where data security and reliability are paramount. For instance, in the energy sector, strict protocols are needed to ensure the integrity and security of data related to grid operations to prevent

malicious interference. Similarly, in transportation, ensuring the accuracy of data used for autonomous vehicle navigation is critical for public safety.

Implementing effective data governance often involves establishing a central data repository or a data lake, complemented by strict access controls and data lineage tracking mechanisms. Metadata management becomes crucial, enabling users to understand the origin, meaning, and usage of data. This helps to break down data silos and fosters a collaborative environment where data can be shared and utilized across different departments and stakeholders. Without strong governance, the potential benefits of big data analytics can be undermined by issues of data trust, accessibility, and security.

The capacity to analyze and act upon this data is increasingly being augmented by the application of
Artificial Intelligence (AI). While big data analytics provides the tools to process and identify patterns in large datasets, AI, particularly machine learning, offers the intelligence to interpret these patterns, make predictions, and even automate decision-making processes. AI algorithms can learn from the data, adapt to changing conditions, and continuously improve their performance over time, making them ideal for the dynamic and complex nature of infrastructure management. The interplay between big data and AI is thus revolutionizing how we approach the planning, operation, maintenance, and resilience of our critical infrastructure.

The convergence of advanced data analytics with the burgeoning capabilities of Artificial Intelligence (AI) marks a profound shift in how engineers approach the design, operation, and stewardship of infrastructure systems. While the preceding discussion has highlighted the critical importance of leveraging vast datasets to understand and optimize these complex networks, AI offers a paradigm shift in *how* we extract value from this data, moving beyond mere observation and analysis towards intelligent interpretation, prediction, and even autonomous action. For the engineering disciplines, AI is not simply another tool in the toolkit; it represents a fundamental evolution, empowering engineers to tackle previously intractable problems and envision infrastructure that is more responsive, efficient, and resilient than ever before.

At its core, Artificial Intelligence refers to the simulation of human intelligence processes by machines, especially computer systems. These processes include learning (the acquisition of information and rules for using the information), reasoning (using rules to reach approximate or definite conclusions), and self-correction. Within the expansive field of AI, several subfields are particularly relevant to engineering applications. **Machine Learning (ML)** is perhaps the most prominent, enabling systems to learn from data without being explicitly programmed. Instead of hard-coding every possible scenario or rule, ML algorithms identify patterns, make predictions, and improve their performance as they are exposed to more data. This is crucial for infrastructure, where the sheer variability of operational conditions, environmental factors, and user demands makes explicit programming impractical. For instance, a machine learning model can learn to predict traffic congestion patterns by analyzing historical traffic flow, time of day, weather, and local events, rather than relying on a static set of rules.

A further refinement within machine learning is
Deep Learning (DL), which utilizes artificial neural networks with multiple layers (hence "deep") to learn complex patterns directly from raw data. Inspired by the structure and function of the human brain, deep learning models excel at processing unstructured data such as images, audio, and natural language, making them invaluable for tasks like visual inspection of infrastructure components or analyzing sensor data that may contain nuanced anomalies. For example, a deep learning model could be trained on thousands of images of bridge structures to automatically detect cracks, corrosion, or other signs of degradation with

remarkable accuracy, far surpassing manual inspection capabilities in speed and consistency.

Understanding the different ways machines can learn is essential for appreciating AI's potential.
Supervised learning involves training a model on a labeled dataset, where the input data is paired with the correct output. The model learns to map inputs to outputs, much like a student learning from examples with known answers. An example in infrastructure would be training a model to predict the remaining useful life of a pump based on historical sensor data (temperature, vibration, flow rate) paired with records of when those pumps actually failed. The model learns the relationship between specific sensor signatures and failure events.

In contrast,
unsupervised learning deals with unlabeled data, where the algorithm's task is to find patterns, structures, or relationships within the data itself. This is useful for discovering hidden insights or categorizing data. For instance, an unsupervised learning algorithm could analyze electricity consumption data from thousands of households to identify distinct patterns of usage, helping utilities understand different consumer behaviors for better demand forecasting and targeted energy efficiency programs, without needing pre-defined categories of "household types."

A third paradigm,
reinforcement learning, involves training an agent to make a sequence of decisions in an environment to maximize a cumulative reward. The agent learns through trial and error, receiving feedback (rewards or penalties) for its actions. This is particularly powerful for optimizing control systems. Consider a smart grid: a reinforcement learning agent could learn to dynamically balance power generation from various sources (renewables, fossil fuels) and manage energy storage to meet demand while minimizing costs and carbon emissions. It would learn

through experience which dispatch strategies are most effective in different grid conditions.

The transformative power of AI in engineering stems from its ability to automate tasks that are either too complex, too time-consuming, or too dangerous for human intervention. This automation can range from routine data processing to highly sophisticated decision-making. Imagine an AI system that continuously monitors thousands of sensors across a vast water distribution network. Instead of engineers sifting through individual alerts, the AI can identify subtle anomalies indicative of leaks, predict their location and severity, and even autonomously dispatch maintenance crews or adjust valve operations to mitigate water loss and service disruption. This proactive approach drastically reduces operational costs and improves the efficiency and reliability of the system.

Furthermore, AI significantly enhances predictive capabilities. While big data analytics can identify correlations, AI, especially machine learning, can build sophisticated predictive models that forecast future events with increasing accuracy. This extends far beyond simple trend extrapolation. For example, in transportation engineering, AI can predict traffic congestion not just based on current conditions, but also by factoring in weather forecasts, upcoming events, and the historical impact of similar conditions. This allows for dynamic rerouting of traffic, adjustments to signal timings, and proactive communication with commuters, smoothing flow and reducing travel times. In structural engineering, AI can analyze sensor data from bridges, buildings, or tunnels to predict the likelihood of material fatigue or structural failure under specific load conditions or environmental stresses, enabling targeted inspections and preventative maintenance before critical issues arise.

The impact of AI is not a distant future prospect; it is already being realized in various engineering domains, offering compelling glimpses of what's to come. In civil engineering, AI-powered drones equipped with computer vision are revolutionizing the inspection of bridges, dams, and high-rise buildings, identifying defects with unprecedented speed and accuracy. Machine learning algorithms are being employed to optimize the design of concrete mixtures, reducing cement usage and improving durability, thereby contributing to more sustainable construction practices. In the realm of energy, AI is instrumental in optimizing the output of renewable energy sources like solar and wind, predicting their intermittency and integrating them seamlessly into the grid. It also plays a crucial role in demand-side management, helping to balance supply and demand in real-time and prevent blackouts.

The early successes in related fields further underscore AI's potential. In medicine, AI is assisting in diagnosis, drug discovery, and personalized treatment plans. In finance, it drives algorithmic trading and fraud detection. These applications, while distinct, share a common thread: the ability of AI to analyze vast, complex datasets, identify subtle patterns, and make intelligent decisions or predictions. As these AI technologies mature and become more accessible, their integration into engineering disciplines, particularly infrastructure, is inevitable and indeed, already underway. For the aspiring engineer, understanding and embracing AI is no longer optional; it is a fundamental requirement for navigating and shaping the future of infrastructure, enabling the creation of systems that are not only functional and robust but also intelligent, adaptive, sustainable, and exceptionally resilient in the face of growing global challenges. The journey from data to insight, and now to intelligent action, is at the heart of this technological revolution, promising a new era of engineered systems.

Chapter 2: Foundational AI Concepts for Engineers

The previous discussion established the foundational role of Artificial Intelligence (AI) and its prominent subfield, Machine Learning (ML), in revolutionizing engineering. We touched upon the general concepts of supervised, unsupervised, and reinforcement learning as the primary modes through which machines acquire intelligence from data. Now, we will delve deeper into each of these core machine learning paradigms, exploring their underlying principles, common algorithms, and, crucially, their specific applications within the broad landscape of engineering. Understanding these paradigms is essential for engineers to effectively harness the power of AI in designing, managing, and optimizing infrastructure systems.

Supervised Learning: Learning from Labeled Examples

Supervised learning is perhaps the most intuitive and widely used machine learning paradigm. Its core principle mirrors human learning from experience where an instructor or a set of examples with known outcomes guides the learner. In supervised learning, algorithms are trained on a dataset that is "labeled," meaning each data point consists of an input feature set and a corresponding correct output or "ground truth." The goal of the algorithm is to learn a mapping function that can predict the output for new, unseen input data. This process is akin to a student studying with flashcards; each card has a question (input) and an answer (output). By going through many such cards, the student learns to associate questions with their correct answers, and eventually, can answer new questions they haven't seen before.

Within supervised learning, two primary types of problems are commonly addressed:
classification and **regression**.

Classification problems involve predicting a discrete category or class label. The output variable is a qualitative or categorical variable. For instance, determining whether an email is spam or not spam, or whether an image contains a cat or a dog, are classic classification tasks. In an engineering context, classification is invaluable for diagnostic and predictive maintenance. Consider the structural integrity of a bridge. Sensor data, such as strain gauge readings, vibration frequencies, and environmental conditions (temperature, humidity), can be fed into a classification model. The model, trained on historical data where specific sensor readings were associated with observed states of structural health (e.g., "sound," "minor damage," "severe damage"), can then classify the current state of the bridge. This allows for early detection of potential issues, enabling proactive maintenance and preventing catastrophic failures. Another example is in water distribution systems, where classification models can analyze pressure and flow sensor data to identify different types of anomalies, such as leaks, burst pipes, or pump malfunctions. Each anomaly type would be a distinct class, allowing for targeted and efficient response.

Regression problems, on the other hand, are concerned with predicting a continuous numerical value. The output variable is quantitative. Examples include predicting a house price based on its features (size, location, number of rooms) or forecasting stock market values. In engineering, regression plays a vital role in forecasting and optimization. For infrastructure, predicting energy consumption is a prime example. By analyzing historical energy usage data, weather patterns, occupancy levels, and building characteristics, regression models can forecast future energy demand. This is critical for power utilities to optimize power generation, manage grid load, and ensure reliable supply. For building management systems, accurate energy consumption forecasts allow for optimized HVAC (Heating, Ventilation, and Air Conditioning) operations, leading to significant energy savings and reduced operational costs. Another regression application is in estimating the remaining useful life (RUL) of critical components in machinery or infrastructure, such as turbines in a power plant or pumps in a water system. By analyzing time-series data from various sensors (temperature, vibration, pressure, power consumption), a regression model can predict how much longer a component is likely to operate effectively before requiring maintenance or replacement. This predictive capability enables a shift from reactive or time-based maintenance to condition-based maintenance, optimizing resource allocation and minimizing downtime.

Several algorithms are employed for supervised learning. **Linear Regression** and **Logistic Regression** are fundamental algorithms for their respective tasks, forming the basis for understanding more complex models. **Decision Trees** and **Random Forests** offer interpretable models that can handle non-linear relationships and interactions between features. **Support Vector Machines (SVMs)** are powerful for classification tasks, particularly in high-dimensional spaces. **Neural Networks**, including deep learning architectures, have shown remarkable success in complex classification and regression problems, especially when dealing with large datasets and intricate patterns, such as image recognition for infrastructure inspection or natural language processing for analyzing maintenance reports.

The efficacy of supervised learning hinges entirely on the quality and relevance of the labeled data. Acquiring and labeling large, accurate datasets can be a significant challenge. Data preprocessing, including feature selection, feature engineering, and handling missing values, is crucial to ensure that the model learns meaningful patterns rather than noise. Furthermore, it's essential to split the data into training, validation, and testing sets. The training set is used to train the model, the validation set to tune hyperparameters and prevent overfitting, and the test set to provide an unbiased evaluation of the model's performance on unseen data.

Unsupervised Learning: Discovering Hidden Patterns

Unsupervised learning represents a different facet of machine learning where the algorithms are presented with unlabeled data. The objective here is not to predict a specific outcome but rather to discover inherent structures, patterns, relationships, or groupings within the data itself. It's akin to a detective sifting through a pile of evidence without any initial suspects or theories, trying to piece together what happened. Unsupervised learning is particularly useful for exploratory data analysis, anomaly detection, and feature extraction, especially when labeled data is scarce or when seeking novel insights.

The two most prominent tasks within unsupervised learning are **clustering** and **dimensionality reduction**.

Clustering involves grouping data points into clusters such that data points within the same cluster are more similar to each other than to those in other clusters. The algorithm identifies natural groupings in the data based on intrinsic similarities in their features. This is extremely useful for segmentation and pattern discovery in large datasets. For example, in transportation engineering, clustering can be applied to traffic flow data collected from various sensors across a city. By clustering traffic segments based on their speed, density, and flow patterns over time, authorities can identify distinct traffic regimes (e.g., peak hour congestion, off-peak smooth flow, event-driven surge) and develop tailored traffic management strategies for each. Similarly, in the energy sector, clustering electricity consumption data from smart meters can reveal different consumer behavior patterns (e.g., households with high daytime usage, those with high evening usage, businesses with consistent demand). This understanding can inform personalized energy efficiency recommendations, dynamic pricing strategies, and more accurate demand forecasting for specific customer segments.

In infrastructure management, clustering can also be applied to categorize the condition of assets based on sensor readings. For instance, by clustering data from various sensors on a fleet of vehicles or a network of pumps, operators might identify distinct "health profiles" corresponding to different stages of wear and tear or different types of emerging issues, even without pre-defined labels for these profiles. This can help in proactive maintenance planning.

Dimensionality Reduction techniques aim to reduce the number of features (dimensions) in a dataset while retaining as much of the important information as possible. High-dimensional data can suffer from the "curse of dimensionality," leading to increased computational costs, difficulty in visualization, and potential overfitting in subsequent modeling. Dimensionality reduction techniques simplify the data by creating new, fewer features that are combinations of the original ones, or by selecting the most relevant subset of original features. This is particularly relevant for large-scale infrastructure monitoring where numerous sensors might generate vast amounts of data.

Principal Component Analysis (PCA) is a widely used dimensionality reduction technique. It transforms the original features into a new set of uncorrelated features called principal components, ordered by the amount of variance they explain in the data. By keeping only the top principal components, the dimensionality of the data is reduced, making it more manageable for visualization and further analysis. For example, imagine a complex system with hundreds of sensors providing real-time data. Applying PCA can reduce these hundreds of data streams into a few principal components that capture the dominant modes of variation in the system. Analyzing these principal components can reveal underlying dynamics or anomalies that might be obscured in the raw, high-dimensional data. This can aid in system diagnostics or identifying unusual operating conditions in power plants, manufacturing facilities, or complex distribution networks.

Another technique,
t-Distributed Stochastic Neighbor Embedding (t-SNE), is often used for visualizing high-dimensional data in a low-dimensional space (typically two or three dimensions), preserving local structure and revealing clusters that might not be apparent otherwise. This is invaluable for engineers exploring complex datasets, providing visual insights into the relationships and groupings within the data.

Unsupervised learning is a powerful tool for uncovering the hidden structure in data, identifying anomalies that deviate from normal patterns, and simplifying complex datasets for further analysis. It is particularly useful in the early stages of a data science project or when dealing with entirely novel data where the nature of patterns is unknown.

Reinforcement Learning: Learning Through Trial and Error

Reinforcement learning (RL) presents a fundamentally different approach to machine learning, inspired by behavioral psychology. Instead of learning from a static dataset (as in supervised or unsupervised learning), an RL agent learns by interacting with an environment. The agent performs actions, and in response, the environment transitions to a new state and provides a reward or penalty signal. The agent's objective is to learn a policy—a strategy or mapping from states to actions—that maximizes its cumulative reward over time. This paradigm is ideal for problems involving sequential decision-making and control in dynamic environments.

The core components of a reinforcement learning system are:

Agent: The learner and decision-maker.
Environment: Everything the agent interacts with.
State: A representation of the current situation in the environment.
Action: A move made by the agent.
Reward: A scalar feedback signal from the environment, indicating how good the action was.
Policy: The agent's strategy for choosing actions based on the current state.

Consider a simple analogy: teaching a robot to navigate a maze. The robot (agent) starts at an entry point (initial state). It can move in different directions (actions). If it hits a wall, it receives a penalty (negative reward). If it moves closer to the exit, it might receive a small positive reward. Reaching the exit grants a significant positive reward. Through repeated attempts (trials and errors), the robot learns which sequences of moves lead to the exit and which lead to dead ends, eventually developing a policy to navigate the maze efficiently.

Reinforcement learning is particularly suited for optimizing control systems and autonomous decision-making in engineering. One of the most promising applications is in
traffic signal control. Traditional traffic signals operate on fixed timers or simple loop detectors, which are often inefficient in dynamic traffic conditions. An RL agent can be trained to control traffic signals

dynamically. The state could include real-time traffic density, queue lengths at intersections, and vehicle arrival rates. The actions could be adjusting signal timings (green light duration for each direction). The reward could be a function that penalizes long wait times for vehicles and congestion, while rewarding smooth traffic flow. By learning from real-time traffic data and experimenting with different signal timing strategies, an RL-based system can optimize traffic flow, reduce travel times, and minimize fuel consumption and emissions across an entire network of intersections.

Another significant application area is in **energy grid management**. In a smart grid, RL agents can learn to optimize power distribution, manage energy storage systems (like batteries), and integrate renewable energy sources dynamically. For instance, an RL agent could learn to decide when to store excess solar energy, when to discharge batteries to meet peak demand, or how to balance supply from intermittent renewable sources with demand, all while considering factors like electricity prices and grid stability. This allows for a more efficient, resilient, and cost-effective energy system.

Robotics and automation also heavily leverage RL. Robots can learn complex manipulation tasks, such as assembling intricate components, by receiving rewards for successful task completion. In infrastructure maintenance, RL could enable robots to learn how to autonomously inspect pipelines, repair minor damages, or perform complex construction tasks in hazardous environments.

Furthermore, RL is being explored for optimizing resource allocation in complex systems. For example, in water management, RL could optimize pump schedules to meet demand while minimizing energy costs, or manage reservoir releases to balance supply needs with flood control.

The challenges in reinforcement learning often lie in the exploration-exploitation dilemma: the agent must explore new actions to discover potentially better strategies, but also exploit its current knowledge to maximize immediate rewards. Designing appropriate reward functions is also critical, as a poorly designed reward can lead to unintended behaviors. Training RL agents can also require significant computational resources and time, especially in complex environments. However, with advancements in algorithms like Deep Reinforcement Learning (which combines deep neural networks with RL), the capabilities of RL systems are rapidly expanding, offering powerful solutions for complex, dynamic decision-making problems in engineering.

In summary, supervised learning excels when labeled data is available for prediction and classification, unsupervised learning shines in pattern discovery and data simplification, and reinforcement learning provides a framework for intelligent decision-making and control in dynamic, interactive environments. Each paradigm offers unique strengths and addresses different types of problems, collectively forming the bedrock of modern AI applications in engineering. Understanding these core paradigms is not just an academic exercise; it is a crucial step towards leveraging AI to build more efficient, intelligent, and sustainable engineered systems.

The effectiveness of any Artificial Intelligence (AI) or Machine Learning (ML) model is intrinsically tied to the quality and preparation of the data it learns from. Even the most sophisticated algorithms will falter if fed raw, unrefined data. This is where data preprocessing and feature engineering become paramount. These are not merely optional steps but rather foundational pillars upon which robust and reliable AI systems are built, especially within the rigorous domain of engineering. They are the meticulous craft of transforming raw data into a format that allows AI models to discern meaningful patterns, generalize effectively to unseen scenarios, and ultimately deliver accurate and actionable insights. Neglecting these stages is akin to building a complex structure on unstable ground – the edifice may appear impressive initially, but its long-term stability and performance are severely compromised.

Data Preprocessing: Laying the Groundwork for Intelligence

Data preprocessing encompasses a suite of techniques designed to clean, transform, and prepare raw data for input into machine learning algorithms. It is a critical, often time-consuming, but indispensable phase in the AI lifecycle. The goal is to address data imperfections, inconsistencies, and formats that could otherwise mislead or confuse the learning process.

Handling Missing Values: Addressing the Gaps in Knowledge

Real-world data is rarely complete. Sensors may malfunction, data collection processes might encounter interruptions, or certain entries might be intentionally left blank. These missing values, often represented as `NaN` (Not a Number), `null`, or specific placeholder values, can cause significant problems. Many machine learning algorithms cannot directly handle missing data and will either crash or produce erroneous results if not addressed.

Several strategies exist for handling missing values, each with its own trade-offs:

Deletion: The simplest approach is to remove rows or columns that contain missing values. Row deletion (listwise deletion) is suitable when the number of missing data points is small relative to the total dataset size, and the missingness is random. However, if a significant portion of data is lost, this can lead to a substantial reduction in sample size, potentially biasing the remaining data and diminishing the model's statistical power. Column deletion is generally discouraged unless a feature is entirely missing or deemed irrelevant, as it discards potentially valuable information.

Imputation: This involves filling in the missing values with estimated or substituted values. Imputation techniques range from simple to sophisticated:
Mean/Median/Mode Imputation: For numerical features, missing values can be replaced with the mean or median of the non-missing values in that column. The median is often preferred as it is less sensitive to outliers. For categorical features, the mode (most frequent category) is used. This is a straightforward and computationally inexpensive method, but it can distort the original variance and covariance of the data, and it doesn't account for relationships between features. For instance, if we are imputing missing temperature readings from a sensor, using the average temperature might not be accurate if the missing data occurred during a specific anomaly or season.

Forward Fill/Backward Fill (for Time-Series Data): In time-series data, where observations are ordered chronologically, missing values can be imputed using the last known value (forward fill) or the next known value (backward fill). This assumes that the value remains constant over short periods, which is often a reasonable assumption for many physical processes. For example, if a vibration sensor reading is missing for a few minutes, it might be reasonable to assume the vibration level stayed similar to the reading just before the gap.

Regression Imputation: A more advanced technique involves using regression to predict the missing values. If a feature has missing values, we can train a regression model using other features as predictors and the feature with missing values as the target. The model then predicts the missing values based on the values of other features for that specific data point. For example, if pressure readings are missing for a specific pipeline segment, we could use flow rate, temperature, and historical pressure data from nearby segments to predict the missing pressure values. This method preserves relationships between variables but can introduce artificial correlation if the imputed values are too close to the regression line.

K-Nearest Neighbors (KNN) Imputation: This method imputes missing values based on the values of their nearest neighbors in the feature space. The algorithm identifies the 'k' most similar data points (neighbors) to the one with the missing value and imputes the missing value using the average (for numerical) or mode (for categorical) of its neighbors. This is a non-parametric approach that can capture complex relationships but is computationally more intensive, especially for large datasets.

Multiple Imputation: Instead of a single imputed value, multiple imputed datasets are created. Each missing value is imputed multiple times, creating several complete datasets. Models are then trained on each of these datasets, and the results are pooled. This method accounts for the uncertainty introduced by imputation and generally leads to more accurate and robust results, though it is more complex to implement.

The choice of imputation method depends heavily on the nature of the data, the type of missingness (e.g., missing completely at random, missing at random, missing not at random), and the specific algorithm being used.

In engineering applications, understanding the physical process that generated the data is often key to choosing the most appropriate imputation strategy. For instance, imputing a missing strain gauge reading during a known seismic event would require a different approach than imputing a missing temperature reading during normal operation.

Dealing with Outliers: Identifying and Managing Extreme Values

Outliers are data points that significantly deviate from the general pattern of the rest of the data. They can arise from various sources: genuine extreme events, measurement errors, data entry mistakes, or simply inherent variability in the system. Outliers can have a disproportionately large impact on statistical measures and machine learning models, particularly those that are sensitive to distance or variance, such as linear regression or clustering algorithms.

Strategies for handling outliers include:

Identification:
Visual Inspection: Box plots, scatter plots, and histograms can help visualize the distribution of data and identify potential outliers.
Statistical Methods:
Z-score: For normally distributed data, data points with a Z-score above a certain threshold (e.g., 2 or 3) are considered outliers. The Z-score measures how many standard deviations a data point is away from the mean.
IQR (Interquartile Range) Method: This method is less sensitive to extreme values than the Z-score. Outliers are typically defined as points

that fall below Q1 - 1.5IQR or above Q3 + 1.5IQR, where Q1 is the first quartile, Q3 is the third quartile, and IQR = Q3 - Q1.
Machine Learning Methods: Algorithms like Isolation Forests or One-Class SVMs are specifically designed to detect anomalies and outliers.

Treatment:
Removal: Similar to handling missing values, outliers can be removed. However, this should be done cautiously, especially if the outliers represent genuine, albeit rare, events that might be of interest. Removing outliers blindly can lead to loss of valuable information.
Transformation: Applying mathematical transformations (e.g., logarithmic, square root) can reduce the skewness of the data and lessen the impact of outliers.
Capping/Winsorizing: Outliers can be "capped" at a certain percentile value. For example, all values above the 95th percentile might be replaced with the value at the 95th percentile. This retains the data point but reduces its extreme influence.
Imputation: In some cases, outliers might be treated as missing values and imputed using methods described earlier.

In engineering, distinguishing between a genuine extreme event and a measurement error is crucial. For instance, an unusual spike in a stress sensor reading on a bridge might indicate an impending structural failure (a genuine extreme event of critical importance) or a faulty sensor (an error). Careful domain expertise is required to decide how to treat such data points.

Data Normalization and Scaling: Standardizing the Playing Field

Many machine learning algorithms are sensitive to the scale of input features. Features with larger values can dominate those with smaller values, even if the latter are more informative. Normalization and scaling techniques bring all features to a comparable range, ensuring that no single feature unduly influences the model's learning process.

Normalization (Min-Max Scaling): This technique rescales features to a fixed range, typically [0, 1] or [-1, 1]. The formula for scaling a feature x to the range [0, 1] is:
`x_scaled = (x - min(x)) / (max(x) - min(x))`
This is useful when algorithms require features to be within a specific bounded interval, such as neural networks. However, it is sensitive to outliers; a single extreme value can compress the range of most of the data.

Standardization (Z-score Scaling): This technique transforms features to have a mean of 0 and a standard deviation of 1. The formula is:
`x*standardized = (x - mean(x)) / std*dev(x)`
Standardization is less sensitive to outliers than normalization and is often preferred for algorithms that assume data is centered around zero or are sensitive to the distribution's shape, such as principal component analysis (PCA) or support vector machines (SVMs). Many algorithms perform better when features are standardized because they assume data follows a Gaussian distribution, or are designed for features with similar scales.

Robust Scaling: This method uses statistics that are robust to outliers, such as the median and the interquartile range (IQR). Features are scaled such that they have a median of 0 and a range that is proportional to the IQR.
`x_scaled = (x - median(x)) / IQR(x)`

This is particularly useful when the dataset contains many outliers.

The choice of scaling technique depends on the algorithm's assumptions and the data characteristics. For instance, if using algorithms sensitive to feature scales like k-means clustering or gradient descent-based methods, scaling is almost always necessary. For tree-based algorithms like decision trees or random forests, scaling is generally not required as they make decisions based on thresholds rather than distances.

Feature Engineering: Crafting Informative Inputs

Feature engineering is the art and science of transforming raw data into features that better represent the underlying problem to the predictive models, leading to improved model accuracy and interpretability. It's about using domain knowledge to create new input variables that capture essential information or relationships that might not be apparent in the raw data. This process is often considered more of an art than a science, requiring creativity, experimentation, and a deep understanding of the problem domain.

Creating New Features from Existing Data

The essence of feature engineering lies in intelligent data transformation and combination.

Polynomial Features: For linear models, creating polynomial combinations of existing features (e.g., `x^2`, `xy`) can help capture non-linear relationships in the data. For instance, if modeling the relationship between the applied force and the deformation of a beam, a linear relationship might be insufficient. Introducing a `force^2` term could better capture the non-linear behavior.

Interaction Features: Combining two or more features to create a new feature that represents their interaction can be powerful. For example, in analyzing energy consumption in a building, the interaction between outdoor temperature and occupancy level might be more predictive than either feature alone. A combined feature like `temperature  occupancy` could capture this synergy.

Aggregations: For data with multiple observations per entity (e.g., sensor readings over time for a piece of equipment), aggregating these readings can create meaningful summary features. For instance, calculating the average, standard deviation, minimum, or maximum of a sensor reading over a specific time window can summarize the equipment's behavior during that period. This is particularly relevant for time-series data.

Encoding Categorical Variables: Machine learning models typically require numerical input. Categorical features (e.g., material type, equipment status, location codes) need to be converted into numerical representations.

One-Hot Encoding: Creates a new binary column for each unique category. For example, if a "material type" feature has categories "steel," "aluminum," and "plastic," one-hot encoding would create three new columns: `is*steel`, `is*aluminum`, `is_plastic`. This is suitable for nominal categories (where order doesn't matter).

Label Encoding: Assigns a unique integer to each category. This is appropriate for ordinal categories (where order matters), such as "low," "medium," "high" being encoded as 0, 1, 2 respectively. However, it can

introduce an artificial ordinal relationship for nominal categories, which some models might misinterpret.
Target Encoding (Mean Encoding): Replaces a category with the average value of the target variable for that category. This can be very effective but requires careful handling to avoid data leakage, often by calculating the encoding on a separate fold of the data.

Feature Engineering for Time-Series Data

Time-series data, common in engineering for monitoring systems, predicting trends, and detecting anomalies, benefits immensely from specific feature engineering techniques:

Lagged Features: Creating features that represent the value of a variable at a previous time step (lag). For example, if predicting a system's temperature, the temperature reading from 1 hour ago (`temperature*lag*1h`) could be a strong predictor. Multiple lags can capture temporal dependencies.

Rolling/Windowed Statistics: Calculating statistics (mean, median, std dev, min, max) over a sliding window of past observations. For instance, `rolling*mean*temperature_1h` would represent the average temperature over the last hour. This smooths out noise and captures trends.

Time-Based Features: Extracting features related to the time of day, day of the week, month, or year. For example, `hour*of*day`, `day*of*week`, `is_weekend`. These can capture cyclical patterns. For infrastructure usage, knowing if it's a weekday or weekend, or a peak or off-peak hour, is often critical for prediction.

Rate of Change/Differencing: Calculating the difference between consecutive time steps (`temperature*t* - *temperature*t-1`). This helps in modeling trends and stationarity.

Domain-Specific Feature Engineering

The most impactful feature engineering often comes from leveraging domain knowledge specific to the engineering discipline.

Structural Engineering:
Stress/Strain Ratios: Combining readings from stress and strain gauges on a component to create a feature representing material properties or an indication of localized stress concentration.
Load Combinations: For bridges or buildings, creating features that represent combinations of different load types (dead load, live load, wind load, seismic load) based on design codes and expected scenarios.
Deflection Calculations: Based on sensor readings, calculating or estimating the deflection of a structural element.

Electrical Engineering:
Power Factor: Combining voltage and current readings to calculate the power factor, an indicator of electrical efficiency.
Harmonic Distortion: Analyzing the frequency spectrum of voltage or current signals to quantify harmonic distortion, which can indicate equipment malfunction or grid issues.

Energy Efficiency Metrics: Creating features that relate energy consumed to output produced (e.g., kWh per unit of manufactured product).

Mechanical Engineering:
Vibration Analysis: Decomposing vibration signals into frequency components (using Fast Fourier Transform - FFT) to identify characteristic frequencies associated with specific rotating machinery issues (e.g., bearing faults, imbalance). The amplitudes of these frequency components become powerful features.
Thermal Gradient: Calculating the difference in temperature between different points in a system to identify potential overheating or inefficient heat dissipation.
Fluid Dynamics Parameters: For pumps or turbines, calculating parameters like flow rate, pressure head, and efficiency from raw sensor data.

Civil/Environmental Engineering:
Water Quality Indices: Combining various sensor readings (pH, dissolved oxygen, turbidity, temperature) into a single index that represents the overall water quality.
Traffic Flow Metrics: From individual vehicle speeds and counts, calculating features like average speed, traffic density, and throughput for different road segments.
Soil Compaction Measures: Engineering derived features from geotechnical sensor data to assess soil stability.

Feature Selection: Choosing the Right Ingredients

While feature engineering involves creating new features, feature selection is the process of selecting the most relevant features from the original and engineered set to build the model. This is crucial for several reasons:

Reduces Overfitting: Too many features, especially irrelevant ones, can lead to models that perform well on training data but poorly on unseen data.
Improves Model Performance: By focusing on informative features, models can learn patterns more effectively.
Reduces Computational Cost: Fewer features mean faster training and inference times.
Enhances Interpretability: A model with fewer features is often easier to understand and explain.

Common feature selection techniques include:

Filter Methods: These methods evaluate the relevance of features based on statistical measures, independent of any specific machine learning model. Examples include correlation coefficients, mutual information, and ANOVA F-tests. For instance, a feature that has a very low correlation with the target variable might be filtered out.

Wrapper Methods: These methods use a specific machine learning model to evaluate subsets of features. They "wrap" the feature selection process around the model training. Examples include Recursive Feature Elimination (RFE) and forward/backward selection. While often more accurate than filter methods, they are computationally more expensive.

Embedded Methods: These methods perform feature selection as part of the model training process. Many algorithms, such as Lasso regression or tree-based models (which inherently provide feature importance scores), have built-in mechanisms for feature selection. Tree-based models, for example, can rank features based on how much they contribute to reducing impurity or variance across the trees.

The interplay between data preprocessing and feature engineering is iterative. Often, initial feature engineering efforts reveal the need for further preprocessing, or preprocessing steps might influence which engineered features are most effective. Thorough data preparation ensures that the subsequent AI model training is not just a mechanical process but a journey guided by well-prepared, informative, and relevant data, leading to intelligent systems that can truly augment engineering capabilities. The time invested in these foundational steps pays significant dividends in the reliability, accuracy, and robustness of the final AI solution.

Ensuring the efficacy and reliability of any artificial intelligence (AI) or machine learning (ML) model is paramount, especially within the demanding field of engineering. Once a model has been trained on meticulously preprocessed and intelligently engineered data, the next critical step is to rigorously evaluate its performance. This evaluation process allows engineers to understand how well the model generalizes to new, unseen data, identify its strengths and weaknesses, and ultimately select the most suitable model for a given application. Without robust evaluation, deploying an AI model would be akin to launching a bridge without stress testing its components – a potentially catastrophic oversight. This subsection delves into the essential model evaluation metrics and techniques that form the bedrock of responsible AI deployment in engineering.

Quantifying Model Performance: Essential Metrics

The way we measure a model's performance depends heavily on the type of problem it is designed to solve. Broadly, these problems fall into two main categories: regression (predicting a continuous value) and classification (predicting a discrete category).

Regression Metrics: Measuring Prediction Accuracy for Continuous Values

Regression tasks are common in engineering for tasks such as predicting material strength, forecasting equipment lifespan, estimating energy demand, or modeling physical phenomena. The goal is to predict a numerical value as accurately as possible. Several metrics are employed to quantify the difference between the predicted values and the actual observed values.

Mean Squared Error (MSE): The Mean Squared Error is a fundamental metric that calculates the average of the squared differences between the predicted values and the actual values. Mathematically, it is represented as:
$MSE = \frac{1}{n} \sum{i=1}^{n} (yi - \hat{y}_i)^2$
where n is the number of data points, yi is the actual value for the i-th data point, and $\hat{y}i$ is the predicted value for the i-th data point. MSE penalizes larger errors more heavily due to the squaring term. This can be advantageous when large deviations are particularly undesirable, such as in predicting structural loads where a significant underestimation could lead to failure. However, the squaring operation also means that MSE is sensitive to outliers; a single extreme error can disproportionately inflate the MSE score. The units of MSE are the square

of the units of the target variable, making it less intuitive for direct interpretation compared to other metrics. For example, if predicting temperature in degrees Celsius, the MSE would be in units of degrees Celsius squared.

Root Mean Squared Error (RMSE): Often preferred over MSE for its interpretability, the Root Mean Squared Error is simply the square root of the MSE:
$RMSE = \sqrt{MSE} = \sqrt{\frac{1}{n} \sum{i=1}^{n} (yi - \hat{y}_i)^2}$
By taking the square root, RMSE brings the error metric back into the original units of the target variable. If predicting temperature in degrees Celsius, RMSE will also be in degrees Celsius. This makes it much easier to understand the typical magnitude of the prediction error. For instance, an RMSE of 2 degrees Celsius indicates that, on average, the model's predictions are off by about 2 degrees. Like MSE, RMSE is also sensitive to outliers due to the squaring operation involved in its calculation. This sensitivity can be a feature or a drawback depending on the application. In monitoring critical systems where deviations from the norm, even if rare, have severe consequences, RMSE's emphasis on larger errors can be beneficial.

Mean Absolute Error (MAE): The Mean Absolute Error calculates the average of the absolute differences between the predicted values and the actual values:
$MAE = \frac{1}{n} \sum{i=1}^{n} |yi - \hat{y}_i|$
MAE offers a different perspective by measuring the average magnitude of errors without considering their direction. It is less sensitive to outliers than MSE and RMSE because it does not square the errors. This can make MAE a more robust choice when dealing with datasets that contain significant extreme values, which might be genuine but rare events. For example, in predicting the lifespan of a component where occasional,

unexpected failures occur due to external factors (e.g., sudden overloads), MAE might provide a more stable estimate of typical prediction error than RMSE. The units of MAE are the same as the target variable, making it as interpretable as RMSE. However, MAE might not sufficiently penalize large errors, which could be critical in certain safety-sensitive engineering applications where minimizing the risk of large deviations is paramount.

R-squared (R^2) or Coefficient of Determination: While not a measure of error magnitude, R^2 is a vital metric that indicates the proportion of the variance in the dependent variable (the target) that is predictable from the independent variables (the features). It ranges from 0 to 1 (or can be negative if the model is worse than predicting the mean).
$R^2 = 1 - \frac{\sum_{i=1}^{n} (y_i - \hat{y}_i)^2}{\sum_{i=1}^{n} (y_i - \bar{y})^2}$
where $\bar{y}$ is the mean of the actual values. An R^2 of 0.80 means that 80% of the variability in the target variable can be explained by the model's features. A higher R^2 generally indicates a better fit, but it's crucial to remember that a high R^2 does not guarantee that the model is unbiased or that it will generalize well. It is possible to achieve a high R^2 on training data by overfitting. For instance, in predicting the load-bearing capacity of a material based on its composition, a high R^2 suggests that the material composition explains a large part of the variation in load capacity.

Adjusted R-squared: This is a modified version of R^2 that adjusts for the number of predictors in the model. As R^2 tends to increase with the addition of more features, even irrelevant ones, Adjusted R^2 penalizes the inclusion of unnecessary features. It is particularly useful when comparing models with different numbers of independent variables.
$Adjusted R^2 = 1 - \frac{(1 - R^2)(n - 1)}{n - k - 1}$

where n is the number of data points and k is the number of predictors. This metric is more indicative of the model's true explanatory power, discouraging the inclusion of features that do not meaningfully improve the model's fit.

Classification Metrics: Evaluating Categorical Predictions

Classification models are used in engineering for tasks such as fault detection (e.g., classifying an anomaly as a bearing failure, an electrical short, or normal operation), predictive maintenance (e.g., classifying a machine as "likely to fail soon" or "healthy"), or image recognition (e.g., classifying a component defect from an inspection image). Evaluating these models requires metrics that consider the counts of correct and incorrect classifications.

A fundamental tool for understanding classification performance is the **Confusion Matrix**. For a binary classification problem (e.g., predicting "fault" vs. "no fault"), the confusion matrix is a table that summarizes the performance by counting the number of True Positives (TP), True Negatives (TN), False Positives (FP), and False Negatives (FN).

True Positive (TP): The model correctly predicted the positive class (e.g., correctly identified a fault when a fault was present).
True Negative (TN): The model correctly predicted the negative class (e.g., correctly identified no fault when no fault was present).
False Positive (FP): The model incorrectly predicted the positive class (e.g., flagged a fault when there was none – a Type I error).
False Negative (FN): The model incorrectly predicted the negative class (e.g., failed to detect a fault when one was present – a Type II error).

From the confusion matrix, several key metrics can be derived:

Accuracy: This is the most intuitive metric and represents the proportion of total predictions that were correct.
$Accuracy = \frac{TP + TN}{TP + TN + FP + FN}$
Accuracy answers the question: "Out of all the predictions made, how many were correct?" While simple, accuracy can be misleading in datasets with imbalanced class distributions. For example, if 99% of components are healthy and only 1% have a fault, a model that always predicts "healthy" will achieve 99% accuracy, but it will be completely useless for detecting faults. This is a common scenario in many engineering anomaly detection problems.

Precision: Precision measures the accuracy of positive predictions. It answers the question: "Of all the instances the model predicted as positive, how many were actually positive?"
$Precision = \frac{TP}{TP + FP}$
High precision means that when the model predicts a positive outcome (e.g., "fault detected"), it is very likely to be correct. In engineering, high precision is crucial when the cost of a false positive is high. For example, triggering an expensive and disruptive shutdown procedure based on a false alarm (FP) would be undesirable.

Recall (Sensitivity or True Positive Rate): Recall measures the model's ability to find all the positive instances. It answers the question: "Of all the actual positive instances, how many did the model correctly identify?"
$Recall = \frac{TP}{TP + FN}$
High recall means the model is good at detecting positive cases. In engineering, high recall is critical when the cost of a false negative is high.

For instance, failing to detect a critical fault (FN) in a power plant turbine could lead to catastrophic failure and immense damage.

F1-Score: The F1-Score is the harmonic mean of Precision and Recall. It provides a single metric that balances both precision and recall, making it a useful metric for imbalanced datasets.
$F1-Score = 2 \frac{Precision Recall}{Precision + Recall}$
The F1-Score is useful when you need to consider both false positives and false negatives. A high F1-Score indicates that the model has good precision and good recall. For example, in a system that flags potential safety hazards, a high F1-score would suggest the system is both good at identifying actual hazards and not producing too many false alarms.

Specificity (True Negative Rate): Specificity measures the model's ability to correctly identify negative instances.
$Specificity = \frac{TN}{TN + FP}$
This is the counterpart to Recall. High specificity means the model is good at correctly identifying instances that do not belong to the positive class.

Area Under the Receiver Operating Characteristic Curve (AUC-ROC): The ROC curve is a graphical plot that illustrates the diagnostic ability of a binary classifier system as its discrimination threshold is varied. It plots the True Positive Rate (Recall) against the False Positive Rate ($FPR = \frac{FP}{FP + TN}$). The AUC-ROC represents the degree or measure of separability of the classes. It tells us how much the model is capable of distinguishing between classes.
An AUC of 1 represents a perfect classifier.
An AUC of 0.5 represents a classifier that is no better than random guessing.
An AUC of 0 represents a classifier that is perfectly wrong.

AUC-ROC is particularly valuable because it provides a single scalar value that summarizes the classifier's performance across all possible thresholds. This is important because the optimal threshold for making a positive/negative prediction often depends on the specific trade-off between precision and recall desired for a given application. In engineering, when seeking a robust anomaly detection system that performs well regardless of the exact decision threshold, AUC-ROC is a strong indicator of overall model quality.

Log Loss (Cross-Entropy Loss): For models that output probability scores for each class (e.g., a probability of 0.8 that a component is faulty), Log Loss penalizes incorrect probabilities. It is a measure of the uncertainty of predictions. Lower log loss indicates better performance. It heavily penalizes confident wrong predictions.

$LogLoss = -\frac{1}{n} \sum_{i=1}^{n} [y_i \log(\hat{p}_i) + (1 - y_i) \log(1 - \hat{p}_i)]$

where y_i *is the true label (0 or 1) and* $\hat{p}_i$ is the predicted probability of the positive class. This metric is crucial when the calibrated probability of an event is as important as the classification itself, such as in risk assessment.

The Crucial Role of Cross-Validation

A common pitfall in model evaluation is testing a model solely on the data it was trained on. This approach invariably leads to an overly optimistic assessment of performance because the model has already "seen" these examples and potentially memorized them, a phenomenon known as **overfitting**. Overfitting means the model performs exceptionally well on the training data but fails to generalize to new, unseen data, rendering it useless in real-world applications. To combat this and obtain a more reliable estimate of a model's generalization ability, various **cross-validation** techniques are employed.

Train-Validation-Test Split

The simplest form of evaluation involves splitting the dataset into three parts:

1.
Training Set: Used to train the model. Typically, 60-80% of the data is allocated here.
2. **Validation Set:** Used to tune hyperparameters (e.g., learning rate, number of layers in a neural network, regularization strength) and to perform model selection. This set provides an unbiased evaluation of a model's performance as it is not used during training. Typically 10-20% of the data.
3. **Test Set:** Used for the final evaluation of the chosen model after all training and hyperparameter tuning are complete. This set acts as a proxy for truly unseen data and provides the most realistic estimate of the model's performance in deployment. Typically 10-20% of the data.

While effective, a single train-validation-test split can still be subject to the luck of the draw. If the split results in a validation or test set that is not representative of the overall data distribution, the evaluation might be skewed.

K-Fold Cross-Validation: A More Robust Approach

K-Fold Cross-Validation is a more robust technique that helps mitigate the issues associated with a single validation set. The process involves the following steps:

1.
Partitioning: The entire dataset (excluding the final test set, if one is reserved) is randomly divided into k equal-sized subsets, called "folds."
2. **Iteration:** The model is trained k times. In each iteration:
One fold is designated as the **validation set**.
The remaining $k-1$ folds are combined to form the **training set**.
The model is trained on the combined training set.
The trained model is evaluated on the validation fold, and its performance metric (e.g., RMSE, Accuracy) is recorded.
3. **Aggregation:** After k iterations, k performance scores are obtained, one for each fold. The final performance estimate is typically the average of these k scores.

A common choice for k is 5 or 10. Using $k=10$ (10-fold cross-validation) is a widely accepted practice, providing a good balance between computational cost and reliability of the performance estimate.

Benefits of K-Fold Cross-Validation:

Reduced Variance: By averaging performance across k different validation sets, K-fold cross-validation provides a more stable and less variable estimate of the model's generalization performance compared to a single train-validation split.
Efficient Data Usage: Every data point gets to be in a validation set exactly once and in a training set $k-1$ times, making more efficient use of the available data. This is particularly valuable in engineering domains

where acquiring large, labeled datasets can be expensive and time-consuming.
Better Hyperparameter Tuning: K-fold cross-validation can be used during the hyperparameter tuning phase. For each combination of hyperparameters, the model is trained and evaluated using K-fold cross-validation. The hyperparameter set that yields the best average cross-validation score is then selected.

Stratified K-Fold Cross-Validation: For classification tasks, especially with imbalanced datasets, it is important to ensure that each fold maintains the same proportion of classes as the original dataset. **Stratified K-Fold Cross-Validation** achieves this by ensuring that each fold contains approximately the same percentage of samples of each target class as the complete set. This prevents situations where a fold might have no examples of a minority class, which would lead to unreliable evaluation.

Leave-One-Out Cross-Validation (LOOCV): This is an extreme case of K-fold cross-validation where k is equal to the number of data points (n). In each iteration, one data point is used as the validation set, and the remaining $n-1$ data points are used for training. LOOCV provides a nearly unbiased estimate of the model's performance but is computationally very expensive, especially for large datasets, as it requires training the model n times. It is generally used when computational resources are not a constraint or for very small datasets.

Considerations for Model Selection and Evaluation

When evaluating and selecting models for engineering applications, several factors beyond raw performance scores should be considered:

Computational Cost: The time and resources required to train and deploy the model. A slightly less accurate model that can provide real-time predictions might be preferable to a highly accurate but computationally prohibitive one.
Interpretability: In many engineering contexts, understanding why a model makes a certain prediction is as important as the prediction itself. Models that offer insights into feature importance or decision logic (like linear models or decision trees) are often favored over "black box" models, even if the latter achieve marginally better performance. This is crucial for debugging, ensuring compliance with regulations, and building trust in the AI system.
Robustness to Data Drift: Real-world engineering systems are dynamic. Sensor characteristics can change, operating conditions can vary, and the underlying physical processes might evolve over time. A model that performs well today might degrade over time if the data distribution shifts (known as data drift). Evaluation should ideally include considerations for how the model might behave under such conditions, perhaps through stress testing or by monitoring performance degradation post-deployment.
Domain-Specific Requirements: The acceptable trade-off between different types of errors (e.g., false positives vs. false negatives) is heavily dictated by the specific engineering domain. A system predicting equipment failure in a nuclear power plant will have very different requirements than a system predicting traffic flow on a highway. The choice of metrics and the interpretation of their values must align with these critical domain requirements. For instance, in predictive maintenance, a slight over-reporting of potential failures (higher FP rate) might be acceptable if it significantly reduces the chance of missing a critical failure (lower FN rate).

In summary, selecting appropriate evaluation metrics and employing rigorous cross-validation techniques are not mere procedural steps; they are integral to the responsible development and deployment of AI in engineering. These practices ensure that the AI models are not only performing well on historical data but are also reliable, generalizable, and trustworthy when applied to the complex and critical challenges faced in engineering practice. They provide the necessary confidence to integrate AI into systems where safety, efficiency, and precision are paramount.

The previous section established the critical importance of rigorously evaluating machine learning models using appropriate metrics and cross-validation techniques. Engineers must ensure that their deployed AI systems are not only accurate on historical data but also generalizable and reliable in real-world scenarios. Now, as we transition to understanding the powerful architectures that underpin many modern AI advancements, we will explore the fundamental building blocks of artificial intelligence: neural networks and their sophisticated extension, deep learning. These concepts are not just theoretical curiosities; they represent a paradigm shift in how we can tackle complex problems in engineering, from analyzing intricate material behaviors to deciphering patterns in vast sensor networks.

At their core, artificial neural networks (ANNs) are computational models inspired by the structure and function of the biological neural networks found in animal brains. Just as our brains are composed of interconnected neurons that process and transmit information, ANNs are built from interconnected processing units, often referred to as nodes or artificial neurons. These artificial neurons are organized into layers, forming a network that can learn to recognize complex patterns and relationships within data. The simplicity of an individual neuron belies the incredible power of these networks when scaled and interconnected. Each artificial neuron receives input signals, processes them, and then produces an output signal. This output is determined by a weighted sum of the inputs, passed through a non-linear function called an activation function. This fundamental operation allows neural networks to model non-linear relationships, a critical capability for many real-world engineering problems that are rarely linear in nature.

Consider a foundational example: predicting the potential for material fatigue in structural components. Historically, engineers relied on empirical formulas and extensive physical testing. With ANNs, we can feed the network data about a material's composition, its stress history, operating temperature, and other environmental factors. Each of these factors can be thought of as an input signal to the network. Inside the network, artificial neurons, organized in layers, process these inputs. For instance, an initial layer might learn to identify basic interactions between stress and temperature. Subsequent layers can then combine these learned features to recognize more complex patterns indicative of fatigue progression. The network learns through a process of trial and error, adjusting the strengths of the connections (weights) between neurons to minimize prediction errors. This ability to learn complex interactions directly from data, without explicit programming of every rule, is what makes neural networks so powerful.

Let's delve deeper into the architecture of a simple feedforward neural network, the most basic type. Such a network consists of at least three types of layers: an input layer, one or more hidden layers, and an output layer.

The **input layer** is where the raw data enters the network. Each node in the input layer corresponds to a feature or attribute of the data. For our material fatigue example, these nodes would represent features like tensile strength, Young's modulus, applied stress, temperature, and cycle count. The number of neurons in the input layer is equal to the number of features in the dataset.
Following the input layer are the **hidden layers**. These layers are where the actual computation and feature extraction occur. Neurons in a hidden

layer receive inputs from the previous layer, perform a weighted sum of these inputs, add a bias term, and then apply an activation function. The "hidden" nature of these layers comes from the fact that their outputs are not directly observable from the outside; they are intermediate representations learned by the network. The number of hidden layers and the number of neurons within each hidden layer are design choices that significantly impact the network's capacity to learn. More layers and more neurons can enable the network to learn more complex patterns, but they also increase the risk of overfitting and computational cost.
Finally, the **output layer** produces the network's prediction. For a regression task, like predicting the remaining useful life of a component, the output layer might have a single neuron with a linear activation function. For a classification task, such as categorizing pavement distress (e.g., "cracks," "potholes," "spalling"), the output layer would have multiple neurons, one for each class, typically using a softmax activation function to produce probabilities for each class.

The magic of how a neural network learns lies in its ability to adjust the weights and biases of its neurons. This adjustment process is guided by an optimization algorithm, most commonly
gradient descent, and the core mechanism for propagating the error backward through the network is called **backpropagation**.

Let's consider the role of activation functions. Without them, a neural network, no matter how many layers it has, would simply be a linear model. Activation functions introduce non-linearity, allowing the network to learn complex, non-linear relationships. Common activation functions include:

Sigmoid: Squashes the input values into a range between 0 and 1. Historically popular, it's often used in output layers for binary classification but can suffer from vanishing gradients.

Tanh (Hyperbolic Tangent): Similar to sigmoid but squashes values into a range between -1 and 1. It is zero-centered, which can sometimes lead to faster convergence than sigmoid.
ReLU (Rectified Linear Unit): Defined as $f(x) = max(0, x)$. It is computationally efficient and has become the default choice for hidden layers in many deep learning architectures. ReLU introduces sparsity by setting negative inputs to zero.
Leaky ReLU: A variation of ReLU that allows a small, non-zero gradient for negative inputs, helping to prevent the "dying ReLU" problem where neurons can become inactive.
Softmax: Primarily used in the output layer for multi-class classification. It converts a vector of numbers into a probability distribution, where all elements sum to 1.

The process of training a neural network involves feeding it a large dataset and iteratively updating its weights and biases to minimize a **loss function**. The loss function quantifies how far the network's predictions are from the actual target values. For regression tasks, common loss functions include Mean Squared Error (MSE) or Mean Absolute Error (MAE), which we discussed in the context of model evaluation. For classification, Cross-Entropy Loss is a popular choice.

Backpropagation is the engine that drives learning in ANNs. Here's a simplified breakdown:

1. **Forward Pass:** Input data is fed through the network, layer by layer, to produce an output prediction.
2. **Loss Calculation:** The loss function is computed, measuring the difference between the predicted output and the actual target.
3. **Backward Pass (Backpropagation):** The error is propagated backward from the output layer to the input layer. Using calculus (specifically, the chain rule), the algorithm calculates the gradient of the loss function with respect to each weight and bias in the network. This

gradient indicates the direction and magnitude of change needed for each parameter to reduce the loss.
4. **Weight Update:** An optimization algorithm, like gradient descent, uses these gradients to update the weights and biases. The goal is to "descend" the loss function landscape towards a minimum. This process is repeated for many iterations (epochs) over the training data until the network converges to a satisfactory level of performance.

To illustrate further, consider a simplified engineering problem: predicting the likelihood of a bridge undergoing excessive vibration based on traffic load and wind speed.

Input Layer: Neurons for 'traffic load' (e.g., weight, speed) and 'wind speed'.
Hidden Layer(s): One or more layers where neurons learn to combine these inputs. For example, a neuron might learn that a combination of high traffic load and high wind speed is more problematic than either individually. Another neuron might learn the effect of resonant frequencies.
Activation Functions: ReLU for hidden layers to introduce non-linearity.
Output Layer: A single neuron with a sigmoid activation function, outputting a probability between 0 and 1 representing the likelihood of excessive vibration.
Loss Function: Binary Cross-Entropy, suitable for this binary classification problem.
Training: The network is fed data from sensors on the bridge, along with known instances of excessive vibration. Backpropagation adjusts weights to minimize the discrepancy between predicted and actual vibration events. Over many cycles, the network learns the complex interplay of factors leading to dangerous vibrations.

This basic structure, where information flows in one direction from input to output, is known as a

feedforward neural network. It's a powerful tool, but it has limitations when dealing with sequential or spatial data. This is where the concept of **deep learning** emerges.

Deep learning is essentially a subfield of machine learning that utilizes neural networks with multiple hidden layers—hence, "deep." The "depth" refers to the number of layers, allowing the network to learn hierarchical representations of the data. Each layer in a deep network learns to detect increasingly complex features based on the output of the previous layer. This hierarchical learning is what makes deep learning so effective for tasks involving intricate data structures like images, audio, and natural language.

Imagine analyzing images of concrete structures for defects. A traditional approach might involve hand-crafted features that look for specific edge patterns or color gradients. A deep neural network, specifically a **Convolutional Neural Network (CNN)**, can learn these features automatically.
The first few layers of a CNN might learn to detect simple edges and corners.
Subsequent layers combine these edges to recognize more complex shapes like curves or textured surfaces.
Deeper layers might learn to identify entire components or patterns of damage, such as hairline cracks or spalling.
This ability to learn representations at multiple levels of abstraction allows deep networks to achieve state-of-the-art performance in tasks like image recognition, object detection, and semantic segmentation—all highly relevant to infrastructure monitoring and inspection.

Another crucial architecture in deep learning is the **Recurrent Neural Network (RNN)**. Unlike feedforward networks, RNNs have connections that loop back on themselves, allowing them to maintain an internal "memory" or state. This makes them exceptionally well-suited for processing sequential data, where the order of information matters. Examples in engineering include:

Time Series Forecasting: Predicting future sensor readings from a complex industrial process (e.g., temperature, pressure, flow rate) to anticipate anomalies or optimize operations. The network learns patterns and dependencies over time.
Predictive Maintenance: Analyzing sequences of operational data from machinery to detect subtle precursors to failure. For instance, a gradual increase in vibration amplitude followed by a change in motor current might be a pattern indicative of an impending bearing failure, which an RNN can learn to recognize.
Natural Language Processing (NLP) for Engineering Reports: Analyzing maintenance logs, inspection reports, or technical documentation to extract key information, identify recurring issues, or even assist in generating summaries. The sequential nature of language makes RNNs ideal for this.

While basic RNNs can suffer from challenges in learning long-term dependencies (the "vanishing gradient problem" again), variations like **Long Short-Term Memory (LSTM)** networks and **Gated Recurrent Units (GRUs)** have been developed to overcome these limitations. LSTMs and GRUs use sophisticated gating mechanisms that control the flow of information, allowing them to selectively remember or forget information over extended sequences. This makes them highly effective for complex tasks like modeling long-term trends in environmental data or predicting the structural integrity of a system over its entire operational lifespan.

The power of deep learning also extends to handling high-dimensional data like large datasets of sensor readings. Imagine monitoring a smart city's power grid, where millions of sensors generate data streams constantly. A deep learning model can be trained to identify anomalous patterns that might indicate equipment malfunction, overload, or even malicious cyber activity. The hierarchical feature extraction inherent in deep networks allows them to sift through this immense volume of data and detect subtle deviations that might be missed by traditional statistical methods.

The transition from traditional machine learning to deep learning represents a significant leap in AI capabilities. While traditional methods often require substantial manual feature engineering—a process where domain experts painstakingly craft relevant input features for the model—deep learning models can learn these features automatically from raw data. This "end-to-end learning" paradigm simplifies the development process and often leads to superior performance, especially for complex, unstructured data.

Consider the application of deep learning in analyzing satellite imagery for infrastructure monitoring. For instance, identifying changes in land use, detecting new construction, or assessing the impact of natural disasters on transportation networks. A CNN can be trained on vast amounts of historical imagery to automatically identify features such as roads, buildings, bridges, and vegetation. By comparing imagery from different time points, it can then detect changes, such as the formation of new cracks on a runway, erosion around a dam, or the extent of flooding impacting critical infrastructure. This automated analysis can significantly speed up the process of monitoring vast geographical areas, allowing engineers to prioritize interventions and allocate resources more effectively.

The success of deep learning is not without its challenges, however. Training deep neural networks can be computationally intensive, often requiring powerful GPUs (Graphics Processing Units) or specialized hardware. Furthermore, deep learning models can be notoriously difficult to interpret, often being referred to as "black boxes." Understanding *why* a deep network makes a particular prediction can be challenging, which is a significant hurdle in safety-critical engineering applications where explainability is paramount. However, ongoing research in areas like **explainable AI (XAI)** is beginning to provide methods for understanding the decision-making process of these complex models, such as techniques that visualize the features learned by different layers or highlight the most influential input features for a given prediction.

Another challenge is the need for large amounts of labeled training data. While deep learning excels at learning from data, it often requires substantial datasets where the desired output is known. In engineering, obtaining such large, meticulously labeled datasets can be expensive and time-consuming. Techniques like **transfer learning** and **data augmentation** are employed to mitigate this. Transfer learning involves taking a model pre-trained on a large, general dataset (e.g., ImageNet for image recognition) and fine-tuning it on a smaller, domain-specific dataset. Data augmentation involves artificially expanding the training dataset by applying transformations to existing data (e.g., rotating, cropping, or adding noise to images) to create new, diverse examples.

In essence, neural networks, particularly in their deep configurations, provide a powerful and flexible framework for engineers to tackle increasingly complex problems. From predicting material behavior under extreme conditions to interpreting vast streams of sensor data for anomaly detection, these models are transforming how we design, build, and maintain the infrastructure that underpins our society. They offer the potential to automate complex analyses, uncover hidden patterns, and ultimately lead to safer, more efficient, and more resilient engineering solutions. As we move forward, understanding these foundational concepts of neural networks and deep learning will be indispensable for any engineer looking to leverage the full potential of artificial intelligence.

The preceding sections have laid the groundwork for understanding the technical underpinnings of artificial intelligence, focusing on neural networks and deep learning architectures. We've explored how these powerful tools can process complex data, learn intricate patterns, and make predictions relevant to a wide array of engineering challenges. However, as we increasingly integrate AI into the fabric of our infrastructure, our professional responsibilities extend beyond mere technical proficiency. A critical, and perhaps the most vital, dimension of AI deployment for engineers is the thorough consideration of its ethical implications. Deploying AI systems, especially in public-facing infrastructure and critical services, is not simply a matter of achieving high accuracy scores; it necessitates a deep commitment to fairness, equity, transparency, and accountability. Ignoring these ethical dimensions can lead to unintended consequences, exacerbating existing societal inequities or creating new ones, and ultimately eroding public trust in the technologies we develop and implement.

One of the most pervasive and insidious ethical challenges in AI is **bias**. AI systems learn from data, and if the data used for training reflects historical or societal biases, the AI system will inevitably inherit and perpetuate those biases. This bias can manifest in numerous ways, leading to unfair or discriminatory outcomes. For instance, consider an AI system designed to optimize traffic light timing across a city. If the historical data used for training over-represents traffic patterns in affluent neighborhoods while under-representing those in lower-income areas, the resulting AI might prioritize traffic flow in the former, leading to longer wait times and reduced mobility for residents in the latter. This is not a hypothetical concern; studies have shown how facial recognition systems exhibit higher error rates for individuals with darker skin tones due to biased training datasets. In engineering contexts, this could translate to discriminatory access to services. Imagine an AI used to allocate resources for infrastructure maintenance, such as prioritizing repairs for roads or utilities. If the historical data doesn't adequately capture the needs of all communities, the AI might inadvertently favor certain areas, leaving others underserved and further entrenching existing disparities. Engineers must therefore be meticulous in scrutinizing their training data for any potential biases. This involves not just demographic representation but also the historical context of the data. Are there patterns of underinvestment or unequal service provision in the past that the data might simply reflect without addressing the underlying inequity? Techniques for bias detection and mitigation, such as re-sampling, re-weighting, or algorithmic fairness constraints, must be integral to the development lifecycle.

Beyond data bias, algorithmic bias itself can emerge. Even with seemingly balanced data, the inherent design or optimization objectives of an algorithm can lead to biased outcomes. For example, an algorithm optimized purely for efficiency, without explicit fairness constraints, might disproportionately impact certain groups. Consider a predictive policing algorithm that relies on historical crime data. If this data is itself a reflection of biased policing practices, the algorithm might predict higher crime rates in certain communities, leading to increased surveillance and potentially a self-fulfilling prophecy of increased arrests in those areas, regardless of actual crime levels. This raises profound questions about **fairness in AI-driven decision-making**. What does it mean for an AI system to be fair? There isn't a single, universally accepted definition of fairness. Engineers might encounter different mathematical formulations of fairness, such as demographic parity (ensuring equal outcome rates across groups), equalized odds (ensuring equal true positive and false positive rates across groups), or individual fairness (treating similar individuals similarly). Choosing which definition of fairness to prioritize is an ethical decision that often involves trade-offs and requires careful consideration of the specific application and its societal impact. In infrastructure, this means asking: If an AI is used to determine eligibility for services like public transportation routes, affordable housing allocation, or even disaster relief distribution, how do we ensure that these decisions are not perpetuating historical disadvantages? Engineers have a responsibility to understand these different fairness metrics and to implement systems that align with principles of equity, ensuring that AI deployment benefits all members of society, not just a select few.

The "black box" nature of many sophisticated AI models, particularly deep neural networks, presents another significant ethical hurdle: the demand for

transparency and interpretability. When an AI system makes a critical decision—whether it's recommending a medical treatment, determining loan eligibility, or identifying a structural defect in a bridge—it is crucial to understand *why* that decision was made. Without interpretability, it becomes incredibly difficult to detect errors, identify biases, or hold anyone accountable when things go wrong. In safety-critical engineering domains, this lack of understanding can be a showstopper. Imagine an AI system that flags a particular bridge as being at high risk of imminent failure. Engineers need to know the specific factors that led to this assessment—was it a particular sensor reading, a historical stress pattern, or a combination of factors? This knowledge is essential for verifying the AI's assessment, designing appropriate mitigation strategies, and ensuring public safety. Furthermore, a lack of transparency can breed distrust. If the public and other stakeholders cannot understand how AI systems are making decisions that affect their lives, they are less likely to accept or trust these technologies. Researchers are actively developing methods for explainable AI (XAI), such as LIME (Local Interpretable Model-agnostic Explanations) and SHAP (SHapley Additive exPlanations), which aim to provide insights into model predictions. Engineers should explore and adopt these techniques where feasible, striving to make AI systems as transparent as possible, especially in high-stakes applications. This might involve choosing simpler, more interpretable models when performance differences are marginal, or developing supplementary explanation modules for complex deep learning systems.

The question of

accountability for AI-generated outcomes is paramount. When an autonomous vehicle causes an accident, who is responsible? Is it the AI developer, the manufacturer of the vehicle, the owner, or the AI system itself? Current legal and ethical frameworks are still grappling with these questions. In engineering practice, however, there is a clear chain of responsibility. Engineers are accountable for the systems they design, build, and deploy. This responsibility extends to understanding the limitations and potential failure modes of AI systems. It means establishing robust testing and validation procedures, implementing oversight mechanisms, and defining clear protocols for what happens when an AI system makes an error or produces an undesirable outcome. For instance, if an AI system is used in an industrial control process, there must be human-in-the-loop oversight and clear procedures for manual intervention if the AI behaves erratically. Accountability also implies a commitment to continuous monitoring and improvement. AI systems are not static; they interact with the real world and can drift in performance over time, or encounter novel situations they were not trained for. Engineers must establish systems for monitoring deployed AI, collecting feedback, and retraining or updating models as necessary to maintain performance and ensure safety and fairness. This proactive approach to accountability is essential for building and maintaining public trust in AI technologies.

The potential for AI to
exacerbate or mitigate societal inequities is a critical consideration that engineers must actively address. AI has the potential to be a powerful force for good, enabling more efficient resource allocation, improving accessibility for people with disabilities, and optimizing services for all. For example, AI can be used to design more accessible public transportation systems, optimize energy grids to reduce costs for low-income households, or provide personalized educational tools. However, without careful design and deployment, AI can also widen existing divides. An AI-powered hiring tool that implicitly favors certain demographic groups can perpetuate employment discrimination. An AI

used in urban planning that prioritizes development in already well-resourced areas can further marginalize underserved communities. Engineers have a moral and professional obligation to consider the broader societal impact of their work. This involves moving beyond purely technical metrics of performance to consider the human and social consequences. It means engaging with diverse stakeholders—including community members, ethicists, social scientists, and policymakers—to ensure that AI systems are developed and deployed in ways that promote equity and social justice.

To foster responsible AI development and deployment in infrastructure projects, engineers should adopt a proactive framework. This framework should include:

1.
Ethical Risk Assessment: Before commencing development, conduct a thorough assessment of potential ethical risks associated with the AI system. This involves identifying potential biases in data and algorithms, considering fairness implications, evaluating transparency needs, and determining accountability mechanisms.
2. **Diverse Development Teams:** Ensure that development teams are diverse in terms of background, perspective, and expertise. This can help identify potential biases and blind spots that a more homogenous team might overlook. Including ethicists, social scientists, and domain experts with a focus on societal impact can be invaluable.
3. **Data Governance and Auditing:** Implement rigorous data governance practices. This includes careful data collection, anonymization where appropriate, and regular auditing of training data for bias. Documenting the provenance and characteristics of training data is crucial.
4. **Fairness-Aware Model Development:** Integrate fairness considerations into the model development process. This may involve selecting appropriate fairness metrics, using bias mitigation techniques, and performing fairness evaluations alongside performance evaluations.

5. **Transparency and Explainability Tools:** Where possible, employ or develop tools and methods for making AI systems more transparent and interpretable. Document the decision-making processes and provide clear explanations for critical outcomes.
6. **Robust Testing and Validation:** Beyond standard performance metrics, design testing protocols that specifically assess fairness, robustness, and potential for unintended consequences across different user groups and scenarios.
7. **Accountability Frameworks:** Clearly define roles, responsibilities, and escalation procedures for AI system performance, errors, and failures. Establish mechanisms for redress and continuous monitoring.
8. **Stakeholder Engagement:** Engage with affected communities, end-users, and other stakeholders throughout the development and deployment lifecycle. Their input is invaluable for understanding real-world impacts and ensuring that AI systems serve the public good.
9. **Continuous Monitoring and Iteration:** AI systems require ongoing vigilance. Implement systems for monitoring deployed AI for performance drift, emergent biases, and unexpected behaviors. Be prepared to iterate, update, or even decommission systems that no longer meet ethical or performance standards.

In conclusion, as engineers, our role in shaping the future of AI is profound. The technical capabilities of neural networks and deep learning are undeniable, offering unprecedented opportunities to innovate and solve complex problems. However, the ethical dimension of AI deployment is not an afterthought; it is an integral part of responsible engineering practice. By proactively addressing issues of bias, fairness, transparency, and accountability, and by committing to developing AI that serves all members of society equitably, we can ensure that the transformative power of artificial intelligence is harnessed for the benefit of humanity, building a more just, resilient, and sustainable future. This requires a conscious effort to embed ethical considerations into every stage of the AI lifecycle, from initial design to long-term maintenance, fostering a culture of responsibility and foresight within the engineering profession.

Chapter 3: Time-Series Forecasting for Resource Demand

Time-series data forms the bedrock of understanding and managing dynamic infrastructure systems. At its core, time-series data is a sequence of data points collected or recorded over successive time intervals. These intervals can be as granular as milliseconds, such as sensor readings from a high-frequency trading system, or as broad as years, like historical records of national GDP. In the context of infrastructure, this temporal aspect is not merely an organizational feature; it is the defining characteristic that allows us to perceive and predict the behavior of complex, evolving systems. Consider the omnipresent flow of electricity. The demand for power is not static; it fluctuates significantly throughout the day, influenced by diurnal cycles, weekly work patterns, and seasonal variations in heating and cooling needs. A utility company relies on understanding these patterns to ensure that generation capacity precisely matches demand at every moment. Any miscalculation can lead to blackouts during peak demand or wasteful overproduction during lulls, both of which have significant economic and societal consequences.

Similarly, water management systems are intrinsically tied to time-series data. Water consumption, whether for residential, commercial, or industrial use, exhibits predictable patterns. Demand typically surges in the morning and evening as people start and end their daily routines, and it can spike during hot summer months due to increased irrigation and cooling. Predicting these fluctuations is vital for reservoir management, pump operation scheduling, and ensuring adequate supply without unnecessary energy expenditure. The operational efficiency of our water infrastructure hinges on the ability to forecast these temporal demands accurately.

Traffic flow is another quintessential example of time-series data in action. Urban planners and traffic engineers meticulously monitor the volume of vehicles traversing roads, highways, and intersections over time. This data reveals rush-hour peaks, slower periods during midday, and the ebb and flow of weekend travel. Forecasting these patterns is crucial for optimizing traffic signal timings, managing congestion, planning for future road capacity needs, and developing effective public transportation strategies. Unforeseen surges in traffic, not anticipated by forecasting models, can cripple urban mobility, leading to lost productivity and increased pollution.

Beyond resource consumption and physical flow, environmental monitoring within infrastructure also generates critical time-series data. Air quality sensors, for instance, record concentrations of pollutants such as particulate matter, ozone, and nitrogen oxides over time. These readings exhibit diurnal and seasonal variations, often influenced by traffic patterns, industrial activity, and meteorological conditions. Understanding these temporal trends is essential for public health advisories, regulatory compliance, and implementing targeted pollution control measures. For example, predicting a spike in ozone levels on a hot, sunny afternoon allows authorities to issue warnings and potentially implement temporary traffic restrictions.

The intrinsic nature of time-series data, particularly within infrastructure, is characterized by several key components that influence its behavior and predictability. These components are crucial for selecting appropriate forecasting models and interpreting their results.

The first, and often most apparent, is
trend. A trend represents the long-term increase or decrease in the data. In infrastructure, this could manifest as a gradual increase in overall electricity demand over decades due to population growth and increasing electrification of various sectors, or a decline in water consumption in a region experiencing depopulation. Identifying and understanding the trend is vital for long-term planning, such as investments in new

generation capacity or the expansion of water distribution networks. Without accounting for trend, short-term forecasts can be significantly misleading, projecting a continuation of recent fluctuations without recognizing the underlying directional shift. For example, if a city is experiencing steady population growth, simply averaging past electricity consumption might underestimate future demand, leading to inadequate infrastructure development. Conversely, a region with declining industrial activity might see a decreasing trend in energy consumption, and failing to recognize this could lead to overinvestment in power generation.

Next is
seasonality. This refers to patterns that repeat over a fixed period, typically within a year. In infrastructure, seasonality is extremely pronounced. Electricity demand, as mentioned, shows strong daily, weekly, and yearly seasonal patterns. Water usage also follows similar seasonal cycles. Traffic volume often exhibits distinct weekly seasonality, with weekdays differing significantly from weekends. Even pollution levels can have seasonal components, with certain pollutants peaking in summer or winter months due to specific atmospheric conditions or human activities like increased heating or cooling. Recognizing seasonality allows for the optimization of operations within these predictable cycles. For instance, scheduling maintenance for power plants during periods of low demand (e.g., overnight on a weekend in spring) is a direct application of understanding seasonal patterns. Without accounting for seasonality, a forecast might predict a higher than actual demand during a holiday season or a lower than actual demand during a heatwave, leading to inefficient resource allocation.

Closely related to seasonality, but often less predictable in its duration, is **cyclicality**. Cyclical patterns are fluctuations that are not of a fixed period, but tend to occur at irregular intervals and may last for several years. In infrastructure, these cycles are often driven by broader economic factors. For example, periods of economic expansion might lead to increased industrial activity and consequently higher energy and water demand, while economic recessions can cause a dip in these demands. These economic cycles can influence the overall trend of infrastructure usage. While seasonality is about predictable, fixed-duration repeats (like daily or yearly), cyclicality is about longer-term, less regular swings that are often tied to external economic or social forces. A forecast that only considers trend and seasonality might be blindsided by a sharp economic downturn that significantly reduces industrial water usage, leading to a projection of continued high demand. Conversely, during an economic boom, ignoring potential cyclical upswings could lead to underestimation of future infrastructure needs.

Finally, there is
randomness, often referred to as noise. This component represents unpredictable, irregular fluctuations in the data that cannot be attributed to trend, seasonality, or cyclicality. These are the short-term, erratic variations that might be caused by a sudden, unforeseen event – a localized power outage affecting demand readings, a major accident causing a temporary traffic gridlock, or a sudden weather anomaly impacting water usage. While individual random fluctuations are unpredictable, their aggregate behavior can sometimes be characterized statistically. Effective time-series forecasting models aim to capture and explain the systematic components (trend, seasonality, cyclicality) and treat the remaining randomness as inherent variability. A good model will minimize the impact of this random noise on the overall forecast, providing a stable prediction despite short-term turbulence. For instance, a sudden, isolated power surge might cause a momentary spike in electricity demand data, but a robust forecasting model will not let this single anomaly derail its prediction for the rest of the day or week, recognizing it as random noise rather than a new trend.

The importance of accurately forecasting these time-series patterns in infrastructure cannot be overstated. It directly impacts operational planning, resource allocation, and the overall stability and efficiency of essential services. For electricity grids, forecasting demand is a continuous, minute-by-minute necessity. Exceeding supply leads to blackouts, damaging equipment and causing significant disruption. Underestimating demand can lead to unnecessary overproduction, wasting fuel and increasing operational costs. Sophisticated forecasting models enable grid operators to optimize power generation, integrate renewable energy sources more effectively (which are inherently variable), and manage energy storage solutions. This not only ensures reliability but also contributes to cost savings and environmental sustainability.

In water management, accurate demand forecasting allows for proactive reservoir management. Knowing how much water will be needed in the coming hours, days, and weeks allows operators to balance supply from various sources, manage reservoir levels to prevent both shortages and floods, and schedule pumping operations to take advantage of lower electricity prices during off-peak hours. This operational efficiency translates directly into reduced costs for water utilities and, consequently, for consumers. Furthermore, it ensures that essential services remain available, particularly during periods of high demand or potential scarcity.

For transportation networks, forecasting traffic volume is key to efficient management. Predictive traffic models inform dynamic traffic light control systems, reroute vehicles around congestion, and guide infrastructure investment. When traffic flow can be predicted, authorities can implement strategies to mitigate bottlenecks before they form, reducing travel times, fuel consumption, and air pollution. This proactive approach to traffic management, powered by accurate time-series forecasting, enhances the overall usability and efficiency of urban mobility.

In essence, time-series data provides the essential temporal lens through which we view the dynamic behavior of infrastructure. By dissecting its components – trend, seasonality, cyclicality, and randomness – and by developing robust forecasting capabilities, engineers and operators can move from reactive problem-solving to proactive, optimized management. This shift is fundamental to ensuring the reliability, efficiency, and cost-effectiveness of the critical services that underpin modern society, directly influencing our daily lives and the economic vitality of our communities. The ability to anticipate, rather than merely react to, the changing demands placed upon our infrastructure is a hallmark of effective engineering and a critical factor in building resilient and sustainable systems for the future.

The realm of time-series forecasting is rich with a variety of statistical methodologies, each offering a distinct approach to unraveling temporal patterns and predicting future values. Among these, classical time-series models stand as foundational pillars, providing robust frameworks that have been refined over decades. These methods are particularly valuable for their interpretability and their effectiveness when dealing with historical data that exhibits clear patterns of trend, seasonality, and autocorrelation. In the context of infrastructure resource demand, understanding these classical techniques offers a crucial starting point, providing a reliable baseline against which more complex, modern approaches can be compared. They are often the first port of call when data is relatively limited, or when the need for transparency in the forecasting process is paramount for decision-makers.

One of the most venerable and widely applied families of classical time-series models is based on the concept of **autoregression**. At its heart, autoregression assumes that future values of a time series are linearly dependent on its past values. The simplest form of this is the **Autoregressive (AR) model**. An AR(p) model posits that the current value of a time series (Y_t) can be explained as a linear combination of its previous p values, plus a random error term. Mathematically, this is expressed as:

$$Y_t = c + \phi_1 Y_{t-1} + \phi_2 Y_{t-2} + ... + \phi_p Y_{t-p} + \epsilon_t$$

Here, c is a constant, $\phi_1, \phi_2, ..., \phi_p$ are the autoregressive coefficients that capture the strength of the relationship between the current value and its past values, and ϵ_t is a white noise error term, assumed to be independent and identically distributed with a mean of zero and a constant variance.

Consider the example of predicting hourly electricity demand in a specific neighborhood. If we observe that demand at 3 PM is strongly correlated with demand at 2 PM, 1 PM, and perhaps even 11 AM, an AR model could capture this dependency. For instance, an AR(2) model might suggest that today's electricity demand is largely determined by yesterday's demand at the same hour and the demand two hours prior, adjusted for some baseline consumption and random fluctuations. The coefficients ϕ_1 and ϕ_2 would indicate how strongly each past hour influences the current hour's demand. A positive ϕ_1 would suggest that if demand was high last hour, it's likely to be high this hour too, reflecting the inertia in consumption patterns.

However, real-world time series often do not exhibit stationarity – a statistical property where the series' statistical characteristics (mean, variance, and autocorrelation) are constant over time. If a time series has a trend, its mean will be increasing or decreasing, violating the stationarity assumption required for basic AR models. To address this, the **Integrated (I)** component was introduced, leading to **Autoregressive Integrated Moving Average (ARIMA)** models.

The "Integrated" part signifies that the time series has been differenced one or more times to make it stationary. Differencing involves calculating

the difference between consecutive observations. For instance, first differencing ($d=1$) calculates $Y'
t = Yt - Y{t-1}$. If this makes the series stationary, then the original series is said to be "integrated of order 1," denoted I(1). If a second differencing is required ($Y''t = Y't - Y'{t-1}$), the series is I(2). The value of d is the order of integration. By differencing, we remove the trend component, allowing us to model the stationary series.

Combining these concepts, an ARIMA(p, d, q) model describes a time series that has been differenced d times to achieve stationarity, and the resulting stationary series can be modeled using an AR(p) process and a **Moving Average (MA)** process. The MA(q) model suggests that the current value of the series is a linear combination of past forecast errors (or shocks) and a current error term. The MA(q) model is expressed as:

$Y
t = c + \epsilont + \theta1 \epsilon{t-1} + \theta2 \epsilon{t-2} + ... +
\thetaq \epsilon{t-q}$

Here, $\theta
1, \theta2, ..., \thetaq$ are the moving average coefficients, and $\epsilont, \epsilon{t-1}, ..., \epsilon{t-q}$ are the error terms from previous periods. The MA component essentially captures the effect of past random shocks on the current observation.

Therefore, an ARIMA(p, d, q) model combines these: it models the d-th difference of the original series as a combination of its past values (AR part) and past forecast errors (MA part).

Let's illustrate with a practical infrastructure example: predicting daily water consumption in a city. Suppose historical data shows a clear upward trend in water usage over the years due to population growth. This trend means the series is non-stationary. We might find that first differencing the daily water consumption resolves this trend, making the series stationary. After differencing ($d=1$), we might discover that the differenced series exhibits autocorrelation patterns that can be well-described by an AR(1) process (meaning yesterday's change in water consumption is a good predictor of today's change) and an MA(1) process (meaning yesterday's unexpected deviation from the forecast is also influential). This would lead to an ARIMA(1, 1, 1) model for daily water consumption. The model would predict today's water usage based on yesterday's usage, the change in usage from yesterday to today, and yesterday's forecast error, all of which are derived from the differenced series.

A key challenge in infrastructure resource management is seasonality. For instance, electricity demand exhibits strong daily and weekly patterns, and water consumption often spikes in summer. Basic ARIMA models do not inherently handle seasonality. This is where
Seasonal ARIMA (SARIMA) models, often denoted as SARIMA(p,d,q)(P,D,Q)m, come into play. These models extend the ARIMA framework by adding seasonal components.

The notation (P,D,Q)m refers to the seasonal part of the model:

P: The order of the seasonal autoregressive component.
D: The order of the seasonal differencing.
Q: The order of the seasonal moving average component.
m: The number of periods in a seasonal cycle (e.g., m=24 for hourly data with a daily cycle, m=7 for daily data with a weekly cycle, m=365 for daily data with a yearly cycle).

A SARIMA model essentially applies the ARIMA logic not only to the non-seasonal component but also to the seasonal component. This means it can account for dependencies on past observations within the same season (e.g., electricity demand yesterday at the same hour) and also dependencies on past observations from previous seasons (e.g., electricity demand on the same day last week).

For example, forecasting hourly electricity demand for a business park might require a SARIMA model. The daily pattern (e.g., high demand during working hours, low demand overnight) suggests a seasonal cycle of m=24. The weekly pattern (e.g., lower demand on weekends) might also be significant. A SARIMA(1,1,1)(1,1,1)24 model could be appropriate. This model would perform regular differencing (d=1) to handle any overall trend, and seasonal differencing (D=1) with a period of 24 hours (m=24) to remove the daily seasonality. It would then model the resulting stationary series using non-seasonal AR(1), MA(1) terms and seasonal AR(1), MA(1) terms. This allows the model to capture how the current hour's demand is influenced by past hours within the same day, and also by the same hour on previous days, effectively modeling both short-term and long-term seasonal effects.

The power of SARIMA lies in its ability to flexibly capture complex seasonal patterns. However, determining the correct orders (p, d, q, P, D, Q) can be a complex task, often involving visual inspection of autocorrelation and partial autocorrelation functions (ACF and PACF plots) of the time series, as well as formal model identification techniques and information criteria like AIC (Akaike Information Criterion) and BIC (Bayesian Information Criterion). For infrastructure managers, this means that while SARIMA is a potent tool, its implementation requires a degree of statistical expertise.

Beyond autoregressive and moving average models, another significant class of classical time-series forecasting methods relies on **exponential smoothing**. These methods assign exponentially decreasing weights to past observations, giving more weight to recent data. The core idea is that the most recent data points are more relevant for predicting the future.

The simplest form is
Simple Exponential Smoothing (SES), suitable for data without a clear trend or seasonality. The forecast for the next period is a weighted average of the current observation and the previous forecast:

$F
*{t+1} = \alpha Y*t + (1 - \alpha) F_t$

Here, $F
*{t+1}$ is the forecast for period $t+1$, $Y*t$ is the observed value in period t, F_t is the forecast for period t, and α is the smoothing parameter (0 < α < 1). A higher α gives more weight to recent observations. SES is useful for very short-term forecasts of stable series, perhaps for predicting immediate fluctuations in a water pump's flow rate that are mostly random noise around a stable average.

When a time series exhibits a
trend, Holt's Linear Trend Method (also known as Double Exponential Smoothing) is employed. It extends SES by adding a component to forecast the trend. It uses two smoothing equations: one for the level (like SES) and one for the trend.

Level: $L
*t = \alpha Y*t + (1 - \alpha) (L*{t-1} + T*{t-1})$
Trend: $T*t = \beta (L*t - L*{t-1}) + (1 - \beta) T*{t-1}$
Forecast: $F*{t+h} = L*t + h T_t$

Here, $L
*t$ is the smoothed level at time t, $T*t$ is the smoothed trend at time t, α is the smoothing parameter for the level, and β is the smoothing parameter for the trend. h is the number of periods ahead to

forecast. Holt's method is effective for series with additive trends. For example, if we observe a steady increase in daily electricity consumption over several weeks, Holt's method could effectively capture this linear growth and extrapolate it into the future.

The most comprehensive of the exponential smoothing methods is the **Holt-Winters Method**, which accounts for both trend and **seasonality**. There are two main variants: additive and multiplicative seasonality.

Additive Holt-Winters:
Level: $L_t = \alpha Y_t + (1 - \alpha) (L_{t-1} + T_{t-1})$
Trend: $T_t = \beta (L_t - L_{t-1}) + (1 - \beta) T_{t-1}$
Seasonal Component: $S_t = \gamma (Y_t - L_t) + (1 - \gamma) S_{t-m}$
Forecast: $F_{t+h} = L_t + h T_t + S_{t+h-m}$ (adjusting for the correct seasonal index)

Multiplicative Holt-Winters:
Level: $L_t = \alpha Y_t/S_{t-m} + (1 - \alpha) (L_{t-1} + T_{t-1})$
Trend: $T_t = \beta (L_t - L_{t-1}) + (1 - \beta) T_{t-1}$
Seasonal Component: $S_t = \gamma (Y_t / L_t) + (1 - \gamma) S_{t-m}$
Forecast: $F_{t+h} = (L_t + h T_t) \times S_{t+h-m}$

Here, γ is the smoothing parameter for the seasonal component, and m is the seasonal period. In the additive method, the seasonal variations are added to the trended level. In the multiplicative method, the seasonal variations multiply the trended level, meaning the seasonal swings become larger as the overall level of the series increases.

The choice between additive and multiplicative seasonality depends on the nature of the data. If the seasonal fluctuations remain relatively constant in magnitude regardless of the level of the series, additive seasonality is appropriate. If the seasonal fluctuations increase or decrease in proportion to the overall level, multiplicative seasonality is better. For instance, predicting hourly water demand in a city might exhibit multiplicative seasonality: during hotter months (higher overall demand), the daily peak demand might be significantly higher in absolute terms than during colder months. A Holt-Winters model with m=24 would be suitable for capturing this pattern. The parameters α, β, and γ are typically optimized to minimize forecast errors on historical data.

Strengths and Limitations in Infrastructure Contexts:

The classical time-series models like ARIMA, SARIMA, and Exponential Smoothing (Holt-Winters) offer significant advantages, particularly in infrastructure applications:

1. **Interpretability:** These models are relatively transparent. The parameters (ϕ, θ, α, β, γ) often have intuitive meanings related to the strength of autocorrelation, the impact of past errors, or the degree of smoothing. This interpretability is crucial for stakeholders who need to understand *why* a forecast is being made, not just *what* the forecast is. For example, understanding that a high ϕ_1 coefficient in an ARIMA model for traffic flow indicates strong persistence in traffic conditions from one hour to the next helps traffic engineers design better control strategies.

2. **Data Efficiency:** Compared to many machine learning models that require vast amounts of data, classical methods can often provide reasonable forecasts with moderate historical datasets. This is a

significant advantage for infrastructure systems where historical data might be available for only a few years, or where specific events might have created gaps or anomalies that require careful handling. For a new water treatment plant, for example, initial demand forecasts might rely on limited historical data, making ARIMA or Holt-Winters a practical choice.

3.
Established Methodology: These models have a long history of successful application and well-developed theoretical underpinnings. Tools and libraries for implementing and diagnosing these models are widely available in statistical software.

4.
Handling of Trend and Seasonality: SARIMA and Holt-Winters are specifically designed to capture common patterns found in infrastructure resource demand, such as growing energy consumption (trend) and diurnal/weekly/annual cycles in water or electricity usage (seasonality).

However, these classical models also have limitations:

1.
Linearity Assumption: Most classical models assume linear relationships between past and future values. Real-world infrastructure systems can exhibit complex, non-linear dynamics (e.g., the sudden surge in demand caused by an unexpected event, feedback loops not captured by simple autoregression).

2.
Univariate Focus: Traditional ARIMA and exponential smoothing models are primarily univariate, meaning they forecast a single time series based on its own past values. They do not inherently incorporate external factors or exogenous variables (e.g., weather conditions, economic indicators, special events) that can significantly influence resource

demand. For instance, predicting electricity demand without considering temperature is a major limitation, as HVAC systems are a primary driver of consumption.

3.
Stationarity Requirements: While the "I" component in ARIMA and seasonal differencing in SARIMA address non-stationarity caused by trends and seasonality, they may struggle with more complex forms of non-stationarity or structural breaks in the data.

4.
Model Identification Complexity: For SARIMA models, identifying the optimal orders (p, d, q, P, D, Q) can be a laborious and subjective process, requiring expertise and potentially a significant amount of trial and error.

5.
Handling of Irregular Events: While these models account for random noise, they are not designed to forecast the impact of highly unusual, unprecedented events that fall outside historical patterns. A severe, unseasonal heatwave or a sudden economic disruption could render forecasts based solely on historical patterns inaccurate.

Despite these limitations, classical time-series models remain indispensable tools in the arsenal of any infrastructure resource manager. They provide a robust and interpretable foundation for forecasting, particularly for stable systems with predictable patterns. They serve as essential baselines, allowing for a clear understanding of fundamental temporal dynamics before considering more sophisticated approaches. For example, forecasting daily water demand for a residential area might begin with a SARIMA model that effectively captures the daily and weekly cycles. The accuracy achieved by this model would then inform whether the added complexity of multivariate models, incorporating weather forecasts or economic activity, is truly necessary and likely to yield significant improvements. The insights gained from understanding the coefficients and performance of these classical models are invaluable for building a comprehensive understanding of resource demand patterns.

The landscape of time-series forecasting has been profoundly reshaped by the advent of machine learning (ML). While classical statistical methods like ARIMA and exponential smoothing have long served as workhorses for predicting resource demand, they often operate under restrictive assumptions, such as linearity and the exclusion of external influencing factors. Machine learning, on the other hand, offers a more flexible and powerful toolkit, capable of uncovering intricate non-linear patterns and seamlessly integrating a multitude of exogenous variables that significantly impact resource consumption. This section delves into the application of prominent machine learning algorithms for time-series forecasting, highlighting their ability to enhance prediction accuracy and provide deeper insights into the drivers of demand for critical infrastructure.

One of the foundational machine learning approaches for regression tasks, including time-series forecasting, is
Support Vector Regression (SVR). Unlike traditional regression methods that aim to minimize the error between predicted and actual values, SVR focuses on finding a function that deviates from the actual values by a value no greater than a predefined margin (ϵ), while simultaneously being as flat as possible. This epsilon-insensitive loss function is key to SVR's robustness. Mathematically, for a given training dataset $\{(x*i*, *y*i)\}*{i=1}^N$, SVR seeks to find a function $f(x)$ that has at most ϵ deviation from the actual $y*i$ for all training data, and is as "flat" as possible. This is typically achieved by minimizing a regularized risk function:

$\min \frac{1}{2} ||w||^2 + C \sum
{i=1}^N L{\epsilon}(f(x*i*) - *y*i)$

Here, w represents the weight vector, $C > 0$ is a regularization parameter that balances the trade-off between minimizing the error and minimizing the flatness, and L_{ϵ} is the epsilon-insensitive loss function defined as:

$L_{\epsilon}(z) = \max(0, |z| - \epsilon)$

For time-series forecasting, the input features (x_i) *can be lagged values of the time series itself, as well as relevant exogenous variables. For instance, to forecast hourly electricity demand,* x_i could include the electricity demand from the previous few hours, the current hour's temperature, humidity, and day of the week. SVR can effectively model non-linear relationships by employing different kernel functions, such as polynomial or radial basis function (RBF) kernels. The RBF kernel, for example, implicitly maps the input data into an infinite-dimensional feature space, allowing for the capture of highly complex, non-linear patterns that linear models or even basic ARIMA might miss.

Consider the example of forecasting the demand for a municipal water supply system. Water demand is notoriously influenced by a variety of factors, including ambient temperature, rainfall, day of the week (weekend vs. weekday usage), and even local events. A simple ARIMA model might struggle to incorporate the intricate, non-linear relationship between temperature and water consumption (e.g., demand might increase exponentially with temperature beyond a certain threshold). An SVR model, however, with an appropriate RBF kernel, can learn these complex dependencies. By feeding it historical water usage, temperature readings, and indicators for weekdays/weekends, the SVR can output a forecast that more accurately reflects the anticipated demand under varying weather conditions and temporal patterns. The choice of kernel and its parameters (like gamma for RBF and the cost parameter C) is crucial and often determined through cross-validation to optimize performance. The epsilon parameter (ϵ) also plays a role, defining the tolerance for errors. A smaller ϵ leads to a more precise model but might overfit noisy data, while a larger ϵ can lead to a smoother model that generalizes better.

Beyond individual models,
ensemble methods have emerged as powerful techniques in machine learning for improving forecasting accuracy and robustness. These methods combine the predictions of multiple base models, often with the goal of reducing variance, bias, or both. Two prominent ensemble techniques widely applied to time-series forecasting are **Random Forests** and **Gradient Boosting**.

Random Forests operate on the principle of bagging (Bootstrap Aggregating) and feature randomness. They construct a multitude of decision trees during training. For each tree, a bootstrap sample of the training data is drawn, and at each node of the tree, a random subset of features is considered for splitting. This randomness in both data sampling and feature selection helps to decorrelate the trees, leading to a more robust ensemble. For a regression task like forecasting, the final prediction is typically the average of the predictions from all individual trees.

In the context of time-series forecasting, Random Forests can be trained to predict future values. The input features can include lagged values of the target variable (e.g., traffic volume in the last 3 hours), exogenous variables (e.g., current weather, time of day, day of the week, presence of a major event), and even features derived from these (e.g., rolling averages of temperature). The ability of Random Forests to handle a large number of input features and their inherent non-linearity makes them well-suited for complex demand patterns. For instance, predicting the load on a public transport system during peak hours might involve features like historical passenger counts, time of day, current weather conditions, and indicators for holidays or special events. A Random Forest can effectively weigh the importance of these diverse factors. The model implicitly performs feature selection, identifying which lags or exogenous variables are most predictive. Feature importance scores derived from Random Forests can also provide valuable insights into the key drivers of demand, aiding infrastructure planners in understanding the underlying dynamics.

Consider the forecasting of public Wi-Fi usage in a city's parks. Usage is highly dependent on factors like time of day, day of the week, weather (sunny vs. rainy), and local events (festivals, concerts). A Random Forest, trained on historical usage data and these exogenous variables, can provide accurate predictions. For example, if a festival is scheduled in a park, a binary feature indicating its presence would be highly influential. The model would learn that on days with festivals, Wi-Fi usage spikes significantly, and it can quantify this increase by averaging the predictions from trees that have encountered similar conditions during training. The ensemble nature reduces the risk of overfitting to specific historical anomalies, making the forecasts more reliable.

Gradient Boosting Machines (GBM), such as XGBoost, LightGBM, and scikit-learn's GradientBoostingRegressor, represent another powerful class of ensemble methods that build models sequentially. Unlike Random Forests, where trees are built independently, GBMs build trees in a stage-wise fashion, with each new tree attempting to correct the errors made by the previous ones. The process involves fitting a new model to the residual errors of the previous ensemble. The objective is to minimize a loss function by adding models that point in the negative gradient direction of the loss function.

The formulation typically involves:

1. Initialize the model with a simple prediction (e.g., the mean of the target variable).
2. For each iteration (tree):
a. Compute the residual errors from the current ensemble's predictions.
b. Fit a new base learner (e.g., a decision tree) to these residuals.
c. Update the ensemble by adding the new learner, scaled by a learning rate.

The learning rate (shrinkage) is a critical parameter that controls the contribution of each tree to the final prediction, helping to prevent overfitting. GBMs are known for their high accuracy and ability to handle complex interactions between features.

For infrastructure resource demand forecasting, Gradient Boosting can be particularly effective. For instance, predicting the peak load on an electrical grid requires a nuanced understanding of how various factors interact. High ambient temperature, combined with specific times of day (afternoon peak) and day of the week (weekday), will lead to different demand profiles than a weekend with moderate temperature. GBMs can capture these complex interaction effects. Imagine forecasting the demand for public transportation in a city. Factors like weather, special events, and even traffic congestion on roads (which might deter people from driving and increase public transport use) can all play a role. A GBM, by sequentially correcting errors, can learn these intricate relationships. For example, it might learn that on a rainy weekday afternoon when there's a major sporting event, public transport demand is exceptionally high due to the combined effects of people avoiding driving in the rain and attending the event. The model would identify these patterns through successive tree additions that focus on reducing the prediction errors for such specific scenarios.

One of the most significant advantages of machine learning models, including SVR, Random Forests, and Gradient Boosting, is their inherent capability to incorporate
exogenous variables. Classical methods, particularly univariate ones, often struggle to leverage external information. However, infrastructure resource demand is rarely solely a function of its own past. External factors can be powerful predictors.

For example, predicting electricity demand is heavily influenced by **weather**. Temperature is a primary driver; higher temperatures increase demand for air conditioning, while lower temperatures increase demand for heating. Humidity, wind speed (affecting heating/cooling loads and renewable energy generation), and solar irradiance (impacting solar power generation) are also relevant. A machine learning model can readily integrate these weather parameters as input features.

Consider a scenario where an electric utility needs to forecast hourly electricity demand for a metropolitan area. They have historical hourly demand data, but also access to hourly weather forecasts (temperature, humidity, wind speed). Using a Random Forest or Gradient Boosting model, they can input not only past demand values (e.g., demand from the previous hour, the same hour yesterday, the same hour last week) but also the forecasted weather conditions for the upcoming hours. The model can learn that a forecasted temperature of 35°C at 3 PM on a Tuesday will lead to a significantly higher demand than a forecasted temperature of 20°C under similar lagged demand conditions. This capability is crucial for proactive grid management, ensuring sufficient generation capacity is available and preventing blackouts. The model can even learn interactions, such as how the impact of high temperature on demand might be exacerbated by high humidity.

Similarly,

economic indicators can significantly influence the demand for resources like water, gas, and electricity, especially in industrial or commercial sectors. For instance, during periods of economic growth, industrial activity often increases, leading to higher energy and water consumption. Conversely, economic downturns can lead to reduced demand. Machine learning models can incorporate macroeconomic variables such as GDP growth, industrial production indices, unemployment rates, and consumer confidence indices. By analyzing historical data where economic conditions correlated with resource consumption patterns, these models can forecast how future economic trends might translate into changes in demand. For a gas utility, for example, forecasting demand might involve not just past demand and temperature, but also the industrial output index for the region. If the index is projected to rise, the model would predict a commensurate increase in industrial gas consumption, even if current weather patterns don't suggest a change.

Special events also play a critical role in modulating resource demand, and machine learning models are adept at handling them. Public holidays, sporting events, festivals, or even major public service disruptions can cause significant deviations from normal demand patterns. These events can be represented as binary (event occurring or not) or categorical features in the ML model. For instance, forecasting water demand for a city might need to account for large public gatherings that increase demand for sanitation services and temporary water kiosks, or conversely, for city-wide evacuations that drastically reduce demand.

Let's expand on the example of forecasting peak electricity demand, specifically considering weather. Peak demand is often critical for grid stability, as it represents the highest point of consumption within a given period, usually occurring on hot summer afternoons when air conditioning load is maximal. Classical models might capture some seasonality, but the precise timing and magnitude of peaks are highly sensitive to meteorological conditions.

A machine learning approach, such as XGBoost, can be configured to forecast hourly electricity demand, with the primary goal of identifying and predicting the timing and magnitude of these peaks. The input features would include:

Lagged Demand: Demand from previous hours (e.g., $t-1, t-2, ..., t-24$) to capture short-term persistence.
Seasonal Features: Hour of the day, day of the week, day of the year, encoded appropriately (e.g., using one-hot encoding or cyclical features).
Weather Data: Forecasted temperature, humidity, dew point, wind speed, and cloud cover for the current and upcoming hours. These are crucial for predicting air conditioning and heating loads.
Event Indicators: Binary flags for public holidays or major local events that might affect consumption patterns.
Special Price Periods: If the utility operates with time-of-use pricing, features indicating high-price periods can be included, as they might influence consumer behavior.

The XGBoost model would be trained on historical data where these features are paired with actual hourly demand. During training, the algorithm iteratively builds decision trees, each aiming to reduce the prediction error (e.g., Mean Squared Error, MSE). The model learns the complex interplay: it might discover that a combination of high temperature (e.g., >30°C), high humidity, and a weekday afternoon leads to a significantly higher demand than any single factor alone. It can also learn that demand peaks might occur slightly earlier or later on weekends, or be suppressed on holidays even if the weather is hot.

To further refine peak demand forecasting, one could also train a model specifically to predict the
probability of a peak event occurring within a certain threshold, or to directly forecast the *maximum demand* within a rolling window (e.g., the next 24 hours). This could involve using different objective functions tailored to the problem. For instance, if the cost of underestimating peak demand (leading to potential blackouts) is much higher than the cost of overestimating it, the model might be optimized to be more conservative, perhaps by adjusting the prediction threshold or using a loss function that penalizes underestimation more heavily.

The interpretability of machine learning models, while sometimes considered a weakness compared to simpler statistical models, is steadily improving. Techniques like SHAP (SHapley Additive exPlanations) and LIME (Local Interpretable Model-agnostic Explanations) allow us to understand the contribution of each feature to a specific prediction. For the electricity demand example, SHAP values could reveal that on a particular hot Tuesday afternoon, the high forecasted temperature contributed the most to the predicted peak demand, followed by the fact that it's a weekday, and then by the demand observed in the previous hour. This level of insight is invaluable for infrastructure operators, allowing them to validate forecasts, identify potential data issues, and build confidence in the predictive system.

In summary, machine learning approaches, particularly advanced regression techniques like SVR and ensemble methods such as Random Forests and Gradient Boosting, offer a significant leap forward in time-series forecasting for resource demand. Their ability to model complex non-linear relationships and seamlessly integrate diverse exogenous variables—weather data, economic indicators, event information—allows for more accurate, nuanced, and actionable predictions. These models move beyond the limitations of classical methods, providing infrastructure managers with a more robust understanding of the multifactorial influences on demand, thereby enabling more effective planning, operation, and resilience of critical services. The continuous development in ML interpretability further enhances their practical utility, transforming raw predictions into actionable insights that inform strategic decision-making.

The frontier of time-series forecasting for resource demand is being dramatically pushed forward by the capabilities of deep learning. While machine learning algorithms like SVR and gradient boosting have proven adept at capturing non-linearities and integrating exogenous factors, deep learning architectures offer an even more sophisticated approach to modeling the complex, sequential nature of demand data. These models, drawing inspiration from the structure of the human brain, can learn intricate patterns and dependencies that might elude traditional methods and even shallower machine learning models.

At the heart of deep learning for sequential data lie
Recurrent Neural Networks (RNNs). Unlike feedforward neural networks, which process data in a single direction, RNNs possess internal memory. This memory allows them to retain information from previous steps in a sequence and use it to inform predictions at current and future steps. This is fundamentally important for time-series data, where the value at time t is often highly dependent on values at $t-1, t-2$, and so on, potentially over very long periods. The core idea of an RNN is the presence of a "recurrent" connection that feeds the output of a hidden layer back into itself, creating a loop.

Mathematically, a basic RNN cell can be described as follows: at time step t, the hidden state $h
*t$ is computed as a function of the current input $x*t$ and the previous hidden state h_{t-1}:

$h

t = *f(W*{hh} h*{t-1}* + *W*{xh} x*t* + *b*h)$

And the output y_t (if needed at each time step) is computed from the hidden state:

$y
t = *g(W*{hy} h*t* + *b*y)$

Here, $W
*{hh}$, $W*{xh}$, and $W*{hy}$ are weight matrices, and $b*h$ and b_y are bias vectors. The functions f and g are typically non-linear activation functions, such as tanh or ReLU.

However, basic RNNs suffer from a significant problem known as the **vanishing gradient problem**. During the training process, gradients can become extremely small as they are backpropagated through many time steps, making it difficult for the network to learn long-term dependencies. Conversely, the **exploding gradient problem** can also occur, where gradients become too large, leading to unstable training.

To address these limitations, more advanced RNN architectures have been developed, most notably
Long Short-Term Memory (LSTM) networks and **Gated Recurrent Units (GRUs)**. These architectures introduce "gates" – mechanisms that control the flow of information within the network, allowing it to selectively remember or forget past information.

Long Short-Term Memory (LSTM) networks are specifically designed to overcome the vanishing gradient problem and effectively learn dependencies over long sequences. An LSTM cell is more complex than a basic RNN cell, featuring three primary gates: the forget gate, the input gate, and the output gate, along with a cell state that acts as a conveyor belt for information.

1.
Forget Gate: Decides what information to throw away from the cell state. It looks at $h{t-1}$ and xt and outputs a number between 0 and 1 for each number in the cell state C_{t-1}. A 1 means "completely keep this," while a 0 means "completely get rid of this."
$ft = \sigma(Wf \cdot [h{t-1}, xt] + b_f)$

2.
Input Gate: Decides which new information to store in the cell state. It has two parts: a sigmoid layer that decides which values to update, and a tanh layer that creates a vector of new candidate values $\tilde{C}_t$ to be added to the state.
$it = \sigma(Wi \cdot [h{t-1}, xt] + b_i)$
$\tilde{C}t = \tanh(WC \cdot [h{t-1}, xt] + b_C)$

3.
Cell State Update: The old cell state $C{t-1}$ is updated to the new cell state Ct. The old state is multiplied by f_t (forgetting the irrelevant parts) and then added to the result of the input gate.
$Ct = ft \cdot C{t-1} + it \cdot \tilde{C}_t$

4.
Output Gate: Decides what to output. It filters the cell state based on the current input and previous hidden state. First, a sigmoid layer determines which parts of the cell state will be output. Then, the cell state is run through tanh (to push values between -1 and 1) and multiplied by the output of the sigmoid gate.
$ot = \sigma(Wo \cdot [h{t-1}, xt] + b_o)$
$ht = ot \cdot \tanh(C_t)$

These gates allow LSTMs to maintain a constant error flow, effectively capturing and utilizing long-range dependencies. This is crucial for forecasting resource demand, where patterns can be influenced by seasonal cycles (yearly), weekly trends, or even long-term economic shifts. For instance, predicting the annual energy consumption of a city requires understanding not just the current weather, but also historical trends influenced by population growth, industrial expansion over years, and long-term energy efficiency initiatives.

Gated Recurrent Units (GRUs) are a simplified variation of LSTMs that have gained popularity due to their comparable performance and reduced computational complexity. GRUs combine the forget and input gates into a single "update gate" and merge the cell state and hidden state. They have two gates: an update gate and a reset gate.

1.
Update Gate (z_t): Similar to the LSTM's forget and input gates, it decides how much of the past information to keep.
$zt = \sigma(Wz \cdot [h{t-1}, xt] + b_z)$

2.
Reset Gate (r_t): Determines how much of the past hidden state to forget when computing the candidate hidden state.
$rt = \sigma(Wr \cdot [h{t-1}, xt] + b_r)$

The candidate hidden state $\tilde{h}_t$ is computed using the reset gate:

$\tilde{h}t = \tanh(Wh \cdot [rt h{t-1}, xt] + bh)$

Finally, the new hidden state h_t is a combination of the previous hidden state and the candidate hidden state, controlled by the update gate:

$h_t = (1 - z_t) h_{t-1} + z_t \tilde{h}_t$

GRUs, with their fewer parameters, can be faster to train and require less data while still being effective at learning long-term dependencies.

Applications of RNNs (LSTMs/GRUs) in Resource Demand Forecasting:

Consider the forecasting of electricity demand for a smart grid. Electricity consumption is influenced by a multitude of factors that evolve over time: daily weather patterns (temperature, humidity), weekly cycles (weekday vs. weekend usage), seasonal variations (heating/cooling demands), holidays, economic activity, and even unforeseen events like power outages or widespread adoption of electric vehicles.

An LSTM or GRU model can be trained to ingest a sequence of historical data points, including:

Lagged Electricity Demand: Past demand values at various intervals (e.g., last hour, same hour yesterday, same hour last week).
Weather Data: Current and forecasted temperature, humidity, wind speed, solar irradiance, cloud cover.
Temporal Features: Hour of the day, day of the week, month of the year, indicators for holidays or special events.
Exogenous Variables: Real-time electricity prices, industrial production indices, population density in specific areas, and data related to EV charging patterns.

The model can then learn complex temporal dependencies. For example, it can capture how a heatwave that started three days ago continues to impact air conditioning load, or how a holiday weekend disrupts typical industrial consumption patterns, even if the weather is otherwise normal. The sequential processing allows the model to understand the "story" behind the demand data, rather than just looking at isolated points in time.

Let's elaborate on the smart grid example. Imagine a utility using an LSTM to forecast hourly electricity demand for the next 24 hours. The model is fed a sequence of data from the past 7 days. This sequence includes hourly demand values, hourly weather observations and forecasts from a local meteorological station, and indicators for whether each day was a weekday, weekend, or public holiday. The LSTM processes this sequence, updating its internal state at each hour.

As the LSTM processes a particularly hot, dry summer day, it learns that demand is high due to air conditioning. If the next day is slightly cooler but still warm, the LSTM, using its learned dependencies, will predict a demand that is lower than the previous day but still elevated, because it has learned the diminishing effect of minor temperature drops. Crucially, if the model also incorporates data on battery charging for electric vehicles and finds a correlation between peak demand hours and increased EV charging activity, it can further refine its forecast. The LSTM's ability to integrate and learn from this rich, sequential, and multi-variate data stream allows it to predict demand with a much higher degree of accuracy, especially during periods of volatility or when multiple influencing factors coincide. This is invaluable for grid operators needing to balance supply and demand, manage reserve capacities, and optimize energy generation from diverse sources, including renewables which are themselves subject to temporal variability.

Another compelling application is in

public transportation demand forecasting. Passenger counts on buses, trains, or subways are highly dynamic, influenced by time of day, day of the week, weather, special events (concerts, sporting matches), school schedules, and even unexpected disruptions like traffic jams or system failures.

An RNN, particularly an LSTM, can effectively model this. Input features might include:

Historical Passenger Counts: Lagged values for routes and stations.
Schedule Information: Departure/arrival times, route type (express, local).
External Factors: Weather forecasts, event calendars, road traffic data, news feeds indicating service disruptions.
Fare/Pricing Information: If dynamic pricing is used.

For instance, predicting demand for a metro line serving a major stadium: the LSTM can learn to associate specific event days and times with exceptionally high passenger volumes, even if the weather is inclement. It can also learn that on normal weekdays, demand peaks occur at typical commute times, but on weekends, these peaks might be later and broader. By observing sequences of data, the model can identify patterns like: "If a football match ends at 5 PM on a Saturday and it's raining, demand at the stadium station will surge by X% for the next 90 minutes." This granular understanding, powered by sequence learning, is vital for deploying sufficient staff, managing train frequency, and ensuring passenger safety and comfort.

The effectiveness of these RNN architectures can be further amplified by incorporating
Convolutional Neural Networks (CNNs). While primarily known for image processing, CNNs have proven surprisingly effective in time-series analysis, particularly for feature extraction. In the context of time-series

forecasting, 1D CNNs can be applied. A 1D CNN uses convolutional filters that slide over the sequential data, detecting local patterns and features. For example, a CNN layer might learn to recognize a "peak demand pattern" characterized by a rapid rise and fall in resource usage over a few hours.

When combined with RNNs, this creates a
Convolutional LSTM (ConvLSTM) or similar hybrid architecture. In a ConvLSTM, the convolutional operations are integrated into the LSTM cell's gating mechanisms. This allows the model to capture both spatial-like structures in the temporal data (via convolutions) and sequential dependencies (via recurrence). For time-series forecasting, this can be powerful. Imagine forecasting demand across multiple interconnected regions or different lines of a transport network. A CNN component within the LSTM could help the model understand patterns specific to certain spatial configurations or local temporal trends, while the LSTM core handles the sequential dependencies across time.

For example, in forecasting water demand for a large metropolitan area with multiple service zones, a ConvLSTM could process demand data and relevant features (temperature, rainfall, population density) for each zone simultaneously. The convolutional layers might identify common demand patterns that occur across adjacent zones during specific weather events, while the recurrent layers track how these patterns evolve over time and propagate through the network of zones. This allows the model to capture complex spatial-temporal dependencies that a simple RNN might miss, leading to more accurate and localized forecasts.

Furthermore,
Transformer networks, originally developed for natural language processing, are increasingly being adapted for time-series forecasting. Transformers rely on a mechanism called "self-attention," which allows the model to weigh the importance of different parts of the input

sequence when making a prediction, regardless of their position. This can be more effective than the fixed sequential processing of RNNs, especially for very long sequences where dependencies might be sparse but critical.

The self-attention mechanism computes attention scores between different time steps, allowing the model to directly relate a prediction at time t to a specific, relevant point in the past (e.g., $t-k$) without needing to propagate through k intermediate steps. This can be highly advantageous for forecasting periodic patterns that might not be perfectly aligned or for capturing abrupt shifts in demand driven by specific, distant events.

In the context of resource demand forecasting, a Transformer model could be trained to predict electricity demand by attending to specific historical demand points and weather conditions that are most predictive of the current or future demand, irrespective of how far in the past they occurred. For instance, predicting demand during a global supply chain disruption might require attending to events from months or even years prior that impacted industrial output and energy consumption, a task at which self-attention excels.

The superiority of deep learning models often lies in their ability to automatically learn relevant features from raw data, reducing the need for extensive manual feature engineering. However, they are also computationally intensive and require substantial amounts of data for effective training. Moreover, while interpretability is improving with methods like attention visualization and SHAP values, understanding the precise reasoning behind a deep learning model's prediction can still be challenging compared to simpler statistical models.

Despite these challenges, the potential for enhanced accuracy and the ability to model highly complex, dynamic demand patterns make deep learning architectures indispensable tools for advanced time-series forecasting in resource management. They enable a more proactive and resilient approach to planning and operating critical infrastructure, ensuring that demand can be met efficiently and reliably in an increasingly complex world. The continuous research and development in this field promise even more sophisticated and robust forecasting capabilities in the near future.

The imperative for precise resource demand forecasting extends beyond energy and transportation, encompassing a critical element for urban sustainability: water. Predicting urban water demand is paramount for efficient water utility operations, ensuring adequate supply while minimizing waste and operational costs. This case study delves into the application of artificial intelligence, particularly advanced time-series forecasting techniques, to tackle the complexities of urban water consumption. We will walk through a practical scenario, illustrating how data-driven approaches can revolutionize how cities manage their most vital resource.

The foundation of any robust forecasting system is high-quality historical data. For our hypothetical city, we begin by acquiring a comprehensive dataset of its water consumption. This data typically comprises hourly or daily aggregated water usage records over several years, often measured in millions of gallons or cubic meters. Such granular data allows us to observe intricate patterns, from diurnal fluctuations driven by daily routines to weekly variations influenced by business hours and residential activity. The raw consumption data, however, only tells part of the story. Water demand is not an isolated phenomenon; it is deeply intertwined with a multitude of external factors, collectively known as exogenous variables.

To build a predictive model that truly captures the dynamics of urban water usage, we must integrate these exogenous variables. A primary influencer is **meteorological data**. Temperature is a key driver: higher temperatures generally correlate with increased water usage for outdoor activities like irrigation and pool filling, as well as increased indoor use for cooling and drinking. Rainfall, conversely, can decrease outdoor water demand. Other meteorological factors like humidity, wind speed, and cloud cover can also play nuanced roles. Beyond weather, the **temporal structure** of demand is crucial. The day of the week significantly impacts consumption; weekdays typically exhibit higher demand due to commercial and industrial activities, as well as typical household routines, compared to weekends when many businesses are closed and residents may alter their usage patterns. Holidays introduce further anomalies, often leading to reduced demand on public services and potentially altered residential usage.

Other important exogenous variables can include:

Population Density and Demographics: While not always available at a granular temporal level for forecasting, broader demographic shifts and population growth in specific service zones can influence long-term demand trends. For short-term forecasting, proxies like the day of the week and holiday indicators can implicitly capture some of these effects by reflecting typical usage patterns of residential versus commercial areas.
Economic Activity: While complex to capture directly for short-term forecasting, general economic indicators could inform longer-term demand projections. For instance, periods of high industrial output might correlate with increased water use in manufacturing.
Water Pricing and Regulations: Changes in water tariffs or the implementation of water conservation policies can directly influence consumption. While such policy changes might occur infrequently, their

impact can be substantial and should be considered in forecasting models, perhaps as step changes or intervention variables.
Event Calendars: Major public events, festivals, or sporting matches can significantly increase water demand in specific areas due to increased foot traffic, event-specific water needs, and potential impacts on public restroom usage.
System-Related Factors: While not exogenous in the strictest sense, information about known leaks, infrastructure maintenance, or changes in water pressure within the distribution network could also refine demand predictions, although this data is often more challenging to integrate into standard forecasting models without specialized sensor networks.

For our case study, we will focus on incorporating **temperature, rainfall, day of the week, and indicators for public holidays** as our primary exogenous variables. The process involves aligning these external data sources with the historical water consumption records, ensuring that each data point corresponds to the correct time period. This alignment is critical for the models to learn the correct relationships between demand and its drivers.

With our data prepared—historical water consumption alongside corresponding exogenous variables—we can now turn to the AI models. A diverse set of algorithms is typically employed to compare their performance and identify the most suitable approach for a given urban water system.

1.
Traditional Statistical Models (e.g., ARIMA): Autoregressive Integrated Moving Average (ARIMA) models, and its extensions like SARIMA (Seasonal ARIMA), are classic time-series forecasting methods. ARIMA models work by identifying linear relationships between past observations and future values, incorporating differencing to handle non-

stationarity and moving averages to capture error patterns. While they can model seasonality and trends, their ability to capture complex non-linear interactions with multiple exogenous variables is limited. They serve as a crucial baseline for comparison, demonstrating the performance gains achievable with more advanced AI techniques.

2.
Machine Learning Models (e.g., Gradient Boosting, Support Vector Regression): Algorithms like **Gradient Boosting Machines (GBM)**, such as XGBoost or LightGBM, are powerful for capturing non-linear relationships. They build an ensemble of decision trees, sequentially correcting errors from previous trees. GBMs can effectively incorporate numerous exogenous variables and capture intricate interactions between them. **Support Vector Regression (SVR)** is another capable algorithm that seeks to find a hyperplane that best fits the data, with parameters that can be tuned to handle non-linearity. These models are typically "stateless," meaning they treat each prediction instance somewhat independently, relying on carefully engineered features derived from the time-series and exogenous data.

3.
Deep Learning Models (e.g., LSTM, GRU): As discussed in the preceding sections, Recurrent Neural Networks (RNNs), particularly **Long Short-Term Memory (LSTM)** and **Gated Recurrent Unit (GRU)** networks, are exceptionally well-suited for sequential data like time-series. Their inherent memory mechanisms allow them to learn long-term dependencies and complex temporal patterns. When applied to water demand forecasting, LSTMs/GRUs can ingest sequences of past consumption data and exogenous variables to predict future demand. They excel at capturing how patterns evolve over time, such as the lingering effect of a heatwave on irrigation needs, which simpler models might struggle to replicate. These models are often trained to predict the next time step or a sequence of future time steps.

For our case study, we will implement and compare these three categories of models:

ARIMA(p, d, q)(P, D, Q)s: A seasonal ARIMA model will be configured to capture daily and weekly seasonality. We will include the exogenous variables (temperature, rainfall, holiday flag) as regressors in an ARIMAX model.
XGBoost: This gradient boosting model will be trained using lagged water demand values, current and lagged exogenous variables, and engineered temporal features (e.g., hour of day, day of week, month, is_holiday).
LSTM: An LSTM network will be designed with an input layer to accept sequences of historical water demand and exogenous variables. The model will have multiple LSTM layers and a final dense layer to output the predicted demand for the next time step (e.g., the next hour).

The training process for these models involves splitting the historical data into training, validation, and testing sets. The training set is used to fit the model parameters, the validation set to tune hyperparameters (e.g., learning rate, number of trees, LSTM units, dropout rates), and the testing set to provide an unbiased evaluation of the final model's performance on unseen data.

Crucially, evaluating the performance of these forecasting models requires a set of appropriate metrics. Common metrics for regression tasks, and thus for time-series forecasting, include:

Mean Absolute Error (MAE): The average of the absolute differences between predicted and actual values. It is easy to interpret as it is in the same units as the target variable.
Mean Squared Error (MSE) and Root Mean Squared Error (RMSE): MSE penalizes larger errors more heavily than MAE. RMSE is the square root of MSE, bringing the error back into the original units. RMSE is widely used and provides a good measure of the overall error magnitude.
Mean Absolute Percentage Error (MAPE): The average of the absolute percentage errors. This metric is useful for understanding forecast accuracy relative to the actual demand, making it scale-independent. However, it can be problematic when actual demand values are close to zero.
R-squared (Coefficient of Determination): Indicates the proportion of the variance in the dependent variable (water demand) that is predictable from the independent variables (historical data and exogenous factors). A value closer to 1 indicates a better fit.

In our case study, we would train and evaluate each model. For instance, let's hypothesize the following results after rigorous hyperparameter tuning and testing on a hold-out set representing a typical summer month:

ARIMAX: Achieves an RMSE of 8.5 million gallons and an MAPE of 7.2%. It captures the basic seasonal patterns and the influence of temperature but struggles with sharp spikes or abrupt changes.
XGBoost: With well-engineered features, it improves performance, achieving an RMSE of 6.2 million gallons and an MAPE of 5.1%. It effectively models the non-linear interactions between weather, day type, and demand.
LSTM: This deep learning model, after extensive training, delivers the best results, with an RMSE of 4.8 million gallons and an MAPE of 3.9%. The LSTM's ability to learn sequential dependencies allows it to better

anticipate demand during rapidly changing conditions, such as the transition from a moderate day to a heatwave, or the impact of a holiday weekend on subsequent demand patterns. The model might reveal, for example, that a 1°C increase in temperature above a certain threshold (e.g., 25°C) triggers a non-linear increase in irrigation demand, a pattern it learned from the sequence of past days.

The superior performance of the LSTM model in this hypothetical scenario is attributed to its capacity to learn complex, non-linear, and time-dependent relationships inherent in water consumption data. It can better account for the inertia in water usage—how yesterday's high demand might influence today's patterns, even if immediate conditions have slightly changed. For example, if there was a prolonged period of hot weather followed by a cooler day, the LSTM might predict slightly higher demand than a simpler model because it has learned that people might still be watering their gardens or that residual effects of high usage persist.

The implications of achieving such accurate forecasts are profound for urban water management. Optimized water treatment and distribution are direct beneficiaries. Instead of over-treating water to ensure a buffer for unpredictable demand or pumping excess water into reservoirs, utilities can operate closer to the actual demand levels. This translates to:

Reduced Energy Consumption: Pumping and treating water are energy-intensive processes. By matching supply more precisely to demand, the energy required for these operations can be significantly lowered, leading to substantial cost savings and a reduced carbon footprint. For a city, this could amount to millions of dollars in annual energy expenditure savings.
Optimized Chemical Usage: Water treatment involves the use of various chemicals. Precisely forecasting demand allows for more accurate dosing

of these chemicals, preventing overuse (which is wasteful and costly) and underuse (which compromises water quality).

Extended Infrastructure Lifespan: Operating the water distribution network under less stress, avoiding unnecessary high-pressure periods or rapid fluctuations, can contribute to the longevity of pipes, pumps, and other critical infrastructure. This reduces the frequency and cost of maintenance and replacement.

Enhanced Water Conservation: Accurate demand forecasts enable utilities to identify periods of unusually high demand that might signal leaks or inefficient usage patterns, prompting targeted investigations and public awareness campaigns. Furthermore, by ensuring sufficient supply where and when needed, it reduces the likelihood of service interruptions or low-pressure situations, which can sometimes lead to contamination risks.

Improved Resilience to Droughts and Scarcity: In regions facing water scarcity or recurring droughts, precise demand forecasting is not just about efficiency; it's about survival. It allows for better planning of water resources, more effective implementation of conservation measures, and optimized allocation during critical periods. Knowing precisely how much water will be needed helps authorities make informed decisions about drawing from reservoirs or implementing stricter consumption limits.

Consider a specific scenario: A city experiences a sudden heatwave, pushing temperatures to record highs. An advanced forecasting system, like the LSTM model, would predict a sharp, sustained increase in water demand, particularly for outdoor irrigation and indoor cooling. Armed with this prediction, the water utility can proactively:

1.

Increase pumping rates in advance: Gradually ramp up water flow from treatment plants to reservoirs, avoiding sudden surges that strain equipment.

2. **Adjust treatment chemical levels:** Ensure adequate chlorine or other disinfectants are present to handle the higher volume and potential variations in raw water quality.
3. **Communicate with the public:** Issue advisories about responsible water use, especially for outdoor activities, if demand is projected to exceed a critical threshold, thereby encouraging voluntary conservation.
4. **Optimize energy procurement:** If the utility has real-time energy pricing, it can schedule energy-intensive pumping operations during off-peak hours leading up to the demand surge.

Conversely, during cooler, rainy periods, the model would predict lower demand. This allows the utility to:

1.
Reduce pumping and treatment: Save energy and chemical costs.
2. **Manage reservoir levels:** Allow reservoirs to replenish, preparing for future demand peaks.
3. **Perform maintenance:** Schedule non-critical maintenance on pumps or treatment systems during periods of low demand, minimizing disruption.

The ultimate outcome is a more resilient, efficient, and cost-effective water management system. For the residents of our hypothetical city, this translates to a more reliable water supply, assurance of water quality, and potentially lower water bills due to operational efficiencies. The integration of AI-driven time-series forecasting for urban water demand is not merely an incremental improvement; it represents a paradigm shift towards smarter, more sustainable urban living. This case study underscores that by leveraging the power of data and sophisticated analytical tools, cities can better manage their most precious resources, ensuring their availability for current and future generations.

Chapter 4: Optimization Under Uncertainty and Constraints

The effective management and development of infrastructure are intrinsically linked to the concept of optimization. At its core, an optimization problem seeks to find the "best" solution from a set of feasible alternatives, according to a specific criterion. In the context of infrastructure, "best" can translate to numerous objectives, such as minimizing costs, maximizing efficiency, ensuring safety, or enhancing sustainability. This pursuit of optimality is not merely an academic exercise; it is fundamental to responsible engineering and public policy, ensuring that limited resources are utilized to achieve the greatest possible benefit for society.

To formally define an optimization problem, we must identify three key components: the objective function, the decision variables, and the constraints. The
objective function is a mathematical expression that quantifies what we are trying to optimize. It represents the goal we want to achieve, whether it's minimizing a cost, maximizing a profit, minimizing travel time, or maximizing the number of people served by a facility. The objective function takes the decision variables as its input and outputs a single value that represents the quality of the solution. For instance, if we are trying to minimize the cost of constructing a new bridge, the objective function would be an equation representing the total cost of materials, labor, and other expenses.

The
decision variables are the parameters or choices that we can control or adjust to influence the outcome of the objective function. These are the levers we can pull to find the optimal solution. In the bridge construction example, decision variables might include the type of materials used (e.g., steel grade, concrete mix), the dimensions of the supporting structures (e.g., span length, pier height), and the construction methods employed. The values of these variables determine the actual cost of the bridge.

Finally,
constraints are limitations or restrictions that must be satisfied for a solution to be considered feasible. These represent the real-world boundaries within which we must operate. Constraints can arise from physical laws, material properties, economic limitations, regulatory requirements, or social considerations. In our bridge example, constraints could include the maximum allowable stress on the materials, the minimum clearance required for river traffic, environmental regulations regarding noise or pollution, budgetary limits, and the geographical topography of the site. Any proposed design that violates these constraints is unacceptable, regardless of how low its theoretical cost might be. The set of all possible values for the decision variables that satisfy all constraints is known as the **feasible region**. The goal of optimization is to find a point within this feasible region that yields the best possible value for the objective function.

The spectrum of optimization problems encountered in infrastructure is vast and diverse, reflecting the complexity and multifaceted nature of engineered systems. Let us consider some common examples to illustrate these concepts.

One prevalent area is the optimization of
construction and maintenance costs. For large-scale projects like highways, airports, or dams, the initial construction cost can be astronomical. Engineers must meticulously select materials, design configurations, and construction sequences to minimize this upfront investment while ensuring the structure's safety and longevity. For instance, optimizing the design of a concrete mix involves balancing the cost of cement, aggregates, and admixtures against desired properties like strength, durability, and workability, subject to specifications for load-bearing capacity and environmental resistance. Similarly, for existing infrastructure, maintenance scheduling can be optimized. Deciding when

to repair a bridge, resurface a road, or replace a pipe involves a trade-off between the cost of immediate intervention and the potential for higher future costs due to deterioration or failure. The objective might be to minimize the total lifecycle cost, which includes both capital and maintenance expenditures over the expected lifespan of the asset.

Another critical area is the optimization of **service coverage and accessibility**. This is particularly relevant for public services and utilities. For example, when deciding where to locate new fire stations, hospitals, or public transportation stops, planners aim to maximize the number of people or areas that can be served within a reasonable response time or distance. This involves selecting optimal locations from a set of potential sites, considering factors like population density, existing infrastructure, traffic patterns, and land availability. The objective might be to minimize the maximum distance to the nearest facility for any resident, or to maximize the population covered within a certain service radius, subject to constraints on the number of facilities that can be built and their individual operating budgets.

Traffic flow optimization is a cornerstone of modern transportation engineering. The goal is typically to **maximize throughput and minimize congestion**. This can involve optimizing traffic signal timings at intersections to synchronize vehicle movements and reduce waiting times. Decision variables here would be the duration of green lights for different traffic streams. Constraints include minimum and maximum signal durations to ensure safety and efficiency, and the cycle length of the signals. More broadly, optimizing the network of roads and public transport routes themselves can alleviate congestion. This could involve decisions about adding new lanes, building bypasses, or adjusting public transport schedules, all aimed at improving the overall efficiency of movement within a city or region. The objective function might be to minimize average travel time for all vehicles in the network, or to minimize the total vehicle-hours of delay.

Energy consumption optimization, especially in buildings and energy grids, is of paramount importance for both economic and environmental reasons. In

building energy management, optimization can focus on minimizing energy use for heating, ventilation, and air conditioning (HVAC), lighting, and other systems. Decision variables could include thermostat setpoints, fan speeds, lighting levels, and the timing of system operation. Constraints would involve maintaining comfortable indoor temperatures, ensuring adequate ventilation, and adhering to occupancy schedules. For **energy grids**, optimization involves balancing supply and demand in real-time, minimizing generation costs, and ensuring grid stability. This can involve deciding which power plants to activate and at what levels, optimizing the dispatch of renewable energy sources, and managing energy storage systems, all while meeting demand and adhering to transmission network constraints. The objective is often to minimize the total cost of electricity generation while maintaining reliability.

These examples highlight that infrastructure optimization is not a monolithic field but rather a collection of specialized domains, each with its unique challenges and methodologies. However, they all share the common thread of seeking the best possible outcome under a defined set of conditions. The process of identifying and formulating these problems—clearly defining the objective, the controllable variables, and the unavoidable limitations—is the crucial first step before any sophisticated analytical techniques can be applied. A well-defined optimization problem is half the solution.

The significance of finding optimal solutions in infrastructure cannot be overstated. Inefficient or suboptimal designs and operational strategies can lead to enormous waste of resources, both financial and environmental. For instance, an inefficiently designed road network might lead to perpetual traffic jams, costing millions of dollars annually in lost productivity and increased fuel consumption. A poorly optimized energy grid might rely too heavily on expensive and polluting fossil fuels when cheaper and cleaner alternatives could be dispatched more effectively. Conversely, well-executed optimization can yield substantial benefits. Optimized traffic signals can reduce commute times and vehicle emissions. Smarter building energy management systems can significantly cut electricity bills and reduce a building's carbon footprint. Careful planning of public transport routes can enhance accessibility and encourage a shift away from private vehicles, leading to less congestion and pollution.

Furthermore, in a world of increasing resource scarcity and environmental concerns, optimization becomes not just a matter of efficiency but of sustainability. Finding the most resource-efficient way to build and operate infrastructure is essential for minimizing environmental impact and ensuring that these systems can serve future generations. This involves considering not only immediate economic costs but also long-term environmental consequences, such as carbon emissions, resource depletion, and habitat disruption.

The challenges in infrastructure optimization often stem from the sheer scale and complexity of the systems involved, the inherent uncertainties in their operation, and the dynamic nature of the environments in which they function. Roads and bridges are subject to weather, traffic loads, and aging. Energy demand fluctuates based on time of day, weather, and economic activity. Water distribution networks can experience leaks and pressure variations. These factors introduce elements of uncertainty that complicate the quest for a single, definitive "optimal" solution.

This is precisely why understanding optimization under uncertainty and constraints, as we will explore further, is so critical. Real-world infrastructure systems rarely operate in a perfectly predictable world. Therefore, optimization approaches must be robust enough to handle variability and adapt to changing conditions. The subsequent sections of this chapter will delve deeper into the methodologies and mathematical frameworks used to tackle these complex optimization problems, laying the groundwork for advanced analyses that incorporate risk, uncertainty, and the multitude of interdependencies inherent in modern infrastructure. We will move from the foundational definition of an optimization problem to specific techniques that allow us to find the best possible outcomes in scenarios that are far from ideal, setting the stage for understanding how sophisticated models can inform better decisions in infrastructure planning and management.

When faced with the task of finding the most efficient or cost-effective solution for infrastructure-related challenges, engineers and planners often turn to a suite of powerful mathematical tools known as deterministic optimization techniques. These methods provide a structured framework for identifying the absolute best outcome among a set of possible choices, assuming that all input parameters and relationships are known with certainty. While the real world is often fraught with unpredictability, understanding these deterministic approaches is fundamental, as they form the bedrock upon which more complex, uncertainty-aware methods are built. They allow us to establish a baseline of optimal performance under ideal conditions, providing a valuable reference point against which real-world performance can be measured and understood. The elegance of deterministic optimization lies in its ability to transform complex decision-making processes into well-defined mathematical problems that can be solved algorithmically.

At the forefront of deterministic optimization is **Linear Programming (LP)**. The power of LP lies in its simplicity and broad applicability. It is used to optimize an objective function that is linear, subject to a set of linear constraints. The objective function in an LP problem represents the quantity to be maximized or minimized – be it profit, cost, time, or resource utilization. This function is expressed as a linear combination of decision variables. For instance, if a construction company is deciding how much of two different types of aggregate to use in a concrete mix to minimize cost, the objective function might be `Cost = c1 *x1 + c2* x2`, where `x1` and `x2` are the quantities of aggregate types 1 and 2, and `c1` and `c2` are their respective costs per unit. The decision variables, `x1` and `x2`, represent the quantities that the company can control.

The constraints in an LP problem are also linear equations or inequalities. These represent the limitations and requirements that must be met. Continuing the concrete mix example, constraints could include:

Material Availability: `x1 <= A1` and `x2 <= A2`, where `A1` and `A2` are the maximum available quantities of aggregate types 1 and 2, respectively.
Strength Requirements: The final concrete mix must meet a certain strength, which might be a linear combination of the aggregates used. For example, `s1 x1 + s2 x2 >= S`, where `s1` and `s2` are strength contributions per unit of aggregate, and `S` is the minimum required strength.
Budget Constraints: The total cost must not exceed a certain budget. `c1 x1 + c2 x2 <= B`, where `B` is the budget.
Non-negativity: Quantities of aggregates cannot be negative, so `x1 >= 0` and `x2 >= 0`.

The core assumption of LP is that all these relationships are linear. This means that if you double the quantity of an aggregate, its cost and contribution to strength also double, with no diminishing returns or synergistic effects. This linearity allows for efficient solution methods, such as the Simplex algorithm, which systematically explores the vertices of the feasible region (the set of all possible solutions that satisfy the constraints) to find the optimal one. The feasible region in LP is a convex polyhedron.

Consider an application in resource allocation for a construction project. Suppose a project manager needs to decide how many hours to allocate to two different tasks: excavation and foundation laying. Let `x1` be the hours spent on excavation and `x2` be the hours spent on foundation laying. The objective is to minimize the total project duration, which might be approximated by a linear function of these hours, considering parallel work possibilities and dependencies. However, a more practical objective might be to minimize the total labor cost. If the cost of labor for excavation is $50/hour and for foundation laying is $60/hour, the objective function is `Minimize Cost = 50
*x1 + 60*x2`.

The constraints could be:

Total Budget: The total expenditure on these two tasks cannot exceed $10,000. So, `50x1 + 60x2 <= 10000`.
Time Deadline: The project must be completed within 200 hours. This might translate to a constraint on the sum of hours if they are sequential, or more complex if parallel. For simplicity, let's assume `x1 + x2 <= 200`.
Excavation Requirement: A minimum of 50 hours of excavation is required. `x1 >= 50`.
Foundation Requirement: A minimum of 30 hours of foundation work is needed. `x2 >= 30`.
Non-negativity: `x1 >= 0`, `x2 >= 0`.

By plotting these constraints, we define a feasible region. The Simplex algorithm, or other LP solvers, would then find the point within this region that yields the lowest cost. LP is incredibly useful for problems involving the allocation of resources (labor, materials, machinery) to different activities, production planning, transportation logistics, and financial portfolio optimization, provided the relationships can be reasonably linearized.

When decision variables are required to be whole numbers, we move into the realm of
Integer Programming (IP). Many real-world decisions are of this discrete nature. For example, you can't build half a bridge, or decide to include 2.7 charging stations. IP problems are an extension of LP, where some or all of the decision variables must take integer values.

Pure Integer Programming requires all variables to be integers. **Mixed Integer Programming (MIP)** allows some variables to be continuous and others to be integers. The addition of the integer constraint significantly increases the complexity of the problem. Unlike LP, where the optimal solution is often found at a vertex of the feasible region, in IP, the optimal integer solution may not lie on any vertex and can be "between" the vertices of the LP relaxation (the problem solved as if the variables were continuous).

Consider the problem of optimally placing charging stations for electric vehicles (EVs) in a city. Let's say we have a set of potential locations, and we need to decide which of these locations to select for building charging stations. The decision variables would be binary: 1 if a station is built at a location, and 0 otherwise. This is a classic example of an IP problem, specifically
Binary Integer Programming, a subset of IP where variables can only take values of 0 or 1.

Suppose a city has 10 potential sites for EV charging stations. We want to select a subset of these sites to maximize coverage of the city's population, while adhering to a budget and ensuring a minimum number of stations are built.

Objective: Maximize total population covered. Let `p*i*` *be the population covered by a station at site `i`. Let* `xi` be a binary variable, `x*i* = *1*` *if a station is built at site `i`, and* `xi = 0` otherwise. The objective is `Maximize Sum(p*i* xi)` for all `i` from 1 to 10.
Budget Constraint: Building a station at site `i` costs `c*i*`. *The total budget is `B`. So, `Sum(c*i x_i) <= B`.
Minimum Stations: A minimum of `K` stations must be built. `Sum(x_i) >= K`.
Other Constraints: Perhaps there are constraints on proximity to major roads, or electrical grid capacity at each potential site, which might also be modeled using binary variables or other integer constraints.

Solving IP problems is computationally more challenging than LP. Algorithms like Branch and Bound, or Branch and Cut, are commonly used. These methods typically start by solving the LP relaxation of the problem. If the solution is integer-feasible, it's a candidate for the optimum. If not, the algorithm "branches" by adding new constraints (e.g., `x
*i <= 0` or* `xi >= 1` for a non-integer variable `x_i`) to divide the problem into sub-problems, and then explores these sub-problems recursively.

Another common type of IP formulation arises in network design. For instance, determining the optimal routing of maintenance crews for a utility company. If there are `N` locations to visit, and each crew can only visit a subset of these locations on a given day, deciding which locations each crew visits (represented by binary variables) and the order in which they visit them (often modeled using assignment variables) can lead to complex IP formulations. For example, the Traveling Salesperson Problem (TSP), a classic NP-hard problem, is typically formulated as an IP.

A further extension involves problems where the relationships between variables are not linear. This is the domain of

Non-Linear Programming (NLP). In NLP, either the objective function or one or more of the constraints (or both) involve non-linear mathematical functions. These functions can represent phenomena like economies of scale (where cost per unit decreases as production increases), diminishing returns, complex physical relationships (e.g., fluid dynamics, stress-strain curves), or interactions between different components of a system.

For example, optimizing the design of a water distribution network might involve non-linear relationships. The pressure loss in a pipe is often proportional to the square of the flow rate, which is a non-linear relationship. If the objective is to minimize the total pumping energy (which depends on pressure and flow) or minimize pipe material cost (which might be related to pipe diameter, and flow rate), the problem can become non-linear.

Let's consider optimizing the operating levels of different power generation units in a utility company. Suppose there are several power plants, each with a different cost function for generating electricity. Some cost functions might be linear (e.g., a simple fossil fuel plant), while others might be quadratic (representing increasing marginal costs as a plant operates at higher capacity due to thermal inefficiencies or wear and tear).

Objective: Minimize the total cost of electricity generation to meet demand. `Minimize Sum(Cost*i*(*x*i))` where `*xi*` *is the output of power plant `i`, and `Cost*i` is its cost function.
Demand Constraint: The total generation must meet the electricity demand `D`. `Sum(x_i) = D`.
Capacity Constraints: Each power plant `i` has a minimum `min*i*` *and maximum `max*i` generation capacity. `min*i* <= *x*i <= max_i`.
Non-linear Cost Functions: For example, `Cost*i*(*x*i) = a*i* xi^2 + b*i* xi + c*i*` *for some plants, and `Cost*j(x*j*) = *d*j *xj* + *e*j` for others.

When the objective function and constraints are non-linear, solving the problem becomes significantly more challenging than with LP or IP. Unlike the convex regions in LP, the feasible regions in NLP can be non-convex, meaning they can have multiple local optima. Algorithms for NLP, such as Gradient Descent, Newton's method, or Sequential Quadratic Programming (SQP), aim to find the optimal solution. However, they often guarantee finding only a local optimum, not necessarily the global optimum, unless the problem has specific convexity properties. For convex problems, the local optimum is also the global optimum. Determining convexity can be a crucial step in analyzing an NLP problem.

The practical applicability of these deterministic methods in infrastructure is vast. For instance, LP is routinely used in traffic assignment problems to determine how drivers choose routes given network conditions and travel times, or in managing fleets of vehicles by optimizing routes and assignments. IP finds its way into facility location problems (e.g., where to build new schools, hospitals, or waste treatment plants), project scheduling with discrete tasks and resource constraints, and designing optimal configurations for communication networks. NLP is essential for more complex engineering designs, such as optimizing the shape of an antenna, the parameters of a control system for a complex chemical process, or the structural integrity of a bridge under various load conditions where material behavior is non-linear.

However, a critical limitation of all these deterministic techniques is their reliance on perfectly known inputs. In the real world of infrastructure, data is rarely perfect. Demand for water, electricity, or transportation fluctuates unpredictably. Material properties can vary. Construction costs are subject to market volatility. Equipment performance can degrade over time. Weather conditions can impact construction schedules and operational efficiency. Applying deterministic optimization without accounting for this inherent variability can lead to solutions that are optimal only under an idealized set of circumstances, and may perform poorly or even fail when faced with real-world deviations. This is precisely where the limitations of deterministic approaches become apparent, paving the way for the introduction of optimization techniques designed to explicitly handle uncertainty. The insights gained from deterministic optimization serve as a crucial foundation, but they highlight the necessity of more sophisticated methods for robust infrastructure management and planning.

The preceding discussion has underscored the pivotal role of deterministic optimization in infrastructure planning and management, establishing a foundational understanding of how to find optimal solutions when all parameters are precisely known. However, the reality of infrastructure systems is that certainty is a luxury rarely afforded. Every facet of their lifecycle, from initial design and construction to ongoing operation and maintenance, is inherently permeated by uncertainty. This pervasive uncertainty manifests in a multitude of forms, influencing everything from the projected demand for services to the very materials used in construction and the reliability of operational components. Ignoring these inherent uncertainties can lead to the development of systems that are brittle, failing to perform as expected when confronted with the unpredictable nature of the real world. Therefore, a crucial evolution in our approach to optimizing infrastructure systems involves embracing and rigorously modeling these uncertainties. This shift from deterministic to stochastic or robust optimization is not merely an academic exercise; it is a pragmatic necessity for building resilient and adaptable infrastructure that can reliably serve society under a wide spectrum of foreseeable and unforeseeable conditions.

One of the primary challenges in modeling uncertainty lies in its very nature: it is often abstract and difficult to quantify precisely. Unlike the concrete numbers used in deterministic models, uncertain parameters are characterized by variability, ambiguity, or a lack of complete information. To effectively incorporate uncertainty into optimization frameworks, we first need robust methods for representing it.

Probability distributions are perhaps the most common and mathematically rigorous tool for modeling uncertainty. When we can collect sufficient historical data or possess expert knowledge about the range and likelihood of possible values for a parameter, we can often fit a probability distribution to it. For instance, the demand for electricity in a city fluctuates daily, seasonally, and annually. While we cannot predict the exact demand for any given hour, we can analyze historical data to understand its statistical properties. This might lead us to model daily peak electricity demand using a normal distribution, a log-normal distribution, or a Weibull distribution, depending on the observed patterns. The mean and variance of such distributions provide a quantitative measure of the expected demand and its variability. Similarly, the time between equipment failures (Mean Time Between Failures, MTBF) is often modeled using exponential or Weibull distributions, reflecting the probabilistic nature of component degradation and failure. The selection of an appropriate probability distribution is critical and relies on statistical analysis of available data and an understanding of the underlying physical processes. Once defined, these probabilistic models allow us to explore how variations in these uncertain parameters might impact the performance and cost-effectiveness of an infrastructure system. For example, if we are designing a water treatment plant, we can use probabilistic models for rainfall and river flow to estimate the range of raw water quality and quantity that the plant might need to handle.

Beyond traditional probability distributions,
fuzzy sets offer a powerful alternative for modeling uncertainty when the boundaries of vagueness are not well-defined or when dealing with

linguistic imprecision. Unlike probability, which deals with the likelihood of an event occurring, fuzzy sets deal with the degree to which an element belongs to a set. This is particularly useful when dealing with subjective assessments or qualitative data that cannot be easily expressed in precise numerical terms. For example, consider the description of soil conditions for a construction project. Terms like "slightly cohesive," "moderately dense," or "highly permeable" are inherently fuzzy. A fuzzy set approach can assign a membership degree (a value between 0 and 1) to a soil sample belonging to each of these categories. This allows for a more nuanced representation of uncertainty than simply assigning a single numerical value or a probability range. Similarly, expert opinions on the likelihood of a specific technology becoming obsolete might be expressed in fuzzy terms, like "highly probable" or "somewhat unlikely." Fuzzy optimization techniques can then operate on these fuzzy parameters to yield solutions that are robust to such imprecision, providing a degree of confidence in the outcome rather than a single definitive answer.

Scenario analysis provides a more intuitive, yet still powerful, method for exploring the implications of uncertainty. This approach involves identifying a set of plausible future scenarios that encompass a range of potential conditions. Each scenario is a self-consistent description of how a set of uncertain parameters might evolve. For example, when planning a new transportation network, scenarios might include:
High Demand Growth: Characterized by rapid population increase, economic boom, and widespread adoption of private vehicles.
Moderate Growth with Modal Shift: Moderate population growth, but with a significant shift towards public transport and active mobility (walking, cycling) due to policy changes and environmental concerns.
Low Growth and Technological Disruption: Stagnant population growth, limited economic development, and the emergence of new mobility technologies (e.g., autonomous vehicles, hyperloop) that fundamentally alter travel patterns.

For each scenario, specific values (or ranges) are assigned to the uncertain variables such as population growth rates, fuel prices, technological adoption curves, and user preferences. Optimization models are then run independently for each scenario to determine the optimal decision (e.g., network design, investment strategy) under those specific conditions. By comparing the outcomes across different scenarios, decision-makers can gain a comprehensive understanding of the potential risks and rewards associated with various choices. This allows for the identification of "robust" solutions – those that perform reasonably well across a wide range of scenarios – or the development of adaptive strategies that can be adjusted as the future unfolds. Scenario analysis is particularly valuable for long-term strategic planning where the range of possible futures is vast and predicting precise probabilities is difficult. It forces planners to think critically about the drivers of change and their potential impact.

A crucial aspect of modeling uncertainty is identifying and characterizing its key sources within infrastructure systems. These sources are diverse and often interconnected:

1. Demand Fluctuations: This is one of the most ubiquitous forms of uncertainty. For public utilities like water, electricity, and gas, demand is influenced by weather, economic activity, population growth, and individual behavior. An electricity grid must be designed to meet peak demand, which can be significantly higher than average demand, and these peaks can be unpredictable. Similarly, transportation networks face uncertainties in commuter volumes, freight traffic, and the impact of special events. For example, the introduction of a new major employer in a city can drastically increase commuting demand on local roads and public transit, a factor that might not have been precisely foreseen during initial planning. Accurate forecasting is challenging, and historical data may not always be a reliable predictor of future demand, especially in the face of societal shifts or new infrastructure development itself.

2. Weather Variability and Climate Change: Weather patterns have a direct impact on the operation and demand for many infrastructure systems. Extreme weather events, such as heatwaves, cold snaps, heavy rainfall, floods, droughts, and storms, can stress systems, cause disruptions, and lead to surges in demand for energy or water. For instance, heatwaves increase electricity demand for cooling, while prolonged cold periods boost demand for heating. Floods can damage critical infrastructure like bridges, roads, and water treatment facilities, necessitating costly repairs and leading to service interruptions. Furthermore, long-term climate change introduces a layer of uncertainty regarding future weather patterns. Projections of sea-level rise, changes in precipitation intensity, and increases in the frequency of extreme events must be considered in the design and adaptation of infrastructure to ensure long-term resilience. A coastal flood defense system, for example, needs to be designed not just for historical flood levels but also for projected future sea levels and storm surge intensities.

3. Equipment Failure and Reliability: Infrastructure systems are composed of numerous physical components that are subject to wear, degradation, and eventual failure. The reliability of these components is rarely absolute. Pumps in a water system, turbines in a power plant, transformers in an electrical grid, and vehicles in a transit fleet all have associated failure rates. These rates are often not constant and can be influenced by operating conditions, maintenance practices, and the age of the equipment. Modeling equipment failure typically involves probabilistic approaches, such as using failure rate data from manufacturers or historical maintenance logs to estimate the probability of component failure over a given period. Understanding these failure probabilities is crucial for designing redundant systems, planning preventive maintenance schedules, and assessing the overall reliability and availability of the infrastructure service. A system designed with insufficient redundancy might be highly efficient under normal operating conditions but could suffer prolonged and widespread outages if a critical component fails unexpectedly.

4. Uncertain Costs and Funding: The financial aspects of infrastructure projects are notoriously subject to uncertainty. Construction costs can escalate due to unforeseen site conditions, material price volatility, labor shortages, or changes in regulatory requirements. Similarly, operating and maintenance costs can deviate from initial estimates due to unexpected repairs, inflation, or changes in energy prices. Funding availability can also be uncertain, depending on government budgets, private investment, and economic conditions. For large-scale projects spanning decades, such as the development of high-speed rail networks or new power generation facilities, forecasting costs and securing adequate funding over the entire project lifecycle is a significant challenge. Scenario analysis or robust optimization techniques can be employed to assess the financial viability of projects under different cost and funding scenarios.

5. Construction and Execution Risks: The process of building or upgrading infrastructure itself is fraught with uncertainties. Construction schedules can be affected by weather delays, supply chain disruptions, labor disputes, or unexpected geological conditions. The quality of construction may also vary, impacting the long-term performance and durability of the asset. For instance, the discovery of contaminated soil on a construction site can lead to significant delays and increased remediation costs, requiring a re-evaluation of project timelines and budgets. Risk management strategies, including contingency planning and flexible contracting, are essential to mitigate the impact of these execution uncertainties.

6. Environmental and Social Factors: Infrastructure development and operation can be influenced by evolving environmental regulations, public opinion, and social acceptance. For example, the permitting process for a new power plant might be delayed or require modifications due to environmental impact assessments or community opposition. The introduction of new technologies or changes in user behavior can also affect the performance and demand for existing infrastructure. The adoption of electric vehicles, for instance, presents both opportunities and challenges for the electricity grid and charging infrastructure.

Understanding and quantifying these uncertainties is the critical first step towards developing infrastructure systems that are not only efficient in their design and operation but also reliable and resilient in the face of real-world variability. This quantification allows us to move beyond simplistic deterministic models and embrace approaches that acknowledge and manage the inherent complexities of the infrastructure landscape. Without this understanding, optimal solutions derived under ideal conditions can quickly become suboptimal, or even entirely unworkable, when faced with the dynamic and unpredictable nature of the environments in which infrastructure operates. This forms the essential bridge to the advanced optimization methodologies discussed in the subsequent sections, which are specifically designed to harness the power of uncertainty quantification for robust decision-making.

The preceding discussion has firmly established the limitations of deterministic optimization in the face of pervasive uncertainty inherent in infrastructure systems. While deterministic models provide a clear optimal solution under idealized conditions, they offer little insight into how that solution might perform when faced with the inevitable deviations and unpredictability of the real world. To bridge this gap and build infrastructure that is truly resilient, we must turn to optimization frameworks that explicitly incorporate and manage uncertainty. This section delves into two primary families of such techniques: Stochastic Optimization and Robust Optimization. These methodologies provide powerful tools for decision-making, enabling us to design and operate infrastructure that is not only efficient but also capable of withstanding a wide range of unforeseeable circumstances.

Stochastic optimization, at its core, seeks to find optimal solutions in problems where some parameters are not fixed values but are instead described by probability distributions. The objective is typically to optimize an expected value or to satisfy certain probabilistic constraints. This approach acknowledges that while we may not know the exact outcome of an uncertain event, we can often characterize its likelihood and distribution. This allows for a more nuanced decision-making process than simply assuming a single, fixed value. Among the various stochastic optimization techniques, chance-constrained programming and two-stage stochastic programming are particularly relevant for infrastructure applications.

Chance-Constrained Programming (CCP) is a framework that directly addresses the probabilistic nature of uncertain parameters by formulating constraints that must be satisfied with a certain minimum probability. Instead of demanding that a constraint be met for all possible realizations of uncertainty (which would be overly restrictive and often lead to infeasible solutions), CCP requires that the constraint be satisfied for at least a specified proportion of the possible outcomes. Mathematically, a typical chance constraint takes the form $P(g(x, \xi) \le 0) \ge \alpha$, where x represents the decision variables, ξ is the random vector encompassing the uncertain parameters, $g(\cdot)$ is a function defining the constraint, and α is the desired probability level (e.g., 95% or 99%).

Consider the example of designing an electricity generation portfolio. A key constraint might be ensuring that the system can meet demand at all times. If electricity demand is uncertain and modeled by a probability distribution, a deterministic approach might simply aim to meet the *expected* demand. However, this could lead to frequent shortages during periods of higher-than-average demand. Using CCP, we could formulate a constraint such as: "The probability that the available generation capacity is greater than or equal to the actual demand must be at least 98%." This approach explicitly accounts for the risk of not meeting demand and allows the decision-maker to set an acceptable level of risk. The challenge with CCP often lies in the computational complexity of solving these problems, especially when dealing with complex probability distributions and numerous uncertain parameters. Analytical solutions are often difficult to obtain, necessitating the use of approximation techniques or specialized algorithms. For instance, if the uncertain demand ξ follows a normal distribution, and the constraint $g(x, \xi)$ is linear in ξ, then the chance constraint can often be reformulated into a deterministic equivalent constraint involving the mean and variance of ξ. However, for non-linear relationships or more complex distributions, specialized algorithms like Monte Carlo simulation-based optimization or sequential quadratic programming with probabilistic constraints may be required.

Another prominent approach within stochastic optimization is **Two-Stage Stochastic Programming with Recourse**. This framework is particularly well-suited for problems where decisions must be made sequentially, with an initial set of decisions taken before the uncertainty is fully realized, followed by corrective actions once the outcomes of the uncertain events become known. In this model, the problem is divided into two stages:

First Stage: Decisions are made under uncertainty. These are often irreversible or costly to change. For example, deciding on the capacity of a power plant to build.
Second Stage: After the realization of the uncertain parameters (e.g., actual electricity demand for the year), recourse actions are taken to mitigate any adverse consequences arising from the initial decisions. For example, purchasing electricity from the spot market or activating backup generators if the built capacity is insufficient.

The objective in a two-stage stochastic program is to minimize the sum of the first-stage decision costs and the expected cost of the second-stage recourse actions. Mathematically, this can be represented as:

Minimize $c^T x + E_{\xi}[Q(x, \xi)]$

Subject to $Ax \le b$

and $x \ge 0$

where x are the first-stage decision variables, c is the cost vector for x, ξ is the random vector of uncertain parameters, A and b define the first-stage constraints, and $Q(x, \xi)$ represents the optimal value of the second-stage problem for a given x and realization of ξ:

$Q(x, \xi) = \min \{q^T y \mid T(\xi)y \ge h - Wx, y \ge 0\}$

Here, y are the second-stage decision variables (recourse actions), q is the cost vector for y, $T(\xi)$ and h are parameters that depend on the realized uncertainty ξ, and W relates the first-stage decisions to the second-stage constraints.

An illustrative example in infrastructure is the planning of a water supply network. A first-stage decision might involve investing in new reservoir capacity or upgrading treatment plants. The uncertainty here could be the future water demand or the frequency and severity of droughts. After these initial investments are made, and if a drought materializes (uncertainty realized), second-stage recourse actions might include implementing water restrictions, purchasing water from neighboring regions, or utilizing emergency backup supplies. The two-stage stochastic program would aim to find the optimal initial investment in infrastructure that minimizes the total cost, considering both the upfront capital expenditure and the expected future costs associated with managing water shortages or surpluses. The expectation $E_{\xi}[\cdot]$ is taken over the probability distribution of the uncertain parameters. When the uncertainty set consists of a finite number of discrete scenarios, the expected value can be computed as a weighted sum over these scenarios. However, if the uncertainty is continuous, numerical integration or approximation techniques are often necessary. The concept of recourse is particularly powerful because it explicitly models the ability to adapt to unfolding events, leading to more resilient and cost-effective long-term strategies.

While stochastic optimization aims to find solutions that perform well on average or satisfy probabilistic guarantees,
Robust Optimization (RO) takes a more conservative approach. Robust optimization seeks solutions that are feasible and perform acceptably well for *all* possible realizations of uncertainty within a predefined uncertainty set. The primary goal is to guarantee performance against the worst-case scenario, thereby hedging against extreme outcomes. This approach is particularly appealing when the probabilities of different uncertainty realizations are difficult to estimate, or when the consequences of a poor outcome are catastrophic.

The core idea in robust optimization is to transform an uncertain optimization problem into a deterministic one by considering the "worst-case" scenario for each constraint and objective function. For a minimization problem, this means finding a solution that minimizes the objective function under the most unfavorable realization of the uncertain parameters within the defined uncertainty set. For a maximization problem, it means maximizing the objective function under the most unfavorable realization.

Consider a robust counterpart of a problem with uncertain parameters ξ. A constraint of the form $g(x, \xi) \le 0$ for all ξ in the uncertainty set $\mathcal{U}$ would be rewritten as:

$$\max_{\xi \in \mathcal{U}} g(x, \xi) \le 0$$

Similarly, an objective function to be minimized, $f(x, \xi)$, would be transformed into minimizing its worst-case realization:

Minimize $\max_{\xi \in \mathcal{U}} f(x, \xi)$

The definition of the uncertainty set $\mathcal{U}$ is crucial in robust optimization. Common choices for $\mathcal{U}$ include:

Box Uncertainty: Each uncertain parameter ξ_i *is confined to an interval* $[\underline{\xi}_i, \bar{\xi}_i]$*. The uncertainty set is then*

$\mathcal{U} = \{\xi \mid \underline{\xi}i \le \xii \le \bar{\xi}i \text{ for all } i\}$. This is a simple and often used uncertainty set.
Ellipsoidal Uncertainty: The uncertainty set is defined by an ellipsoid, often centered around a nominal value. For example, $(\xi - \hat{\xi})^T \Sigma^{-1} (\xi - \hat{\xi}) \le \rho^2$, where $\hat{\xi}$ is the nominal value, Σ is a covariance matrix, and ρ controls the size of the ellipsoid. This set captures some correlation between uncertain parameters.
Polyhedral Uncertainty: The uncertainty set is defined by a finite number of linear inequalities. This allows for flexible modeling of uncertain relationships.

The power of robust optimization lies in its ability to transform problems with complex uncertainty into tractable deterministic optimization problems, often solvable using standard optimization solvers, provided the uncertainty set has a suitable structure. For instance, for problems with linear objective and constraints and box uncertainty, the robust counterpart can often be reformulated as a larger-scale linear program.

Let's illustrate the application of robust optimization in infrastructure with an example of network design. Suppose we are designing a transportation network, and the demand for each link is uncertain and can vary within certain bounds. A deterministic approach might optimize the network for the
expected demand. However, if the actual demand on some links turns out to be at the upper end of their range, the network might become severely congested, leading to unacceptable delays and economic losses. A robust optimization approach would instead aim to design a network that guarantees a certain level of service (e.g., maximum travel time or minimum throughput) even under the *worst possible combination* of demands within the predefined uncertainty bounds.

Consider a resource allocation problem, such as assigning limited maintenance crews to a set of infrastructure assets that may require repair. The time to failure for each asset is uncertain. A robust approach would ensure that the maintenance schedule is feasible and effective even if the failures occur at the earliest possible times within their predicted ranges. This means that resources are allocated to satisfy the most demanding realization of failures, ensuring resilience against unexpected breakdowns. The cost of robust solutions is typically higher than their deterministic counterparts because they must account for the worst-case scenarios. However, this "premium" often represents a valuable insurance policy against potentially catastrophic failures or performance degradations. The trade-off between robustness and cost is a central theme in robust optimization, and selecting the appropriate uncertainty set is critical to balancing this trade-off effectively. A smaller, more restrictive uncertainty set leads to more robust solutions but potentially higher costs, while a larger, less restrictive set might result in lower costs but less guaranteed performance.

The choice between stochastic optimization and robust optimization often depends on the specific characteristics of the problem and the decision-maker's risk tolerance. Stochastic optimization, particularly when using probability distributions, is favored when there is good historical data or expert knowledge to accurately characterize the likelihood of different outcomes, and when optimizing for expected performance or probabilistic guarantees is acceptable. Robust optimization, on the other hand, is preferred when the consequences of poor performance are severe, when precise probability distributions are hard to ascertain, or when a guarantee of performance under any conceivable (within the defined set) scenario is paramount.

In essence, stochastic optimization methods provide a spectrum of approaches to dealing with uncertainty. Chance-constrained programming allows for probabilistic guarantees on constraint satisfaction, while two-stage stochastic programming explicitly models the sequential nature of decision-making and the ability to adapt to realized uncertainties through recourse actions. Robust optimization, by contrast, offers a more conservative approach, focusing on worst-case performance within a defined uncertainty set, thus providing a degree of resilience against unforeseen events, even if their precise probabilities are unknown. Both families of techniques are indispensable for modern infrastructure planning and management, enabling the development of systems that are not only efficient but also reliable and adaptable in the face of an uncertain future. Their application allows us to move beyond the limitations of deterministic thinking and embrace a more pragmatic and resilient approach to infrastructure development, ensuring that these vital systems can continue to serve society effectively under a wide array of conditions. The decision on which approach to employ hinges on a careful assessment of the available data, the specific risks involved, and the desired level of assurance against adverse outcomes.

The preceding discussion has underscored the indispensable role of stochastic and robust optimization in equipping infrastructure systems with resilience against uncertainty. However, the effectiveness of these powerful frameworks hinges critically on the accuracy and timeliness of information regarding future states, particularly in dynamic and complex environments. This is precisely where Artificial Intelligence (AI) emerges as a transformative force, offering novel capabilities to predict uncertain variables and to facilitate real-time decision-making within optimization contexts. This subsection will explore the synergistic integration of AI with optimization under uncertainty, with a specific focus on its application in enhancing the resilience of power grids. We will examine how AI algorithms can generate predictions of future grid states, such as renewable energy generation and electricity demand, and how these predictions can be seamlessly incorporated into advanced optimization frameworks. Furthermore, we will delve into AI-driven techniques, such as Approximate Dynamic Programming (ADP) and Reinforcement Learning (RL), which enable adaptive control strategies for maintaining system stability and reliability in the face of fluctuating inputs and unforeseen component failures.

The modern power grid is a quintessential example of a complex, dynamic infrastructure system facing pervasive uncertainty. The increasing penetration of renewable energy sources, such as solar and wind power, introduces significant variability into generation profiles. These sources are inherently intermittent, dependent on weather conditions that are difficult to predict with absolute certainty over extended periods. For instance, a sudden cloud cover can drastically reduce solar photovoltaic output, while a drop in wind speed can curtail wind turbine generation. Simultaneously, electricity demand, influenced by factors like temperature, economic activity, and time of day, also exhibits dynamic and often unpredictable patterns. Adding to this complexity are the potential for unexpected equipment failures, transmission line outages, or cyber-physical attacks, all of which can disrupt grid operations.

Traditional optimization approaches, even those incorporating stochastic or robust methodologies, often rely on pre-defined scenarios or probability distributions that may not fully capture the nuanced, real-time fluctuations of the power system. This is where AI, particularly machine learning (ML) techniques, offers a paradigm shift. AI excels at identifying intricate patterns and correlations within vast datasets, enabling it to learn from historical data and make sophisticated predictions about future states. For power grids, this translates into the ability to forecast renewable energy generation with improved accuracy, often on short-term (minutes to hours) and medium-term (days to weeks) horizons. Techniques like Recurrent Neural Networks (RNNs), Long Short-Term Memory (LSTM) networks, and Transformer models have proven highly effective in time-series forecasting for solar irradiance, wind speed, and consequently, the expected power output from these renewable sources.

Similarly, AI can significantly enhance the accuracy of electricity demand forecasting. By analyzing historical demand data alongside a multitude of influencing factors such as weather forecasts, calendar events (holidays, weekends), and even social media sentiment, ML models can provide more precise short-term and long-term demand predictions. For example, sophisticated deep learning models can capture non-linear relationships between ambient temperature and air conditioning load, or between economic indicators and industrial electricity consumption, leading to more accurate load profiles than conventional statistical methods.

The integration of these AI-driven predictions into optimization frameworks for power grids is a critical step towards achieving enhanced resilience. Instead of relying on static or generalized scenario sets, optimization problems can be formulated with AI-generated, dynamic forecasts of uncertain parameters. For instance, a unit commitment problem, which determines which power generation units to activate and at what output levels to meet forecasted demand at the lowest cost while respecting operational constraints, can be re-optimized frequently using the latest AI-generated demand and renewable generation forecasts. This allows the grid operator to adapt the generation schedule in near real-time, ensuring that the system is always operating with the most up-to-date information about anticipated conditions.

Beyond forecasting, AI itself can be employed to directly derive adaptive control strategies. This is particularly relevant for operational decisions that need to be made continuously and dynamically. Two prominent AI paradigms for this purpose are Approximate Dynamic Programming (ADP) and Reinforcement Learning (RL).

Approximate Dynamic Programming (ADP) is a powerful technique that extends the principles of dynamic programming to problems with large state spaces or continuous state and action spaces, which are characteristic of power grid operations. Dynamic programming typically involves solving for the optimal value function, which represents the best achievable future reward (or cost) from a given state. In large-scale systems, computing this exact value function can be computationally intractable. ADP addresses this by using parameterized approximation functions (e.g., neural networks) to estimate the value function.

In the context of a resilient power grid, ADP can be used to develop control policies that optimize system performance under uncertainty. Consider the problem of managing energy storage systems (e.g., batteries). The optimal charging and discharging strategy for a battery depends on a multitude of factors: current grid state (frequency, voltage), electricity prices, forecasted demand, forecasted renewable generation, and the possibility of grid contingencies. An ADP-based controller can learn an optimal policy for managing the battery by iteratively improving its approximation of the value function. The "state" in this context could include variables like the current state of charge of the battery, time of day, day of the week, and short-term forecasts of key grid parameters. The "action" would be the rate of charge or discharge. The "reward" or "cost" could be defined based on factors like minimizing operational costs, maximizing grid stability (e.g., maintaining frequency within a tight band), and preserving the battery's lifespan. The ADP algorithm would simulate various scenarios, update its value function approximation based on the observed outcomes, and gradually converge to a policy that makes near-optimal decisions in real-time. This allows the battery to be used strategically not only for economic arbitrage but also for providing ancillary services that enhance grid resilience, such as frequency regulation or voltage support, in response to unpredictable events.

Reinforcement Learning (RL) offers a complementary and often more direct approach to learning control policies in dynamic environments. RL agents learn by interacting with an environment, receiving rewards or penalties based on their actions, and adjusting their behavior to maximize cumulative future rewards. Unlike ADP, which often starts with a value function approximation, RL agents can learn policies directly (policy-based RL) or learn value functions and derive policies from them (value-based RL), or a combination of both (actor-critic methods).

For power grid resilience, RL can be employed to train intelligent agents capable of making decisions to maintain stability and reliability under a wide range of conditions, including extreme events. For example, an RL agent could be trained to control distributed energy resources (DERs) such as rooftop solar inverters, electric vehicle charging stations, and small-scale energy storage units. The agent's objective would be to collectively contribute to grid stability. The state space would include local measurements (voltage, frequency, power flow), local generation and load, and potentially aggregated information from the wider grid. Actions could involve adjusting the power output of DERs, curtailing load, or dispatching storage. Rewards would be designed to incentivize actions that contribute to grid stability, such as maintaining voltage within acceptable limits, supporting frequency regulation, or helping to absorb surplus renewable generation. Penalties would be imposed for actions that destabilize the grid.

A significant advantage of RL in this context is its ability to learn robust policies through experience. By training the RL agent on a diverse set of simulated scenarios, including normal operations, fluctuations in renewables, demand spikes, and even simulated component failures or cyber-attacks, the agent can develop adaptive behaviors that generalize well to unseen situations. This allows the grid to respond more intelligently and autonomously to disturbances, reducing reliance on slow-acting human operator interventions or pre-programmed responses that might be inadequate for novel events.

Consider a specific application: managing grid frequency in the presence of rapid renewable generation fluctuations and load changes. Traditionally, this is handled by primary and secondary frequency control reserves. An RL agent could be trained to provide a more dynamic and optimized form of frequency response by coordinating the actions of a fleet of aggregated DERs. The agent would learn to anticipate frequency deviations based on incoming data and proactively adjust the power output of DERs to counteract these deviations, potentially offering a faster and more precise response than traditional methods. This distributed control approach, enabled by AI, can significantly enhance the grid's ability to absorb disturbances without cascading failures.

The integration of AI into optimization for resilient grids is not without its challenges. One primary concern is the "black box" nature of some advanced AI models, particularly deep neural networks. Understanding why an AI model makes a particular decision can be difficult, which can be a barrier to adoption in critical infrastructure where transparency and explainability are paramount. Research into explainable AI (XAI) is crucial for addressing this. XAI techniques aim to provide insights into the decision-making process of AI models, allowing operators to understand the reasoning behind an AI-driven control action, thereby building trust and facilitating validation.

Another challenge is the computational burden associated with training and deploying complex AI models, especially for real-time applications. Training deep learning models can require significant computational resources and large amounts of data. However, advancements in hardware (e.g., GPUs, TPUs) and efficient training algorithms are continuously improving this aspect. For real-time deployment, techniques such as model compression, knowledge distillation, and efficient inference engines are employed to enable AI models to run effectively on embedded systems or within tight operational timeframes.

Furthermore, ensuring the cybersecurity of AI-driven control systems is of utmost importance. AI models themselves can be vulnerable to adversarial attacks, where malicious inputs are crafted to deliberately mislead the model into making incorrect decisions. Robust cybersecurity measures, including data sanitization, anomaly detection in input data, and secure model deployment strategies, are essential to protect AI-enabled power grids from such threats.

The concept of hybrid optimization, which combines traditional optimization techniques with AI, represents a promising avenue. For example, AI could be used to learn an approximation of a complex objective function or constraint that is otherwise intractable for analytical optimization. Alternatively, AI could be used to guide the search process of an optimization algorithm, focusing computational effort on more promising regions of the solution space. For instance, an AI model could predict which operational scenarios are most likely to be critical or lead to instability, allowing a robust optimization algorithm to focus its worst-case analysis on those specific scenarios, thereby improving computational efficiency without sacrificing resilience.

The potential impact of AI-driven optimization on power grid resilience is profound. By enabling more accurate prediction of uncertain factors, facilitating adaptive real-time decision-making through ADP and RL, and allowing for the creation of distributed intelligent control strategies, AI can transform the power grid from a relatively rigid system into a flexible, self-healing network. This enhanced adaptability is crucial for navigating the increasing complexity and volatility of future energy landscapes, ensuring the reliable and sustainable delivery of electricity even under the most challenging circumstances. The continuous advancements in AI, coupled with a deeper understanding of its integration with established optimization principles, promise to unlock new levels of resilience and efficiency for critical infrastructure worldwide.

Chapter 5: AI for Infrastructure Monitoring and Anomaly Detection

The relentless march of technological advancement, coupled with the increasing complexity of modern infrastructure, necessitates a paradigm shift in how we manage and maintain these vital systems. Gone are the days when periodic inspections and scheduled maintenance were sufficient to ensure the longevity and reliability of critical assets. Today, the interconnected nature of infrastructure, from sprawling power grids and intricate transportation networks to essential water and gas pipelines, demands a more dynamic, responsive, and, above all, real-time approach to oversight. This is where the concept of real-time infrastructure monitoring emerges not as a mere enhancement, but as an indispensable cornerstone for ensuring safety, efficiency, and resilience.

At its core, real-time infrastructure monitoring involves the continuous collection and analysis of data from a distributed network of sensors embedded within or affixed to infrastructure assets. These sensors act as the eyes and ears of the system, capturing a diverse array of parameters that reflect the current state and performance of the infrastructure. For instance, on a bridge, sensors might track strain gauges to measure structural stress, accelerometers to detect vibrations caused by traffic, and thermometers to monitor temperature-induced expansion or contraction. In a pipeline network, pressure sensors, flow meters, and acoustic sensors can provide immediate insights into operational pressures, fluid movement, and potential leaks. For power lines, sensors can monitor current, voltage, temperature, and even ambient weather conditions like wind speed and ice accumulation. In the realm of buildings, sensors can track occupancy, energy consumption, structural integrity, and environmental conditions. The sheer volume and velocity of data generated by these sensor networks are staggering, transforming infrastructure management from a reactive, event-driven discipline into a proactive, data-informed discipline.

The paramount importance of this continuous data stream lies in its ability to provide an unprecedentedly granular and up-to-the-minute understanding of an infrastructure's condition. Unlike traditional inspection methods, which offer snapshots in time and are prone to human error or the limitations of accessibility, real-time monitoring offers a constant flow of information. This allows operators and engineers to move beyond simply reacting to failures and instead to anticipate them. Early indicators of stress, wear, or anomaly can be detected as they manifest, often long before they escalate into critical issues. For example, a gradual increase in vibration levels on a bridge, a subtle shift in pressure within a pipeline, or a localized temperature anomaly on a power line could be the first signs of an impending problem. Real-time monitoring systems, equipped with appropriate analytical capabilities, can flag these nascent issues, allowing for timely interventions. This proactive approach is not just about preventing catastrophic failures, which can have devastating human and economic consequences, but also about optimizing maintenance strategies. Instead of adhering to rigid, time-based maintenance schedules that might be either too early or too late, maintenance can be triggered by actual need, leading to more efficient allocation of resources and reduced unnecessary work.

The benefits of implementing real-time monitoring are multifaceted and far-reaching, directly impacting safety, operational efficiency, and economic viability. Safety is arguably the most critical advantage. By continuously assessing structural integrity and operational parameters, real-time monitoring significantly reduces the risk of unexpected failures that could endanger lives. Imagine a scenario where sensors on a bridge detect accumulating fatigue due to heavy traffic and adverse weather. This real-time data can trigger immediate restrictions on vehicle weight or speed, or even prompt a temporary closure, averting a potential collapse. Similarly, in a water distribution system, a sudden and unexplained drop in pressure, detected by real-time sensors, could indicate a major leak, allowing authorities to isolate the affected section, repair the damage swiftly, and prevent widespread water loss and potential contamination. The ability to detect and respond to anomalies before they become emergencies is the bedrock of enhanced infrastructure safety.

Beyond safety, operational efficiency is dramatically improved. For transportation networks, real-time monitoring of traffic flow, bridge load capacities, and tunnel conditions can inform dynamic route management and traffic control strategies, reducing congestion and travel times. In the energy sector, real-time monitoring of power generation, transmission lines, and substations allows for more precise load balancing, optimized energy distribution, and faster identification and isolation of faults, thereby minimizing power outages. For water and wastewater systems, real-time monitoring of flow rates, water quality, and pump status enables operators to optimize system performance, reduce energy consumption, and ensure efficient delivery of services. The insights gained from continuous data streams allow for better operational planning, resource allocation, and performance tuning, leading to a more streamlined and cost-effective operation.

Reduced downtime is another significant benefit, directly translating into economic savings and improved service continuity. Infrastructure failures are not only dangerous but also incredibly costly, both in terms of repair expenses and the economic impact of disrupted services. A prolonged power outage can cripple businesses, a major pipeline rupture can disrupt supply chains, and a critical transportation artery becoming impassable can have cascading economic effects. Real-time monitoring, by enabling early detection and proactive intervention, drastically reduces the likelihood and duration of such failures. Predictive maintenance, informed by real-time data, allows for planned downtime during periods of low demand or inconvenience, rather than forcing emergency shutdowns. This shift from reactive repairs to proactive, predictive maintenance leads to substantial cost savings by avoiding expensive emergency services, minimizing lost productivity, and preserving the lifespan of assets, thereby deferring costly replacements.

Furthermore, real-time monitoring facilitates better resource management. With a clear and continuous understanding of asset condition and performance, organizations can make more informed decisions about where and when to allocate resources for maintenance, repair, and upgrades. Instead of relying on generalized schedules or guesswork, resource allocation can be precisely targeted to areas of greatest need or highest risk, as identified by the real-time data. This ensures that limited budgets are spent most effectively, maximizing the return on investment in infrastructure upkeep. For example, a municipality managing a vast network of water mains can use real-time sensor data to prioritize pipe replacement projects in areas showing the most signs of wear and stress, rather than replacing pipes on a fixed age-based schedule that might be inefficient. This data-driven approach to resource allocation is crucial for maximizing the lifespan and performance of aging infrastructure.

The integration of real-time monitoring is not merely about deploying sensors; it is about building a comprehensive ecosystem that collects, processes, analyzes, and acts upon the data generated. This ecosystem typically comprises several key components. First are the sensors themselves, which must be robust, reliable, and capable of operating in the often-harsh environments where infrastructure is situated. The selection of appropriate sensor technology is critical, depending on the type of infrastructure, the parameters to be measured, and the required accuracy and frequency of data collection. Second is the communication infrastructure, which is essential for transmitting the vast amounts of data from the sensors to a central processing unit or cloud platform. This can involve wired networks, wireless technologies like cellular or LoRaWAN, or even satellite communication for remote locations. The reliability and security of this communication link are paramount. Third is the data processing and analytics platform. This is where the raw sensor data is cleaned, aggregated, and analyzed. Advanced analytics, often incorporating AI and machine learning, are employed to identify patterns, detect anomalies, predict future behavior, and generate actionable insights. Finally, there are the human operators and automated systems that receive these insights and initiate appropriate actions, whether it be dispatching a maintenance crew, adjusting operational parameters, or issuing alerts.

The transition to real-time infrastructure monitoring represents a fundamental shift towards what can be termed "proactive infrastructure stewardship." It moves away from a legacy of reactive problem-solving towards a future where infrastructure systems are managed with a deep, data-driven understanding of their current state and likely future trajectory. This proactive approach is crucial for maintaining the integrity and functionality of essential services in an era of increasing environmental challenges, aging assets, and growing demands. By embracing real-time monitoring, we are not just observing our infrastructure; we are actively and intelligently managing it to ensure its continued reliability and safety for generations to come. This continuous flow of actionable intelligence forms the bedrock upon which advanced AI-driven solutions for anomaly detection and predictive maintenance can be built, transforming our approach to infrastructure management from one of repair to one of continuous, intelligent optimization.

The foundation of any robust infrastructure monitoring system lies in the diverse array of sensors deployed to capture crucial data. These sensors act as the distributed nervous system of our built environment, continuously feeding information about the state, performance, and health of critical assets. The type of sensor selected is paramount and is dictated by the specific infrastructure being monitored, the parameters of interest, and the operational environment. These sensors can broadly be categorized based on the type of data they collect, ranging from physical stresses and environmental influences to operational fluid dynamics and subtle acoustic signatures.

One of the most critical categories of sensors focuses on **structural health monitoring (SHM)**. These sensors are indispensable for understanding the physical integrity of structures like bridges, buildings, dams, and tunnels. **Strain gauges** are a prime example, meticulously measuring the deformation of a material under load. When attached to a structural element, such as a steel beam on a bridge or a concrete column in a building, a strain gauge can detect minute changes in length caused by traffic, wind, seismic activity, or even temperature fluctuations. This data is vital for assessing how a structure is responding to its environment and operational loads, allowing engineers to identify areas experiencing excessive stress or fatigue that might not be visible through conventional inspections. The raw output from strain gauges is typically an electrical signal proportional to the strain, which can then be amplified and digitized for analysis. The accuracy of strain gauges can be affected by temperature, so many modern gauges incorporate temperature compensation mechanisms or are used in conjunction with separate temperature sensors.

Complementing strain gauges are **accelerometers**. These devices measure acceleration, which can be used to infer dynamic loads and vibrations acting on a structure. For instance, accelerometers installed on a bridge can detect the vibrations induced by passing vehicles. By analyzing the frequency and amplitude of these vibrations, engineers can gain insights into the bridge's dynamic characteristics and identify any anomalies that might indicate damage or a change in structural behavior. Unusual vibration patterns, such as a sudden increase in amplitude or a shift in dominant frequencies, could signal the presence of cracks, loose components, or even the onset of resonance. Accelerometers are also crucial for monitoring seismic activity and assessing the response of structures to earthquakes. They can also be used to detect subtle movements or deformations that might not be captured by static strain measurements. The data from accelerometers is time-series in nature, providing a continuous record of motion.

Beyond direct structural strain, **environmental sensors** play a pivotal role in understanding the external factors that influence infrastructure integrity and performance. **Temperature sensors** are ubiquitous, measuring ambient air temperature, surface temperatures of materials (like concrete or asphalt), or internal temperatures of components (like transformers in a power substation). Temperature variations cause materials to expand and contract, leading to thermal stresses. Monitoring these changes is essential for predicting structural behavior, especially in long spans or complex assemblies where differential expansion can be significant. For example, on a long bridge, monitoring the temperature of the deck and supports can help predict expansion and contraction ranges, informing the design and operation of expansion joints. Similarly, in the oil and gas industry, monitoring the temperature of pipelines can be critical for preventing issues related to material embrittlement at low temperatures or increased corrosion rates at high temperatures.

Humidity sensors are important for assessing conditions that can accelerate corrosion or degradation of materials. In coastal environments or areas with high rainfall, monitoring humidity levels can provide an early warning of increased risk to steel structures or reinforced concrete. **Anemometers**, which measure wind speed and direction, are essential for structures exposed to significant wind loads, such as tall buildings, bridges, and wind turbines. High wind speeds can induce substantial dynamic forces, and monitoring these conditions in real-time allows for immediate assessment of structural response and potential safety risks. For example, during extreme weather events, real-time wind data from sensors on a bridge can be correlated with accelerometer data to assess the dynamic response and determine if traffic restrictions are necessary.

Operational parameter sensors are tailored to the specific function of the infrastructure. In water and wastewater systems, **flow meters** are essential for measuring the volume of fluid passing through pipes. These sensors are critical for detecting leaks (indicated by unaccounted-for flow), monitoring system capacity, and optimizing pumping operations. Various technologies exist, including ultrasonic, electromagnetic, and mechanical flow meters, each with its own advantages depending on the fluid characteristics and pipe diameter. **Pressure sensors** are equally vital in these systems, monitoring the internal pressure within pipelines. Sudden drops or spikes in pressure can indicate blockages, pipe bursts, or pump failures. In power grids, **voltage and current sensors** (like transformers and current sensors) are fundamental for monitoring electricity flow, detecting faults, and ensuring grid stability. Real-time measurement of voltage and current allows operators to balance loads, identify power quality issues, and quickly isolate sections of the grid experiencing anomalies.

For gas pipelines,
pressure and flow sensors are crucial for detecting leaks and ensuring safe operating pressures. **Acoustic sensors** are also increasingly employed to detect the subtle sound signatures associated with leaks in pipelines, even small ones that might not immediately register on pressure or flow meters. In transportation infrastructure, **traffic sensors** (such as inductive loops, radar, or cameras) provide real-time data on vehicle count, speed, and occupancy, enabling dynamic traffic management and congestion prediction.

Asset condition sensors provide insights into the degradation or wear of components over time. **Vibration sensors**, distinct from accelerometers used for structural response, can be used to monitor the condition of rotating machinery like pumps, turbines, or engines. Excessive vibration levels in machinery often indicate wear in bearings, imbalance in rotating parts, or misalignment, all of which are precursors to failure. Analyzing the frequency spectrum of vibration can help diagnose the specific type of fault. **Acoustic emission sensors** are highly sensitive devices that detect high-frequency stress waves generated by crack initiation and propagation, or other localized damage mechanisms. These sensors can be used in critical structures like pressure vessels, pipelines, and aircraft components to detect nascent damage that might be invisible to other monitoring methods.

The data generated by these diverse sensor types forms a rich tapestry of information. These
data streams can vary significantly in their nature and frequency. Many sensors, particularly those for SHM, environmental monitoring, and operational parameters, generate **continuous time-series data**. This means a constant stream of readings is collected at a defined sampling rate (e.g., multiple readings per second for accelerometers, hourly readings for temperature). This high-frequency data is invaluable for capturing dynamic events and subtle trends.

Other sensors might operate on an
event-based or **threshold-based** principle. For example, a leak detection sensor might only transmit data when it detects a significant pressure drop or a specific acoustic signature above a certain threshold. Similarly, a traffic sensor might report traffic volume and speed periodically (e.g., every five minutes) but could also generate an alert if an unusual slowdown or incident is detected. This approach can significantly reduce the volume of data transmitted, especially for parameters that do not change rapidly.

Furthermore, some data streams are
discrete or categorical. For instance, a status indicator on a pump might report whether it is operational, idle, or in a fault state. The data from a camera vision system, while ultimately composed of pixels, is often

processed to extract categorical information such as "vehicle present," "obstacle detected," or "lane occupied."

The effectiveness of any sensor network hinges on careful **sensor placement**. Strategic placement ensures that sensors are located where they can capture the most representative and critical data. For SHM, sensors are typically placed at locations known to be critical stress points, near potential fault zones, or on elements that are most susceptible to damage. For operational parameters, sensors are installed at key points in the flow or power path to accurately reflect system performance. Environmental sensors are positioned to capture relevant external conditions. Factors such as accessibility for installation and maintenance, protection from environmental hazards, and the proximity to data collection points also influence placement decisions.

Calibration is another fundamental aspect of data acquisition. Sensors must be regularly calibrated to ensure that their readings are accurate and reliable. Over time, sensor drift, environmental exposure, or physical damage can lead to inaccurate measurements. A rigorous calibration schedule, often involving comparison with known standards or cross-referencing with redundant sensors, is essential for maintaining data integrity. Without proper calibration, the data collected by even the most sophisticated sensors can be misleading, leading to incorrect assessments and potentially costly errors in decision-making.

The journey of sensor data from its point of origin to where it can be analyzed involves robust **data transmission** mechanisms. The choice of communication technology depends on factors such as the volume and frequency of data, the distance to the central processing unit, power availability, and the required reliability and security. For sensors in close proximity or within established infrastructure networks, wired connections (e.g., Ethernet, fiber optics) often offer high bandwidth and reliability. However, for many infrastructure applications, especially those involving widely distributed assets or remote locations, wireless technologies are indispensable.

Cellular networks (3G, 4G, 5G) provide broad coverage and relatively high bandwidth, making them suitable for transmitting moderate to large volumes of data from sensors located in urban or semi-urban areas. For applications requiring low power consumption and long-range communication, technologies like **LoRaWAN (Long Range Wide Area Network)** and **NB-IoT (Narrowband Internet of Things)** are gaining traction. These protocols are designed to transmit small amounts of data infrequently over several kilometers, making them ideal for battery-powered sensors deployed in remote or difficult-to-access locations, such as agricultural fields, remote pipelines, or distributed environmental monitoring stations. In extremely remote or challenging environments, **satellite communication** might be the only viable option for transmitting sensor data, albeit often at a higher cost and with lower bandwidth.

Regardless of the transmission method, ensuring the **reliability** and **security** of the data stream is paramount. Redundant communication paths, error detection and correction mechanisms, and robust encryption protocols are often employed to protect data integrity and prevent unauthorized access or manipulation. The sheer volume of data generated by extensive sensor networks also necessitates efficient data compression and aggregation techniques before transmission to minimize bandwidth requirements and associated costs. This entire process of data acquisition, from sensor selection and placement to calibration and secure transmission, forms the critical front-end of any AI-driven infrastructure monitoring system, providing the raw material upon which intelligent analysis and actionable insights are built.
Before delving into the sophisticated realms of artificial intelligence for anomaly detection, it's crucial to acknowledge and appreciate the

foundational statistical methods that have long served as the bedrock for identifying deviations from normal operational patterns. These classical techniques, while perhaps less adaptive than their AI counterparts, offer interpretable insights and remain highly effective for detecting clear, statistically significant outliers. They provide a vital baseline against which more advanced methods can be measured and often serve as a crucial first line of defense in monitoring systems, flagging immediate and unambiguous departures from expected behavior. Understanding these statistical approaches is not merely an academic exercise; it's essential for appreciating the evolution of anomaly detection and for situations where their simplicity and transparency are distinct advantages.

One of the most enduring and widely adopted statistical tools for process control and anomaly detection is the
control chart. Developed by Walter Shewhart in the 1920s, control charts are graphical tools used to monitor a process over time. They consist of a central line representing the process mean, an upper control limit (UCL), and a lower control limit (LCL). Data points are plotted chronologically, and any point falling outside the control limits, or exhibiting specific non-random patterns within the limits, is considered an indication of an anomaly or an out-of-control state.

The most basic form is the
Shewhart chart, often referred to as an X-bar chart when monitoring the mean of subgroups, or an individuals chart (X chart) when monitoring individual data points. For instance, imagine monitoring the pressure within a critical water main. Historical data is used to calculate the average pressure (the central line) and the standard deviation. From these, the UCL and LCL are established, typically at ±3 standard deviations from the mean. If a pressure reading from a real-time sensor exceeds the UCL or drops below the LCL, it signifies a potential anomaly. This could indicate a sudden pressure surge due to a valve malfunction or a rapid pressure drop, possibly signaling a significant leak. The simplicity of the Shewhart chart makes it easy to implement and interpret; an

excursion beyond the boundaries is an immediate red flag requiring investigation. However, it can be less sensitive to small, persistent shifts in the process mean, as these might not immediately cross the ±3 standard deviation limits.

To address the limitations of Shewhart charts in detecting small but persistent shifts, the
Cumulative Sum (CUSUM) chart was developed. Instead of monitoring individual data points or subgroup averages directly, CUSUM charts accumulate deviations from a target value over time. They are particularly adept at detecting small, sustained shifts that might go unnoticed by Shewhart charts. For a CUSUM chart, we typically track two values: an upper cumulative sum and a lower cumulative sum. The upper sum increases with observations above the target and decreases with observations below it, while the lower sum does the opposite. If either sum exceeds a predefined threshold (often called a decision interval), an anomaly is detected. Consider the temperature readings from a data center's cooling system. A CUSUM chart could be used to monitor the temperature of the air returning to the cooling units. If there's a gradual increase in temperature due to a slow degradation of the cooling unit's efficiency, or a persistent blockage in airflow, a Shewhart chart might not flag it until the temperature breaches a critical high limit. A CUSUM chart, however, would detect the cumulative effect of these small upward deviations, signaling a problem before it escalates to a critical failure. This makes CUSUM charts highly valuable for proactive maintenance and for identifying gradual degradation rather than sudden failures.

Beyond control charts, a broad class of
outlier detection methods relies on understanding the expected statistical distribution of the monitored data. The fundamental principle is to define what constitutes "normal" behavior based on a statistical model and then identify data points that deviate significantly from this model.

One of the simplest and most intuitive methods is the **Z-score**. The Z-score measures how many standard deviations a particular data point is away from the mean of the dataset. The formula for a Z-score is: $Z = (x - \mu) / \sigma$, where x is the data point, μ is the mean of the distribution, and σ is the standard deviation. A common threshold for identifying an outlier using Z-scores is a value greater than 3 or less than -3, corresponding roughly to data points outside the 99.7% confidence interval for a normal distribution. For example, if we are monitoring the vibration levels of a critical pump, we can calculate the mean and standard deviation of vibration readings during normal operation. If a new reading has a Z-score exceeding 3, it suggests that the vibration level is unusually high and warrants investigation, potentially indicating a bearing failure or imbalance. The Z-score method assumes that the data is normally distributed, which may not always be the case.

When the data is not normally distributed, or when the presence of outliers makes the calculation of mean and standard deviation unreliable (as extreme values can heavily skew these statistics), the **Interquartile Range (IQR)** method offers a more robust approach. The IQR is the difference between the 75th percentile (Q3) and the 25th percentile (Q1) of the data. The range from Q1 to Q3 encompasses the middle 50% of the data. Outliers are typically defined as points that fall below Q1 - 1.5 *IQR or above Q3 + 1.5* IQR. This method is less sensitive to extreme values than the Z-score method because it relies on percentiles, which are less affected by outliers. Consider monitoring the latency of network packets within an industrial control system. If some packets experience extremely high latency due to intermittent network congestion or a temporary hardware issue, these extreme values can inflate the standard deviation and mean, making Z-score analysis less effective. Using the IQR method, we can establish bounds for "normal" latency that are more resilient to these occasional extreme events, allowing us to identify truly anomalous latency patterns that deviate from the typical spread of the middle 50% of observations.

Another common approach involves fitting various **statistical distributions** to the data and identifying points with a low probability of occurring under the fitted distribution. For instance, if we assume the data follows an exponential distribution (common for time-to-failure data), we can calculate the probability density function (PDF) or cumulative distribution function (CDF) for each observed data point. Points with very low PDF values or very high CDF values (depending on the definition of anomaly) can be flagged. This could be applied to monitoring the flow rate in a chemical processing pipeline. If the flow rate typically follows a specific distribution reflecting normal process variations, a sudden, significant drop or surge that falls into the extremely low probability tail of that distribution would be flagged as an anomaly, potentially indicating a pump failure, a blockage, or a valve malfunction.

The effectiveness of these statistical methods hinges on several critical assumptions. Many of these techniques implicitly or explicitly assume that the underlying data generating process is **stationary**, meaning its statistical properties (like mean, variance, and autocorrelation) do not change over time. In real-world infrastructure, this assumption is often violated due to gradual wear and tear, changes in operational modes, seasonality, or external environmental factors. When a process is non-stationary, what was considered "normal" might shift, leading to false alarms or missed detections. For example, a gradual increase in temperature due to aging insulation in an electrical transformer might cause a sensor reading to eventually cross a static threshold, but if the threshold was set based on initial, healthy performance, it might miss the subtle, continuous degradation.

Furthermore, these methods often assume a specific **distribution** for the data, most commonly the normal (Gaussian) distribution. However, many real-world infrastructure metrics, such as traffic flow, sensor noise, or event occurrences, may follow non-normal distributions like Poisson, exponential, or Weibull distributions. Applying methods designed for normal distributions to data that deviates significantly can lead to poor performance.

The concept of
"normal operation" is also a critical dependency. Statistical methods require a well-defined baseline period of normal operation to establish parameters like the mean, standard deviation, or percentiles. If this baseline period itself contained anomalies, or if the definition of "normal" is poorly chosen, the anomaly detection system will be flawed from the outset. For instance, if a baseline period for monitoring bridge strain during normal traffic also included a period of unexpected heavy load or strong winds, the calculated "normal" range would be wider than it should be, potentially masking future anomalies.

Despite these limitations, these statistical methods offer significant advantages, particularly in terms of
interpretability and computational efficiency. The underlying logic is transparent and easy to explain to domain experts. For example, stating that a pressure reading is "three standard deviations above the mean" provides a clear, quantifiable reason for flagging it. Computationally, they are often very light, requiring minimal processing power and memory, making them suitable for deployment on resource-constrained edge devices or for analyzing vast streams of data in real-time where complex AI models might be too slow or power-hungry. They are also excellent for detecting acute, unambiguous events. A sudden, massive spike in temperature or a complete drop to zero in a flow meter reading is unequivocally anomalous and will be readily detected by these methods.

In summary, traditional statistical methods provide a robust and interpretable toolkit for identifying deviations in infrastructure monitoring data. Control charts like Shewhart and CUSUM charts offer visual and quantitative means to track process stability over time, flagging excursions beyond established limits or persistent shifts. Outlier detection techniques, such as Z-scores and IQR-based methods, leverage statistical distributions to quantify how unusual a particular data point is compared to historical norms. These methods excel at identifying clear, statistically significant anomalies and offer computational efficiency and transparency, making them invaluable as a first-stage analysis or for simpler monitoring tasks. They lay the groundwork for understanding deviations, offering a critical baseline before more sophisticated AI-driven anomaly detection approaches are considered.

Before delving into the sophisticated realms of artificial intelligence for anomaly detection, it's crucial to acknowledge and appreciate the foundational statistical methods that have long served as the bedrock for identifying deviations from normal operational patterns. These classical techniques, while perhaps less adaptive than their AI counterparts, offer interpretable insights and remain highly effective for detecting clear, statistically significant outliers. They provide a vital baseline against which more advanced methods can be measured and often serve as a crucial first line of defense in monitoring systems, flagging immediate and unambiguous departures from expected behavior. Understanding these statistical approaches is not merely an academic exercise; it's essential for appreciating the evolution of anomaly detection and for situations where their simplicity and transparency are distinct advantages.

One of the most enduring and widely adopted statistical tools for process control and anomaly detection is the
control chart. Developed by Walter Shewhart in the 1920s, control charts are graphical tools used to monitor a process over time. They consist of a central line representing the process mean, an upper control limit (UCL), and a lower control limit (LCL). Data points are plotted chronologically, and any point falling outside the control limits, or exhibiting specific non-random patterns within the limits, is considered an indication of an anomaly or an out-of-control state.

The most basic form is the
Shewhart chart, often referred to as an X-bar chart when monitoring the mean of subgroups, or an individuals chart (X chart) when monitoring individual data points. For instance, imagine monitoring the pressure within a critical water main. Historical data is used to calculate the average pressure (the central line) and the standard deviation. From these, the UCL and LCL are established, typically at ±3 standard deviations from the mean. If a pressure reading from a real-time sensor exceeds the UCL or drops below the LCL, it signifies a potential anomaly. This could indicate a sudden pressure surge due to a valve malfunction or a rapid pressure drop, possibly signaling a significant leak. The simplicity of the Shewhart chart makes it easy to implement and interpret; an excursion beyond the boundaries is an immediate red flag requiring investigation. However, it can be less sensitive to small, persistent shifts in the process mean, as these might not immediately cross the ±3 standard deviation limits.

To address the limitations of Shewhart charts in detecting small but persistent shifts, the
Cumulative Sum (CUSUM) chart was developed. Instead of monitoring individual data points or subgroup averages directly, CUSUM charts accumulate deviations from a target value over time. They are particularly adept at detecting small, sustained shifts that might go unnoticed by Shewhart charts. For a CUSUM chart, we typically track two values: an upper cumulative sum and a lower cumulative sum. The upper sum increases with observations above the target and decreases with observations below it, while the lower sum does the opposite. If either sum exceeds a predefined threshold (often called a decision interval), an anomaly is detected. Consider the temperature readings from a data center's cooling system. A CUSUM chart could be used to monitor the temperature of the air returning to the cooling units. If there's a gradual increase in temperature due to a slow degradation of the cooling unit's efficiency, or a persistent blockage in airflow, a Shewhart chart might not

flag it until the temperature breaches a critical high limit. A CUSUM chart, however, would detect the cumulative effect of these small upward deviations, signaling a problem before it escalates to a critical failure. This makes CUSUM charts highly valuable for proactive maintenance and for identifying gradual degradation rather than sudden failures.

Beyond control charts, a broad class of **outlier detection methods** relies on understanding the expected statistical distribution of the monitored data. The fundamental principle is to define what constitutes "normal" behavior based on a statistical model and then identify data points that deviate significantly from this model.

One of the simplest and most intuitive methods is the **Z-score**. The Z-score measures how many standard deviations a particular data point is away from the mean of the dataset. The formula for a Z-score is: $Z = (x - \mu) / \sigma$, where x is the data point, μ is the mean of the distribution, and σ is the standard deviation. A common threshold for identifying an outlier using Z-scores is a value greater than 3 or less than -3, corresponding roughly to data points outside the 99.7% confidence interval for a normal distribution. For example, if we are monitoring the vibration levels of a critical pump, we can calculate the mean and standard deviation of vibration readings during normal operation. If a new reading has a Z-score exceeding 3, it suggests that the vibration level is unusually high and warrants investigation, potentially indicating a bearing failure or imbalance. The Z-score method assumes that the data is normally distributed, which may not always be the case.

When the data is not normally distributed, or when the presence of outliers makes the calculation of mean and standard deviation unreliable (as extreme values can heavily skew these statistics), the **Interquartile Range (IQR)** method offers a more robust approach. The IQR is the difference between the 75th percentile (Q3) and the 25th percentile (Q1) of the data. The range from Q1 to Q3 encompasses the middle 50% of the data. Outliers are typically defined as points that fall below Q1 - 1.5 *IQR or above Q3 + 1.5* IQR. This method is less sensitive to extreme values than the Z-score method because it relies on percentiles, which are less affected by outliers. Consider monitoring the latency of network packets within an industrial control system. If some packets experience extremely high latency due to intermittent network congestion or a temporary hardware issue, these extreme values can inflate the standard deviation and mean, making Z-score analysis less effective. Using the IQR method, we can establish bounds for "normal" latency that are more resilient to these occasional extreme events, allowing us to identify truly anomalous latency patterns that deviate from the typical spread of the middle 50% of observations.

Another common approach involves fitting various **statistical distributions** to the data and identifying points with a low probability of occurring under the fitted distribution. For instance, if we assume the data follows an exponential distribution (common for time-to-failure data), we can calculate the probability density function (PDF) or cumulative distribution function (CDF) for each observed data point. Points with very low PDF values or very high CDF values (depending on the definition of anomaly) can be flagged. This could be applied to monitoring the flow rate in a chemical processing pipeline. If the flow rate typically follows a specific distribution reflecting normal process variations, a sudden, significant drop or surge that falls into the extremely low probability tail of that distribution would be flagged as an anomaly, potentially indicating a pump failure, a blockage, or a valve malfunction.

The effectiveness of these statistical methods hinges on several critical assumptions. Many of these techniques implicitly or explicitly assume that the underlying data generating process is **stationary**, meaning its statistical properties (like mean, variance, and autocorrelation) do not change over time. In real-world infrastructure, this assumption is often violated due to gradual wear and tear, changes in operational modes, seasonality, or external environmental factors. When a process is non-stationary, what was considered "normal" might shift, leading to false alarms or missed detections. For example, a gradual increase in temperature due to aging insulation in an electrical transformer might cause a sensor reading to eventually cross a static threshold, but if the threshold was set based on initial, healthy performance, it might miss the subtle, continuous degradation.

Furthermore, these methods often assume a specific **distribution** for the data, most commonly the normal (Gaussian) distribution. However, many real-world infrastructure metrics, such as traffic flow, sensor noise, or event occurrences, may follow non-normal distributions like Poisson, exponential, or Weibull distributions. Applying methods designed for normal distributions to data that deviates significantly can lead to poor performance.

The concept of **"normal operation"** is also a critical dependency. Statistical methods require a well-defined baseline period of normal operation to establish parameters like the mean, standard deviation, or percentiles. If this baseline period itself contained anomalies, or if the definition of "normal" is poorly chosen, the anomaly detection system will be flawed from the outset. For instance, if a baseline period for monitoring bridge strain during normal traffic also included a period of unexpected heavy load or strong winds, the calculated "normal" range would be wider than it should be, potentially masking future anomalies.

Despite these limitations, these statistical methods offer significant advantages, particularly in terms of **interpretability and computational efficiency**. The underlying logic is transparent and easy to explain to domain experts. For example, stating that a pressure reading is "three standard deviations above the mean" provides a clear, quantifiable reason for flagging it. Computationally, they are often very light, requiring minimal processing power and memory, making them suitable for deployment on resource-constrained edge devices or for analyzing vast streams of data in real-time where complex AI models might be too slow or power-hungry. They are also excellent for detecting acute, unambiguous events. A sudden, massive spike in temperature or a complete drop to zero in a flow meter reading is unequivocally anomalous and will be readily detected by these methods.

In summary, traditional statistical methods provide a robust and interpretable toolkit for identifying deviations in infrastructure monitoring data. Control charts like Shewhart and CUSUM charts offer visual and quantitative means to track process stability over time, flagging excursions beyond established limits or persistent shifts. Outlier detection techniques, such as Z-scores and IQR-based methods, leverage statistical distributions to quantify how unusual a particular data point is compared to historical norms. These methods excel at identifying clear, statistically significant anomalies and offer computational efficiency and transparency, making them invaluable as a first-stage analysis or for simpler monitoring tasks. They lay the groundwork for understanding deviations, offering a critical baseline before more sophisticated AI-driven anomaly detection approaches are considered.

Machine Learning Algorithms for Anomaly Detection

As infrastructure systems become increasingly complex and generate vast volumes of data, the limitations of traditional statistical methods in capturing subtle anomalies or adapting to evolving operational patterns become more apparent. This is where machine learning (ML) algorithms offer a powerful paradigm shift. ML models can learn intricate relationships within data, identify patterns that are not easily defined by simple statistical rules, and adapt to changing dynamics, making them exceptionally well-suited for anomaly detection in modern infrastructure.

The application of ML in this domain broadly falls into three categories: unsupervised, supervised, and semi-supervised learning.

Unsupervised Anomaly Detection

Unsupervised learning is perhaps the most prevalent approach for anomaly detection in infrastructure monitoring, primarily because obtaining large, perfectly labeled datasets of anomalies is often prohibitively difficult or impossible. Unsupervised methods aim to learn the "normal" patterns from unlabeled data and identify instances that deviate significantly from these learned patterns.

Clustering-based methods are a cornerstone of unsupervised anomaly detection. The core idea is that normal data points tend to group together into clusters, representing distinct operational states or modes. Anomalies, by definition, do not conform to these normal groupings and thus will either not belong to any cluster or will form very small, sparse clusters.

K-Means Clustering: This popular algorithm partitions data points into a pre-defined number of clusters, K. Each data point is assigned to the cluster whose centroid (mean) is nearest. After training, an anomaly can be identified if it is far from any cluster centroid. The distance threshold can be determined empirically or through statistical measures applied to the cluster distances. For example, in monitoring the vibration patterns of rotating machinery, K-Means could identify different operational states (e.g., steady operation, startup, shutdown). A vibration signature that is significantly distant from the centroids of all these identified "normal" operational states could indicate an incipient fault, such as a bearing wear or an imbalance, that doesn't fit neatly into any established operational profile. However, K-Means has a significant drawback: it requires specifying the number of clusters (K) beforehand, which can be challenging in dynamic infrastructure environments. It also assumes clusters are spherical and of similar size, which may not always be true.

DBSCAN (Density-Based Spatial Clustering of Applications with Noise): DBSCAN offers a more flexible approach than K-Means. It groups together data points that are closely packed together (points with many neighbors within a specified radius, ϵ), marking points that lie alone in low-density regions as outliers or noise. DBSCAN does not require the number of clusters to be specified and can discover arbitrarily shaped clusters. This makes it particularly useful for detecting anomalies in complex, high-dimensional data where normal behavior might manifest in non-spherical or interconnected regions. Consider monitoring the energy consumption patterns of smart buildings. DBSCAN could identify distinct clusters corresponding to different occupancy levels and operational schedules. A data point that falls into a low-density region, far from any established cluster, might signify an unusual energy drain, such as a system malfunction or an unauthorized appliance operating outside normal parameters. The parameters ϵ (maximum distance between samples for one to be considered as in the neighborhood of the other) and `min_samples` (the number of samples in a neighborhood for a point to be considered as a core point) are crucial and require careful tuning.

One-Class Support Vector Machines (OC-SVM) are another powerful unsupervised technique. Unlike standard SVMs that learn a boundary to separate two classes, OC-SVM learns a boundary that encompasses all (or most) of the "normal" data points. The algorithm aims to find a hypersphere (or hyperplane in higher dimensions) that encloses the majority of the training data in a high-dimensional feature space, effectively learning the boundary of the normal data distribution. Any new data point that falls outside this learned boundary is classified as an anomaly. OC-SVM is effective in scenarios where anomalies are rare and diverse, and the definition of "normal" might be complex. For instance, in monitoring the operational parameters of a fleet of drones, OC-SVM could be trained on flight logs of healthy drones. If a drone exhibits unusual flight characteristics—perhaps deviating significantly from the typical flight envelope in terms of altitude, speed, or battery usage—it would be flagged as an anomaly by the OC-SVM, potentially indicating a software glitch, a hardware issue, or external interference. The effectiveness of OC-SVM relies on the kernel choice and regularization parameter (ν), which influence the trade-off between capturing all normal data and allowing for some misclassifications.

Other unsupervised methods include:

Isolation Forests: This algorithm works by randomly partitioning the data. Anomalies, being rare and different, are expected to be isolated closer to the root of the decision trees in the forest, requiring fewer partitions to be separated from the rest of the data. The "anomaly score" is typically based on the average path length to isolate a data point. This method is efficient and scales well to large datasets. For example, detecting fraudulent transactions in an IoT payment system could benefit from Isolation Forests. Anomalous transactions, being infrequent and exhibiting unique characteristics, would likely be isolated quickly by the random splits in the trees, thus receiving a high anomaly score.

Autoencoders (a type of Neural Network): Autoencoders are neural networks trained to reconstruct their input. They consist of an encoder that compresses the input data into a lower-dimensional latent representation and a decoder that reconstructs the original input from this representation. When trained on normal data, the autoencoder learns to reconstruct normal patterns effectively, resulting in a low reconstruction error. Anomalies, however, will be poorly reconstructed, leading to a high reconstruction error. This high error can then be used as an anomaly score. Consider monitoring the thermal imaging of critical electrical components in a power grid. An autoencoder trained on normal thermal signatures could identify subtle changes that indicate developing faults (e.g., hot spots, uneven heat distribution) that might be missed by simple thresholding. These subtle deviations would result in a higher reconstruction error for the abnormal thermal pattern.

Supervised Anomaly Detection

Supervised anomaly detection requires a dataset where instances are explicitly labeled as either "normal" or "anomalous." The ML model is trained to distinguish between these two classes. This approach is highly effective when sufficient labeled data is available, as it allows the model to learn precise decision boundaries.

Classification Algorithms: Standard classification algorithms such as Logistic Regression, Support Vector Machines (SVMs) with appropriate kernels, Decision Trees, Random Forests, Gradient Boosting Machines (e.g., XGBoost, LightGBM), and Neural Networks can be employed. The training process involves feeding labeled examples of both normal and anomalous behavior to the model. For instance, in monitoring the structural integrity of bridges, historical sensor data (strain gauges, accelerometers) might be labeled. If data points corresponding to known failure modes (e.g., fatigue cracks, overload events) are labeled as "anomalous" and healthy operational data as "normal," a supervised classifier can be trained to predict the class of new, incoming data.

A significant challenge in supervised anomaly detection is **class imbalance**. Anomalies are, by definition, rare. This means the dataset will overwhelmingly consist of "normal" instances. Standard training procedures can lead to models that are biased towards the majority class, performing poorly in identifying the rare anomalous events. Techniques to address class imbalance include:

Resampling: Oversampling the minority class (anomalies) or undersampling the majority class (normal data).
Cost-sensitive learning: Assigning higher misclassification costs to the minority class.
Generating synthetic data: Using algorithms like SMOTE (Synthetic Minority Over-sampling Technique) to create artificial anomalous instances based on existing ones.

For example, in monitoring the performance of a fleet of wind turbines, detecting anomalies such as blade icing or gearbox failures is critical. If historical data includes labeled examples of these failures, a supervised model like a Random Forest could be trained. However, if only a handful of failure instances exist compared to thousands of normal operation records, the Random Forest might learn to predict "normal" for almost every input. Applying SMOTE to generate more synthetic but representative failure data can help the model learn to identify these rare events more effectively.

Semi-Supervised Anomaly Detection

Semi-supervised learning strikes a balance between unsupervised and supervised methods. It leverages a large amount of unlabeled data to learn the general structure of normal behavior and a small amount of labeled data (which may contain both normal and anomalous instances, or just normal instances) to refine the model or to directly detect known anomalies. This is particularly useful when labeled anomaly data is scarce but not entirely absent, or when the cost of labeling is high.

One common semi-supervised approach is to train a model exclusively on **normal data** (similar to unsupervised methods but with the explicit knowledge that the training data is purely normal). This model then acts as a detector for any deviation from this known normal state. For example, if we have a dataset of sensor readings from a healthy pump system, an autoencoder or OC-SVM trained solely on this data will learn the characteristics of normal operation. When new data arrives, a high reconstruction error (for autoencoders) or an out-of-bounds prediction (for OC-SVM) will indicate an anomaly. If there are a few labeled anomalies, this information can be used to set more precise thresholds or fine-tune the model's sensitivity.

Another semi-supervised strategy involves using a small set of labeled data to guide the learning process on a larger unlabeled dataset. Techniques like
label propagation or **transductive learning** can be employed. For instance, imagine monitoring the traffic flow in a smart city network. We might have a vast amount of unlabeled traffic sensor data. We might also have a few instances explicitly labeled as "traffic jam" or "accident." A semi-supervised model could first learn the general patterns of traffic flow from all the data and then use the few labeled examples to specifically identify and classify instances of traffic jams or accidents. This approach is valuable because manually labeling every type of traffic

disruption is impractical, but having even a few examples can significantly improve the model's ability to detect and categorize them.

Hybrid Approaches:

It's important to note that in practice, many advanced anomaly detection systems employ **hybrid approaches**, combining multiple techniques to leverage their respective strengths. For example:

1. **Feature Engineering + Unsupervised Learning**: Statistical or domain-expert-driven features are extracted from raw sensor data, and then an unsupervised algorithm like Isolation Forest or DBSCAN is applied to these features. This can improve the performance of unsupervised methods by providing more informative input.
2. **Unsupervised Pre-training + Supervised Fine-tuning**: An autoencoder is trained on a large corpus of unlabeled infrastructure data to learn a good feature representation. This learned representation is then used as input to a supervised classifier trained on a smaller set of labeled anomaly data. This approach benefits from the ability of unsupervised learning to capture complex data structures and the precision of supervised learning for specific anomaly types.
3. **Ensemble Methods**: Multiple anomaly detection models (e.g., K-Means, Isolation Forest, Autoencoder) are trained, and their anomaly scores are combined (e.g., by averaging, voting, or training another meta-model) to make a final decision. This often leads to more robust and accurate detection by mitigating the weaknesses of individual models.

The choice of ML algorithm depends heavily on the specific infrastructure context, the type and volume of data available, the nature of expected anomalies, and the interpretability requirements. For instance, monitoring the vibration of a critical pump might favor unsupervised methods like Isolation Forests or autoencoders due to the difficulty of labeling all potential fault conditions. In contrast, a system monitoring for cybersecurity threats within a network might have access to some labeled attack data, making supervised or semi-supervised methods more appropriate.

Ultimately, machine learning provides a sophisticated and adaptable toolkit for anomaly detection in infrastructure monitoring. By moving beyond static statistical rules, these algorithms can uncover subtle deviations, adapt to evolving system dynamics, and provide a more proactive and resilient approach to maintaining the integrity and operational efficiency of critical infrastructure. The continuous advancement in ML techniques, coupled with increasing computational power and data availability, promises even more powerful and nuanced anomaly detection capabilities in the future.

The evolution of anomaly detection in infrastructure monitoring has reached a sophisticated frontier with the advent of deep learning techniques. While traditional statistical methods and foundational machine learning algorithms have provided invaluable tools, deep learning offers unparalleled capabilities in handling complex, high-dimensional data and uncovering subtle, intricate patterns that might elude simpler models. These advanced methods are particularly adept at learning intricate, non-linear relationships within vast datasets, making them ideal for the multifaceted challenges of modern infrastructure, from smart grids and transportation networks to industrial control systems and environmental monitoring. This section will explore two prominent deep learning architectures that are revolutionizing anomaly detection: Autoencoders and Generative Adversarial Networks (GANs).

Autoencoders for Anomaly Detection

Autoencoders are a class of unsupervised neural networks designed for efficient data representation learning. Their fundamental principle is to learn a compressed representation of the input data, known as the "latent space" or "bottleneck," and then reconstruct the original data from this compressed representation. The network is trained to minimize the difference between the original input and its reconstruction, thereby forcing it to learn the most salient features of the data. When trained exclusively on data representing normal operational states, an autoencoder becomes exceptionally proficient at reconstructing typical patterns. Anomalous data, by its very nature, deviates from these learned normal patterns. Consequently, when an autoencoder is presented with an anomaly, it struggles to reconstruct it accurately, leading to a significant discrepancy between the input and the output. This discrepancy, often quantified as a "reconstruction error," serves as a powerful indicator of an anomaly.

The architecture of a typical autoencoder comprises two main parts: an encoder and a decoder. The encoder progressively reduces the dimensionality of the input data through a series of layers (often dense or convolutional layers), transforming it into a lower-dimensional latent representation. This bottleneck layer captures the essential characteristics of the input. The decoder then takes this latent representation and expands it back, layer by layer, attempting to reconstruct the original input. The number of layers, the type of layers (e.g., fully connected, convolutional, recurrent), the activation functions, and the size of the bottleneck are all hyperparameters that can be tuned to suit the specific dataset and problem.

Consider the application of autoencoders in monitoring the structural health of a large infrastructure asset, such as a bridge. A bridge is equipped with numerous sensors—strain gauges, accelerometers, temperature sensors, GPS modules—generating a continuous stream of high-dimensional time-series data. This data reflects the bridge's response to various loads (traffic, wind, seismic activity) and environmental conditions. Training an autoencoder on data collected during periods of known stable and safe operation allows it to learn the complex interplay between these sensor readings under normal conditions. The encoder learns to compress the multi-sensor data into a compact representation that captures the essence of typical structural behavior. The decoder learns to reconstruct the typical multi-sensor readings from this latent representation.

When an unusual event occurs—perhaps a subtle structural fatigue initiating a crack, an abnormal distribution of weight due to a specific traffic pattern, or a response to a gust of wind that is slightly outside the normal range—the autoencoder will struggle to reconstruct the corresponding sensor readings accurately. The resulting high reconstruction error signals that the observed data deviates significantly from the learned normal patterns. For instance, if a strain gauge on a specific beam begins to exhibit a reading that, in combination with other sensor readings, deviates from the autoencoder's learned understanding of normal load distribution and material response, the reconstruction error will likely spike. This could indicate a developing structural compromise that might not be immediately apparent through simpler threshold-based monitoring or even basic statistical analysis. The autoencoder can flag these subtle deviations, enabling proactive inspection and maintenance before a critical failure occurs.

Variations of autoencoders further enhance their utility for anomaly detection in sequential data, which is common in infrastructure monitoring.
Recurrent Neural Networks (RNNs), such as Long Short-Term Memory (LSTM) or Gated Recurrent Unit (GRU) networks, can be incorporated

into the autoencoder architecture. These recurrent autoencoders are specifically designed to process sequential data and can learn temporal dependencies within the data streams. This is crucial for infrastructure where the behavior of systems over time is as important as instantaneous readings. For example, in monitoring the operational parameters of a fleet of autonomous vehicles or the flow patterns in a complex water distribution network, the temporal evolution of sensor readings provides vital context. A recurrent autoencoder trained on normal traffic patterns or water flow sequences can effectively detect anomalies that manifest as deviations in the sequence of events or the timing of changes, rather than just unusual individual data points.

Convolutional Autoencoders (CAEs) are another powerful variant, particularly useful for data with a grid-like topology, such as image data or spatial sensor arrays. In infrastructure, this might include thermal imaging of electrical equipment, visual inspection data from drones, or sensor grids deployed on large structures. CAEs use convolutional layers in both the encoder and decoder. These layers are adept at capturing spatial hierarchies and local patterns. For instance, if monitoring the thermal signature of a power transformer, a CAE trained on normal thermal images can detect subtle anomalies like the formation of hot spots or unusual temperature gradients across the surface, which might indicate internal winding degradation or cooling system issues. These patterns, captured by the convolutional filters, would lead to a higher reconstruction error for the anomalous thermal image.

The key to using autoencoders for anomaly detection lies in defining the anomaly score and setting an appropriate threshold. The anomaly score is typically the reconstruction error. Common error metrics include Mean Squared Error (MSE) or Mean Absolute Error (MAE) between the original input and its reconstruction. Once trained, the autoencoder is used to process a validation dataset or real-time data. The distribution of reconstruction errors for normal data is analyzed to determine a threshold. Any data point that yields a reconstruction error exceeding this threshold is flagged as an anomaly. This threshold can be set statistically, for example, to capture a certain percentile (e.g., 99th percentile) of the reconstruction errors observed during normal operation.

However, autoencoders are not without their challenges. Determining the optimal architecture, including the depth, width, and bottleneck size, can be a complex hyperparameter tuning task. Moreover, if the training data is not sufficiently representative of "normal" operation—for instance, if it inadvertently includes subtle anomalies—the autoencoder might learn to reconstruct these anomalies as well, reducing its effectiveness. Careful data curation and preprocessing are therefore paramount.

Generative Adversarial Networks (GANs) for Anomaly Detection

Generative Adversarial Networks (GANs) represent a more recent and potent advancement in deep learning, offering a novel paradigm for anomaly detection. GANs consist of two neural networks, a generator and a discriminator, trained in a zero-sum game. The generator's objective is to create synthetic data samples that are indistinguishable from real data, while the discriminator's objective is to distinguish between real data samples and those generated by the generator. Through this adversarial process, the generator learns to produce highly realistic synthetic data, and the discriminator becomes adept at identifying subtle deviations from real data patterns.

While GANs are primarily known for their generative capabilities, their structure and training process can be ingeniously adapted for anomaly detection. The core idea is to train a GAN on normal data. Once trained, the discriminator becomes an expert at identifying data that does not conform to the normal distribution learned during training. Alternatively, the generator can be leveraged to "normalize" or "explain" anomalous data.

One prominent GAN-based approach for anomaly detection involves training a GAN on normal data. After training, the discriminator network can be used directly. When presented with a new data sample, the discriminator outputs a probability score indicating how likely the sample is to be from the normal training distribution. A low probability score suggests that the sample is anomalous. This is analogous to how a classifier works, but the discriminator has learned from a potentially complex, high-dimensional distribution of normal data.

Another sophisticated GAN-based approach, often referred to as AnoGAN, uses the generator's ability to map latent space vectors to the data space. For anomaly detection, AnoGAN aims to find a latent space representation (z) for a given test data point (x) such that the generated sample from the generator ($G(z)$) is as close as possible to x, and z is a typical latent representation. The anomaly score is then derived from the difference between the test data point and its closest reconstruction from the generator, along with a measure of how "typical" the latent representation z is. Essentially, for an anomaly, there might not exist a latent representation z from which the generator can produce a sample closely resembling x, or the latent representation required might be an unusual one.

Consider monitoring the complex sensor data streams from a cutting-edge research facility or a large-scale industrial plant. These systems generate data with intricate correlations and temporal dependencies. Training a GAN on the normal operating data allows the generator to learn the underlying probability distribution of this normal behavior. The discriminator, in turn, becomes highly sensitive to any data that deviates from this learned distribution. If a sensor experiences an unexpected malfunction, or if a process parameter drifts into an uncharacteristic state, the discriminator will likely classify this data point with low confidence as "real" (i.e., normal), thereby signaling an anomaly.

For example, imagine monitoring the pressure and temperature readings within a complex chemical reactor. These parameters are not independent; they have a sophisticated relationship influenced by the ongoing chemical reactions, catalysts, and external conditions. A GAN trained on data representing stable and efficient reactor operation can learn this intricate relationship. If a subtle perturbation occurs—perhaps a minor impurity in the feedstock or a slight deviation in catalyst activity—that causes the pressure and temperature to drift into a state that is statistically unlikely under normal conditions, the discriminator will flag it. This could indicate an emerging issue that requires immediate attention, such as the formation of unwanted byproducts or a potential safety hazard.

Furthermore, GANs can be used in a "feature extraction" capacity. The discriminator network, after being trained on normal data, can act as a feature extractor. The outputs from its intermediate layers can be used as a new set of features that are highly discriminative of normal versus anomalous data. These features can then be fed into a simpler anomaly detection model, such as an OC-SVM or an Isolation Forest, potentially leading to improved performance.

The complexity of implementing and training GANs is a significant consideration. They are notoriously difficult to train, often suffering from issues like mode collapse (where the generator produces only a limited variety of samples) or vanishing gradients. Careful architectural design, hyperparameter tuning, and judicious choice of loss functions are crucial for successful GAN training. However, when successfully trained, GANs offer a powerful mechanism for anomaly detection, particularly in scenarios where anomalies are subtle, high-dimensional, and lack clear statistical definitions.

Applications in Advanced Infrastructure Monitoring

The deep learning techniques discussed—Autoencoders and GANs—are not merely theoretical constructs; they are increasingly being deployed to tackle real-world challenges in infrastructure monitoring.

In
transportation systems, for instance, deep learning can be applied to detect anomalies in traffic flow data. Recurrent autoencoders can learn the normal temporal patterns of traffic congestion, speed, and density on road networks. Deviations from these learned patterns, such as sudden inexplicable slowdowns or unusually dense clusters of vehicles in unexpected locations, can be flagged. Similarly, GANs can analyze video feeds from traffic cameras to detect unusual events like accidents, debris on the road, or erratic driver behavior that deviates from normal driving patterns.

For
power grids, deep learning models can monitor sensor data from substations, transmission lines, and distributed energy resources. Autoencoders can detect anomalies in voltage, current, and frequency readings that might indicate equipment malfunctions, cyber-attacks, or cascading failures. GANs can be used to generate realistic scenarios of grid disturbances, helping to train more robust anomaly detection systems or to test the resilience of the grid.

In
water management and distribution networks, deep learning can identify anomalies in flow rates, pressure levels, and water quality sensor data. Autoencoders can detect leaks, pipe bursts, or contamination events by identifying deviations from normal operational profiles. GANs can learn the complex dynamics of water flow and pressure across the network, enabling the detection of subtle anomalies that might go unnoticed by traditional monitoring systems.

The inherent complexity of modern infrastructure, characterized by interconnectedness, vast data volumes, and dynamic operational conditions, makes deep learning an indispensable tool. While traditional methods offer a valuable baseline, deep learning approaches like autoencoders and GANs provide the advanced capabilities needed to discern subtle, complex, and evolving anomalies. Their ability to learn intricate patterns directly from data, without explicit feature engineering or predefined rules, allows for more adaptive, sensitive, and comprehensive anomaly detection systems. As these technologies continue to mature, they promise to play an ever-increasing role in ensuring the reliability, safety, and efficiency of our critical infrastructure. The ongoing research in areas like attention mechanisms, graph neural networks for network-based data, and self-supervised learning further expands the horizons for deep learning in anomaly detection, pushing the boundaries of what is possible in safeguarding the built environment.

Chapter 6: Predictive Maintenance and Asset Management

The evolution of maintenance philosophies for critical infrastructure has been a journey marked by increasing sophistication, driven by a growing understanding of asset behavior and the imperative to minimize disruption and cost. For decades, the dominant approach, and often the only feasible one, was reactive maintenance. This strategy is fundamentally defined by its "fix-it-when-it-breaks" mentality. Maintenance tasks were only initiated after a component or system had already failed, causing an operational disruption. While seemingly straightforward, this approach carries inherent and significant drawbacks. The most immediate and impactful consequence of reactive maintenance is unplanned downtime. When a critical asset fails unexpectedly, operations grind to a halt, leading to lost productivity, missed deadlines, and potential revenue loss. The severity of this downtime can range from minor inconveniences to catastrophic disruptions, depending on the criticality of the asset.

Beyond the direct impact of downtime, reactive maintenance often incurs higher repair costs. Emergency repairs are typically more expensive than planned maintenance. Technicians may need to be called in on short notice, overtime rates may apply, and the necessary replacement parts might need to be sourced urgently, often at a premium. Furthermore, a failure in one component can often cascade, leading to secondary damage to other parts of the system, thereby increasing the overall repair bill. This reactive approach also makes resource allocation and inventory management extremely inefficient. It is difficult to predict which parts will be needed, when, and in what quantity. This can lead to either an overstocking of parts that may never be used or, conversely, a shortage of critical components when an unexpected failure occurs, further exacerbating downtime. From a safety perspective, allowing assets to operate until failure poses significant risks. Equipment that is nearing the end of its life or operating in a compromised state can present hazards to personnel and the environment.

In response to the shortcomings of purely reactive maintenance, preventive maintenance strategies emerged. This approach aims to reduce the likelihood of failure by performing maintenance tasks at predetermined intervals, regardless of the actual condition of the asset. This is often based on manufacturer recommendations, historical data, or regulatory requirements. For example, a pump might be scheduled for inspection and servicing every six months, or a vehicle might undergo an oil change every 5,000 miles. The rationale is that by performing regular, scheduled maintenance, wear and tear can be managed, and potential issues can be identified and addressed before they lead to failure.

While preventive maintenance represents an improvement over a purely reactive strategy, it too has its limitations and associated costs. The primary issue with time-based preventive maintenance is that it can be both inefficient and ineffective. Maintenance is performed on a schedule, not based on the actual need of the asset. This can lead to two types of inefficiencies. Firstly, components that are still in good working order may be replaced prematurely, leading to unnecessary expenditure on parts and labor. This is often referred to as "over-maintenance." For instance, replacing a perfectly functional bearing simply because its scheduled maintenance interval has arrived incurs costs that could have been avoided. Secondly, and perhaps more critically, scheduled maintenance may not be frequent enough to catch an impending failure. If a component experiences accelerated wear due to unforeseen operating conditions or manufacturing defects, it can still fail between scheduled maintenance checks. In this scenario, the preventive measure fails to prevent the failure, leading to the same unplanned downtime and associated costs as reactive maintenance, but with the added expense of the scheduled maintenance that did not avert the issue.

The scheduling itself can also be a logistical challenge. Coordinating maintenance across a large fleet of assets or a complex industrial facility requires careful planning. If maintenance is performed too frequently, it can disrupt operations unnecessarily. If performed too infrequently, the risk of failure increases. Furthermore, preventive maintenance often involves significant upfront investment in terms of labor and parts, which may not always yield a proportional reduction in failures. This can lead to higher overall maintenance costs compared to a more optimized approach. The fundamental flaw lies in its lack of awareness of the asset's actual condition. It treats all assets of a certain type, regardless of their operating environment or individual usage patterns, in the same way. This "one-size-fits-all" approach is inherently suboptimal in a world where assets operate under diverse and dynamic conditions.

The limitations and inefficiencies inherent in both reactive and preventive maintenance strategies have paved the way for a more intelligent and data-driven approach: predictive maintenance. This paradigm shift fundamentally alters how maintenance is conceived and executed. Instead of waiting for failure (reactive) or performing maintenance based on an arbitrary schedule (preventive), predictive maintenance focuses on anticipating failures
before they occur. It leverages the power of data, advanced analytics, and increasingly, artificial intelligence and machine learning, to understand the health and condition of an asset in real-time or near real-time.

The core principle of predictive maintenance is to monitor the operational parameters of an asset and analyze the data collected to identify subtle indicators of degradation or impending failure. This involves tracking a multitude of variables, such as vibration levels, temperature, pressure, electrical current, sound, operational speed, and any other measurable characteristic that can provide insight into the asset's performance and health. By analyzing trends, patterns, and anomalies within this data, it becomes possible to predict when a component is likely to fail. This allows maintenance teams to schedule interventions at the optimal time – not too early, leading to wasted resources, and not too late, leading to an unexpected failure.

The transition from reactive and preventive to predictive maintenance is not merely an incremental improvement; it represents a fundamental paradigm shift. It moves maintenance from a cost center, often seen as a necessary evil, to a strategic enabler of operational efficiency, reliability, and safety. This shift is fueled by several converging factors. Firstly, the exponential growth in sensor technology has made it more feasible and cost-effective to collect vast amounts of data from virtually any asset. Secondly, advancements in data storage and processing capabilities allow for the management and analysis of this "big data." Finally, the maturation of analytical techniques, including statistical modeling, machine learning, and deep learning, provides the tools to extract meaningful insights from this data, transforming raw measurements into actionable intelligence.

The benefits of adopting a predictive maintenance strategy are multifaceted and profound, impacting nearly every aspect of asset management and operational efficiency. One of the most significant advantages is the dramatic reduction in unplanned downtime. By anticipating failures, maintenance can be scheduled during planned operational windows, minimizing disruption to production or service delivery. This leads to increased asset availability and reliability, directly contributing to higher productivity and revenue.

Cost savings are another major benefit. While implementing a predictive maintenance system may involve an initial investment in sensors, software, and training, the long-term financial returns are substantial. By avoiding catastrophic failures and their associated secondary damage, repair costs are reduced. Furthermore, by performing maintenance only when it is needed, the expenditure on parts and labor is optimized, eliminating the waste associated with unnecessary preventive tasks. Maintenance teams can be more efficient, as they are working with a clear understanding of the specific issues that need addressing, rather than conducting general inspections or replacements. This also allows for better inventory management, as replacement parts can be ordered proactively and with greater certainty.

Safety is significantly enhanced through predictive maintenance. Assets that are showing early signs of degradation can be identified and serviced before they pose a risk to personnel or the environment. This is particularly crucial in industries with high-risk operations, such as manufacturing, energy, and transportation. For example, detecting subtle increases in vibration in a rotating machine could indicate a bearing that is about to fail, preventing a potential catastrophic mechanical failure that could cause injury or significant damage.

Moreover, predictive maintenance provides invaluable insights into asset performance and operational efficiency. By analyzing the data, operators can gain a deeper understanding of how their assets are performing under various conditions. This understanding can lead to adjustments in operational parameters, improvements in energy efficiency, and extended asset lifespan. For instance, if data reveals that a particular operational setting consistently leads to accelerated wear on a component, that setting can be modified to prolong the component's life. This holistic view of asset health and performance fosters a culture of continuous improvement.

The implementation of predictive maintenance is not a monolithic process but rather a spectrum of maturity. At its most basic level, it might involve simple threshold monitoring, where alerts are triggered if a sensor reading exceeds or falls below a predefined limit. While this is a step above reactive maintenance, it is still quite rudimentary. More advanced stages involve trend analysis, where deviations from normal operational behavior over time are identified. The most sophisticated level, and where artificial intelligence and machine learning play a crucial role, involves complex pattern recognition, root cause analysis, and the forecasting of failure probabilities and remaining useful life (RUL).

For example, consider a fleet of large industrial pumps. In a reactive system, maintenance is performed only when a pump stops working. In a preventive system, all pumps might undergo a check-up every three months. With a predictive approach, each pump is outfitted with vibration, temperature, and acoustic sensors. The data from these sensors is continuously collected and analyzed. An AI model might detect a slight, but consistent, increase in vibration at a specific frequency band in one of the pumps, accompanied by a minor rise in operating temperature. This pattern, learned from historical data of similar pumps that eventually failed, might indicate the early stages of bearing wear. The system can then predict that this bearing is likely to fail within the next four to six weeks. This allows maintenance planners to schedule the replacement of the bearing during a planned shutdown, order the necessary part in advance, and avoid an unexpected and costly failure. The same approach can be applied to a vast array of assets, from wind turbines and aircraft engines to railway tracks and power transformers, revolutionizing how maintenance is performed and how assets are managed throughout their lifecycle. This transition is not just about technology; it's about a strategic shift towards a proactive, data-informed, and ultimately more resilient operational framework.

The efficacy of any predictive maintenance (PdM) model is inextricably linked to the quality, relevance, and comprehensiveness of the data it consumes. Without a robust foundation of accurate and well-structured data, even the most sophisticated algorithms will falter, producing unreliable predictions and ultimately undermining the entire predictive maintenance initiative. Therefore, understanding the diverse data streams essential for building these models, alongside the methodologies for their collection, integration, and validation, is paramount to achieving successful asset management and minimizing operational disruptions.

At the heart of most predictive maintenance systems lies **sensor data**. These are the real-time or near real-time measurements generated by various transducers attached to the asset, providing a continuous pulse on its operational status and physical condition. The type of sensor data collected is highly dependent on the asset and the potential failure modes being monitored. For instance, in rotating machinery such as pumps, motors, or turbines, **vibration analysis** is a cornerstone. Sensors like accelerometers detect minute tremors that, when analyzed for frequency, amplitude, and patterns, can reveal issues such as imbalance, misalignment, bearing wear, or gear tooth damage long before they manifest as audible noise or significant performance degradation. A subtle increase in specific vibration frequencies, for example, might indicate the initial stages of a bearing spalling, a problem that, if left unaddressed, could lead to catastrophic failure and extensive downtime.

Equally critical is **temperature data**. Excessive heat is a universal indicator of abnormal operation or impending failure. Thermocouples, RTDs (Resistance Temperature Detectors), or infrared cameras can monitor bearing temperatures, motor windings, gearbox oil, or even exhaust gas temperatures in engines. A steady, gradual increase in temperature, or a sudden spike beyond expected operating ranges, can signal issues like insufficient lubrication, overloaded operation, electrical resistance problems, or inadequate cooling. For example, a motor that is running hotter than usual might be experiencing increased friction due to worn bearings, or it could be operating at a load exceeding its design specifications. The ability to track these temperature trends over time allows for the early detection of thermal issues.

Pressure data is vital for systems involving fluids or gases, such as hydraulic systems, pipelines, or compressors. Pressure sensors can detect anomalies like leaks (indicated by a drop in pressure), blockages (causing a rise in pressure upstream or a drop downstream), or pump/compressor performance degradation. For example, a sustained drop in hydraulic system pressure, even under normal load, might point to a developing leak in a hose or seal, or a failing pump. Monitoring these pressure profiles can prevent major system failures and fluid loss.

Electrical data, including voltage, current, power factor, and resistance, is indispensable for assets like electric motors, transformers, and switchgear. Monitoring current draw, for instance, can reveal motor overloads or developing winding faults. A motor drawing significantly more current than usual under a constant load suggests increased resistance or mechanical strain, potentially indicating a failing winding or a jammed bearing. Power factor deviations can signal issues within transformers or complex electrical machinery. Analyzing these electrical signatures provides a direct insight into the health of the electrical components.

Beyond these common sensor types, other data streams can be invaluable depending on the application.
Acoustic sensors can detect abnormal noises, such as grinding, whistling, or knocking sounds, which might indicate mechanical wear or the presence of foreign objects. **Flow meters** monitor the rate at which fluids or gases are moving through a system, helping to identify blockages, leaks, or pump inefficiencies. **Strain gauges** measure deformation, useful for monitoring the structural integrity of components under load. The strategic placement and selection of these sensors are critical to capture the most relevant indicators of potential failure modes for a given asset.

However, sensor data alone, especially raw sensor readings, often requires context. This is where **operational history data** becomes indispensable. This encompasses how the asset has been used over time. Key parameters here include load, speed, operational cycles, start-stop events, environmental conditions (ambient temperature, humidity), and the specific operational modes the asset has been subjected to. Understanding the operational context allows PdM models to differentiate between normal variations in sensor readings due to changing operational demands and anomalous readings indicative of a fault. For example, a rise in motor temperature might be considered normal if the asset's load has significantly increased, but if the temperature rises while the load remains constant, it signals a potential problem. Operational data helps build a baseline of "normal" behavior under various conditions, making deviations more apparent. Historical operational data can also reveal how different operating patterns contribute to wear and tear, informing maintenance strategies and potentially guiding operational adjustments to extend asset life.

Complementing sensor and operational data are **maintenance logs and historical repair data**. This invaluable repository documents every maintenance activity performed on an asset. It includes details about when maintenance was conducted, the type of maintenance (e.g., inspection, lubrication, repair, replacement), the specific components serviced or replaced, the parts used, the labor involved, and the personnel who performed the work. This historical data is crucial for several reasons. Firstly, it helps in identifying recurring issues or specific components that have a higher propensity for failure. If a particular type of bearing is consistently failing prematurely across a fleet of assets, this historical data will highlight it, allowing for proactive measures like using a more robust bearing type or adjusting lubrication schedules.

Secondly, maintenance logs provide crucial information for training and validating predictive models. When a failure eventually occurs, correlating the sensor and operational data leading up to that event with the documented maintenance history and the nature of the failure itself helps the model learn to associate specific patterns with particular fault types. For example, if the maintenance logs indicate that a specific vibration signature consistently preceded a gearbox failure, the PdM model can learn to flag that signature as a high-risk indicator for future gearbox issues. This data also helps in estimating the Remaining Useful Life (RUL) of components. By analyzing how long a component lasted before its last replacement, and under what conditions, models can refine their predictions for the lifespan of similar components.

Inspection reports also contribute significantly to the data landscape for predictive maintenance. These are often generated during scheduled maintenance checks or specialized inspections (e.g., visual inspections, non-destructive testing like ultrasonic or eddy current testing). These reports provide qualitative and quantitative observations about the asset's condition, such as the presence of cracks, corrosion, leaks, wear marks, or loose connections. While sensor data provides continuous, quantitative insights, inspection reports offer periodic, expert-driven assessments that can capture visible or detectable defects that sensors might miss. For instance, a visual inspection might reveal external damage to a casing or the early signs of corrosion on a pipe, which could then be further investigated or correlated with other sensor data. Integrating these findings into the PdM framework enriches the understanding of the asset's overall health.

Finally, and perhaps most critically for training and validating predictive models, are

failure records. This data meticulously documents instances where an asset or component has actually failed. It typically includes the date and time of failure, the circumstances leading up to it, the root cause of the failure (if determined), the impact of the failure (e.g., downtime duration, severity of damage), and the actions taken for repair or replacement. Failure records are the ground truth for predictive models. They allow data scientists to test their models by feeding them historical data and seeing if the model correctly predicted the failure. This feedback loop is essential for refining algorithms, improving prediction accuracy, and understanding the model's limitations. The more comprehensive and detailed these failure records are, the more effectively models can be trained to recognize the precursor signatures of different failure modes.

The sheer volume and variety of this data present significant challenges. **Data collection** must be systematic and robust. This often involves deploying a network of sensors, ensuring reliable data acquisition systems, and establishing protocols for manual data entry (for logs and inspections). For new installations, integrating data acquisition capabilities from the design phase onwards is far more efficient than retrofitting. For existing assets, a phased approach to sensor deployment, prioritizing critical components and failure modes, is often practical.

Data integration is another major hurdle. Data often resides in disparate systems. Sensor data might come from SCADA (Supervisory Control and Data Acquisition) systems, IoT platforms, or dedicated data loggers. Maintenance logs and work orders are typically managed within Computerized Maintenance Management Systems (CMMS) or Enterprise Asset Management (EAM) software. Inspection reports might be stored in separate databases or even paper-based systems. To build a holistic view of asset health, all these data sources must be brought together and harmonized. This requires robust data integration strategies, often involving data lakes, data warehouses, or specialized integration platforms. These platforms need to extract data from source systems, transform it into a consistent format, and load it into a central repository where it can be accessed and analyzed by PdM models. Establishing standardized data formats and unique identifiers for assets and components across all systems is crucial for successful integration.

Beyond collection and integration, **data quality and integrity** are paramount. "Garbage in, garbage out" is a truism in data science, and PdM is no exception. Inaccurate, incomplete, or inconsistent data can lead to flawed predictions, false alarms, and missed critical events. Therefore, rigorous data validation and cleaning processes are essential. This involves:

Data Validation: Implementing checks to ensure data falls within plausible ranges (e.g., temperature within expected operating limits), has correct data types, and adheres to format specifications. For example, a vibration reading of "XYZ" or a temperature of -500°C would immediately be flagged as erroneous.
Outlier Detection and Handling: Identifying and addressing anomalous data points that may be due to sensor malfunctions, transmission errors, or genuine, but extreme, operational events. The strategy for handling outliers might range from removal to transformation, depending on the context and the nature of the outlier.
Missing Data Imputation: Developing strategies to deal with gaps in the data. This could involve using statistical methods to estimate missing values based on available data (e.g., interpolation for time-series data) or marking them appropriately so that models can account for their absence.
Data Normalization and Scaling: Ensuring that data from different sensors and sources are on comparable scales. For example, vibration data might be measured in m/s^2 or g, while temperature is in °C or °F. Normalizing these values allows them to be used together effectively in analytical models.
Data Labeling: For supervised learning models, accurately labeling historical data with the corresponding event (e.g., "normal operation," "bearing fault type A," "motor overload") is critical. This is often the most

time-consuming and expert-intensive part of the process, relying heavily on maintenance logs and failure records.

Data quantity is also a significant factor. While some basic anomaly detection can be performed with limited data, training sophisticated predictive models, especially those employing machine learning, requires a substantial volume of historical data. This includes sufficient examples of both normal operation and various types of failures. For rare failure modes, collecting enough data can be a challenge, often necessitating the use of simulation techniques or transfer learning from similar assets. The "more data is better" adage holds true, but it must be balanced with the quality and relevance of that data.

Furthermore, the
relevance of the data cannot be overstated. Collecting vast amounts of data that do not provide insight into the asset's condition or potential failure modes is an inefficient use of resources. The selection of sensors, the parameters monitored, and the historical information captured must be directly linked to the physics of failure for the specific asset. This requires a deep understanding of the asset's design, its operating environment, and its known failure mechanisms. Collaboration between domain experts (engineers, maintenance technicians) and data scientists is crucial in identifying the most relevant data streams and features for effective PdM.

In essence, the data requirements for predictive maintenance models form a complex ecosystem. It is a multi-faceted interplay of real-time sensor feeds, historical operational context, detailed maintenance and failure records, and expert observations. Successfully navigating this ecosystem requires a strategic approach to data collection, robust integration capabilities, and an unwavering commitment to ensuring data quality and integrity. Without this foundational data infrastructure, the promise of predictive maintenance remains largely theoretical, unable to translate into tangible improvements in asset reliability, operational efficiency, and cost reduction. The investment in establishing and maintaining this data pipeline is not merely an IT or operational expense; it is a strategic imperative that underpins the entire predictive maintenance value proposition.

The advent of machine learning (ML) has revolutionized the field of predictive maintenance, moving beyond simple threshold-based alerts to sophisticated, data-driven prognostics. At its core, ML enables systems to learn from historical data and identify patterns that precede equipment failure. This learning capability allows for more accurate, nuanced, and timely predictions, ultimately enhancing asset reliability and optimizing maintenance schedules. The power of ML in failure prediction lies in its ability to process vast amounts of complex data, uncover subtle relationships, and adapt to evolving operational conditions.

One of the most common applications of ML in failure prediction involves **classification algorithms**. These algorithms are designed to categorize data points into predefined classes. In the context of predictive maintenance, the primary objective is often to predict the probability of an asset failing within a specific future timeframe. For instance, a binary classification model might predict whether a component is likely to fail in the next 7 days (Yes/No). More advanced models can output a probability score, indicating the likelihood of failure, which allows maintenance teams to prioritize interventions based on risk.

Logistic Regression is a foundational classification algorithm often employed for its interpretability. It models the probability of a binary outcome (failure vs. no failure) as a function of one or more predictor variables (e.g., vibration amplitude, temperature trends, load history). While relatively simple, logistic regression can be effective when the relationship between features and the probability of failure is approximately linear in the log-odds space. For example, one could use logistic regression to predict the probability of a conveyor belt idler failing within the next month based on its recorded vibration levels and operating hours. The model would learn a set of coefficients that best map these input features to the observed failure outcomes in historical data. A higher coefficient for vibration, for instance, would indicate that increased vibration levels significantly contribute to the likelihood of failure.

Moving towards more complex, non-linear relationships, **Support Vector Machines (SVMs)** offer a powerful approach. SVMs work by finding an optimal hyperplane that best separates data points belonging to different classes. In failure prediction, this means finding a boundary that effectively distinguishes between instances that led to failure and those that did not. SVMs are particularly adept at handling high-dimensional data and can be configured with different kernels (e.g., radial basis function, polynomial) to capture complex, non-linear decision boundaries. Consider a scenario where predicting the failure of an industrial pump depends on a combination of factors like flow rate, discharge pressure, bearing temperature, and motor current. These factors might interact in non-linear ways, making linear models less effective. An SVM can learn these intricate relationships, identifying a more precise separation between operational states that are indicative of impending failure and those that represent normal operation. The "support vectors" are the data points closest to the decision boundary, highlighting the critical examples that define the model's classification capability.

Decision Trees and their ensemble counterparts, such as **Random Forests** and **Gradient Boosting Machines**, are widely adopted due to their robustness, ease of use, and inherent ability to handle a mix of data types and complex interactions. A decision tree recursively partitions the data based on feature values, creating a tree-like structure where each leaf node represents a class prediction (failure or no failure). Random Forests build upon this by constructing multiple decision trees on bootstrapped samples of the data and aggregating their predictions (e.g., by voting). This ensemble approach significantly reduces the risk of overfitting and improves generalization performance. For instance, to predict the likelihood of a critical valve failing in a chemical processing plant, a Random Forest model could incorporate data on cycle counts, fluid pressure and temperature at various points, actuator speed, and diagnostic codes logged by the valve's controller. The model would learn a series of rules derived from these features – e.g., "IF cycle count > 100,000 AND actuator speed < 80% THEN probability of failure increases." The collective wisdom of hundreds of such trees provides a more reliable prediction than any single tree could offer. Gradient Boosting Machines, another ensemble technique, sequentially build trees, with each new tree attempting to correct the errors of the previous ones, often leading to even higher accuracy.

Beyond predicting the
likelihood of failure, a more ambitious goal is to estimate the **Remaining Useful Life (RUL)** of an asset or component. This shifts the problem from classification to **regression**, where the ML model predicts a continuous value – the number of operational hours, cycles, or days until failure. This is incredibly valuable for planning maintenance proactively, allowing organizations to schedule replacements or overhauls just before failure, thereby maximizing asset utilization while avoiding catastrophic breakdowns.

Linear Regression, similar to its classification counterpart, is a simple starting point for RUL estimation. It assumes a linear relationship between predictor variables and the RUL. However, in most real-world scenarios, the degradation of an asset is a non-linear process. As a component wears down, its degradation rate may accelerate. Therefore, more sophisticated regression techniques are typically required.

Polynomial Regression can capture some non-linear trends by introducing polynomial terms of the features into the model. For example, if a bearing's vibration amplitude increases over time in a parabolic fashion as it degrades, a polynomial regression model could potentially capture this trend. However, determining the correct degree of the polynomial can be challenging, and higher-degree polynomials can lead to overfitting.

Machine Learning Regression Models like Support Vector Regression (SVR) and ensemble methods such as Random Forest Regressors and Gradient Boosting Regressors are far more adept at modeling complex, non-linear degradation curves. SVR extends the principles of SVM to regression tasks, seeking to find a function that deviates from the actual target values by a certain threshold (epsilon) while being as flat as possible. Random Forest Regressors and Gradient Boosting Regressors operate similarly to their classification counterparts, but instead of predicting a class, they predict a continuous RUL value. These models can effectively learn the patterns of degradation from sensor data and historical RUL information. For instance, imagine tracking the cumulative stress on a bridge support over its operational lifetime, alongside various environmental factors like temperature fluctuations and load cycles. A Random Forest Regressor could be trained on this data, where the target variable is the known RUL of similar bridge supports. The model would learn how different combinations of stress, load, and environmental exposure contribute to the degradation rate, ultimately providing an estimate of how much longer the current support is likely to remain within safe operational parameters.

A specific example of RUL prediction might involve the fleet of aircraft jet engines. Each engine is equipped with numerous sensors monitoring parameters like exhaust gas temperature, turbine speed, and fuel flow. As an engine accumulates flight hours, certain components, such as turbine blades, undergo wear and tear, leading to subtle changes in these sensor readings. ML models can be trained on historical data from thousands of flights, correlating these sensor patterns with the eventual time to overhaul or replacement of specific components. The goal is to predict the RUL of critical engine sub-assemblies, allowing airlines to schedule maintenance between flights, minimizing disruption and maximizing safety and efficiency. For instance, a model might identify a specific trend in exhaust gas temperature fluctuations that historically precedes a particular type of turbine failure. By monitoring this trend in real-time, the model can then estimate the remaining life before such a failure is likely to occur, prompting a maintenance intervention at the most opportune moment.

Beyond standard classification and regression, **Survival Analysis** techniques provide a powerful framework for modeling the time until an event occurs, which is directly applicable to failure prediction. Unlike traditional regression, which might assume a fixed "target" RUL, survival analysis explicitly models the probability of an event (failure) occurring over time, accounting for censored data. Censored data occurs when an observation ends before the event of interest (failure) has happened. For example, if an asset is still operational at the end of the observation period, its failure time is "right-censored."

Traditional survival analysis methods include the **Kaplan-Meier estimator** for estimating survival functions and the **Cox Proportional Hazards model** for assessing the impact of covariates on the hazard rate (the instantaneous risk of failure). The Cox model is particularly useful as it allows the inclusion of predictor variables (e.g., operating conditions, maintenance history) to understand how they influence the time to failure, without making strong assumptions about the specific shape of the survival function.

More recently, ML has been integrated with survival analysis to create more powerful predictive models.

Random Survival Forests extend the Random Forest concept to survival data, allowing for the estimation of survival curves and the prediction of hazard ratios based on complex feature interactions. These models can handle high-dimensional data and non-linear relationships, making them suitable for analyzing the vast datasets generated by modern industrial assets.

An illustrative example of survival analysis in action could be predicting the lifespan of tires on a fleet of heavy-duty vehicles. Factors like mileage, tire pressure, load, driving speed, and road surface conditions all influence tire wear and the probability of failure (e.g., blowout or excessive wear requiring replacement). Survival analysis, particularly with ML enhancements, can model the "time to failure" for each tire. This allows fleet managers to predict when individual tires will need replacement, optimizing tire inventory, scheduling rotations, and ensuring safety by preventing premature tire failures that could lead to costly downtime or accidents. If a particular batch of tires shows a higher hazard rate under specific operating conditions, survival analysis can highlight this, prompting investigation into manufacturing defects or recommending different tire types for certain routes.

Another domain where these techniques are crucial is in the management of civil infrastructure, such as bridges. Sensors embedded in bridge components can monitor strain, vibration, and environmental factors. Predicting the RUL of critical elements like expansion joints or support bearings involves understanding cumulative damage and the probability of failure under varying stress and environmental loads. Survival analysis can model the probability of a specific failure mode occurring within a given timeframe, accounting for the fact that bridges can operate for decades without failure. By analyzing sensor data correlated with historical maintenance records and known degradation mechanisms, ML-enhanced survival models can provide crucial insights into the long-term reliability of the structure, informing decisions about inspection schedules and necessary repairs or retrofits.

The application of machine learning for failure prediction is not without its challenges. The accuracy and reliability of these models are heavily dependent on the quality and quantity of historical data, particularly data that clearly labels past failures and their precursors. The interpretability of complex "black-box" models, such as deep neural networks, can also be a concern, as maintenance engineers often need to understand *why* a prediction is being made to trust and act upon it. Furthermore, the continuous evolution of operating conditions and the emergence of novel failure modes require models to be regularly retrained and validated. Despite these hurdles, the ongoing advancements in ML algorithms and computational power are continuously enhancing the capabilities of predictive maintenance, making it an indispensable tool for modern asset management.

The progression from traditional machine learning techniques to the realm of deep learning marks a significant leap in the sophistication and efficacy of Prognostics and Health Management (PHM) systems. While the previously discussed ML algorithms have proven their worth in identifying failure precursors and estimating Remaining Useful Life (RUL), deep learning architectures offer unparalleled capabilities in learning intricate, hierarchical representations of data. This is particularly crucial in PHM, where subtle degradation patterns, non-linear system dynamics, and complex interdependencies between sensor readings can be indicative of impending failure. The ability of deep learning models to automatically extract relevant features from raw data, without extensive manual feature engineering, democratizes the process and unlocks insights previously inaccessible with conventional methods.

Among the most potent deep learning architectures for PHM are Recurrent Neural Networks (RNNs), and their specialized variants like Long Short-Term Memory (LSTM) networks. Time-series sensor data, intrinsic to monitoring industrial equipment, often exhibits temporal dependencies – the state of the system at one point in time is influenced by its history. Standard feedforward networks struggle to capture these long-range dependencies effectively. RNNs, by incorporating feedback loops, allow information to persist, enabling them to process sequences of data and learn from past observations. LSTMs, a prominent type of RNN, are specifically designed to overcome the vanishing gradient problem that often plagues standard RNNs when dealing with very long sequences. They achieve this through a gating mechanism (input, forget, and output gates) that selectively controls the flow of information, allowing them to remember relevant past states and forget irrelevant ones. This makes LSTMs exceptionally well-suited for analyzing the continuous stream of sensor data from machinery. For instance, consider a fleet of wind turbines. Each turbine generates terabytes of data daily from vibration sensors, temperature probes, accelerometers, and rotational speed encoders. Subtle anomalies in vibration patterns, gradually increasing bearing temperatures, or slight deviations in rotational speed, when viewed over extended periods, can signal the early stages of gearbox or bearing degradation. An LSTM network, trained on historical operational data that includes recorded sensor readings leading up to known failures, can learn to identify these complex, evolving patterns. It can discern that a specific sequence of increasing RMS vibration values, coupled with a slow rise in gearbox oil temperature and a marginal decrease in rotational efficiency, is a strong precursor to a catastrophic bearing failure. The LSTM's ability to "remember" the initial onset of these trends, even if they are initially minor, allows for much earlier detection than traditional threshold-based alarms or simpler ML models that might only consider localized snapshots of data.

The power of LSTMs extends beyond simple anomaly detection. They can be trained to directly predict RUL by learning the mapping between sequences of sensor readings and the time remaining until failure. Imagine a complex chemical processing plant where the operational integrity of a reactor pump depends on a multitude of parameters: inlet pressure, outlet flow rate, motor current, impeller speed, and internal temperature. As the pump ages and its internal components (seals, impeller, bearings) wear down, these parameters will change in correlated, often non-linear ways. An LSTM model, fed with historical data of these parameters leading up to pump failures, can learn the degradation trajectory. When presented with current real-time sensor data, the LSTM can extrapolate this learned trajectory to estimate the remaining operational hours or cycles before the pump is likely to fail. This proactive estimation allows maintenance teams to schedule pump refurbishment or replacement during planned downtime, avoiding unexpected shutdowns that could halt production and incur significant financial losses. Furthermore, the interpretability of these models, while more challenging than simpler methods, is advancing. Techniques like attention mechanisms within LSTMs can highlight which specific time steps or sensor readings were most influential in the RUL prediction, offering valuable diagnostic insights.

Beyond sequential data, another class of deep learning models, Convolutional Neural Networks (CNNs), has found significant application in PHM, particularly in the analysis of visual data. In many industries, inspections of critical assets are conducted visually, either by human inspectors or automated systems equipped with cameras. These inspections aim to identify physical signs of wear, corrosion, cracks, or other forms of damage. CNNs, originally developed for image recognition tasks, excel at automatically learning hierarchical features from images. They can identify patterns at different scales, from detecting minute hairline cracks on a metal surface to recognizing the overall extent of corrosion on a structural component. For example, in the aerospace industry, the structural integrity of aircraft fuselages, wings, and engine components is paramount. Regular visual inspections are performed to detect fatigue cracks, delamination in composite materials, or erosion. A CNN model trained on a vast dataset of images of aircraft components, meticulously labeled with the presence and severity of various defects, can learn to perform these inspections with remarkable accuracy and consistency. When presented with a new inspection image, the CNN can automatically identify and localize potential defects, classifying them by type and severity. This not only speeds up the inspection process but also reduces the subjective variability inherent in human inspections, leading to more reliable defect detection.

Consider the inspection of rail tracks. Cracks, wear, and deformities in rail lines can lead to derailments. Traditionally, inspections might involve manual visual checks or specialized inspection trains with basic sensors. By deploying cameras along the tracks and feeding the imagery into a trained CNN, it's possible to automate the detection of rail surface defects. The CNN can learn to distinguish between normal wear patterns and critical defects like fissures, spalling, or excessive rail head wear that require immediate attention. The output could be a map highlighting the location and type of defects, allowing maintenance crews to prioritize repairs efficiently and prevent potential accidents. Similarly, in the oil and gas sector, underwater pipelines are subject to corrosion, pitting, and physical damage. Remote Operated Vehicles (ROVs) equipped with cameras can capture images of these pipelines. A CNN can analyze these images to detect and classify signs of degradation, providing crucial data for assessing the integrity of the pipeline and planning necessary maintenance or repairs. The network learns to recognize subtle variations in surface texture, color, and shape that indicate the presence of these damaging phenomena, often before they become readily apparent to the human eye.

The synergy between different deep learning architectures further amplifies their predictive power. Hybrid models, combining CNNs and LSTMs, are increasingly being employed for complex PHM tasks. For instance, in the analysis of video feeds from industrial equipment, a CNN can first process individual frames to extract salient visual features (e.g., signs of abnormal vibration in moving parts, leakage, or discoloration). These extracted features can then be fed into an LSTM network to analyze their temporal evolution over a sequence of frames. This allows for the detection of not just static defects but also dynamic anomalies. Imagine monitoring a critical rotating machine, like a compressor. A CNN might identify a slight visual wobble in a shaft, while an LSTM, processing the sequence of these visual anomalies over time, can determine if this wobble is increasing, indicating a developing imbalance or bearing failure, and subsequently estimate the RUL.

The ability of deep learning models to capture highly complex, non-linear relationships is a significant advantage over traditional ML methods, which may struggle with intricate interactions between multiple sensor readings or with subtle, multi-modal degradation pathways. For example, the failure of a complex electro-mechanical system might not be caused by a single parameter exceeding a threshold but by a subtle, long-term interplay of factors such as gradual temperature increase, fluctuating electrical load, and increasing acoustic emissions, all occurring within specific operational contexts. Deep learning models, with their layered structure, can learn these intricate feature interactions and learn representations of the system's health state that are far more nuanced and predictive. This leads to more accurate failure predictions and, consequently, more optimized maintenance scheduling. Instead of scheduling maintenance based on time intervals or simple "trigger" conditions, maintenance can be scheduled precisely when it is needed, just before failure is imminent, thereby maximizing asset utilization and minimizing the risk of unscheduled downtime.

Furthermore, deep learning techniques are proving invaluable in handling the sheer volume and variety of data generated by modern industrial assets, often referred to as "Big Data." As sensorization becomes more pervasive, the datasets become exponentially larger and more complex, containing high-frequency time-series data, images, acoustic signals, and logs. Manually engineering features from such diverse data sources would be an insurmountable task. Deep learning models, through their hierarchical feature learning capabilities, can process this raw, high-dimensional data directly, automatically identifying the most relevant patterns for prediction. This scalability is critical for implementing PHM across large fleets of assets, where individual asset health must be monitored continuously and comprehensively.

One notable area where deep learning is making strides is in the field of generative models, such as Generative Adversarial Networks (GANs). GANs can be used to generate synthetic sensor data that mimics real-world degradation patterns. This is particularly useful when historical data of actual failures is scarce, a common problem in many industrial applications. By training a GAN on limited failure data, one can generate a larger, more diverse synthetic dataset that can then be used to train more robust predictive models. This augmentation of training data can significantly improve the accuracy and generalization capabilities of prognostics models, especially for rare failure modes. For instance, if a specific, rare failure mode of a turbine component has only occurred a handful of times in decades of operation, GANs can help create a richer dataset of similar failure precursors, enabling an LSTM to learn the associated patterns more effectively.

Another advanced deep learning approach involves the use of transformers, a neural network architecture that has revolutionized natural language processing. While initially designed for sequential text data, transformers are increasingly being adapted for time-series analysis in PHM. Their self-attention mechanism allows them to weigh the importance of different parts of the input sequence, enabling them to capture long-range dependencies and contextual information even more effectively than LSTMs in some scenarios. This could be beneficial in understanding how events that occurred very early in an asset's operational history might still have a significant impact on its future reliability.

However, the adoption of deep learning in PHM is not without its challenges. The immense computational resources required for training deep neural networks can be a barrier, especially for smaller organizations. Furthermore, the "black-box" nature of many deep learning models remains a concern. While they can achieve high predictive accuracy, understanding the underlying reasons for a particular prediction can be difficult, which can hinder trust and adoption by domain experts who need to validate the model's reasoning. Research into explainable AI (XAI) techniques is actively addressing this by developing methods to visualize and interpret the decisions made by deep learning models. Techniques like SHAP (SHapley Additive exPlanations) and LIME (Local Interpretable Model-agnostic Explanations) are being explored to provide insights into which input features and data points contribute most to a prediction. For example, if a deep learning model predicts an imminent failure, XAI techniques could highlight that specific sensor readings from the vibration sensor at a particular time, combined with a gradual increase in motor temperature over the past week, were the primary drivers of this prediction. This level of interpretability is crucial for gaining confidence in the model's outputs and for guiding maintenance actions.

Despite these challenges, the transformative potential of deep learning in PHM is undeniable. By enabling systems to learn from complex, high-dimensional data and to capture subtle, non-linear degradation patterns, deep learning is pushing the boundaries of predictive maintenance. It promises to deliver more accurate RUL estimations, earlier failure detection, and ultimately, more resilient and efficient asset management strategies, paving the way for truly autonomous and optimized industrial operations.

The integration of predictive maintenance (PdM) capabilities into the broader framework of asset management systems represents a pivotal evolution in how organizations approach the stewardship of their critical infrastructure and equipment. Moving beyond the isolated execution of diagnostic and prognostic tasks, this integration aims to weave PdM insights into the very fabric of operational and strategic decision-making. It is about transforming raw data-driven predictions into actionable intelligence that directly influences the entire asset lifecycle, from acquisition and deployment through to eventual decommissioning. The ultimate objective is to cultivate a holistic asset lifecycle management (ALM) approach, ensuring that each asset not only performs optimally throughout its intended service life but also contributes maximum economic value while simultaneously mitigating the inherent risks and substantial costs associated with unforeseen failures.

At its core, this integration bridges the gap between the technical realm of condition monitoring and failure prediction and the managerial domain of resource planning and capital allocation. When a predictive maintenance system, powered by advanced analytics or deep learning algorithms, forecasts an impending failure with a certain probability and estimates a Remaining Useful Life (RUL), this information must be channeled into the relevant asset management processes. This isn't merely about notifying a maintenance team; it's about empowering them with foresight to proactively adjust schedules, optimize spare parts procurement, reallocate resources, and even influence long-term capital expenditure plans. The shift is from a reactive or even proactive maintenance posture to a truly predictive and optimized strategy that synchronizes maintenance activities with the actual, evolving health of the asset, rather than with arbitrary time-based schedules or simple threshold breaches.

Consider the operationalization of RUL estimates. If a PdM system predicts that a critical pump in a manufacturing plant has an RUL of 200 operating hours, this figure becomes a powerful input for the maintenance scheduling module within the asset management system. Instead of relying on a fixed preventive maintenance interval of, say, every 500 operating hours, the maintenance planner can now schedule the pump's servicing or replacement precisely within that 200-hour window. This allows for maintenance to be performed during planned downtime, minimizing production disruption. Furthermore, the precision of this forecast allows for optimization against other operational demands. If the plant is expecting a high-demand period, the maintenance manager might aim to service the pump at the 180-hour mark, ensuring it is fully operational for the peak demand. Conversely, if there is a period of lower production, they might extend the service slightly, up to the 210-hour mark, as long as the probability of early failure remains acceptably low. This dynamic scheduling, informed by real-time asset health, represents a significant departure from traditional, less flexible maintenance planning.

The implications for spare parts inventory management are equally profound. Traditional inventory strategies often rely on historical consumption data and lead times, leading to either excessive stockholding of frequently used parts (to avoid stock-outs) or insufficient inventory of less frequently needed but critical components. Predictive maintenance transforms this by enabling a demand-driven, just-in-time (JIT) approach to spare parts. When the RUL of an asset, such as a gearbox, is predicted to be nearing its end, the asset management system can automatically trigger a request for the specific required spare parts. This allows procurement to order these parts well in advance, leveraging bulk discounts or ensuring their availability from suppliers without the need for carrying large, idle inventories of every conceivable part. This reduces capital tied up in inventory, minimizes storage costs, and crucially, reduces the risk of parts obsolescence. For specialized or expensive components, this just-in-time approach is particularly valuable. Instead of maintaining a $1 million spare turbine rotor 'just in case', a utility could receive an RUL prediction that warrants ordering the rotor six months in advance, securing it from the manufacturer at a more predictable cost and schedule, rather than facing a catastrophic outage and an emergency, premium-priced procurement.

Resource allocation also benefits immensely from integrated PdM. Maintenance teams are often multidisciplinary, comprising skilled technicians, engineers, and specialized equipment operators. In traditional models, resources are allocated based on a pre-defined maintenance schedule or on an emergency response basis. With PdM, resource needs become predictable and quantifiable. If multiple assets across a facility are predicted to require similar maintenance tasks within the same timeframe, the asset management system can help consolidate these needs. This allows for the efficient scheduling of teams and equipment, minimizing idle time for both personnel and specialized tools. For instance, if a fleet of specialized inspection drones is required for a series of pipeline integrity checks, and several of these checks are flagged for near-future maintenance based on PdM alerts, the system can optimize the deployment of these drones and their associated teams to cover all necessary inspections efficiently, rather than having them deployed piecemeal. This coordinated approach maximizes the utilization of expensive and specialized resources.

Beyond immediate operational maintenance, predictive maintenance insights play a critical role in long-term capital investment planning and asset replacement strategies. Asset management systems that incorporate PdM data can provide a more accurate picture of the true health and remaining economic life of an asset. This enables organizations to move away from arbitrary replacement cycles dictated by accounting depreciation or vendor recommendations, and towards data-driven decisions about when to repair, refurbish, or replace an asset. For example, if a fleet of trucks is consistently showing RUL predictions that indicate significant upcoming maintenance costs, the asset management system, armed with this data, can inform financial planners about the impending capital expenditure required for replacements. This allows for better budgeting, phased replacement strategies that align with capital availability, and the potential to defer major investments if PdM indicates that current assets can safely operate for a longer period with targeted interventions. This data-driven forecasting of capital needs is invaluable for financial stability and strategic growth.

The concept of "holistic asset lifecycle management" is the overarching goal that this integration serves. It means viewing an asset not as an isolated piece of equipment, but as a component within a larger system, with a defined beginning and end, and with value to be extracted at every stage. Predictive maintenance contributes to this by providing a continuous feedback loop on the asset's performance and health. This feedback informs decisions not only about maintenance but also about the design of future assets. If certain failure modes are consistently predicted and observed across a fleet of assets, this information can be fed back to design engineers to improve future iterations. For example, if vibration sensors on a particular model of industrial motor consistently predict bearing failures within a specific operating environment, this insight can lead to design modifications, such as improved sealing or a different bearing material, for the next generation of motors. This continuous improvement cycle, driven by real-world operational data and predictive insights, is central to maximizing the total economic value and service life of assets.

Furthermore, the integration of PdM into asset management systems facilitates a more robust approach to risk management. By understanding the likelihood and potential impact of equipment failures, organizations can better quantify and manage operational risks. The RUL predictions, combined with information about the criticality of the asset to operations, allow for a more sophisticated assessment of risk exposure. If a critical asset is predicted to fail soon, and the consequences of such a failure (production downtime, safety hazards, environmental impact) are high, the asset management system can prioritize its repair or replacement, thus proactively mitigating that risk. Conversely, if a less critical asset is approaching its RUL, the risk mitigation strategy might involve closer monitoring rather than immediate intervention. This nuanced approach to risk allows for more efficient allocation of resources, focusing attention and capital where they will have the greatest impact on overall risk reduction.

The strategic advantage gained from this integration cannot be overstated. Organizations that effectively leverage PdM within their asset management systems are able to achieve higher asset availability, reduced maintenance costs, extended asset lifespan, improved safety records, and enhanced operational efficiency. They are better equipped to respond to market demands, optimize production schedules, and maintain a competitive edge. This moves maintenance from being a cost center to becoming a strategic enabler of business objectives. The predictive insights become an integral part of the operational intelligence that drives informed business decisions. This holistic view ensures that investments in asset management are optimized for both performance and economic return over the entire lifecycle of the asset. The insights derived from PdM are not just about preventing breakdowns; they are about maximizing the value that each asset delivers to the organization. This requires a systems-level thinking where PdM data is not siloed but is a vital input to all relevant asset management functions.

Chapter 7: AI in Infrastructure Design and Planning

The advent of artificial intelligence within the realm of infrastructure design and planning has ushered in a transformative methodology known as generative design. This sophisticated approach moves beyond the traditional, iterative process of human-led design, where engineers and planners meticulously craft and refine individual concepts. Instead, generative design leverages AI algorithms to autonomously explore an expansive and complex design space, systematically generating a multitude of potential solutions. These solutions are not born from random iteration but are meticulously sculpted by a set of predefined objectives and stringent constraints. For infrastructure projects, this capability is particularly revolutionary. Imagine optimizing the intricate layout of a new highway network, the precise placement of a sprawling urban pipeline system, or the foundational design for a complex of buildings. Generative design can analyze these scenarios, seeking to achieve a delicate balance between competing demands. It can strive to minimize the ecological footprint of a development by identifying routes that avoid sensitive habitats, reduce the cost of construction through efficient material usage and simplified logistics, or maximize the operational efficiency of utilities by ensuring optimal flow and accessibility.

The power of generative design lies in its ability to process and analyze an unprecedented number of design permutations in a fraction of the time it would take human teams. Where a human designer might explore a handful of distinct approaches, AI can evaluate thousands, even millions, of variations, uncovering novel and often unexpected solutions. This is particularly critical when dealing with the inherent complexities of infrastructure development, where site-specific conditions, geological surveys, environmental regulations, and performance requirements must all be integrated into a coherent and optimized plan. For instance, when designing a new metro line, engineers must consider not only the most direct route between stations but also the impact on existing infrastructure, soil stability, groundwater levels, and the potential for noise pollution in residential areas. Generative design algorithms can be fed all these variables. They can then explore an array of tunnel alignments, station locations, and construction methods, identifying pathways that might be less intuitive to a human designer but are, in fact, more efficient, cost-effective, or environmentally benign. The algorithm would systematically test different gradient profiles for the tunnels, various depths for station excavation, and even different approaches to mitigating seismic risks, all while adhering to strict safety codes and budgetary limitations.

Consider the application of generative design to the intricate network of pipelines that form the backbone of modern urban life – water, sewage, gas, and telecommunications. Historically, the routing of these essential conduits has been a complex undertaking, often involving significant excavation and disruption. Generative design can transform this process. By inputting data such as existing underground utilities, geological strata, property boundaries, and anticipated future demand, AI can generate optimal routing solutions. These solutions would aim to minimize the number of road crossings, reduce the depth of required excavations, avoid areas with problematic soil conditions, and potentially even identify synergies between different pipeline types to share trenching where feasible. The algorithm could be programmed to prioritize minimizing disruption to traffic flow during construction, or to ensure that the most cost-effective materials are utilized for different sections of the network based on pressure requirements and soil corrosivity. Furthermore, it can explore scenarios for future expansion, designing the initial layout with built-in flexibility to accommodate new services or increased capacity without requiring costly re-excavation.

The process typically begins with the articulation of clear objectives and constraints. For a road network, objectives might include minimizing travel time between key points, reducing the number of traffic signals, and limiting the visual impact on surrounding landscapes. Constraints could encompass maximum allowable gradient to ensure accessibility for all vehicles, minimum setback distances from residential properties, preservation of existing green spaces, and adherence to specific construction material limitations. Once these parameters are defined, the AI engine initiates its search. It might start with a basic skeletal network and, through a process of iterative refinement, begin to flesh out the details. For example, it could explore variations in curve radii, lane configurations, and junction designs, constantly evaluating each iteration against the defined objectives and constraints. The output is not a single "best" solution but rather a portfolio of viable designs, each with its own set of trade-offs. This allows human planners to make informed decisions, selecting the design that best aligns with their overall project goals and priorities, even if it means accepting a slightly longer travel time in exchange for significantly reduced environmental impact.

The ability of generative design to conceive solutions that diverge from conventional thinking is a significant advantage. Human designers, while highly skilled, often operate within established paradigms and familiar design patterns. Generative design, unburdened by these ingrained habits, can propose unconventional geometries or material distributions that might be overlooked. For instance, in the design of bridge structures, generative design could explore lattice-like or organic forms that minimize material usage while maintaining structural integrity, leading to more aesthetically pleasing and sustainable constructions. Similarly, for the layout of solar farms, generative design could optimize the placement and orientation of panels not just for maximum sunlight exposure but also to minimize land use, reduce shading on adjacent panels, and account for the specific topography of the site to simplify maintenance access. The AI can simulate countless configurations of panel arrays, considering factors such as inter-panel spacing, tilt angles, and even the impact of wind patterns, to arrive at a layout that is both highly productive and harmoniously integrated into its environment.

Moreover, the speed and scale at which generative design can operate are invaluable in the context of infrastructure projects, which often face tight deadlines and budget pressures. The ability to rapidly generate and evaluate a wide spectrum of design possibilities allows for a more thorough exploration of the design space, reducing the risk of overlooking a superior solution. This accelerated process can also facilitate more timely decision-making. Instead of weeks or months spent on initial concept development and revision, preliminary designs can be generated in days or even hours, providing stakeholders with concrete options to review and discuss. This allows for earlier identification of potential challenges or opportunities, enabling proactive adjustments and preventing costly changes later in the project lifecycle.

The integration of real-world data is crucial for the effectiveness of generative design in infrastructure. This includes geographical information systems (GIS) data for terrain, soil conditions, and existing infrastructure; environmental data such as flood plains and ecological habitats; traffic flow data; and even socioeconomic data related to population density and accessibility needs. When these data layers are fed into the AI algorithms, the generated designs become highly contextualized and relevant to the specific site. For example, when designing a water distribution network for a new urban development, the generative design tool would consider not only the required flow rates and pressure but also the detailed topography of the area to minimize pumping energy. It would also incorporate information about the soil type to select appropriate pipe materials resistant to corrosion or settlement. The algorithm could even be tasked with optimizing the placement of fire hydrants to ensure adequate coverage while minimizing the visual clutter and potential disruption they might cause in public spaces.

The output of a generative design process is often presented as a series of design options, each visualized and accompanied by key performance indicators. These might include projected construction costs, estimated operational energy consumption, predicted environmental impact scores, and anticipated maintenance requirements. This rich dataset empowers human decision-makers with the information needed to compare different solutions objectively. For instance, a city planner might be presented with three viable designs for a new pedestrian bridge. Design A might be the most aesthetically striking but also the most expensive to build. Design B might offer the lowest construction cost but have a higher environmental footprint due to the materials used. Design C might strike a balance, offering good aesthetics and moderate cost, with a focus on sustainable material sourcing. The AI has effectively done the heavy lifting of exploring myriad possibilities, presenting the human experts with a curated selection of well-defined choices, allowing them to apply their judgment and project-specific priorities to make the final selection.

Furthermore, generative design can be applied to optimize the performance of existing infrastructure. For instance, it can be used to reconfigure traffic signal timings across a city to improve traffic flow and reduce emissions, or to optimize the placement of sensors for monitoring the structural health of bridges. In the context of smart cities, generative design algorithms can be employed to plan the most efficient deployment of charging stations for electric vehicles, ensuring they are strategically located to meet demand while minimizing their impact on the urban landscape and electrical grid. The AI can simulate various usage patterns and charging behaviors to identify optimal locations and capacities for these stations, considering factors such as proximity to residential areas, commercial centers, and major transportation routes.

The iterative nature of generative design also allows for continuous improvement and adaptation. As new data becomes available – perhaps from post-construction monitoring or changes in usage patterns – the design parameters can be updated, and the AI can generate revised layouts or modifications. This is particularly important for infrastructure that needs to remain functional and efficient for decades, if not centuries. For example, a system designed to manage stormwater runoff could be continually optimized using real-time rainfall data and sensor feedback, with the generative design algorithms suggesting adjustments to drainage pathways or reservoir capacities to better cope with changing climate patterns.

The successful implementation of generative design in infrastructure requires a robust data infrastructure and a collaborative approach between AI specialists and domain experts. The AI algorithms are only as good as the data they are fed, and the interpretation of the generated solutions requires the deep understanding and experience of civil engineers, urban planners, environmental scientists, and other infrastructure professionals. This synergy ensures that the AI-generated designs are not only technically sound and efficient but also socially responsible, environmentally sustainable, and aligned with the long-term vision for the infrastructure. The goal is not to replace human expertise but to augment it, providing tools that amplify creativity, accelerate innovation, and lead to more resilient, efficient, and sustainable infrastructure for the future. This partnership between human ingenuity and artificial intelligence is poised to redefine the very landscape of infrastructure development, enabling us to build better, smarter, and more responsive environments. The ability to explore a vast design space, identify optimal solutions based on complex criteria, and present a curated set of viable options empowers infrastructure professionals to tackle challenges with unprecedented efficiency and creativity, ultimately leading to a built environment that is more functional, sustainable, and responsive to the needs of society.

The selection of materials is a cornerstone of any infrastructure project, profoundly influencing its cost, performance, longevity, and environmental footprint. Traditionally, this process has relied on the accumulated knowledge and experience of engineers, who meticulously evaluate material specifications, consult extensive databases, and conduct rigorous testing. However, the sheer volume of available materials, coupled with the complexity of their performance characteristics under diverse environmental and operational stresses, presents a formidable challenge. Artificial intelligence offers a powerful new paradigm for optimizing this critical decision-making process, moving beyond human intuition and static data to uncover material selections that are both innovative and rigorously validated.

AI's capability to process and analyze vast datasets is directly applicable to the nuanced world of material science and engineering. By training machine learning models on comprehensive databases that detail the properties of countless materials – from traditional concrete and steel to advanced composites, engineered timber, and recycled aggregates – AI can identify patterns and correlations that might elude human observation. These databases encompass a wide array of attributes: mechanical properties such as tensile strength, compressive strength, elasticity, and fatigue resistance; physical properties like density, thermal conductivity, and fire resistance; and chemical properties related to corrosion resistance and reactivity. Beyond these intrinsic characteristics, AI can also integrate data pertaining to manufacturing processes, supply chain logistics, and the cost implications associated with each material. This holistic approach ensures that the material selection is not based on isolated performance metrics but on a comprehensive understanding of its lifecycle implications.

A key area where AI excels is in predicting material performance under specific, real-world conditions. Infrastructure is rarely static; it is subjected to a dynamic interplay of environmental factors, operational loads, and potential hazards. AI models, trained on historical performance data, simulation results, and sensor readings from existing structures, can forecast how different materials will behave over time when exposed to conditions such as extreme temperatures, moisture, chemical attack, seismic activity, and prolonged stress. For instance, when designing a bridge in a coastal environment, AI can analyze data on salt spray, humidity, and the specific loads the bridge will bear, then recommend materials that exhibit superior corrosion resistance and mechanical integrity under these precise conditions. This might lead to the selection of specialized concrete admixtures, high-performance steel alloys, or advanced polymer coatings, all identified by the AI as optimal for the given environmental context, far surpassing generic recommendations.

The imperative for sustainable infrastructure development further amplifies the value of AI in material selection. The concept of "embodied energy" – the total energy consumed in the extraction, manufacturing, and transportation of a material – is a critical consideration in reducing the carbon footprint of construction. AI algorithms can be tasked with quantifying and comparing the embodied energy of various material options, factoring in regional differences in energy production and transportation distances. Furthermore, AI can assess the recyclability and reusability of materials, promoting a circular economy approach. For example, in the design of a new building, AI could analyze the structural requirements and then propose a mix of materials that balances strength and durability with low embodied energy and high potential for end-of-life recycling. This might involve recommending timber from sustainably managed forests for certain structural elements, specifying recycled steel for reinforcement, or identifying innovative geopolymer concretes that utilize industrial byproducts instead of traditional cement. The AI can present a clear trade-off analysis, showing how different material combinations impact not only initial cost and performance but also long-term environmental sustainability goals.

Consider the design of a large-scale water management system, such as a dam or a complex network of pipes. The materials chosen for these projects must withstand immense hydrostatic pressure, resist erosion from water flow, and remain inert to prevent contamination. AI can analyze geological data of the site, hydrological models of water flow, and data on the chemical composition of the water itself. Based on this comprehensive input, the AI can recommend specific types of concrete formulations with tailored aggregate sizes and cementitious binders to maximize durability and minimize permeability. It could also suggest specialized liners or coatings for pipes, drawing from a vast library of polymers and composites, to ensure long-term protection against abrasion and chemical degradation. The AI's ability to cross-reference performance data across thousands of material variants allows it to identify the most cost-effective and resilient solutions for these demanding applications, potentially uncovering novel material pairings that human engineers might not have considered.

The economic implications of material selection are also significantly enhanced by AI. Beyond the upfront purchase cost, AI can factor in the long-term expenses associated with maintenance, repair, and eventual replacement. By analyzing data on the historical failure rates and maintenance needs of different materials in similar applications, AI can predict the total lifecycle cost of a project. This predictive capability allows for a more informed investment decision, prioritizing materials that, while potentially having a higher initial cost, offer substantial savings over the lifespan of the infrastructure due to their superior durability and reduced maintenance requirements. For instance, when designing a road or pavement, AI can analyze traffic volume, expected wear patterns, climate, and the performance history of various asphalt mixes or concrete formulations. It can then recommend a pavement design that minimizes long-term repair costs and disruption to traffic, even if it involves a slightly more expensive initial surface material.

The optimization of concrete mixes is a classic example of AI's potential in material selection. Concrete is a complex composite material, and its properties are highly dependent on the proportions of cement, aggregates (sand, gravel), water, and admixtures. AI can analyze a vast number of potential mix designs, each with varying ratios of these components, and predict the resulting compressive strength, workability, durability, and setting time. This is particularly valuable when designing for specific performance requirements, such as high-strength concrete for tall buildings, self-compacting concrete for complex formwork, or concrete resistant to freeze-thaw cycles in cold climates. By feeding AI with data on local aggregate availability and cost, along with desired performance metrics, engineers can rapidly identify the optimal concrete mix that maximizes performance while minimizing cost and environmental impact. The AI can even suggest specific types and dosages of admixtures, such as fly ash or silica fume, to enhance durability and reduce the cement content, thereby lowering embodied carbon.

Beyond traditional materials, AI is also instrumental in the adoption of advanced composites and novel materials. These materials, such as fiber-reinforced polymers (FRPs), engineered wood products, and nanomaterials, offer exceptional strength-to-weight ratios, corrosion resistance, and design flexibility. However, their application can be complex due to a less established body of knowledge and performance data compared to conventional materials. AI can bridge this gap by processing research findings, laboratory test results, and performance data from pilot projects. For example, in the design of a lightweight bridge or a façade system, AI can analyze the structural loads and environmental exposures, then recommend specific FRP configurations (e.g., carbon fiber, glass fiber, resin types) that offer the best balance of strength, stiffness, durability, and cost. This allows engineers to confidently incorporate these cutting-edge materials, unlocking new possibilities in structural design and material efficiency.

The AI-driven material selection process typically involves several key steps. Firstly, project-specific requirements are defined, including performance criteria (strength, durability, fire resistance), environmental constraints (sustainability targets, local climate), economic considerations (budget, lifecycle cost), and aesthetic preferences. Secondly, a comprehensive dataset of potential materials, including their properties, costs, and historical performance, is curated and fed into the AI model. The AI then employs various machine learning techniques, such as regression analysis, classification, and optimization algorithms, to evaluate the suitability of each material against the defined requirements. Finally, the AI outputs a ranked list of recommended materials or material combinations, often accompanied by predictive performance data, lifecycle cost analyses, and sustainability metrics. This empowers the human engineer to make a final, informed decision, leveraging the AI's analytical power to supplement their own expertise.

The integration of AI in material selection is not about replacing the engineer but about augmenting their capabilities. It provides them with a powerful tool to explore a far broader range of possibilities, analyze complex interactions, and make more data-driven decisions. This leads to infrastructure that is not only more robust and cost-effective but also more sustainable and resilient, capable of meeting the challenges of the 21st century and beyond. The continuous learning nature of AI also means that as more data becomes available from ongoing projects and research, the accuracy and effectiveness of these material selection models will continue to improve, driving further innovation in the field of infrastructure engineering. This evolving partnership between human intelligence and artificial intelligence promises to redefine the very foundations of how we build our world, ensuring that the materials we choose serve us well, for generations to come.

The intelligent selection of sites for infrastructure development, coupled with a thorough assessment of associated risks, represents a critical juncture in the lifecycle of any major project. Historically, this complex undertaking has relied heavily on the seasoned judgment of planners and engineers, who would painstakingly gather and interpret a multitude of data points. This process often involved extensive fieldwork, manual analysis of maps and surveys, consultation with local communities, and a deep understanding of historical precedents and potential environmental impacts. However, the sheer scale and complexity of modern infrastructure projects, alongside the growing imperative to build resilient and sustainable systems, have increasingly strained the limitations of traditional methods. Artificial intelligence is emerging as a transformative force in this domain, offering unparalleled capabilities to process vast datasets, identify subtle patterns, and predict potential challenges with a level of precision previously unattainable.

AI's prowess in analyzing diverse and voluminous datasets makes it exceptionally suited for the intricate task of site selection. By integrating and processing a wide array of information – including high-resolution satellite imagery, topographical maps, geological surveys, demographic projections, land use patterns, socioeconomic data, and climate models – AI can identify optimal locations for a broad spectrum of infrastructure. Consider, for instance, the placement of a new renewable energy facility, such as a wind farm or a solar power plant. AI algorithms can sift through terabytes of data to pinpoint areas that offer the most favorable wind speeds or solar irradiance, while simultaneously considering proximity to existing grid infrastructure for efficient power transmission. Furthermore, these algorithms can evaluate factors like land availability, zoning regulations, environmental impact assessments, and potential visual or noise pollution concerns, presenting a holistic picture of suitability for each potential site. This data-driven approach moves beyond simple adjacency to grid connections or open land, enabling a more nuanced and strategic selection that maximizes operational efficiency and minimizes negative externalities.

Beyond energy infrastructure, AI's application extends to other critical sectors. For the siting of a new waste disposal facility, AI can analyze geological stability, groundwater vulnerability, proximity to residential areas, transportation logistics, and long-term containment feasibility. Similarly, when planning new transportation hubs – be it airports, railway stations, or logistics centers – AI can optimize locations based on current and projected traffic flows, accessibility for diverse user groups, potential for integration with other transport modes, and the economic impact on surrounding regions. The ability of AI to perform multi-criteria optimization allows for the simultaneous consideration of numerous, often competing, factors, leading to site selections that are not only technically sound but also economically viable and socially responsible. This is particularly valuable when balancing the need for proximity to populations or resources with the requirement for buffer zones or minimal environmental disruption.

Geospatial data analysis forms a cornerstone of AI-assisted site selection. Advanced AI models, particularly those employing deep learning techniques, can interpret complex spatial relationships from satellite imagery, aerial photography, and geographic information systems (GIS). For example, when selecting a location for a new hospital or emergency services facility, AI can analyze population density, travel times from various neighborhoods under different traffic conditions, accessibility for emergency vehicles, and proximity to potential hazard zones. It can identify areas that are currently underserved or that are projected to experience significant population growth, ensuring that critical services are strategically positioned for maximum reach and effectiveness. The AI can also learn to identify subtle features within the landscape, such as optimal drainage patterns or areas less prone to subsidence, which might be easily overlooked in manual analyses.

The integration of demographic and socioeconomic data further refines site selection. AI can analyze census data, income levels, employment statistics, and population growth trends to understand the needs and characteristics of communities. This information is crucial for locating public facilities, educational institutions, or commercial developments. For a new public school, for instance, AI can forecast future student enrollment based on housing development patterns and birth rates, suggesting optimal locations that minimize busing distances and ensure equitable access for all children. This predictive capability is invaluable for long-term urban planning, allowing for proactive development that aligns with demographic shifts rather than reactive responses.

However, site selection is only one part of the equation. A fundamental aspect of AI's contribution lies in its ability to conduct comprehensive risk assessments. Infrastructure projects are inherently exposed to a multitude of potential hazards, ranging from natural disasters to operational failures. AI can analyze historical data on seismic activity, flood patterns, extreme weather events, landslide occurrences, and soil instability to predict the likelihood and potential severity of these risks at various potential sites. By processing data from geological surveys, meteorological records, and sensor networks, AI models can generate detailed risk maps, highlighting areas with high susceptibility to earthquakes, flooding, or subsidence.

Consider the development of a new bridge or tunnel. AI can analyze historical flood data, river flow rates, predicted changes in precipitation patterns due to climate change, and the proposed structure's elevation relative to water levels to assess flood risk. It can also analyze geological data to predict the potential for soil liquefaction or landslides in the vicinity of the construction site, particularly if it is in a seismically active zone or on a slope. This information is vital for determining the most suitable location, designing appropriate protective measures, and setting appropriate construction standards. For example, if an AI model identifies a high risk of seismic activity at a particular site for a new building, it can recommend deeper foundations, seismic isolation systems, or the use of more robust structural materials.

The assessment of geological risks is a prime example of AI's utility. By analyzing borehole data, seismic refraction surveys, and ground-penetrating radar readings, AI can create detailed three-dimensional models of subsurface conditions. This allows for the identification of hidden geological faults, unstable soil layers, or underground water channels that could pose significant risks to the structural integrity of an infrastructure project. For underground infrastructure like subways or utility tunnels, AI can predict the excavation challenges, the potential for groundwater ingress, and the need for specific ground support systems, thereby informing both the site selection and the detailed design process.

Furthermore, AI can integrate real-time environmental monitoring data with historical records to predict and assess emerging risks. For instance, in coastal areas, AI can analyze sea-level rise projections, storm surge data, and coastal erosion rates to identify sites that are increasingly vulnerable to inundation or extreme weather damage. This foresight allows planners to either select less vulnerable locations or to incorporate enhanced resilience measures, such as elevated platforms, robust seawalls, or alternative foundation designs, into the project from the outset. This proactive approach to risk management is essential for ensuring the long-term viability and safety of infrastructure in the face of a changing climate.

The application of AI in risk assessment extends to operational hazards as well. For facilities like power plants or chemical processing units, AI can analyze historical incident data, operational parameters, and maintenance records to identify potential failure points and predict the likelihood of accidents. This can inform the selection of sites that offer better access for emergency response, are located away from densely populated areas, or have favorable geological conditions that minimize the impact of any potential event. The AI can also simulate various failure scenarios to assess the effectiveness of proposed safety protocols and emergency response plans, guiding the development of more robust and reliable infrastructure.

The synergistic relationship between AI-assisted site selection and risk assessment provides a powerful framework for informed decision-making. By using AI to simultaneously identify potential locations and evaluate their associated hazards, engineers and planners can avoid costly errors, minimize project delays, and ensure the long-term resilience and sustainability of critical infrastructure. For example, when planning a new highway or railway line, AI can analyze topographical data to find the most cost-effective route (minimizing earthworks and bridges) while also assessing the risk of landslides, flooding, or areas of unstable soil along potential corridors. This integrated approach allows for the identification of routes that not only meet functional requirements but also minimize environmental impact and construction risks.

The process typically begins with defining the project's functional requirements and constraints. These might include the need for specific capacity, proximity to certain points, environmental performance targets, and budget limitations. Subsequently, AI algorithms are fed with vast datasets encompassing geographic, environmental, demographic, and geological information. These algorithms then undertake a multi-faceted analysis. For site selection, they might employ techniques such as spatial clustering, suitability analysis, and optimization algorithms to identify areas that best meet the defined criteria. Concurrently, for risk assessment, machine learning models, including regression analysis, anomaly detection, and probabilistic forecasting, are utilized to quantify the likelihood and potential impact of various natural and man-made hazards.

The output from these AI systems is not a definitive answer but rather a suite of ranked options, each accompanied by detailed analyses of suitability, risks, and potential mitigation strategies. For instance, the AI might present three optimal site locations for a new data center, along with detailed reports on the seismic hazard, flood risk, power availability, and connectivity for each. It could also suggest specific design modifications or operational procedures needed to address identified risks at each location. This empowers human experts to make the final, informed decision, leveraging AI's analytical power to explore a far wider range of possibilities and gain deeper insights into potential challenges than would be possible with traditional methods.

The continuous learning capability of AI further enhances its value in this domain. As new data becomes available – through ongoing geological monitoring, updated climate models, or the performance of existing infrastructure – AI models can be retrained and refined. This ensures that site selection and risk assessments remain current and adaptive, crucial for projects with long lifespans in a rapidly evolving world. The ability to learn from real-world performance and unexpected events allows AI to continuously improve its predictive accuracy, leading to increasingly robust and resilient infrastructure planning for future generations. This ongoing refinement is paramount as we face increasingly complex environmental and societal challenges.

The dynamic nature of our planet and the evolving demands of society necessitate an approach to infrastructure development that is not only robust in the present but also resilient and adaptable to the uncertainties of the future. Artificial intelligence offers a groundbreaking pathway to achieve this foresight through sophisticated simulation capabilities. By leveraging AI, we can move beyond static design principles and explore the potential performance of infrastructure under a wide spectrum of plausible future scenarios. This allows engineers and planners to proactively identify weaknesses, optimize designs for longevity, and ensure that critical assets can withstand the challenges that lie ahead, thereby safeguarding public safety, economic stability, and environmental well-being.

One of the most pressing future scenarios that AI-powered simulations can help us address is the impact of climate change. As global temperatures rise, we are witnessing profound shifts in weather patterns, sea levels, and the frequency and intensity of extreme events. For coastal infrastructure, such as ports, bridges, and seawalls, the simulated impact of sea-level rise and increased storm surges is a critical area of investigation. AI can integrate sophisticated climate models that project future sea-level changes with detailed topographical data of a proposed site. By running simulations, engineers can visualize how a specific bridge design might be inundated during a storm surge of a certain magnitude under a mid-century or end-of-century climate projection. This allows for the evaluation of different foundation heights, the effectiveness of proposed protective barriers, and the identification of optimal locations that are less vulnerable. For instance, an AI simulation might reveal that a particular proposed bridge design, while functionally sound today, would experience critical structural stress or even complete inundation under a worst-case sea-level rise scenario combined with a Category 4 hurricane. Armed with this knowledge, designers can then explore design alternatives, such as elevating the roadway, incorporating advanced flood-resistant materials, or even reconsidering the site altogether, thereby preventing potentially catastrophic failures and enormous costs associated with disaster recovery and reconstruction.

Beyond coastal regions, the increased intensity of rainfall events and the potential for more severe inland flooding present another significant challenge that AI simulations can help mitigate. For infrastructure like urban drainage systems, wastewater treatment plants, and even underground transportation networks, the ability to simulate performance under extreme precipitation events is crucial. AI can be used to develop highly granular hydrological models that account for factors like impervious surface cover, soil saturation levels, and the capacity of existing and proposed storm drains. By simulating scenarios with rainfall intensities exceeding historical records, based on climate projections, engineers can test the capacity of the designed system to handle the increased water volume. An AI-driven simulation might demonstrate that a proposed stormwater management system, designed to current standards, would be overwhelmed during a "100-year storm" event projected to occur more frequently in the future. This would prompt a reassessment of pipe sizes, detention basin volumes, and the inclusion of green infrastructure solutions, such as permeable pavements or bioswales, which can help absorb excess water. For underground structures, simulations can reveal the likelihood of water ingress and the effectiveness of waterproofing and pumping systems under prolonged inundation. This proactive approach avoids the costly and disruptive consequences of flooded subway lines or overwhelmed sewage systems, ensuring the continuity of essential services.

The projected shifts in global temperatures also have implications for infrastructure that relies on stable environmental conditions. For example, the performance of thermal power plants, data centers that require significant cooling, and even the durability of road surfaces and railway tracks can be affected by rising ambient temperatures. AI simulations can model the thermal stress on materials and the increased energy demands for cooling systems under future heatwave scenarios. By simulating the operation of a proposed data center during a prolonged period of significantly higher average temperatures and more frequent heatwaves, AI can predict the strain on cooling infrastructure and the potential for system failures. This could lead to the integration of more efficient cooling technologies, the use of heat-reflective materials in construction, or the strategic placement of facilities in areas projected to experience less extreme temperature increases. Similarly, for road and rail infrastructure, AI simulations can assess the impact of increased temperatures on material deformation, rutting, and the risk of rail buckling, guiding the selection of more resilient materials and construction techniques.

Population growth and urbanization are also powerful drivers that AI-driven simulations can help infrastructure planners anticipate and manage. As cities expand and populations increase, the demand for services such as transportation, water supply, energy, and waste management escalates. AI can analyze demographic projections, migration patterns, and land-use changes to forecast future demand on existing and proposed infrastructure. For a public transportation network, AI simulations can model the impact of projected population increases in suburban areas on commuter flows, public transit ridership, and congestion on arterial roads. By simulating traffic patterns under these future conditions, planners can identify bottlenecks, assess the need for new transit lines or expanded capacity, and optimize route planning to serve growing communities effectively. This goes beyond simply extrapolating current trends; AI can incorporate complex interactions between land use, transportation choices, and economic development to provide a more nuanced and accurate picture of future demand. For instance, a simulation might reveal that a planned expansion of a highway system, while adequate for current traffic, will become saturated within two decades due to projected residential growth in a particular corridor, necessitating a shift in investment towards public transit solutions or more integrated mobility strategies.

Furthermore, AI-powered simulations are invaluable for testing the adaptability of infrastructure designs to evolving policy and regulatory landscapes. Governments may introduce new environmental standards, energy efficiency mandates, or safety regulations that could impact the long-term viability of existing designs. AI can be used to simulate the performance of an infrastructure project against these potential future policy shifts. For example, if a government is considering implementing stricter regulations on carbon emissions from industrial facilities, AI simulations can model the operational efficiency and emissions profile of a proposed power plant under these future regulatory conditions. This allows for the design of facilities that are not only compliant with current standards but also capable of meeting future, more stringent requirements, thereby avoiding costly retrofits or premature decommissioning. Similarly, simulations can assess the impact of new urban planning policies, such as requirements for increased green space or pedestrian-friendly designs, on the functionality and cost-effectiveness of proposed developments.

The complexity of these future scenarios, involving interconnected environmental, social, and economic factors, often exceeds the capabilities of traditional simulation methods. This is where AI truly shines. Machine learning algorithms can learn from vast datasets of historical performance, sensor data, and environmental monitoring to build highly predictive models. These models can then be integrated into simulation frameworks to capture non-linear relationships and emergent behaviors that might be missed by simpler analytical tools. For instance, simulating the long-term resilience of a complex network, such as an electrical grid or a water distribution system, requires understanding how failures in one component can cascade and affect others. AI can learn these intricate dependencies and simulate the system's response to various disruptions, whether they are caused by extreme weather, cyber-attacks, or component degradation. This allows for the identification of critical vulnerabilities and the development of robust redundancy and response strategies.

The process of using AI for future scenario simulation typically involves several key steps. First, specific future scenarios of interest are defined. These might include a range of climate change impacts (e.g., low, medium, and high emissions pathways), population growth projections for different regions, or hypothetical policy changes. Second, relevant data is gathered. This includes historical environmental data, climate model outputs, demographic statistics, land-use maps, engineering design specifications, and data on the performance of existing infrastructure. Third, AI models are trained using this data to create predictive simulations. These models can range from sophisticated physics-based simulations enhanced with AI for parameter estimation and optimization, to purely data-driven machine learning models that learn complex relationships directly from data. Fourth, the trained AI models are used to run simulations of the proposed infrastructure design under the defined future scenarios. This involves inputting the design parameters and then observing the simulated performance metrics over time, under various conditions. Finally, the simulation results are analyzed to assess the robustness, adaptability, and long-term viability of the design. This analysis can identify critical failure points, areas where performance may degrade, and opportunities for design optimization or the implementation of adaptive management strategies.

For example, consider the simulation of a large-scale water reservoir system. Future scenarios might include prolonged droughts, increased demand due to population growth, and more intense rainfall events leading to potential dam overtopping. AI models could simulate water levels, inflow and outflow rates, and the structural integrity of the dam under these combined conditions. The simulation might reveal that under a severe drought scenario followed by exceptionally heavy rainfall, the reservoir's capacity would be insufficient, leading to water shortages, and simultaneously, the dam's spillway might not be adequate to handle the peak inflow, posing a risk of overtopping. This would then inform decisions about increasing storage capacity, reinforcing the spillway, or developing more sophisticated water allocation strategies.

Another crucial aspect is the simulation of the interaction between different infrastructure systems. In reality, transportation, energy, water, and communication networks are all interconnected. A disruption in one system can have cascading effects on others. AI is particularly adept at modeling these complex interdependencies. For instance, simulating the impact of a major power outage (perhaps caused by a severe storm) on transportation systems could reveal how traffic light failures lead to gridlock, how electric vehicle charging stations become inoperable, and how public transport reliant on electricity grinds to a halt. This holistic simulation capability allows planners to design more resilient, integrated infrastructure systems that can withstand shocks and recover quickly.

The iterative nature of AI-powered simulation is also a significant advantage. The output of a simulation is not necessarily a final verdict but rather a starting point for further refinement. If a simulation reveals a potential weakness, designers can modify the design, update the simulation parameters, and run new simulations to test the effectiveness of the changes. This iterative process, guided by AI's analytical power, allows for a continuous improvement loop, leading to increasingly optimized and resilient infrastructure designs. This is far more efficient and cost-effective than discovering design flaws after construction, which can lead to expensive retrofits or premature replacement.

Ultimately, the integration of AI-powered simulations into infrastructure design and planning represents a paradigm shift. It moves us from a reactive approach, where we often address problems after they arise, to a proactive and predictive one. By rigorously testing designs against a spectrum of plausible futures – from the slow-burn effects of climate change to the sudden shocks of extreme weather events and the continuous pressure of societal growth – we can build infrastructure that is not only functional and efficient today but also robust, adaptable, and sustainable for generations to come. This foresight is not merely an advantage; it is a necessity for building the resilient societies of the 21st century and beyond.

The advent of artificial intelligence heralds a transformative era for urban planning and the intricate design of interconnected infrastructure networks. As our metropolises grow in complexity and population density, the challenges of ensuring efficient service delivery, sustainable resource management, and an enhanced quality of life for residents become increasingly formidable. Traditional urban planning approaches, often relying on static data analysis and linear projections, struggle to keep pace with the dynamic, multi-faceted nature of urban environments. AI, with its capacity to process vast datasets, identify subtle patterns, and model complex interactions, offers a powerful suite of tools to address these challenges comprehensively.

At its core, AI empowers urban planners to move beyond fragmented sectoral considerations and embrace a holistic, systems-thinking approach. Instead of designing transportation, energy, water, and communication networks in isolation, AI can analyze the intricate interdependencies between these critical urban systems. By understanding how changes in one sector might propagate and impact others, planners can design more resilient, efficient, and integrated urban infrastructure. For instance, AI algorithms can ingest data from traffic sensors, public transit usage, weather forecasts, and even social media trends to predict mobility patterns with unprecedented accuracy. These predictions can then inform the dynamic optimization of public transit routes, ensuring that buses and trains are deployed where and when they are most needed, thereby reducing congestion, minimizing travel times, and improving passenger experience. Furthermore, AI can identify optimal locations for new transit stops or hubs based on projected population growth, employment centers, and existing pedestrian flows, creating a more responsive and demand-driven public transportation system.

The optimization of energy infrastructure, often referred to as "smart grids," is another area where AI is making significant inroads. Modern cities consume vast amounts of energy, and ensuring a stable, reliable, and increasingly renewable energy supply is paramount. AI can analyze energy consumption patterns across different districts and time periods, predict peak demand loads, and optimize the distribution of electricity from various sources, including renewable ones like solar and wind power. This predictive capability allows for more efficient energy generation and storage, reducing waste and reliance on fossil fuels. For example, AI can forecast periods of high solar energy production and low demand, prompting the system to store excess energy in batteries for later use during periods of low production and high demand. Conversely, during periods of exceptionally high demand, AI can intelligently manage load shedding or activate demand-response programs, encouraging consumers to reduce their energy usage during critical times through incentives. This level of granular control and predictive optimization not only enhances grid stability but also facilitates a smoother transition towards a greener energy future.

Similarly, AI is revolutionizing the design and management of urban water systems. Water scarcity and aging infrastructure are pressing concerns for many cities worldwide. AI can analyze water consumption data, identify leakage points in distribution networks through sensor data anomaly detection, and predict future water demand based on population growth and climate projections. This allows for more efficient water management, reducing water loss and ensuring equitable distribution. For example, AI models can simulate the impact of drought conditions on water supply and demand, enabling planners to develop proactive water conservation strategies and optimize the operation of reservoirs and treatment plants. Moreover, AI can assist in the design of more resilient and efficient wastewater management systems. By analyzing data on sewage flow, pollutant levels, and rainfall, AI can help optimize the capacity and operation of treatment facilities, predict and mitigate the impact of combined sewer overflows during heavy rainfall, and even identify opportunities for water recycling and reuse.

The concept of the "smart city" is intrinsically linked to the intelligent integration of AI across all urban infrastructure domains. AI acts as the central nervous system, enabling seamless communication and coordination between different services. Waste management, for instance, can be significantly enhanced by AI. Smart bins equipped with sensors can report their fill levels, allowing AI algorithms to optimize collection routes for waste management vehicles. This reduces fuel consumption, minimizes traffic disruption caused by garbage trucks, and ensures that waste is collected efficiently before it overflows. Beyond simple route optimization, AI can analyze waste generation patterns across the city to inform policy decisions, such as the placement of new recycling facilities or the implementation of targeted waste reduction campaigns in areas with particularly high generation rates.

Furthermore, AI's ability to model complex urban dynamics extends to land-use planning and development. By analyzing factors such as demographic trends, economic activity, housing demand, and transportation accessibility, AI can help planners identify optimal locations for new residential, commercial, and industrial developments. This can lead to more sustainable urban growth patterns that minimize sprawl, reduce commuting distances, and preserve valuable green spaces. For example, AI could simulate the impact of a proposed new housing development on local traffic congestion, school enrollment, and demand for public services, providing planners with crucial data to make informed decisions. It can also help in identifying areas that are underserved by existing infrastructure, guiding the prioritization of investments in new utilities or transportation links.

The design of communication networks, the backbone of any smart city, is also profoundly influenced by AI. With the ever-increasing demand for high-speed internet, mobile connectivity, and the proliferation of Internet of Things (IoT) devices, AI plays a crucial role in designing and managing robust and scalable communication infrastructure. AI algorithms can analyze network traffic patterns, predict congestion points, and dynamically allocate bandwidth to ensure optimal performance. This includes managing the deployment of 5G networks, ensuring seamless coverage, and optimizing the placement of cell towers and fiber optic cables based on predicted usage and terrain analysis. AI can also be used to enhance cybersecurity for these networks, detecting and responding to threats in real-time, thereby protecting critical urban services from disruption.

A critical aspect of AI's contribution to urban planning and network design is its capacity to foster citizen engagement and personalize urban services. By analyzing anonymized data on how residents interact with their city – how they move, where they shop, what services they use – AI can help identify community needs and preferences. This information can then be used to tailor urban planning decisions and service delivery to better meet the specific requirements of different neighborhoods and demographic groups. For example, AI-driven platforms could be used to gather citizen feedback on proposed development projects, analyze sentiment from public forums, and even predict the impact of new infrastructure on different communities, thereby fostering a more inclusive and participatory planning process. Imagine an AI system that can simulate the impact of a new park on a neighborhood's social cohesion and physical activity levels, based on existing usage patterns of similar facilities in other parts of the city and demographic profiles of the residents.

The interconnectedness of urban systems means that designing one without considering the others can lead to unforeseen consequences. AI's strength lies in its ability to model these interdependencies. For instance, a new public transportation initiative, while seemingly beneficial for mobility, might increase energy demand for powering electric trains or buses, which in turn could strain the local power grid if not planned in conjunction with energy infrastructure upgrades. AI can simulate these cascading effects, allowing planners to anticipate and mitigate potential conflicts. It can model how increased electric vehicle adoption, while reducing tailpipe emissions, will necessitate significant upgrades to charging infrastructure and the electrical grid's capacity to handle the increased load, especially during peak charging hours. By considering these interdependencies, AI enables the creation of truly integrated urban systems where each component supports and enhances the others.

The application of AI in urban planning and network design is not merely about efficiency; it is also about creating more sustainable and livable cities. By optimizing resource use, reducing waste and pollution, and improving the functionality of urban services, AI contributes to a higher quality of life for residents. For example, AI-powered traffic management systems can reduce vehicle idling times, thereby lowering air pollution and noise levels in urban centers. Smart energy grids can integrate more renewable energy sources, reducing the city's carbon footprint. Optimized water management systems can conserve precious water resources, and efficient waste management reduces the environmental impact of landfills. Ultimately, AI empowers cities to grow and evolve in a way that is both environmentally responsible and socially equitable.

As AI technologies continue to mature, their role in shaping our urban future will only become more pronounced. The ability to perform complex simulations, analyze vast datasets, and predict future trends allows for a level of foresight and precision in urban planning that was previously unattainable. This empowers city leaders and planners to make more informed, data-driven decisions, leading to the development of cities that are not only functional and efficient but also resilient, sustainable, and truly responsive to the needs of their inhabitants. The ongoing integration of AI into the fabric of urban development promises to unlock new possibilities for creating smarter, greener, and more livable urban environments for generations to come.

Chapter 8: Socio-Technical Dimensions: Equity and Accessibility

The pursuit of equitable infrastructure services is not merely a matter of technical efficiency or economic viability; it is fundamentally a social justice imperative. At its core, equity in this context signifies the fair and just distribution of both the benefits derived from infrastructure and the burdens associated with its development and maintenance, across all strata of society. This means that essential services and the opportunities they unlock should be accessible to everyone, regardless of their socioeconomic status, race, ethnicity, geographic location, age, or ability. It extends beyond mere equal access to encompass the actual lived experience of service delivery and the avoidance of disproportionate negative impacts on vulnerable populations.

When we speak of infrastructure, we are referring to the foundational physical and organizational structures and facilities needed for the operation of a society or enterprise. This encompasses a wide array of systems: transportation networks that move people and goods; energy grids that power our homes and industries; water and sanitation systems that safeguard public health; communication networks that connect us; and public spaces that foster community life. The equitable provision of these services means that a family living in a low-income neighborhood should have the same reliable access to clean water, affordable and consistent electricity, safe and efficient public transportation, and high-speed internet as a family residing in an affluent area. It also means that the placement of undesirable infrastructure, such as waste treatment facilities or polluting industrial sites, should not be disproportionately concentrated in communities that already bear the brunt of environmental and social disadvantages.

The historical trajectory of infrastructure development in many parts of the world reveals a persistent pattern of inequity. In numerous instances, investments in infrastructure have followed existing patterns of wealth and power, leading to underinvestment in marginalized communities and exacerbating existing disparities. This can manifest in several ways. For example, public transportation systems might be robust and frequent in wealthier districts, offering convenient commutes to employment centers, while in poorer neighborhoods, routes may be infrequent, unreliable, and fail to connect residents to essential services and job opportunities. This lack of mobility can trap individuals and families in cycles of poverty, limiting their access to education, healthcare, and better-paying jobs. The benefits of connectivity, which is increasingly crucial in the digital age, are thus unequally distributed.

Similarly, access to clean and reliable water is a fundamental human right, yet many communities, particularly those in developing nations or in underserved rural and urban areas within developed nations, lack this basic necessity. Infrastructure failures, inadequate maintenance, or inequitable distribution policies can lead to persistent water shortages, contamination, or prohibitively high costs, disproportionately impacting low-income households and communities of color. These communities often bear the brunt of water-related health issues and the economic burden of seeking alternative, often more expensive, water sources. The construction and upkeep of these vital systems are therefore not neutral acts; they carry profound social consequences.

The provision of affordable and reliable energy is another critical dimension of infrastructure equity. In many regions, energy poverty remains a significant challenge, where households struggle to afford the electricity needed for basic needs like heating, lighting, and cooking. This can lead to severe health consequences, such as respiratory illnesses from indoor air pollution caused by burning solid fuels, and can hinder educational outcomes for children who cannot study in well-lit environments. Furthermore, the transition to cleaner energy sources, while environmentally necessary, must be managed equitably. Without careful planning, the costs of new energy infrastructure, such as the upgrading of grids or the implementation of new technologies, could be passed on to consumers in a way that further burdens those least able to pay, or the benefits of renewable energy installations could be concentrated in wealthier areas, leaving disadvantaged communities reliant on older, less efficient, and more polluting energy sources.

The digital divide represents a contemporary manifestation of infrastructure inequity. In an era where access to information, online education, remote work opportunities, and essential government services increasingly relies on reliable internet connectivity, the lack of access in many communities creates a profound disadvantage. Low-income urban neighborhoods, rural areas, and remote indigenous communities often suffer from a lack of broadband infrastructure, or they may have access only to slow, expensive, and unreliable services. This digital exclusion not only limits economic opportunities but also hinders social participation and access to vital information, further marginalizing already vulnerable populations. Ensuring equitable digital access is therefore as crucial as ensuring access to water or electricity.

The very process of planning and implementing infrastructure projects can also be a source of inequity if not managed with a strong commitment to social justice. Often, decisions about where to build new roads, power plants, or waste disposal sites are made without meaningful consultation with the communities most likely to be affected. This can lead to the imposition of burdens on communities that have historically been excluded from decision-making processes, reinforcing cycles of environmental racism and social injustice. For instance, highways have historically been routed through predominantly Black and low-income neighborhoods, disrupting communities, increasing pollution, and decreasing property values, while simultaneously facilitating commutes for more affluent populations.

Therefore, the concept of equity in infrastructure services must be integrated into the very fabric of planning, design, construction, and operation from the outset of any project. It cannot be an afterthought or a mere compliance checklist. This requires a proactive approach that involves identifying potential impacts on different communities, engaging stakeholders in a genuine and inclusive manner, and designing solutions that actively promote fairness and reduce disparities. It means prioritizing investments in underserved areas, ensuring that the benefits of modernization reach everyone, and establishing mechanisms for accountability and redress when inequities arise. This foundational understanding of equity sets the stage for examining how socio-technical systems can be designed and managed to achieve a more just and inclusive urban future.

Understanding and addressing infrastructural disparities is a complex undertaking that begins with a clear and robust methodology for identification and measurement. Without precise tools and techniques to pinpoint where and how these inequities manifest, any efforts towards achieving greater equity will remain superficial and ineffectual. This subsection delves into the critical approaches required to diagnose the extent of infrastructural disadvantages, moving beyond anecdotal evidence to establish quantifiable metrics and spatial understandings of service gaps. It is through rigorous analysis that we can effectively advocate for targeted interventions and hold stakeholders accountable for delivering equitable access to essential services.

A cornerstone in identifying infrastructure disparities lies in the meticulous analysis of socio-economic data. This involves disaggregating demographic information – such as income levels, educational attainment, racial and ethnic composition, age, and disability status – and overlaying it with data pertaining to infrastructure provision. For instance, mapping household income against access to reliable public transportation routes can vividly illustrate how lower-income neighborhoods are often served by less frequent, more circuitous, and ultimately less effective transit options. Similarly, correlating areas with high concentrations of elderly populations or individuals with mobility impairments with the availability of accessible sidewalks, curb cuts, and accessible public transit stops can reveal critical gaps in planning that prioritize convenience over inclusivity. The granularity of this analysis is paramount; aggregated data can mask significant disparities within seemingly uniform geographic areas. By examining data at the census tract or even block group level, we can uncover pockets of severe under-service that might otherwise be overlooked. This data-driven approach allows for a more objective assessment of need and highlights the specific populations that are being disproportionately burdened or excluded by current infrastructure configurations.

Complementing socio-economic analysis, Geographic Information Systems (GIS) offer an indispensable tool for visualizing and quantifying spatial disparities in infrastructure access and quality. GIS allows for the creation of detailed maps that depict the physical distribution of infrastructure services and their proximity to different population groups. For example, by inputting the locations of water treatment plants, sewer lines, and potable water sources, alongside data on the housing units they serve, GIS can map areas experiencing inadequate water pressure, frequent service interruptions, or contamination risks. This spatial layering can also identify "service deserts," areas that are geographically distant from essential services, such as hospitals, well-equipped schools, or reliable broadband internet infrastructure. Furthermore, GIS can be used to analyze the reach of existing services, calculating the percentage of a population within a certain radius of a bus stop, a charging station for electric vehicles, or a public park. The ability to perform spatial queries and analyses enables researchers and policymakers to understand the geographic dimensions of inequity, identifying communities that are literally on the wrong side of the infrastructure divide. This visual representation is often more compelling and easier to grasp than raw statistical data, making it a powerful tool for advocacy and public awareness campaigns.

Beyond quantitative data, understanding the lived experiences of residents is crucial for a comprehensive assessment of infrastructure disparities. Community surveys, focus groups, and participatory mapping exercises provide invaluable qualitative insights that data alone cannot capture. These methods allow for the collection of information on the perceived reliability, affordability, and quality of services, as well as the direct impacts of infrastructure on daily life. For instance, a survey might reveal that while a neighborhood has a bus route, residents find it unreliable, overcrowded, or unsafe, leading them to avoid using it. Similarly, focus groups could uncover how the lack of safe pedestrian infrastructure discourages walking, impacting public health and community cohesion. Participatory mapping allows community members to identify and annotate areas where they experience specific infrastructure challenges, such as poorly lit streets, broken sidewalks, or areas prone to flooding – issues that might not be readily apparent from official infrastructure maps. These qualitative methods are essential for understanding the nuances of inequity, moving beyond mere access to consider the actual user experience and the socio-cultural implications of infrastructure design and delivery.

To effectively communicate and track progress in addressing these disparities, specific metrics and indices are required. One such concept is the "infrastructure gap," which quantifies the difference in the level or quality of infrastructure provision between different groups or geographic areas. This gap can be measured across various dimensions: for example, the gap in average commute times between affluent and low-income neighborhoods, the difference in the number of households with access to high-speed internet, or the disparity in the frequency and reliability of public transit services. Another valuable metric is a "service equity index," which could be a composite score that combines multiple indicators of infrastructure access and quality, weighted according to their importance for well-being and opportunity. This index would allow for a more holistic assessment of equity, considering factors such as water quality, energy affordability, transportation accessibility, and digital connectivity. Developing standardized metrics is crucial for enabling comparisons across different cities, regions, and even countries, and for establishing benchmarks against which progress can be measured over time. These metrics serve as crucial performance indicators, guiding resource allocation and policy development towards a more equitable distribution of infrastructural benefits.

Historical planning biases have often led to deeply entrenched infrastructure disparities that continue to affect communities today. For instance, the legacy of redlining and discriminatory housing policies in many countries has resulted in the underinvestment of infrastructure in predominantly Black and minority neighborhoods. These communities often suffer from aging water and sewer systems, inadequate public transportation, fewer parks and green spaces, and limited access to broadband. A case study might examine a city where historically, new highway construction was prioritized to connect suburban residential areas with downtown business districts, often cutting through existing low-income and minority neighborhoods. This not only displaced residents but also created physical barriers, increased noise and air pollution, and further isolated these communities from economic opportunities. The lack of investment in their public transit systems, compared to wealthier areas, then compounded these disadvantages, making it harder for residents to access jobs, education, and essential services. Another example could involve rural areas where the cost of extending fiber optic cable for broadband internet is deemed too high by private providers, leaving entire communities digitally disconnected, while neighboring, more affluent suburban or urban areas enjoy robust high-speed internet access. Such case studies serve as potent reminders that current disparities are not accidental but are often the result of deliberate, albeit sometimes historical, policy choices that need to be actively unraveled and rectified.

Furthermore, the measurement of disparities must also consider the quality and reliability of existing infrastructure, not just its presence or absence. A neighborhood may have access to electricity, but if the grid is old and prone to frequent power outages, or if electricity prices are prohibitively high due to inefficient generation or transmission, then this does not represent equitable service. Similarly, while a community might have a public library, if its operating hours are limited, its resources are outdated, or it is difficult to access due to poor transportation links, its value and utility are significantly diminished. Measuring "digital inclusion" goes beyond simply counting the number of households with an internet subscription; it involves assessing the speed, reliability, affordability, and usability of that connection, as well as the digital literacy of the users. These qualitative aspects of infrastructure provision are critical for ensuring that access translates into tangible benefits and opportunities for all members of society.

The process of identifying and measuring these disparities is not a one-time exercise but an ongoing endeavor. Infrastructure needs and technologies evolve, and so too do the ways in which inequities can manifest. Continuous monitoring, regular data collection, and adaptive measurement techniques are therefore essential to ensure that policies remain relevant and effective in promoting genuine infrastructure equity. This requires a commitment from governments, utility providers, and urban planners to invest in the data infrastructure and analytical capabilities needed to perform these assessments regularly. It also necessitates a willingness to listen to community voices and to integrate their experiences into the measurement framework. By employing a robust and multifaceted approach to identifying and quantifying infrastructure disparities, we lay the groundwork for informed decision-making and the development of targeted strategies that can lead to a more just and inclusive distribution of essential services and their benefits.

Artificial Intelligence (AI) presents a transformative opportunity to address historical and systemic inequities in the distribution of infrastructure resources. By moving beyond conventional planning methods that may perpetuate existing biases, AI can offer a more dynamic, data-driven, and potentially fairer approach to resource allocation. The core of AI's contribution lies in its unparalleled capacity to process vast amounts of complex data, identify intricate patterns, and make predictions or recommendations that can lead to more equitable outcomes. This is particularly crucial in sectors like public transportation, water and sanitation, energy, and digital connectivity, where disparities in access and quality disproportionately affect marginalized communities.

One of the most promising applications of AI in this domain is through sophisticated demand-driven resource allocation. Traditional infrastructure planning often relies on historical usage data, which can inadvertently entrench existing patterns of under-service if those patterns were established by discriminatory practices or systemic neglect. AI, however, can analyze a broader spectrum of real-time and predictive data to understand the actual needs of a population, regardless of historical provision. For instance, AI-powered transit optimization systems can analyze anonymized mobility data, demographic information, and even social media sentiment to identify areas with unmet transportation needs. These systems can then dynamically adjust bus routes, schedules, and vehicle deployment to better serve low-income neighborhoods, areas with high concentrations of elderly or disabled individuals, or communities that are geographically distant from essential services and employment centers. Instead of simply maintaining routes that have historically received the most ridership (often in more affluent areas), AI can help identify underserved corridors and propose modifications to improve accessibility for those who rely most heavily on public transit. This might involve creating new feeder routes, increasing service frequency during peak demand in overlooked areas, or even suggesting the deployment of smaller, more flexible transit options like on-demand microtransit services in areas where fixed routes are less efficient. The goal is not just to provide *any* service, but to provide *equitable* service that genuinely enhances mobility and opportunity for all.

Similarly, in the realm of water and sanitation infrastructure, AI can play a critical role in prioritizing upgrades and maintenance. Water systems in older, historically disinvested neighborhoods often suffer from aging pipes, leading to frequent breaks, contamination risks, and service disruptions. AI can integrate data from sensor networks within the water infrastructure (measuring pressure, flow rates, water quality), alongside historical maintenance records, geospatial data on pipe age and material, and demographic information, to predict areas most at risk of failure or most severely impacted by current deficiencies. By applying predictive analytics, AI can identify specific pipe segments or entire network sections that are likely to fail or are contributing to poor water quality in low-income communities. This allows utility providers to move from a reactive maintenance model to a proactive, preventative one. Instead of waiting for a major pipe burst to occur in a vulnerable neighborhood, AI can flag these areas for preemptive repair or replacement, thereby minimizing disruptions and ensuring more consistent access to safe, clean water. Furthermore, AI can analyze patterns of water usage and demand in conjunction with infrastructure capacity to optimize water pressure across a network, ensuring that areas that have historically experienced low pressure due to their distance from main pumping stations or pipe limitations receive adequate service. This data-driven approach to infrastructure investment ensures that limited capital is directed where it can have the greatest impact on equity and public health, particularly for communities that have been historically underserved.

The energy sector also stands to benefit significantly from AI-driven equitable resource distribution. Smart grid technologies, powered by AI, can optimize energy distribution, detect faults, and manage demand more efficiently. For communities that are disproportionately affected by power outages or high energy costs, AI can help identify systemic issues. For example, AI can analyze historical outage data in conjunction with weather patterns, grid infrastructure age, and socio-economic demographics to pinpoint areas where the grid is least resilient. This information can then inform strategic investments in grid modernization, such as upgrading transformers, reinforcing power lines, or deploying distributed energy resources like microgrids in vulnerable neighborhoods. Beyond reliability, AI can also contribute to energy affordability. By analyzing energy consumption patterns and forecasting demand, AI can help utilities implement more dynamic pricing strategies or identify opportunities for energy efficiency programs tailored to specific communities. For instance, AI could identify low-income households that are likely to benefit most from weatherization programs or solar panel installations, facilitating targeted outreach and resource allocation to reduce energy burdens for these households. This ensures that the benefits of energy modernization and efficiency are not confined to more affluent areas but are actively channeled to those who need them most.

Digital infrastructure, particularly broadband internet access, is another critical area where AI can foster equity. The "digital divide" remains a significant barrier to education, employment, and civic participation. AI can analyze existing broadband infrastructure maps, population density, and socio-economic data to identify areas that are either entirely unserved or underserved by reliable high-speed internet. Moreover, AI can go beyond simply mapping physical infrastructure to analyzing actual internet performance metrics (speed, latency, reliability) collected from user devices or network probes. This provides a more accurate picture of the digital experience on the ground. Based on these insights, AI can help optimize the deployment of new broadband infrastructure, such as fiber optic cables or 5G towers, by identifying the most impactful locations for investment. This might involve prioritizing areas where a significant portion of the population lacks access or where existing services are substandard and unaffordable. Furthermore, AI can be used to manage and optimize shared broadband resources, ensuring fair access and preventing congestion in areas with high demand. The goal is to leverage AI's analytical power to make the business case for expanding broadband into less profitable or harder-to-reach communities, thereby closing the digital divide and ensuring that everyone has the opportunity to participate in the digital economy and society.

Beyond these specific sectors, AI's ability to create comprehensive digital twins or sophisticated simulations of urban environments can offer a powerful tool for evaluating the equity implications of various infrastructure development or policy proposals. Before any new project is approved or any policy is enacted, AI can model its potential impacts on different demographic groups and geographic areas. For example, an AI simulation could predict how a new highway expansion might affect air quality in nearby low-income neighborhoods, or how a change in public transit fares might impact the ability of residents in underserved areas to access jobs. By quantifying these potential disparities before they materialize, policymakers can make more informed decisions and adjust plans to mitigate negative equity outcomes. This proactive approach to equity assessment, facilitated by AI, represents a significant departure from traditional methods that often react to inequities after they have become entrenched.

However, the implementation of AI for equitable resource distribution is not without its challenges. A primary concern is the potential for AI systems to inherit and amplify existing biases present in the data they are trained on. If historical data reflects discriminatory practices in service provision or resource allocation, an AI algorithm trained on this data might inadvertently perpetuate these biases. For instance, if past investments in public transport were lower in certain minority neighborhoods, an AI system might learn that these areas have lower "demand" for transit improvements, thus deprioritizing them for future investment. Addressing this requires careful data curation, bias detection algorithms, and ongoing auditing of AI system outputs. Techniques like adversarial debiasing and fairness-aware machine learning are crucial to ensure that AI models are designed to promote equity, not undermine it.

Another critical consideration is transparency and explainability (XAI). For AI-driven decisions regarding resource allocation to be accepted and trusted, especially by communities that have historically been marginalized, the reasoning behind these decisions must be understandable. "Black box" AI models that make recommendations without clear justification can breed suspicion and distrust. Developing AI systems that can explain their decision-making processes in clear, accessible terms is therefore paramount. This allows for scrutiny, feedback, and ultimately, greater accountability. Communities affected by infrastructure decisions should be able to understand why certain areas are prioritized over others, or why particular solutions are proposed. This transparency is essential for building trust and ensuring that AI serves as a tool for empowerment rather than an opaque arbiter of resource distribution.

Furthermore, the deployment of AI in this context necessitates a significant investment in data infrastructure and analytical capacity. Governments, utility companies, and public agencies need the technical expertise and the digital tools to collect, manage, and analyze the vast amounts of data required for effective AI implementation. This includes investing in sensor networks, data storage, computing power, and skilled personnel who can develop, deploy, and maintain AI systems. For many municipalities, particularly those in underserved areas, these investments may be a significant hurdle. Therefore, collaborative efforts, public-private partnerships, and targeted funding initiatives may be required to ensure that the benefits of AI for equitable resource distribution are accessible to all communities, not just those that are already well-resourced.

Finally, the human element remains indispensable. While AI can provide powerful data-driven insights and optimizations, it cannot replace the need for community engagement and human judgment. AI should be viewed as a tool to augment, not supplant, human decision-making and participatory processes. Community input is vital for understanding nuanced local needs, validating AI-generated insights, and ensuring that proposed solutions are culturally appropriate and socially acceptable. The most effective applications of AI for equitable resource distribution will likely emerge from a symbiotic relationship between advanced AI capabilities and robust community engagement, where data analytics inform and empower human-led planning and decision-making. This collaborative approach ensures that AI is used responsibly and ethically to build infrastructure that truly serves the needs of all citizens, fostering a more just and equitable society.

The transformative potential of Artificial Intelligence (AI) in reshaping infrastructure and resource allocation for greater equity is undeniable, as discussed in the preceding sections. However, the pursuit of fairness through AI must extend beyond the equitable distribution of resources themselves to encompass the accessibility of the very systems that manage and deliver these resources. As AI becomes increasingly embedded in the fabric of our urban environments and public services – from transit systems and energy grids to communication networks and utility management – it is imperative that these AI-driven systems are designed with inclusivity at their core. Failure to do so risks creating new digital divides and reinforcing existing inequalities, effectively barring certain segments of the population from benefiting from technological advancements. This subsection delves into the critical principles and practical considerations for ensuring that AI-driven infrastructure systems are universally accessible, particularly for individuals with disabilities, thereby preventing new forms of exclusion and fostering truly equitable access to essential services.

A foundational principle for achieving this inclusivity is the adoption of Universal Design. This philosophy, originating in architecture and product design, advocates for creating environments and products that are usable by all people, to the greatest extent possible, without the need for adaptation or specialized design. When applied to AI-driven systems, Universal Design means proactively considering the diverse needs of users from the outset of the design process, rather than attempting to retrofit accessibility features later. For AI-powered systems, this translates into designing interfaces, control mechanisms, data presentation, and service delivery pathways that are inherently usable by individuals with a wide range of abilities, including those with visual, auditory, motor, and cognitive impairments.

Consider the realm of public transportation, a sector where AI is increasingly being deployed for route optimization, real-time information dissemination, and even autonomous vehicle operation. For an AI-driven transit system to be truly accessible, its interfaces and information delivery must cater to diverse user needs. For individuals with visual impairments, this might involve AI-powered navigation aids that provide detailed, real-time audio guidance through stations and onto vehicles. These systems could leverage computer vision to identify platform edges, bus numbers, and available seating, offering spoken turn-by-turn directions. Beyond simple GPS, AI can analyze the immediate environment to describe obstacles or unexpected changes. For example, an AI assistant could inform a visually impaired passenger that a temporary barrier has been placed on the platform or that their usual boarding spot is currently occupied by a service vehicle. Furthermore, intelligent audio announcements on vehicles, dynamically generated by AI based on passenger location and destination, can provide more granular information than standard pre-recorded announcements, ensuring timely and relevant updates for all.

Similarly, voice-controlled interfaces are paramount for enhancing accessibility in public transit. AI-powered natural language processing (NLP) can enable users to query transit information, plan journeys, or report issues using spoken commands. This is invaluable for individuals with motor impairments who may find it difficult to operate touchscreens or keyboards, as well as for users who are multitasking or have limited dexterity. An AI chatbot integrated into a transit app could allow a user to ask, "What's the next bus to downtown from this stop?" or "Is the number 15 bus running on time?" and receive an accurate, spoken response. The AI's ability to understand a wide range of accents and speech patterns, continuously improved through machine learning, is critical for broad adoption. Moreover, these voice interfaces should not be limited to simple information retrieval; they should also facilitate the booking of accessible seating, requesting assistance, or reporting service disruptions in real-time, providing a direct communication channel to transit authorities or support staff.

The digital platforms through which users access essential services, such as utility management or public service portals, also require a strong commitment to accessibility. AI can play a crucial role in making these platforms usable for everyone. For instance, AI-driven content summarization and simplification tools can help individuals with cognitive disabilities or those who are not fluent in the primary language of the platform to understand complex information about billing, service updates, or application procedures. Imagine an AI that can take a dense utility bill with complex jargon and present a simplified summary highlighting the amount due, the payment deadline, and any available assistance programs, all in clear, concise language. Screen reader compatibility, a long-standing accessibility requirement, can be enhanced by AI that not only reads content but also understands the semantic structure of web pages and applications, providing more contextually relevant information to visually impaired users. AI can also personalize the user interface, adapting font sizes, color contrasts, and layout based on individual preferences or detected needs, further promoting ease of use.

Preventing new forms of exclusion through technology means being acutely aware of the potential pitfalls. One significant risk is the reliance on biometric identification systems powered by AI, such as facial recognition or fingerprint scanning, for accessing services or verifying identity. While these technologies offer convenience and security, they have been shown to exhibit biases, with lower accuracy rates for individuals with darker skin tones or certain facial features. If access to essential services like healthcare portals, government benefits, or even public Wi-Fi relies solely on such biased AI systems, it could systematically exclude already marginalized groups. Therefore, alternative, non-biometric authentication methods, perhaps reinforced by AI-driven anomaly detection rather than absolute identification, must always be available and equally convenient. The design of these authentication systems should prioritize robustness and fairness, undergoing rigorous testing across diverse demographic groups before deployment.

Another critical aspect is the accessibility of AI-driven decision-making processes themselves. While the previous chapter discussed the importance of transparency and explainability in AI for infrastructure allocation, this extends to the user-facing aspects of AI services. If an AI system denies a user a service, flags their application for review, or modifies their service level, the reasoning behind this decision must be accessible and understandable. For instance, if an AI-powered credit assessment system for utility payment plans flags a user as high-risk, the system should be able to clearly articulate the factors contributing to this assessment in plain language, allowing the user to understand what information led to the decision and how they might improve their standing. This requires AI systems to be designed not only to make decisions but also to generate comprehensible justifications, potentially tailored to different levels of technical understanding, and delivered through accessible channels.

Furthermore, the continuous learning nature of AI presents both opportunities and challenges for accessibility. As AI systems evolve and adapt based on new data, it is crucial to ensure that these adaptations do not inadvertently degrade accessibility. For example, an AI that learns to predict user behavior to streamline service delivery might, if not carefully monitored, optimize for the "average" user in a way that marginalizes less common usage patterns or needs associated with disabilities. Regular audits and testing by diverse user groups are essential to identify and rectify any emergent accessibility issues. This includes testing AI-driven interfaces on a variety of assistive technologies, such as screen readers, magnifiers, alternative input devices, and switch access systems, to ensure seamless integration and functionality.

The deployment of AI in public spaces, such as intelligent traffic management systems or smart city kiosks, also necessitates careful consideration of accessibility. Pedestrian navigation systems, for example, can be significantly enhanced by AI that analyzes real-time traffic flow, public transport movements, and pedestrian volumes to provide optimal, safe routes. For individuals with mobility impairments, these AI systems could prioritize routes that avoid steep inclines, uneven surfaces, or high-traffic intersections, and proactively alert them to potential hazards or temporary obstacles like construction zones. Similarly, smart city kiosks, often serving as information hubs or service points, must be designed with adjustable height interfaces, tactile controls, and clear audio output options, all informed by AI that can adapt the display and interaction based on user input or sensor data indicating potential difficulties.

Beyond physical and digital interfaces, the very delivery of services through AI must be equitable. For instance, AI-powered demand-responsive transit services, while offering flexibility, must be designed to avoid creating "exclusion zones." If the AI algorithm prioritizes efficiency by serving densely populated areas or lucrative routes, it might inadvertently leave individuals in less densely populated or more remote areas, who may rely heavily on these services due to disability or lack of private transport, with inadequate or nonexistent options. Ensuring equitable service delivery requires AI models that explicitly incorporate fairness metrics, such as ensuring a minimum service level or response time for all users, regardless of their location or socio-economic status, and that these metrics are regularly monitored and adjusted.

The development and maintenance of accessible AI-driven systems also demand a diverse and inclusive workforce within the AI industry itself. Teams that design, develop, and deploy AI should reflect the diversity of the populations they serve. This includes individuals with disabilities, who can provide invaluable insights into user needs and potential usability barriers. Inclusive design processes, participatory design workshops involving end-users, and the establishment of accessibility standards and guidelines within organizations are crucial steps. Furthermore, ongoing training for AI developers and product managers on accessibility principles and best practices is essential to foster a culture of inclusivity.

In conclusion, the integration of AI into infrastructure and public services presents a profound opportunity to advance equity. However, this potential can only be fully realized if accessibility is treated not as an add-on, but as a core requirement from the inception of any AI-driven system. By embracing Universal Design principles, leveraging AI to create tailored assistive technologies, ensuring transparency and understandability of AI decisions, and proactively addressing potential biases, we can build AI systems that empower all individuals, including those with disabilities. This approach moves beyond simply providing equitable access to resources and ensures equitable access to the technologies that manage and deliver those resources, thereby fostering a truly inclusive and just society in the age of artificial intelligence. The focus must remain on harnessing AI's power to break down barriers, not erect new ones, ensuring that technological progress serves humanity in its entirety.

The preceding discussion has emphasized the critical importance of accessibility in AI-driven infrastructure and services, ensuring that technological advancements do not inadvertently create new barriers for individuals with disabilities. Moving forward, this section explores another vital dimension of socio-technical AI integration: fostering genuine community engagement and enabling participatory design in infrastructure development. As AI becomes more adept at processing information and facilitating communication, its potential to democratize decision-making processes and ensure that infrastructure projects truly serve the needs and reflect the values of the communities they impact becomes increasingly apparent. This is not merely about distributing resources equitably, but about empowering communities to co-create the very systems that shape their lives.

Traditionally, public engagement in infrastructure projects has often been a top-down process. While mechanisms like public consultations, town hall meetings, and surveys exist, they can be time-consuming, resource-intensive, and may not always effectively capture the nuanced perspectives of all stakeholders. Certain groups, including those with limited time, mobility challenges, or language barriers, might find it difficult to participate. Furthermore, the sheer volume and complexity of information involved in infrastructure planning can be overwhelming, making it hard for the general public to grasp the implications of proposed designs or to articulate their concerns effectively. AI offers promising avenues to bridge these gaps, transforming passive recipients of infrastructure into active participants in its design and evolution.

One of the most significant contributions AI can make is in the analysis of vast amounts of public feedback. In today's hyper-connected world, opinions, concerns, and suggestions are disseminated across a multitude of platforms – social media, online forums, community group websites, direct feedback channels, and even through digital versions of traditional surveys and petitions. Manually sifting through this deluge of information to identify recurring themes, key priorities, and minority concerns is an arduous, if not impossible, task for human teams alone. AI-powered natural language processing (NLP) and sentiment analysis tools can automate and enhance this process considerably. These tools can be trained to identify keywords, recognize emotional tones, and categorize feedback according to specific infrastructure components or impact areas. For instance, an AI system could be deployed to monitor public discourse around a proposed new transit line. It could identify frequent mentions of concerns about noise pollution in specific residential areas, the need for improved accessibility at certain stations, or the desire for more green spaces to be integrated into station designs. This automated analysis allows project planners to gain a more comprehensive and rapid understanding of community sentiment, ensuring that the diverse voices of the populace are heard and considered.

Moreover, AI can help identify and amplify the voices of underrepresented or marginalized communities. By analyzing demographic data in conjunction with feedback patterns, AI can highlight areas where engagement is low or where specific concerns from vulnerable populations might be overlooked. For example, an AI system could flag that feedback from neighborhoods with a high proportion of elderly residents or non-native English speakers is significantly lower than in other areas. This insight would prompt project teams to implement targeted outreach strategies, such as offering consultations in community centers frequented by these groups, providing information in multiple languages, or developing simplified feedback mechanisms that cater to their specific needs and communication preferences. This proactive approach ensures that participatory design is not just an abstract ideal but a tangible practice that actively seeks out and incorporates the perspectives of all community members, thereby fostering greater equity in infrastructure development.

Beyond just understanding existing feedback, AI can also play a crucial role in facilitating dialogue and promoting informed participation. Interactive AI-powered platforms can be developed to provide communities with accessible and engaging ways to learn about proposed projects and to contribute their ideas. Imagine an AI-driven simulation or visualization tool that can take complex architectural plans or engineering schematics and translate them into easily understandable 3D models or immersive virtual reality experiences. These visualizations can dynamically demonstrate the potential impacts of different design choices, such as how a new building might affect sunlight in a residential area, how a redesigned intersection might alter traffic flow, or how a new park could be integrated into the urban landscape. By allowing community members to virtually "walk through" proposed developments and see their potential consequences firsthand, AI can demystify complex technical information and empower individuals to provide more informed and constructive feedback.

These AI-powered visualization tools can go further by enabling participatory scenario planning. Communities could, through intuitive interfaces, adjust parameters of a proposed design – perhaps altering the height of a building, changing the type of materials used, or modifying the layout of public spaces. The AI could then instantly render these changes and provide an immediate, visual representation of the outcome, along with an analysis of potential trade-offs, such as cost implications or environmental impacts. This iterative process, guided by AI, allows for a co-creative environment where citizens can actively contribute to shaping the project's trajectory, moving beyond simply reacting to proposals to actively shaping them. This is particularly valuable for ensuring that projects align with local values and priorities, such as preserving historical character, promoting sustainable practices, or enhancing social cohesion.

Furthermore, AI can assist in generating and evaluating design alternatives that are specifically tailored to community preferences. By integrating community feedback analysis with generative design algorithms, AI systems can propose a range of design options that not only meet technical requirements but also resonate with identified community needs and aesthetic preferences. For instance, if a community expresses a strong preference for natural materials and a desire for more communal gathering spaces in the design of a new public library, an AI could generate multiple architectural concepts that incorporate these elements, presenting them to the community for further refinement. This moves the process from a single designer's vision to a collaborative exploration of possibilities, informed by the collective intelligence of the community and amplified by AI's computational power.

The role of AI in participatory design also extends to improving the efficiency and effectiveness of community engagement initiatives. AI can help in identifying the most effective communication channels and engagement methods for different demographic groups, based on historical data and real-time analysis of participation rates. For example, an AI might suggest that for a particular demographic, direct outreach through community liaisons and localized workshops is more effective than broad social media campaigns, while for another group, interactive online platforms with gamified elements might yield higher engagement. This data-driven approach allows organizations to allocate their engagement resources more strategically, ensuring that efforts are focused on reaching the right people through the right channels, thereby maximizing participation and inclusivity.

AI can also facilitate the creation of "digital twins" of existing infrastructure or proposed developments. These dynamic, data-rich digital models can serve as living laboratories for community engagement. Residents can interact with the digital twin to understand the operational aspects of services, visualize the impact of proposed upgrades, and even test the efficacy of different management strategies. For instance, in managing an urban water system, a digital twin powered by AI could allow community members to explore how different water conservation policies might affect supply during drought periods, or how new infrastructure investments could mitigate flood risks. This level of transparency and interactive exploration fosters a deeper understanding and greater trust in the infrastructure and the decision-making processes surrounding it.

However, the integration of AI into community engagement and participatory design is not without its challenges and requires careful consideration. Ensuring that AI tools themselves are accessible and inclusive is paramount, echoing the points made in the previous section. The interfaces used to interact with AI feedback analysis tools or visualization platforms must be usable by individuals with diverse abilities. If the tools used to gather community input are themselves barriers to participation, the very purpose of using AI will be undermined.

Furthermore, ethical considerations surrounding data privacy and algorithmic bias are critical. When AI is used to analyze public feedback, it is essential to ensure that individual privacy is protected and that data is anonymized where appropriate. Equally important is addressing the potential for AI algorithms to perpetuate or amplify existing societal biases. For example, if an AI is trained on historical engagement data that reflects a lack of participation from certain groups, it might inadvertently prioritize feedback that aligns with the patterns of more vocal or dominant segments of the population, further marginalizing underrepresented voices. Rigorous testing, bias detection, and mitigation strategies are crucial to ensure that AI-driven engagement processes are fair and equitable.

Transparency in how AI is used in these processes is also non-negotiable. Communities have a right to know when and how AI is being employed to analyze their feedback or to generate design options. Explaining the capabilities and limitations of AI tools in clear, accessible language can build trust and encourage greater participation. This transparency should extend to how the insights derived from AI analysis are used to inform decision-making, ensuring that AI serves as a tool to augment human judgment and community deliberation, rather than replacing it. The ultimate decisions must remain in the hands of accountable human stakeholders, informed by both expert knowledge and the collective wisdom of the community.

Finally, the successful integration of AI into participatory design necessitates a shift in organizational culture and skillsets. Public agencies and infrastructure developers need to invest in training their staff on AI literacy, data analysis, and ethical AI deployment. They also need to foster a culture that values and actively seeks out community input, viewing AI not as a substitute for human interaction but as a powerful enabler of more meaningful and effective engagement. This involves moving from a mindset of simply informing the public to one of genuinely co-creating solutions with them.

In conclusion, AI offers transformative potential for enhancing community engagement and participatory design in infrastructure projects. By leveraging AI for sophisticated analysis of public feedback, creating immersive and interactive visualization tools, and facilitating the generation of community-centric design alternatives, we can move towards infrastructure development that is more responsive, equitable, and socially accepted. When thoughtfully and ethically deployed, AI can empower communities to become active partners in shaping their environments, ensuring that the infrastructure of the future is not just technically sound but also deeply rooted in the needs, values, and aspirations of the people it serves. This approach moves beyond simply making infrastructure accessible to ensuring that its creation and evolution are themselves accessible, inclusive, and democratically driven processes.

Chapter 9: AI in Water Resource Management

The landscape of water resource management is inherently complex, characterized by a confluence of escalating demands and diminishing supplies, all amplified by the intricate web of human activity and environmental pressures. At the forefront of these challenges is the relentless growth in global population. As more people inhabit the planet, the per capita demand for water intensifies, not only for direct consumption like drinking and sanitation but also indirectly through increased food production and industrial output. This burgeoning demand places an unprecedented strain on finite freshwater resources, pushing many regions towards, or already past, their sustainable limits. Managing this escalating demand requires a delicate balancing act, considering the fundamental human right to water while also acknowledging the ecological needs of rivers, lakes, and aquifers that sustain life.

Compounding the pressure of increased demand is the escalating reality of climate change. Altered precipitation patterns, prolonged droughts, and more intense rainfall events disrupt traditional water availability and predictability. Regions historically blessed with consistent water supplies are now experiencing unprecedented arid conditions, while others face the destructive force of flash floods that can overwhelm existing infrastructure and contaminate water sources. These climate-induced shifts mean that water managers can no longer rely on historical data alone to forecast future availability. The variability and uncertainty introduced by climate change necessitate adaptive strategies, robust contingency planning, and a fundamental rethinking of how water is stored, distributed, and conserved. The ephemeral nature of rainfall, once a reliable cornerstone of water management, is becoming a significant challenge, requiring innovative solutions for capturing and utilizing water when and where it is available, and for mitigating the impacts of its absence.

Furthermore, a significant portion of the world's water infrastructure is aging and in a state of disrepair. Decades of underinvestment and deferred maintenance have led to deteriorating pipelines, treatment plants, and reservoirs. This decay results in substantial water losses through leaks, which in some urban areas can account for a significant percentage of the total water supplied. Beyond simple loss, these compromised systems become breeding grounds for contaminants, posing serious public health risks. Old pipes can leach harmful substances into the water, and inadequate treatment facilities may fail to remove emerging contaminants like pharmaceuticals, microplastics, and industrial chemicals. The imperative to upgrade and modernize this aging infrastructure is therefore twofold: to conserve precious water resources and to safeguard public health. The cost and complexity of such overhauls are substantial, often requiring significant capital investment and long-term strategic planning.

The efficient treatment and distribution of water present another formidable hurdle. As water sources become more stressed and potentially more polluted, the energy and chemical inputs required for purification increase. Many existing treatment plants are not equipped to handle the complexity of modern contaminants, necessitating costly upgrades or the development of entirely new treatment technologies. Equally challenging is the distribution of treated water. Maintaining adequate pressure across vast networks, ensuring equitable access to all communities, and minimizing losses during transport are ongoing operational complexities. In many developing regions, the lack of even basic distribution networks means that access to safe water remains a distant dream for millions, highlighting the global disparities in water management capabilities.

The interconnectedness of water systems with other critical sectors cannot be overstated, and this interdependency introduces further layers of complexity to water resource management. Agriculture, for instance, is the largest consumer of freshwater globally, accounting for approximately 70% of all water withdrawals. Meeting the food security needs of a growing population inherently means increased agricultural water demand. However, current irrigation practices are often inefficient, leading to significant waste. Balancing the needs of agriculture with those of other sectors and the environment requires integrated strategies that promote water-efficient farming techniques, such as drip irrigation and precision agriculture, and explore alternative water sources for irrigation, like treated wastewater or desalinated water, where feasible and appropriate.

Industry also plays a pivotal role in the water equation. Manufacturing processes, energy production (particularly thermal power plants that require vast amounts of cooling water), and resource extraction are all significant water users. Industrial discharges, if not properly treated, can introduce a cocktail of pollutants into water bodies, jeopardizing both human and ecological health. Managing industrial water use involves a dual focus: encouraging water conservation and efficiency within industrial processes and implementing stringent regulations for wastewater treatment and discharge. The pursuit of a circular economy, where water is recycled and reused within industrial processes, offers a promising avenue for reducing overall water footprint.

Crucially, water systems are inextricably linked to natural ecosystems. Rivers, lakes, wetlands, and groundwater aquifers are not merely sources of water for human use; they are vital habitats for biodiversity, essential components of biogeochemical cycles, and natural regulators of water flow and quality. When human demand exceeds sustainable limits, or when water bodies are heavily polluted, these ecosystems suffer severe degradation. Reduced river flows can lead to the loss of aquatic life, wetlands can dry up, and groundwater depletion can cause land subsidence and saltwater intrusion in coastal areas. Effective water management must therefore adopt an ecosystem-based approach, recognizing that the health of human water security is directly dependent on the health of the natural environment. This requires setting aside adequate environmental flows for rivers, protecting critical wetland areas, and managing groundwater extraction sustainably.

The cumulative effect of these challenges—rising demand, climate variability, aging infrastructure, inefficient treatment and distribution, and the complex interdependencies with agriculture, industry, and ecosystems—creates a pressing need for more intelligent, integrated, and sustainable water management strategies. Traditional approaches, often fragmented and reactive, are proving increasingly inadequate to address the scale and complexity of the issues at hand. There is a clear and urgent call for a paradigm shift towards proactive, holistic, and technologically informed solutions to ensure water security for current and future generations. This is precisely where the potential of artificial intelligence begins to emerge as a transformative force.

The intricate dance between water availability and its consumption is a defining challenge of our era. To navigate this complexity effectively, a profound understanding of future water dynamics is indispensable. This understanding hinges on accurate forecasting of both water demand and supply. Artificial intelligence, with its burgeoning capabilities in pattern recognition, predictive modeling, and complex data analysis, offers a transformative approach to this critical aspect of water resource management. By leveraging AI, water managers can move from reactive measures to proactive strategies, ensuring more resilient and sustainable water systems.

The demand for water is not static; it fluctuates based on a myriad of factors, many of which are dynamic and interconnected. Predicting these fluctuations accurately is paramount for efficient resource allocation, infrastructure planning, and operational optimization. AI excels at dissecting these intricate demand drivers. At the municipal level, for instance, water demand is influenced by population density, socio-economic status, daily routines, and most significantly, weather patterns. Hotter days lead to increased usage for cooling and outdoor activities, while colder periods see a dip. AI-powered time-series forecasting models are particularly adept at capturing these temporal dependencies. Models such as Long Short-Term Memory (LSTM) networks, a type of recurrent neural network, are revolutionizing this field. LSTMs can learn long-range dependencies in sequential data, making them ideal for predicting water demand over days, weeks, or even months. They can ingest vast amounts of historical data, including past consumption patterns, temperature forecasts, humidity levels, and even event calendars (e.g., holidays or local festivals that might influence water usage). Unlike traditional statistical methods, LSTMs can automatically identify and learn complex, non-linear relationships between these variables, leading to more precise predictions. For example, an LSTM model trained on city-wide water consumption data, alongside meteorological data from the past decade, can forecast the likely demand for the upcoming weekend, factoring in an anticipated heatwave. This allows water utilities to adjust pumping schedules, optimize reservoir levels, and ensure sufficient treatment capacity is available, thereby preventing shortages and minimizing the need for energy-intensive operations during peak demand.

Beyond municipal consumption, AI also plays a crucial role in forecasting agricultural and industrial water demand, sectors that are typically the largest water consumers. Agricultural demand is intricately linked to crop types, irrigation methods, soil moisture levels, and, critically, weather forecasts. AI models can integrate satellite imagery data, which provides insights into crop health and soil conditions, with meteorological predictions to estimate crop water needs. Precision agriculture, an area where AI is already making significant inroads, relies on such granular forecasts. For instance, an AI system can predict the exact water requirements for a specific field of corn on a given day, factoring in the predicted rainfall, evapotranspiration rates, and the growth stage of the crop. This allows for highly targeted irrigation, minimizing water wastage and optimizing yield. Traditional methods often rely on generalized irrigation schedules, which can lead to significant over or under-watering. AI-driven forecasting enables a shift towards a need-based approach, where water is applied only when and where it is needed.

Similarly, industrial water demand is influenced by production schedules, operational efficiency, and the type of industry. Manufacturing processes, cooling systems in power plants, and mining operations all have distinct water consumption profiles. AI can be employed to forecast these demands by analyzing production data, energy consumption patterns, and historical water usage logs. For example, an AI model for a thermal power plant could predict the cooling water requirements based on the anticipated electricity generation load and ambient temperature. This allows plant operators to optimize cooling tower operations and water intake from the source, contributing to both water conservation and energy efficiency. Furthermore, AI can help identify anomalies in industrial water usage, potentially signaling leaks or inefficiencies that might otherwise go unnoticed.

The efficacy of these demand forecasting models is significantly enhanced by their ability to learn from and adapt to evolving conditions. As climate change alters historical weather patterns and economic activity shifts, the underlying drivers of water demand can change. AI models, particularly those employing machine learning techniques, can be continuously retrained with new data, allowing them to adapt to these shifts and maintain their predictive accuracy over time. Techniques like ARIMA (AutoRegressive Integrated Moving Average) models, while more traditional, can still provide valuable baseline forecasts, especially when combined with exogenous variables that capture external influences like economic indicators or population growth projections. However, LSTMs and other deep learning architectures often surpass ARIMA in complex, real-world scenarios where data is noisy and non-linear relationships abound.

Just as critical as predicting how much water will be needed is forecasting how much water will be available. Water supply forecasting is essential for managing reservoirs, allocating water rights, planning for droughts and floods, and ensuring the long-term sustainability of water resources. AI offers powerful tools for predicting the availability of water from various sources, including rivers, lakes, groundwater aquifers, and reservoirs.

Rainfall is the primary source of freshwater, and forecasting its patterns is fundamental to understanding future water supply. AI, particularly through sophisticated meteorological models that incorporate vast datasets from weather stations, satellites, and radar systems, can significantly improve rainfall predictions. These models can identify complex atmospheric patterns and predict precipitation intensity, duration, and spatial distribution with greater accuracy than conventional methods. For instance, deep learning models have shown promise in downscaling global climate model outputs to predict regional rainfall patterns with higher resolution, which is crucial for local water management decisions.

Beyond direct rainfall, snowmelt is a critical contributor to water supply in many regions, particularly those with mountainous terrain. The timing and volume of snowmelt are heavily influenced by temperature and precipitation. AI models can integrate snowpack data, temperature forecasts, and historical melt rates to predict when and how much water will be released into river systems. This is vital for reservoir operators who need to manage releases to meet downstream demands while also preparing for potential flood risks. For example, an AI system could analyze real-time satellite imagery of snow cover, combined with a 10-day temperature forecast, to predict the peak melt runoff into a major river basin, allowing for proactive reservoir management.

River flow forecasting is another area where AI is making substantial contributions. By analyzing historical flow data, rainfall, snowmelt, upstream reservoir releases, and even factors like soil moisture and land use, AI models can predict future river levels and discharge rates. This is crucial for hydropower generation, navigation, ecosystem health (by ensuring environmental flows), and water supply to downstream users. LSTMs and other recurrent neural networks are particularly effective here, as river flow is a classic example of a time-series phenomenon with strong temporal dependencies. These models can learn from past events, such as the impact of a series of storms on river levels, and use this knowledge to predict the response to future weather events.

Groundwater availability also benefits from AI-driven forecasting. While often perceived as a stable resource, groundwater levels are influenced by recharge rates (often linked to rainfall and snowmelt) and abstraction rates. AI can integrate hydrogeological data, pumping records, and meteorological forecasts to predict future groundwater levels. This is especially important in regions heavily reliant on groundwater, where over-extraction can lead to aquifer depletion, land subsidence, and saltwater intrusion in coastal areas. Machine learning models can identify the complex interactions between surface water and groundwater, providing a more holistic view of water availability.

The accuracy of these AI-driven supply forecasts directly translates into significant operational benefits. For water treatment plants, accurate supply forecasts enable better planning of raw water intake, optimization of treatment processes to match anticipated water quality variations, and more efficient chemical usage. For reservoir management, precise forecasts of inflow and outflow allow for maximizing water storage during periods of abundance, minimizing evaporation losses, and ensuring sufficient releases for downstream users and environmental needs. In distribution networks, better supply forecasts, coupled with demand forecasts, allow for proactive pressure management, reduction of energy consumption associated with pumping, and quicker identification and response to leaks or bursts.

Furthermore, the integration of both demand and supply forecasts powered by AI creates a powerful synergy for integrated water resource management. By simultaneously predicting what will be needed and what will be available, water managers can gain a comprehensive foresight into potential imbalances. This allows for the proactive implementation of strategies such as water conservation campaigns, adjustments to irrigation schedules, optimization of inter-basin transfers, and the strategic pre-positioning of resources to mitigate the impacts of predicted shortages or surpluses. The ability to anticipate future water conditions with a higher degree of certainty empowers water authorities to make more informed, sustainable, and economically sound decisions, ultimately contributing to greater water security in an increasingly uncertain world. The continuous learning and adaptation capabilities of AI ensure that these forecasting systems remain relevant and effective even as the water landscape evolves.

The efficient delivery of water to consumers is a complex logistical challenge, and the infrastructure through which this vital resource flows—the water distribution network—is a critical component of urban and rural life. These networks, often extensive and aging, are susceptible to various inefficiencies, from excessive energy consumption to physical losses through leaks. Artificial intelligence is emerging as a powerful ally in transforming these networks from passive conduits into intelligent, responsive systems capable of optimizing their performance. This section delves into how AI-driven techniques are revolutionizing the management and operation of water distribution networks, leading to enhanced efficiency, reduced costs, and improved service delivery.

One of the most significant areas where AI is making a substantial impact is in the optimization of pumping schedules. Pumping stations are major energy consumers within a water distribution system, and their operation is intrinsically linked to meeting fluctuating water demands while maintaining adequate pressure throughout the network. Traditional methods of scheduling pumping often rely on historical demand patterns and fixed operational rules, which can be suboptimal and lead to excessive energy expenditure. AI algorithms, particularly machine learning models, can analyze real-time data from sensors deployed throughout the network, including flow rates, pressure levels, and reservoir statuses, alongside sophisticated demand forecasts. By processing this vast amount of data, AI can predict future demand with greater accuracy and, crucially, determine the most energy-efficient pumping strategies.

Consider the application of reinforcement learning (RL) in this context. An RL agent can be trained to make decisions about when to activate pumps, how fast to run them, and which pumps to utilize, with the objective of minimizing energy costs while ensuring that pressure thresholds are met and demand is satisfied. The "state" for the RL agent might include current pressure readings, reservoir levels, and the time of day, while "actions" could involve turning pumps on/off or adjusting their speed. The "reward" function would be designed to incentivize energy savings and penalize deviations from desired pressure levels or unmet demand. Through trial and error in a simulated environment, or by learning from historical operational data, the RL agent can discover highly optimized pumping schedules that adapt dynamically to changing conditions. For instance, an AI could learn to take advantage of lower electricity tariffs during off-peak hours by strategically filling reservoirs when demand is low, thereby reducing overall operational expenditure without compromising supply reliability. Furthermore, AI can optimize pump sequencing, considering the efficiency curves of different pumps and the overall load on the system to select the most economical combination of operational units. This sophisticated control can lead to substantial reductions in energy consumption, a significant portion of operational budgets for water utilities.

Beyond energy optimization, AI plays a crucial role in managing pressure levels within the distribution network to minimize water losses. Leaks are an inevitable reality in water distribution systems, particularly in older infrastructure. These leaks can be exacerbated by high internal pressures, leading to significant quantities of treated water being lost before it even reaches the consumer. Conversely, maintaining pressure that is too low can lead to service interruptions and potential ingress of contaminants into the pipes. AI algorithms can analyze pressure sensor data from various points across the network to identify patterns indicative of leakage. By understanding the typical pressure profiles under different demand conditions, AI can flag deviations that suggest the presence of a leak.

Machine learning models, such as anomaly detection algorithms (e.g., Isolation Forests or One-Class SVMs), can be trained on historical pressure data to establish a baseline of normal network behavior. When real-time data diverges significantly from this baseline in a localized area, the AI can flag it as a potential leak. This allows water utilities to move from a reactive approach of responding to customer complaints about low pressure or visible water loss to a proactive strategy of early leak detection. Moreover, AI can help pinpoint the likely location of these leaks by analyzing the spatial distribution of pressure drops and flow anomalies. By integrating this information with network topology, AI can guide maintenance crews to the most probable leak sites, reducing the time and resources required for detection and repair. This not only conserves water but also prevents costly secondary damage that can result from prolonged undetected leaks, such as road subsidence or damage to underground utilities.

The optimization of pressure management also extends to dynamic pressure zoning. Many systems operate with a single, often high, pressure setting across large areas to ensure adequate supply to the highest points. AI can enable dynamic pressure management by creating multiple pressure zones that can be adjusted in real-time. By precisely controlling pressure within each zone based on local demand and elevation, AI can significantly reduce the overall pressure in the system. This reduction in average pressure directly translates to a reduction in the volume of water lost through existing leaks and also decreases the likelihood of new leaks occurring or existing ones worsening. The sophisticated control offered by AI allows for a level of granularity in pressure management that was previously unfeasible, leading to substantial water savings and extended pipe lifespan.

Furthermore, AI can be employed to optimize the hydraulic performance of the network, ensuring that water flows efficiently from source to tap. This involves determining the most efficient routes for water flow, managing valve operations, and optimizing the configuration of the network to meet demand at minimal cost. For instance, during periods of high demand, AI can determine the optimal combination of pumping and valve settings to ensure that water reaches all areas of the network with minimal energy expenditure and pressure loss. This might involve dynamically adjusting the opening of certain valves to reroute flow or to bypass less efficient pumping stages.

Consider a scenario where a section of the network experiences an unexpected increase in demand due to a fire or a large public event. AI can rapidly analyze the available capacity, pump availability, and valve states to calculate the optimal adjustments required to meet this surge in demand while minimizing disruption to other parts of the network. This involves complex hydraulic modeling and real-time decision-making, capabilities that AI is uniquely suited to provide. By continuously monitoring flow rates and pressures, AI can also identify areas of the network that are experiencing stagnation or inadequate flow, which can lead to water quality issues. By optimizing flow paths and valve operations, AI can ensure that water is continuously moving through the system, maintaining water quality and reducing the risk of dead ends.

The integration of AI with smart sensor networks is fundamental to achieving these optimizations. Modern water distribution systems are increasingly equipped with a variety of sensors measuring flow, pressure, water quality parameters (like chlorine residual or turbidity), and acoustic signals that can detect leaks. AI algorithms can ingest and process the massive datasets generated by these sensors in real-time. This allows for a holistic understanding of the network's performance, enabling predictive maintenance, proactive leak detection, and dynamic operational adjustments. For example, by analyzing acoustic data from sensors along a pipe, AI can not only detect the presence of a leak but also estimate its size and location with greater accuracy than traditional methods. This data can then be fed into the AI's pressure optimization algorithms to prioritize repairs in areas where leakage is most significant.

Moreover, AI can help identify areas within the network that are consistently exhibiting signs of stress or inefficiency. This could include regions with persistently low pressure, high energy consumption for pumping, or frequent reports of water quality issues. By analyzing these patterns over time, AI can provide valuable insights to water utilities for strategic planning, such as identifying which sections of the network are candidates for rehabilitation or upgrades. For example, if an AI system consistently identifies that a particular older section of the network requires significantly higher pumping pressure to maintain adequate service compared to newer sections, it would flag this as an area requiring urgent attention and investment. This data-driven approach to infrastructure management moves away from cyclical replacement schedules towards a more needs-based and cost-effective approach.

The impact of AI on water distribution networks extends to improved customer service and operational resilience. By ensuring a more reliable supply of water at consistent pressure and proactively addressing issues like leaks and bursts, AI-driven optimization contributes to higher customer satisfaction. Furthermore, the enhanced visibility and control that AI provides make the network more resilient to disruptions, such as equipment failures or extreme weather events. For instance, if a pump fails, an AI system can quickly reconfigure the network to reroute water, adjust pressures, and minimize the impact on consumers, potentially avoiding widespread outages.

The adoption of AI in water distribution networks represents a significant paradigm shift. It moves beyond simple automation towards intelligent, adaptive systems that can continuously learn and improve their performance. The benefits are manifold: significant reductions in energy consumption and operational costs, substantial savings in water due to minimized leakage, extended lifespan of infrastructure through optimized pressure management, improved water quality, and enhanced resilience of the entire system. As AI technologies continue to mature and sensor networks become more pervasive, the potential for optimizing water distribution networks will only grow, paving the way for more sustainable and efficient water management practices globally. The ability to continuously monitor, analyze, and adapt the operation of these complex systems in real-time allows water utilities to navigate the challenges of increasing demand, aging infrastructure, and climate variability with greater confidence and effectiveness. The data-driven insights generated by AI are not merely operational enhancements; they are strategic tools that empower water managers to make more informed decisions about investment, maintenance, and long-term planning, ultimately ensuring the security and sustainability of water resources for generations to come.

The continuous and vigilant oversight of water quality is paramount for public health, environmental protection, and the sustainable management of water resources. Traditional methods of water quality monitoring, often relying on periodic manual sampling and laboratory analysis, can be time-consuming, labor-intensive, and prone to delays. These approaches are inherently reactive, meaning that by the time a contamination event is detected, it may have already spread, potentially impacting a large number of consumers or ecosystems. In the face of increasing water scarcity, aging infrastructure, and the growing threat of anthropogenic pollution, the need for more robust, timely, and predictive monitoring systems has never been greater. This is where Artificial Intelligence (AI) emerges as a transformative force, offering the capability to revolutionize how we detect, understand, and respond to changes in water quality.

The advent of sophisticated in-situ sensors has laid the groundwork for AI-driven water quality monitoring. These sensors, deployed strategically in water bodies, treatment plants, and distribution networks, can continuously measure a wide array of physico-chemical parameters in near real-time. These typically include pH, temperature, dissolved oxygen, turbidity, conductivity, chlorine residual, and specific ion concentrations. More advanced sensors can also detect the presence of specific organic compounds, heavy metals, or microbial indicators. However, the sheer volume and velocity of data generated by these sensor networks can be overwhelming for human operators. AI, particularly machine learning (ML) and deep learning (DL) algorithms, excels at sifting through this data deluge to identify meaningful patterns, subtle deviations, and critical anomalies that might otherwise go unnoticed.

One of the primary applications of AI in water quality monitoring is anomaly detection. An anomaly, in this context, refers to a data point or a sequence of data points that deviates significantly from what is considered normal or expected behavior. These deviations can serve as early indicators of potential pollution events, equipment malfunctions in treatment facilities, or breaches in the integrity of the distribution system. ML algorithms are adept at learning the complex, often non-linear, relationships between various water quality parameters under different environmental and operational conditions. Once a model has been trained on a dataset representing "normal" water quality, it can then be used to identify instances where the incoming sensor data falls outside this learned normal behavior.

Various ML techniques are employed for anomaly detection. Unsupervised learning methods, such as clustering algorithms (e.g., K-Means) or density-based approaches (e.g., DBSCAN), can group data points based on their similarity. Outliers that do not belong to any cluster or form very small clusters can be flagged as anomalies. More specialized algorithms like Isolation Forests or One-Class Support Vector Machines (OC-SVMs) are specifically designed to identify anomalies without needing prior knowledge of what constitutes an anomaly. These methods effectively build a model of the normal data distribution and then identify data points that are unlikely to have been generated from that distribution. For instance, an Isolation Forest works by randomly selecting a feature and then randomly selecting a split value for that feature to partition the data. Anomalies, being rare and different, tend to be isolated in fewer splits, making them easier to detect.

Consider a scenario where a river is monitored by a network of sensors. Under normal conditions, parameters like turbidity might fluctuate within a certain range, driven by rainfall or seasonal changes. However, if an industrial facility upstream experiences a spill, the turbidity levels could suddenly spike to unprecedented values, or a subtle, sustained increase might occur if there's a slow leak of effluent. An AI-powered anomaly detection system, trained on historical data, would flag this deviation immediately. This real-time alert allows water managers and environmental agencies to initiate an investigation much faster than would be possible with traditional sampling. This rapid response is crucial for containing the pollution, mitigating its spread, and assessing the impact on downstream water users and aquatic ecosystems.

Deep learning models, with their ability to automatically learn hierarchical features from raw data, offer even more sophisticated capabilities for anomaly detection, especially when dealing with complex temporal patterns. Recurrent Neural Networks (RNNs), particularly Long Short-Term Memory (LSTM) networks, are well-suited for analyzing time-series data, which is characteristic of sensor readings. An LSTM model can learn the typical temporal evolution of water quality parameters. For example, it can learn how turbidity typically rises after a heavy rainfall and then gradually subsides. If, after a rainfall, the turbidity remains high for an extended period or behaves in an unusual pattern, the LSTM can identify this as an anomaly, potentially indicating an uncharacteristic source of pollution, such as increased runoff carrying pollutants from urban areas or agricultural fields. Autoencoders, another type of deep learning architecture, can also be used for anomaly detection. An autoencoder is trained to reconstruct its input. If the input data is anomalous, the autoencoder will have a higher reconstruction error, signaling that the data deviates from the patterns it learned during training.

Beyond simply detecting anomalies, AI can provide valuable insights into the potential
causes of these anomalies. By analyzing the correlation between the anomalous sensor readings and other available data, such as weather patterns, land-use data, discharge records from industrial sites, or operational logs from water treatment plants, AI can help pinpoint the most probable source of the contamination. For example, if an anomaly is detected downstream of a wastewater treatment plant, and the AI also identifies an increase in specific chemical markers or a drop in dissolved oxygen that correlates with the plant's operational status or recent discharge reports, it strengthens the hypothesis that the plant is the source. This causal inference capability significantly aids in the enforcement of environmental regulations and the implementation of targeted mitigation strategies.

Furthermore, AI models can be employed for predictive water quality assessment. Instead of just reacting to anomalies, AI can forecast potential future quality issues based on current conditions and predicted environmental changes. For instance, by integrating meteorological forecasts (e.g., predicted rainfall intensity and duration) with hydrological models and real-time water quality data, AI can predict the likelihood of algal blooms in reservoirs or the potential for increased turbidity and pathogen runoff into surface water bodies following heavy precipitation. This predictive capability allows water utilities to take preemptive actions, such as increasing chemical treatment at water plants, diverting raw water intake to cleaner sources, or issuing advisories to consumers. This proactive stance is a paradigm shift from traditional reactive monitoring and treatment, fundamentally enhancing the safety and reliability of water supplies.

The application of AI in water quality monitoring is not limited to natural water bodies. It is equally critical within water treatment plants and distribution networks. In treatment facilities, AI can monitor the performance of various treatment stages, such as coagulation, flocculation, sedimentation, filtration, and disinfection. By analyzing sensor data from each stage (e.g., turbidity after sedimentation, residual chlorine after disinfection), AI can detect deviations that indicate a malfunction or suboptimal performance. For example, if the residual chlorine level drops unexpectedly, it could signal a problem with the chlorination system or an increased demand for chlorine due to a higher influent load, potentially leading to inadequate disinfection. An AI system can flag this immediately, alerting operators to investigate and adjust the process, thereby preventing the delivery of insufficiently treated water. Similarly, AI can optimize the dosage of treatment chemicals based on real-time influent characteristics, ensuring effective treatment while minimizing chemical consumption and operational costs.

Within the vast and complex water distribution networks, AI plays a vital role in maintaining water quality as it travels from the treatment plant to the consumer's tap. Water quality can degrade due to factors such as aging pipes, biofilm formation, stagnant water in dead-end mains, or re-contamination events. AI can analyze data from sensors placed throughout the network to detect signs of potential degradation. For instance, a sustained increase in turbidity or a drop in residual chlorine in a specific zone of the network could indicate issues like pipe corrosion, sediment resuspension, or a compromised section of the pipe. AI can correlate these readings with network hydraulics, such as flow rates and residence times, to identify areas at high risk of water quality deterioration. This enables proactive interventions, such as targeted flushing of pipes, inspection of specific sections, or early repair of infrastructure.

The integration of AI with the Internet of Things (IoT) is central to the effectiveness of these advanced monitoring systems. The proliferation of low-cost, robust sensors capable of wireless communication enables the creation of comprehensive sensor networks that provide a granular view of water quality across wide geographical areas and complex infrastructure. AI algorithms process the data streams from these IoT devices, extracting actionable intelligence. Furthermore, AI can also leverage data from non-traditional sources. For example, social media posts reporting unusual odors or tastes of tap water, or citizen science initiatives collecting local water quality data, can be analyzed using natural language processing (NLP) and ML techniques to identify potential widespread issues that might not be immediately apparent from sensor data alone.

The benefits of employing AI in water quality monitoring are multifaceted. Firstly, it significantly enhances public health protection by enabling early detection and rapid response to contamination events, thereby minimizing the risk of waterborne diseases. Secondly, it leads to more efficient and cost-effective water management. By predicting potential issues and enabling proactive interventions, AI reduces the need for costly emergency responses and remediation efforts. Optimized chemical dosing in treatment plants and reduced water losses due to better leak detection also contribute to cost savings. Thirdly, AI-driven monitoring supports environmental protection by providing better tools to track pollution sources and assess the impact of human activities on aquatic ecosystems. Finally, it fosters greater public trust and confidence in the safety and reliability of drinking water supplies.

However, the successful implementation of AI for water quality monitoring also presents challenges. The accuracy and reliability of AI models are heavily dependent on the quality and quantity of training data. Ensuring data integrity, handling sensor drift or failure, and addressing the inherent variability of natural water systems are critical considerations. Furthermore, the interpretation and validation of AI-generated insights require domain expertise from water quality scientists and engineers. Ethical considerations, data privacy, and cybersecurity also need to be addressed, particularly when dealing with critical infrastructure data. The development of robust, explainable AI (XAI) models is also crucial to build trust and facilitate the adoption of these technologies by water utilities and regulatory bodies. Despite these challenges, the trajectory is clear: AI is poised to become an indispensable tool in the ongoing effort to safeguard and sustainably manage our planet's most precious resource. The transition from reactive to predictive and proactive water quality management, driven by AI, represents a significant leap forward in ensuring safe, reliable, and high-quality water for all.

The imperative to design and operate water systems that can withstand disruptions, whether from extreme weather events, aging infrastructure, or evolving demand patterns, has never been more pronounced. This calls for a fundamental shift in how we conceptualize and manage our water grids, moving from static, reactive approaches to dynamic, predictive, and adaptive strategies. Artificial Intelligence (AI) offers the technological backbone for this transformation, enabling the creation of truly resilient water grids capable of ensuring continuous delivery of safe and reliable water services even under the most challenging circumstances. This case study illustrates how AI can be holistically applied to achieve such resilience, integrating multiple facets of water resource management into a cohesive, intelligent system.

At the core of designing a resilient water grid lies the ability to accurately forecast both water demand and supply. Traditional forecasting methods often rely on historical averages and simple trend analyses, which prove insufficient in the face of increasing climate variability and unpredictable consumption patterns. AI, through advanced machine learning algorithms, can analyze a far richer tapestry of data to generate highly accurate predictions. For demand forecasting, AI models can ingest real-time data from smart meters, weather forecasts (including temperature, humidity, and precipitation), socio-economic indicators, and even event calendars (e.g., public holidays, major sporting events) to predict water usage at granular spatial and temporal scales. For instance, a convolutional neural network (CNN) might be trained to recognize spatial patterns of demand across a city based on sensor data and satellite imagery indicating urban activity, while a recurrent neural network (RNN) can capture the temporal dynamics of daily, weekly, and seasonal consumption. This allows water utilities to anticipate peak loads, understand how extreme heat waves might drastically increase demand in specific neighborhoods, or how prolonged drought conditions might lead to voluntary or mandated conservation measures altering consumption profiles. Such foresight is crucial for optimizing pumping schedules, managing reservoir levels, and ensuring sufficient treatment capacity is available when and where it is needed most.

Simultaneously, AI is indispensable for robust supply-side forecasting. This involves not only predicting the availability of raw water sources, factoring in rainfall patterns, snowmelt, and the performance of upstream infrastructure, but also assessing the operational capacity of treatment plants and the integrity of the distribution network. For surface water sources, AI can integrate hydrological models with real-time sensor data from rivers and reservoirs, alongside long-term climate projections, to forecast water availability months or even years in advance. This aids in strategic water allocation and investment decisions. For groundwater, AI can model recharge rates and predict sustainable extraction levels, preventing over-pumping and aquifer depletion. Furthermore, AI can predict the performance of critical treatment processes. For example, by analyzing influent water quality data and operational parameters of a filter bed, an AI model can predict when the filter will reach its hydraulic capacity or when its effectiveness in removing turbidity will diminish, allowing for scheduled backwashing or maintenance before performance degrades and impacts downstream water quality.

With accurate demand and supply forecasts in hand, AI can then optimize the entire water distribution network. This involves dynamically managing the flow of water through pipes, the operation of pumps, and the regulation of pressure to meet predicted demand while minimizing energy consumption and water losses. Reinforcement learning algorithms are particularly well-suited for this task. An AI agent can learn optimal control strategies for a network of pumps and valves by receiving rewards for meeting demand at required pressure levels, minimizing energy expenditure, and minimizing the detection of leaks. For example, if the AI forecasts a surge in demand in a particular district due to a heatwave, it can proactively adjust pump speeds and open specific valves to reroute water from less-stressed areas or from storage reservoirs, ensuring consistent supply without over-pressurizing the system or causing unnecessary wear on equipment. This dynamic control also plays a critical role in maintaining water quality. By managing flow rates and pressure, AI can help prevent issues like biofilm growth in pipes, which thrive in low-flow or stagnant conditions, and can also reduce the likelihood of backflow or ingress of contaminants into the distribution system.

The monitoring of water quality, as discussed in the previous context, is a vital component of a resilient grid. AI's role here extends beyond anomaly detection to proactive intervention and informed decision-making. By continuously analyzing data from in-situ sensors across the distribution network, AI can identify subtle changes in water chemistry that might indicate potential issues. For instance, a gradual increase in turbidity in a specific pipe segment, coupled with a decrease in residual chlorine, might not immediately trigger alarms in a traditional system. However, an AI system, by correlating these readings with historical data, pipe material, age, and flow patterns, might predict the formation of an internal deposit or the early stages of a biofilm development. This prediction allows for targeted interventions, such as flushing that specific pipe segment or adjusting disinfection strategies in that zone, thereby preventing the deterioration of water quality before it becomes a significant problem for consumers. Moreover, AI can integrate real-time water quality data with hydraulic models to understand how water quality parameters are propagating through the network, allowing for more precise identification of contamination sources or the impact of operational changes.

A crucial aspect of infrastructure resilience is the ability to predict and prevent failures. AI-powered predictive maintenance is revolutionizing how water utilities manage their aging assets, particularly pumps and pipes. For pumps, AI models can analyze vibration data, motor current, temperature readings, and operational history to predict when a pump is likely to fail. By identifying patterns indicative of bearing wear, seal degradation, or impeller damage, the AI can flag a pump for scheduled maintenance
before it breaks down catastrophically. This not only prevents service disruptions but also avoids the costly emergency repairs and potential collateral damage associated with equipment failure. The economic benefits are substantial, as proactive maintenance is generally less expensive than reactive repairs.

For pipes, which form the vast majority of a water grid's physical infrastructure, AI can predict the likelihood of failure (e.g., bursts, leaks) based on a multitude of factors. These include pipe material, age, diameter, soil conditions, historical leak data, pressure fluctuations, and proximity to other utilities. By overlaying these data layers, AI models can generate risk maps, highlighting sections of the network that are most vulnerable to failure. For example, a cast-iron pipe laid in corrosive soil, experiencing frequent pressure transients, and with a history of minor leaks, would be flagged as high-risk. This allows water managers to prioritize rehabilitation or replacement efforts, focusing limited resources on the areas where they will have the greatest impact on overall network resilience and minimizing disruptive service interruptions. Furthermore, AI can analyze acoustic sensor data deployed along pipelines to detect subtle acoustic signatures indicative of leaks, even very small ones that might otherwise go undetected for extended periods, leading to significant water loss and potential structural damage to surrounding areas.

The integration of these AI capabilities—demand and supply forecasting, distribution optimization, water quality monitoring, and predictive maintenance—creates a truly adaptive and resilient water grid. This integrated intelligence allows utilities to move from a static operational mode to a dynamic, self-optimizing system. For example, during an unforeseen event like a major power outage affecting a pumping station, the AI can rapidly reconfigure the network, rerouting water from alternative sources, adjusting pressures in surrounding zones to maintain supply, and alerting field crews to the issue and its impact. Similarly, if a significant contamination event is detected at the source, the AI can immediately identify which parts of the distribution network are potentially affected, adjust treatment processes to mitigate the impact, and issue targeted advisories to affected consumers, all within minutes.

The resilience of a water grid is further tested by the impacts of climate variability and climate change. Increasing frequency and intensity of droughts, floods, and extreme temperature events pose significant challenges. AI provides the tools to build adaptive strategies. For instance, in drought-prone regions, AI-driven demand management systems can automatically adjust water restrictions based on real-time reservoir levels and weather forecasts, communicating these changes directly to consumers through smart devices or utility portals. In flood-prone areas, AI can integrate rainfall forecasts with hydrological models and sensor data from drainage systems to predict the likelihood of localized flooding affecting water infrastructure, enabling proactive measures to protect critical facilities. Moreover, by modeling the long-term impacts of climate change on water availability and demand, AI can inform strategic planning for infrastructure upgrades and water resource development, ensuring the system remains robust for decades to come.

The implementation of such an AI-driven resilient water grid is not without its complexities. It requires significant investment in sensor networks, data infrastructure, and skilled personnel capable of developing, deploying, and managing these advanced systems. Cybersecurity becomes paramount, as a compromised AI system could have catastrophic consequences. Ensuring data privacy and ethical deployment of AI, particularly concerning consumer data from smart meters, is also crucial. Furthermore, building trust in AI-generated recommendations among operators and stakeholders requires transparency and explainability of the AI models (Explainable AI or XAI). Nevertheless, the potential benefits—uninterrupted access to safe water, significant operational cost savings, reduced environmental impact, and enhanced public health—far outweigh the challenges. This case study serves as a blueprint, demonstrating how a holistic application of AI can transform water grids from vulnerable networks into intelligent, adaptive, and resilient systems, capable of navigating the complexities of the 21st century and beyond. It represents the culmination of how AI, across various domains of water resource management, converges to create a system that is not just efficient, but fundamentally secure and sustainable.

Chapter 10: AI in Energy Systems and Smart Grids

The energy landscape is undergoing a profound metamorphosis, driven by a confluence of environmental imperatives, technological advancements, and evolving societal demands. For decades, the global energy infrastructure has been largely predicated on centralized power generation, primarily from fossil fuels. This model, while instrumental in powering industrialization and economic growth, is increasingly proving unsustainable. The escalating urgency to mitigate climate change has placed renewable energy sources—such as solar and wind power—at the forefront of global energy strategies. These sources, however, are inherently intermittent, presenting a significant challenge to grid stability and reliability. The sun does not always shine, and the wind does not always blow, meaning their output fluctuates, creating a dynamic and unpredictable supply that traditional grid management systems are ill-equipped to handle.

This variability necessitates a paradigm shift in how electricity grids are conceived and operated. The era of simply dispatching power from large, fossil-fuel-fired plants to meet demand is giving way to a more complex reality. The integration of variable renewable energy (VRE) sources requires sophisticated forecasting, real-time balancing, and flexible grid operations. Grid operators now face the intricate task of managing a system where supply can change dramatically within minutes, demanding an unprecedented level of agility and predictive capability. Furthermore, the proliferation of distributed energy resources (DERs) is fundamentally altering the traditional one-way flow of electricity. Rooftop solar panels on homes and businesses, small-scale wind turbines, and increasingly, battery storage systems, are generating power closer to the point of consumption. While this decentralization offers numerous benefits, including increased resilience and reduced transmission losses, it also introduces new layers of complexity in grid management. The grid must now contend with bi-directional power flows, a multitude of small-scale generators, and the challenge of coordinating these diverse assets to ensure overall system stability.

The demand for energy efficiency and enhanced reliability further complicates this evolving picture. Consumers, both industrial and residential, are increasingly aware of energy costs and environmental impacts, leading to a greater drive for efficiency. Smart appliances, energy-efficient building designs, and behavioral changes are contributing to more sophisticated demand patterns. Simultaneously, the increasing reliance on electricity for critical infrastructure, from data centers to transportation, heightens the expectation for uninterrupted power supply. Outages, even brief ones, can have significant economic and societal consequences, making reliability a paramount concern. Traditional grid management systems, often based on decades-old infrastructure and manual control processes, struggle to cope with the sheer volume and velocity of data generated by modern energy systems, let alone the complexities of integrating these new sources and demands. These legacy systems are not designed for the real-time, data-intensive, and highly dynamic environment of today's energy landscape. The limitations of these traditional approaches are becoming increasingly apparent as the grid grapples with the challenges of intermittency, distributed generation, and the imperative for greater efficiency and reliability. This is precisely where Artificial Intelligence (AI) emerges as not just a beneficial tool, but an indispensable necessity for navigating these transformative changes and forging a sustainable energy future. AI offers the advanced analytical capabilities, predictive power, and automation potential required to manage the intricate web of modern energy systems.

The integration of renewable energy sources, particularly solar and wind power, has been a cornerstone of global decarbonization efforts. Governments worldwide have set ambitious targets for renewable energy deployment, incentivized by policy frameworks and driven by a growing awareness of climate change impacts. Solar photovoltaic (PV) technology has seen remarkable cost reductions and efficiency improvements over the past decade, making it economically competitive with, and often cheaper than, traditional fossil fuel sources in many regions. Similarly, wind turbine technology has advanced significantly, with larger, more efficient turbines capable of harnessing wind resources more effectively. This surge in renewable energy adoption, however, has introduced unprecedented challenges to grid operators. Unlike conventional power plants that can be ramped up or down to match demand, solar and wind power generation is inherently dependent on weather conditions. Solar output is directly affected by cloud cover, time of day, and season, while wind power fluctuates with wind speed and direction. This intermittency means that the supply of electricity from these sources can vary significantly and unpredictably over short timescales.

Managing this variability requires sophisticated forecasting techniques. Grid operators need to predict the output of solar and wind farms with a high degree of accuracy to ensure that they can compensate for any shortfalls or manage any surpluses. Traditional forecasting methods, often based on historical weather patterns, are insufficient for the rapid fluctuations characteristic of renewable energy generation. This is where AI, particularly machine learning algorithms, offers a transformative solution. AI models can analyze vast datasets, including real-time weather observations, satellite imagery, atmospheric conditions, and historical performance data from renewable energy installations, to generate much more accurate and timely generation forecasts. For instance, deep learning models can identify complex patterns in weather data that human analysts might miss, leading to improved predictions of solar irradiance and wind speeds. Recurrent Neural Networks (RNNs) are particularly adept at capturing the temporal dependencies in time-series data, making them suitable for predicting how wind or solar output might evolve over the next few minutes, hours, or days. The ability to accurately forecast renewable energy generation is critical for maintaining grid stability. It allows operators to optimally schedule the dispatch of other generating assets, such as battery storage systems or flexible conventional power plants, to fill the gaps left by intermittent renewables or to absorb excess generation.

The rise of distributed energy resources (DERs) represents another significant shift in the energy landscape. Rooftop solar panels installed on homes and commercial buildings, combined with advances in battery storage technology, are enabling consumers to generate and store their own electricity. This decentralization of power generation has profound implications for grid management. Traditionally, electricity flowed from large power plants in a predictable, one-way direction to consumers. With DERs, power can flow in multiple directions, with excess solar energy being fed back into the grid, or stored in batteries for later use. This bi-directional flow complicates grid operations, requiring advanced monitoring and control systems. Managing a grid with millions of small-scale, interconnected energy sources is a far more complex undertaking than managing a system with a few hundred large power plants.

AI plays a crucial role in managing the complexity introduced by DERs. AI-powered platforms can aggregate and coordinate the output of numerous distributed assets, effectively creating virtual power plants (VPPs). A VPP is a network of distributed energy resources that are managed collectively by an AI system to provide grid services, such as supplying power during peak demand periods or providing grid stabilization services. AI algorithms can optimize the charging and discharging of batteries, taking into account electricity prices, grid conditions, and the owner's energy needs. For example, an AI system can learn to discharge a home's battery when electricity prices are highest or when the grid is under strain, and recharge it when prices are low or when there is an abundance of renewable energy. This dynamic management of DERs not only benefits individual consumers by reducing their electricity bills but also contributes to overall grid stability and efficiency by providing valuable grid services. Furthermore, AI can help identify and predict the behavior of DERs, allowing grid operators to better understand and manage the aggregate impact of these resources on the grid. This includes forecasting the collective contribution of rooftop solar to local electricity supply or anticipating the demand response capabilities of aggregated battery storage.

The pursuit of greater energy efficiency and enhanced reliability is intrinsically linked to the transformation of energy systems. As energy prices fluctuate and environmental concerns grow, consumers are increasingly seeking ways to reduce their energy consumption and optimize their usage patterns. This drive for efficiency is leading to the adoption of smart home technologies, energy-efficient appliances, and smart building management systems. These technologies generate a wealth of data about energy consumption patterns, which, when analyzed by AI, can reveal opportunities for significant savings. AI algorithms can identify anomalies in energy usage, suggest optimal times for operating high-consumption appliances, and even automate adjustments to building systems to minimize energy waste. For example, AI can learn the occupancy patterns of a building and adjust heating, ventilation, and air conditioning (HVAC) systems accordingly, significantly reducing energy consumption without compromising comfort.

Reliability, the ability of the grid to deliver uninterrupted power, remains a paramount concern for consumers and utility operators alike. The increasing reliance on electricity for critical services, from healthcare to communication networks, means that any disruption can have severe consequences. AI contributes to enhanced reliability in several ways. Firstly, through predictive maintenance, AI can anticipate equipment failures before they occur. By analyzing sensor data from transformers, transmission lines, and other grid components, AI models can identify subtle signs of degradation or impending failure. This allows utility companies to schedule maintenance proactively, preventing costly outages and extending the lifespan of critical infrastructure. For instance, AI can analyze the temperature, vibration, and electrical load data of a transformer to predict when it might fail, allowing for its replacement or repair during a planned maintenance window.

Secondly, AI can improve the speed and effectiveness of grid response to disturbances. In the event of an outage, AI-powered systems can quickly pinpoint the location and cause of the fault, isolate the affected section of the grid, and reroute power from alternative sources to minimize the impact on consumers. This rapid diagnostic and response capability is crucial for maintaining grid stability and reducing the duration of power interruptions. Furthermore, AI can enhance grid resilience against extreme weather events. By integrating weather forecasts with grid operational data, AI systems can predict how potential disruptions, such as storms or heatwaves, might impact grid performance. This allows operators to take preemptive measures, such as strengthening vulnerable infrastructure or implementing demand-side management strategies, to mitigate the risk of widespread outages. The combination of increased efficiency and improved reliability, enabled by AI, is essential for building a modern, sustainable, and customer-centric energy system that can meet the demands of the 21st century. These advancements are not merely incremental improvements; they represent a fundamental re-imagining of how energy is generated, distributed, and consumed.

The critical need for precise energy forecasting is amplified by the increasing penetration of variable renewable energy (VRE) sources and the dynamic nature of electricity demand. Traditional grid management systems, often designed for predictable, baseload power generation, are ill-equipped to handle the inherent unpredictability of solar and wind power, nor the evolving patterns of electricity consumption. Artificial Intelligence (AI) offers a powerful suite of tools to address these challenges, enabling a more resilient, efficient, and reliable energy future.

This subsection delves into the application of AI for both forecasting energy demand and predicting the generation output of renewable sources, highlighting the sophisticated methodologies and the profound impact these capabilities have on the modern energy grid.

Forecasting Electricity Demand with AI

Accurate electricity demand forecasting is the bedrock of efficient grid operations. Utilities and grid operators must anticipate how much power will be needed at any given moment to ensure supply consistently meets demand, avoiding both wasteful overproduction and disruptive shortages. Traditionally, demand forecasting relied on statistical methods, historical data, and expert judgment, which, while useful, struggled to capture the increasingly complex and dynamic factors influencing consumption. AI, particularly machine learning (ML) and deep learning (DL) algorithms, has revolutionized this domain by enabling the analysis of vast and diverse datasets to identify intricate patterns and make highly precise predictions.

ML models, such as Support Vector Machines (SVMs) and Random Forests, can effectively model the non-linear relationships between demand and various influencing factors. However, deep learning architectures, especially Recurrent Neural Networks (RNNs) like Long Short-Term Memory (LSTM) networks and Gated Recurrent Units (GRUs), have proven particularly adept at handling time-series data, which is fundamental to demand forecasting. These models can learn from sequential patterns, temporal dependencies, and long-term trends within the historical electricity consumption data.

The inputs to these AI-driven demand forecasting models are multifaceted and often include:

Historical Load Data: This forms the baseline, providing insights into typical consumption patterns over hours, days, weeks, and years. ML models can learn daily peaks and troughs, weekly variations, and seasonal trends from this data.
Weather Data: Temperature, humidity, cloud cover, and wind speed have a significant impact on electricity demand. For example, extreme temperatures drive up demand for heating and cooling. AI models can correlate minute-by-minute weather data with real-time load data to predict how upcoming weather will influence consumption. Advanced models can even incorporate weather forecasts from multiple meteorological services, weighing their predictions based on historical accuracy.
Time of Day and Day of Week: Consumption patterns vary significantly between weekdays and weekends, and at different times of the day (e.g., morning peak, evening peak). AI models inherently capture these cyclical patterns.
Calendar Events and Holidays: Special events, public holidays, and even major sporting events can cause deviations from normal demand profiles. AI can be trained to recognize the impact of these events by incorporating calendar data. For instance, demand during a major national holiday might be significantly lower than a typical workday, while a championship football game could lead to a surge in demand during its broadcast.
Economic Indicators: Factors such as industrial output, retail sales, and employment rates can correlate with aggregate electricity demand, especially in industrial and commercial sectors. While these are often longer-term indicators, AI can help integrate them for more nuanced forecasting.

Socio-demographic Data: Population density, household income, and urbanization trends can provide insights into overall consumption patterns, especially when forecasting demand at a regional or city level.
Electricity Prices and Market Signals: In deregulated markets, consumer behavior can be influenced by electricity prices. AI models can learn to predict how price fluctuations might affect demand, particularly for flexible loads that can be shifted to off-peak hours.
Real-time Sensor Data: The proliferation of smart meters and IoT devices provides granular, real-time data on energy consumption at the household or building level. AI can leverage this data to refine short-term forecasts and identify anomalies or emerging trends instantaneously.

Consider a scenario where a heatwave is forecast for the upcoming weekend. A traditional forecasting method might simply extrapolate from previous hot weekends. An AI model, however, would integrate the detailed temperature forecasts, the day of the week, historical data from similar heatwaves, and potentially even real-time social media sentiment analysis indicating public responses to the heat. This allows for a far more granular and accurate prediction of peak demand, enabling grid operators to secure sufficient generation capacity and ensure grid stability.

The accuracy of these AI-driven demand forecasts has direct implications for grid efficiency and cost. Overestimating demand leads to the dispatch of more generation capacity than necessary, often relying on expensive peaking plants that are typically less efficient and more polluting. Underestimating demand can result in brownouts or blackouts, leading to significant economic losses and public dissatisfaction. By providing forecasts with greater precision, AI helps utilities optimize the dispatch of generation resources, reduce reliance on inefficient fossil fuel peaker plants, and integrate renewables more seamlessly. This translates into lower operational costs, reduced emissions, and a more reliable power supply.

Forecasting Renewable Energy Generation with AI

The integration of variable renewable energy (VRE) sources like solar and wind power into the grid is a cornerstone of decarbonization, but their inherent intermittency poses significant operational challenges. Unlike conventional power plants that can be dispatched at will, the output of solar panels is dependent on solar irradiance, and wind turbines rely on wind speed and direction. Accurate forecasting of VRE generation is therefore crucial for grid operators to balance supply and demand, maintain grid stability, and ensure economic dispatch of electricity. AI, with its ability to process complex meteorological data and identify subtle patterns, is indispensable in this regard.

AI models for renewable energy generation forecasting typically fall into two categories: short-term forecasting (minutes to hours ahead) and medium-to-long-term forecasting (hours to days or even weeks ahead). Both leverage sophisticated ML and DL techniques.

1. Solar Power Forecasting:

AI models for solar power forecasting primarily utilize meteorological data, satellite imagery, and historical performance data from solar installations. Key inputs include:

Solar Irradiance: This is the most direct predictor of solar output. AI models analyze data from ground-based pyranometers and satellite-

based solar radiation models to predict irradiance levels at specific locations. Deep learning models, especially Convolutional Neural Networks (CNNs), are adept at interpreting satellite images to predict cloud cover movement and its impact on irradiance.
Temperature: While less direct than irradiance, ambient temperature can affect the efficiency of photovoltaic (PV) panels, particularly at very high temperatures.
Cloud Cover and Type: The presence, density, and type of clouds significantly influence solar output. AI models can learn to differentiate between fast-moving, thin clouds that cause transient dips and dense, persistent cloud formations that lead to prolonged reductions in generation.
Historical PV Performance Data: Training data includes past generation output from the specific solar farm or plant, correlated with concurrent weather conditions. This allows the AI to learn the plant's specific response characteristics, including degradation over time or the impact of soiling on panels.
Atmospheric Aerosol Content: Aerosols in the atmosphere can scatter and absorb sunlight, reducing its intensity reaching the panels. Advanced models can incorporate data on aerosol optical depth from satellite measurements.
Soiling and Shading: While often managed through maintenance and site selection, AI can help predict potential impacts of dust accumulation or temporary shading from adjacent structures or vegetation, especially when combined with real-time sensor data or visual inspection data.

For short-term solar forecasting, LSTMs and GRUs are widely used to capture the rapid fluctuations in irradiance caused by passing clouds. For longer-term forecasts, models might incorporate ensemble methods, combining predictions from multiple algorithms and weather models to improve robustness. For instance, an AI system can analyze real-time satellite imagery showing a band of clouds approaching a solar farm and predict a sharp drop in generation within the next 30 minutes, allowing grid operators to ramp up other resources preemptively.

2. Wind Power Forecasting:

Wind power forecasting is even more complex due to the chaotic nature of wind and the significant impact of terrain and turbine characteristics. AI models for wind forecasting utilize a combination of meteorological data, wind farm operational data, and sometimes computational fluid dynamics (CFD) models. Key inputs include:

Wind Speed and Direction: These are the primary drivers of wind turbine power output. Forecasts from numerical weather prediction (NWP) models are crucial, but AI models can refine these predictions using local measurements and historical data.
Atmospheric Pressure and Temperature Gradients: These factors influence wind patterns.
Turbulence Intensity: High turbulence can reduce turbine efficiency and increase wear and tear. AI can help predict periods of high turbulence.
Wind Farm Layout and Turbine Characteristics: The wake effect, where the turbulent wake of one turbine reduces the wind speed available to downstream turbines, is a critical factor. AI models can incorporate the specific layout of a wind farm and the performance curves of individual turbines to predict the aggregate output, accounting for these wake interactions.
Historical Wind Turbine Performance: Similar to solar, historical generation data correlated with wind conditions allows AI to learn the specific behavior and limitations of a wind farm.
Terrain Data: Topographical features can significantly alter local wind patterns. Advanced models can integrate digital elevation models.

AI techniques like Random Forests, Gradient Boosting Machines, and deep learning models, including CNNs and LSTMs, are employed. CNNs can be used to analyze spatial patterns in wind fields derived from NWP models, while LSTMs are effective at capturing the temporal dynamics of wind speed. For example, an AI model might predict that a large wind farm's output will decrease by 50% over the next two hours as a weather front passes, and this prediction informs the grid operator's decision to draw power from a battery storage system or a fast-ramping gas turbine.

The Impact of AI Forecasting on Grid Operations and Market Integration:

The accuracy and granularity of AI-driven demand and VRE generation forecasts have profound implications for grid operations and the electricity market:

Improved Grid Stability and Reliability: By providing more accurate predictions, AI-powered forecasting allows grid operators to better anticipate and manage imbalances between supply and demand. This reduces the need for costly and inefficient operating reserves, minimizes the risk of overloads or under-frequency events, and enhances the overall reliability of the power system, especially with higher VRE penetration.
Optimized Dispatch of Generation Resources: Accurate forecasts enable utilities to optimally schedule the dispatch of all available generation resources, including VRE, battery storage, and dispatchable conventional power plants. This leads to more efficient use of assets, reduced fuel consumption, and lower operational costs. For instance, if a solar farm is forecast to produce less power than expected, the AI can automatically signal for battery storage to discharge or for a gas peaker plant to start up, minimizing the delay and ensuring supply continuity.

Enhanced Integration of Renewables: The ability to forecast VRE output with high confidence is critical for enabling higher penetration levels of solar and wind power. Grid operators can more confidently integrate these intermittent resources into the grid when they have a clear understanding of their expected output.
More Efficient Electricity Markets: In competitive electricity markets, accurate demand and VRE forecasts are essential for market participants to make informed bidding and trading decisions. AI-powered forecasts can help generators optimize their offers, reduce market risk, and facilitate more efficient price discovery. This also supports the integration of new market services, such as ancillary services provided by distributed energy resources.
Reduced Emissions: By enabling better integration of renewables and optimizing the dispatch of less polluting generation sources, AI-driven forecasting directly contributes to reducing greenhouse gas emissions. The ability to minimize the use of fossil fuel peaker plants, which are often highly carbon-intensive, is a significant environmental benefit.

In essence, AI-driven forecasting transforms the complex and often opaque process of energy supply and demand management into a more predictable and controllable system. It empowers grid operators and market participants with the foresight needed to navigate the challenges of a rapidly evolving energy landscape, paving the way for a cleaner, more reliable, and more economically efficient energy future. The continuous refinement of these AI models, fueled by ever-increasing volumes of data from smart grids and advanced sensors, promises even greater accuracy and more sophisticated applications in the years to come.

The transition to a smart grid, characterized by two-way communication, distributed energy resources (DERs), and dynamic demand patterns, necessitates sophisticated control and optimization strategies. While accurate forecasting lays the groundwork for understanding future energy states, the real-time management of grid operations requires AI-powered systems capable of making intelligent decisions under rapidly changing conditions. This subsection explores how artificial intelligence is revolutionizing the optimization and control of smart grids, enabling them to operate more efficiently, reliably, and cost-effectively than ever before.

One of the foremost applications of AI in smart grid control is the optimization of energy dispatch from a diverse portfolio of sources. Modern grids are no longer solely reliant on large, centralized fossil fuel power plants. Instead, they integrate a complex mix of conventional generation, variable renewable energy (VRE) sources such as solar and wind, and energy storage systems. AI algorithms are crucial for determining the most efficient and economical way to dispatch these resources to meet fluctuating demand while adhering to grid stability constraints. This involves sophisticated optimization models that can process real-time data on generation availability, energy prices, grid conditions, and forecasted demand. For instance, AI can be employed to dynamically manage the charging and discharging cycles of battery energy storage systems (BESS). During periods of low demand and high renewable generation, excess energy can be stored in batteries. Conversely, when demand peaks or renewable output dips, the stored energy can be discharged, acting as a buffer and reducing reliance on more expensive or polluting dispatchable generation. AI algorithms can learn optimal charging strategies based on historical price data, forecasted load profiles, and the degradation characteristics of the battery to maximize its economic benefit while preserving its lifespan.

Furthermore, AI plays a pivotal role in managing the integration of distributed energy resources (DERs) like rooftop solar panels and electric vehicles (EVs). The decentralized nature of these resources presents both opportunities and challenges. AI can aggregate and control these distributed assets, transforming them from individual loads or sources into a virtual power plant (VPP). By forecasting the collective output of DERs and coordinating their operation, AI can provide grid services such as frequency regulation or peak shaving. For example, during a system-wide peak demand event, an AI system controlling a fleet of EVs plugged into charging stations can intelligently curtail or delay charging for a brief period, thereby reducing the overall load on the grid without significantly impacting individual users. This demand-side management capability is a cornerstone of smart grid efficiency.

Demand-side management (DSM) itself is significantly enhanced by AI. Beyond simply forecasting demand, AI can actively influence it. Through smart pricing signals, personalized recommendations delivered via mobile apps, or automated control of smart appliances and building management systems, AI can incentivize consumers to shift their electricity consumption away from peak hours. This can be achieved through various strategies. For example, AI algorithms can analyze an individual household's consumption patterns and preferences, along with real-time electricity prices and grid needs, to propose optimal times for running high-energy-consuming appliances like washing machines or dishwashers. In industrial settings, AI can orchestrate the operation of flexible loads, such as large industrial motors or HVAC systems, to align with grid conditions, potentially earning financial incentives for load reduction. Reinforcement learning (RL) is a particularly promising AI technique in this domain. RL agents can learn to interact with the grid and consumers to optimize energy usage over time by receiving rewards (e.g., cost savings, grid stability contributions) and penalties (e.g., high costs, grid instability). An RL agent controlling smart thermostats in thousands of homes could learn to collectively reduce peak demand by making small, coordinated adjustments to temperature setpoints, adapting its strategy based on real-time feedback from the grid.

Beyond energy dispatch and demand management, AI is indispensable for maintaining the operational integrity and resilience of the smart grid. Voltage control, a critical aspect of grid stability, is being transformed by

AI. In traditional grids, voltage is regulated through manual adjustments or relatively simple automated systems. However, with the influx of intermittent VRE and rapidly changing loads, maintaining voltage within acceptable limits across a wide network becomes increasingly complex. AI-powered voltage control systems can analyze real-time voltage measurements from numerous points across the grid, predict potential voltage deviations, and proactively adjust reactive power injection from distributed sources like inverters of solar panels, static var compensators, or by controlling capacitor banks. This predictive and adaptive approach helps prevent voltage sags or swells that could damage equipment or disrupt service.

Fault detection, localization, and isolation are also areas where AI is making significant strides. In conventional grids, locating a fault can be a time-consuming process, often requiring manual inspection. AI algorithms can analyze high-frequency data streams from sensors, smart meters, and protective relays to detect anomalies indicative of a fault almost instantaneously. Furthermore, by correlating data from multiple sources and learning typical fault signatures, AI can rapidly pinpoint the location of the fault, enabling quicker dispatch of repair crews and reducing outage durations. This capability is crucial for grid self-healing, where the grid can automatically reconfigure itself around a fault to minimize the impact on consumers. For example, if a line fault is detected, an AI system could automatically open circuit breakers upstream and downstream of the fault and then attempt to reroute power through alternative paths, restoring service to unaffected areas within seconds or minutes. This ability to intelligently isolate faults and reconfigure the network rapidly is a hallmark of a truly resilient smart grid.

The concept of a "self-healing" grid is heavily reliant on AI's ability to perceive, reason, and act autonomously. When a disturbance occurs, such as a sudden loss of a major generation unit or a transmission line failure, the grid must react instantaneously to maintain stability. AI systems can monitor thousands of parameters simultaneously and execute complex control actions in real-time. This might involve rapidly adjusting generator outputs, reconfiguring power flows, or shedding non-critical loads to prevent cascading failures. Techniques like Model Predictive Control (MPC), often augmented with AI for parameter estimation and adaptation, can forecast the grid's future state and compute optimal control sequences to counteract disturbances. For instance, in response to a simulated generator trip, an AI-driven control system could simultaneously increase the output of other online generators, adjust tap changers on transformers to manage voltage, and dispatch battery storage to absorb any initial frequency deviations, all within milliseconds.

Moreover, AI can optimize the operation of grid infrastructure for efficiency beyond simple dispatch. This includes optimizing power flow to minimize transmission losses, scheduling maintenance proactively based on predictive analytics of equipment health, and managing the integration of electric vehicles in a way that avoids overloading local distribution networks. For example, AI can analyze historical charging data, transformer load data, and forecasted EV adoption rates for a specific neighborhood to predict when and where grid upgrades might be necessary. This allows utilities to plan infrastructure investments more effectively, avoiding costly emergency upgrades and ensuring the grid can accommodate future demand.

The complexity of smart grid control problems often involves high-dimensional state spaces and dynamic environments, making traditional control methods insufficient. This is where advanced AI techniques, particularly reinforcement learning, shine. RL agents can learn optimal control policies through trial and error, without explicit programming for every possible scenario. In smart grids, an RL agent could learn to manage the charging and discharging of distributed batteries to provide ancillary services like frequency regulation. The agent would observe the grid's frequency deviations and receive rewards for contributing to frequency stabilization, gradually learning a policy that effectively uses the battery's capacity to smooth out power fluctuations. Similarly, RL can be applied to optimize the coordinated operation of DERs for voltage regulation in distribution networks, learning complex interaction dynamics between numerous distributed inverters.

The challenges in implementing AI for smart grid control are significant. These include the need for vast amounts of high-quality data, robust cybersecurity measures to protect critical infrastructure from cyberattacks, the development of explainable AI (XAI) to build trust and facilitate regulatory approval, and the need for standardization to ensure interoperability between different systems and vendors. However, the potential benefits—a more reliable, efficient, sustainable, and affordable electricity supply—are driving rapid innovation and adoption. As AI capabilities continue to advance, its role in orchestrating the complex dance of energy supply and demand in smart grids will only become more profound, enabling a seamless transition to a future powered by clean, abundant energy. The ability of AI to continuously learn and adapt to new data, changing grid conditions, and evolving energy sources makes it an indispensable tool for navigating the complexities of the modern and future energy landscape.

For instance, consider the challenge of managing voltage stability in a distribution feeder with a high penetration of rooftop solar PV. Without AI, grid operators might have to curtail solar production during periods of low load and high solar output to prevent voltage rise. An AI-powered system, however, could leverage the smart inverters of these PV systems and potentially connected battery storage. Using reinforcement learning, an AI agent could learn to dynamically adjust the reactive power output of the inverters, or the charge/discharge rate of batteries, to absorb excess voltage. The agent would continuously monitor voltage levels, learn the impact of its control actions, and optimize these settings to keep voltage within the desired range. This would allow for higher solar penetration without curtailment, maximizing the utilization of clean energy resources. This level of granular, real-time control is beyond the scope of traditional methods, highlighting AI's transformative potential.

Another critical application lies in the coordination of electric vehicle charging. As EV adoption surges, their cumulative charging demand can place immense strain on local distribution transformers and feeders, potentially leading to overloads and outages. AI can facilitate "smart charging" by communicating with EVs and charging infrastructure. This AI system would consider factors such as the driver's departure time, their minimum required State of Charge (SoC), the electricity price, and the current load on the local grid. Based on this information, it could schedule charging to occur during off-peak hours, coordinate charging among multiple EVs in a neighborhood to avoid exceeding transformer capacity, or even utilize the EV battery as a temporary power source for the grid (Vehicle-to-Grid, or V2G) during peak demand periods. Reinforcement learning can be used here to learn optimal charging and discharging strategies that balance the driver's needs with grid stability and economic benefits, adapting to daily variations in demand and electricity prices. The AI could learn, for example, that on Tuesdays, the local feeder is particularly stressed between 5 PM and 7 PM, and therefore it should prioritize delaying charging for EVs in that area on Tuesdays, while perhaps allowing faster charging on less constrained days.

Furthermore, AI's role extends to optimizing the operational efficiency of grid components themselves. For example, predictive maintenance powered by AI can analyze sensor data from transformers, circuit breakers, and other critical assets to forecast potential failures. By identifying early signs of wear and tear, AI can trigger maintenance orders before a component fails catastrophically, preventing costly downtime and service disruptions. This proactive approach contrasts with traditional reactive maintenance strategies and significantly enhances grid reliability. AI algorithms can learn complex patterns in vibration data, temperature fluctuations, or oil analysis results that are indicative of impending issues, patterns that might be too subtle for human operators to detect. The ability to predict failures and schedule maintenance optimally, considering factors like spare part availability and workforce scheduling, leads to substantial cost savings and improved asset utilization.

The integration of AI into grid control is not merely about improving existing processes; it is about enabling entirely new capabilities and paradigms. For instance, AI can facilitate the formation and operation of microgrids, which are localized energy systems that can disconnect from the main grid and operate autonomously. AI is essential for managing the complex energy flows within a microgrid, balancing local generation (e.g., solar, wind, combined heat and power) with local demand and storage. During grid outages, AI can orchestrate the microgrid's transition to islanded mode, ensuring continuous power supply to critical loads. Once the main grid is restored, AI can manage the seamless reconnection. This capability is vital for enhancing resilience in the face of extreme weather events or other disruptions that can impact the broader electricity network.

In summary, the optimization and control of smart grids are profoundly enhanced by artificial intelligence. From optimizing the dispatch of diverse energy resources and enabling sophisticated demand-side management, to ensuring voltage stability, rapidly detecting and isolating faults, and facilitating self-healing capabilities, AI is transforming grid operations. Advanced techniques like reinforcement learning are proving particularly adept at handling the dynamic and complex nature of modern energy systems. As smart grids continue to evolve with increasing levels of distributed generation and electrification, AI will be an indispensable engine driving their efficiency, reliability, and sustainability. The continuous influx of data from smart meters, sensors, and IoT devices will further fuel the learning and adaptation of these AI systems, paving the way for an intelligent and resilient energy future.

The seamless operation of our modern energy systems, from the vast networks of transmission lines that crisscross continents to the intricate substations and distributed generation assets, hinges on the unwavering reliability of its physical components. Traditionally, maintenance strategies have oscillated between two primary approaches: reactive maintenance, where repairs are undertaken only after a failure occurs, and time-based preventive maintenance, which schedules interventions at predetermined intervals, regardless of the actual condition of the equipment. While these methods have served the industry for decades, they are inherently inefficient and costly. Reactive maintenance leads to unexpected downtime, often impacting millions of consumers and causing significant economic losses. Preventive maintenance, on the other hand, can result in unnecessary servicing of healthy equipment, while failing to catch components that are degrading faster than expected, thereby still risking failure. This is where the transformative power of Artificial Intelligence (AI) in predictive maintenance for energy infrastructure comes to the fore, ushering in an era of proactive, condition-based asset management.

At its core, predictive maintenance leverages AI to move beyond simply reacting to failures or adhering to rigid schedules. Instead, it focuses on understanding the health of critical infrastructure components in real-time and forecasting when a failure is likely to occur. This is achieved by meticulously analyzing vast streams of data generated by sensors embedded within the infrastructure itself. These sensors collect a multitude of parameters, including vibration patterns, temperature fluctuations, acoustic emissions, electrical signatures, oil quality, and operational performance metrics. AI algorithms, particularly machine learning models, are then employed to sift through this complex data, identify subtle anomalies, and discern patterns that indicate nascent degradation or an elevated probability of future failure.

Consider the colossal turbines that form the backbone of conventional power generation. These are sophisticated machines operating under immense mechanical stress and thermal loads. AI models can analyze vibration data from the turbine shaft, bearings, and blades. Anomalous vibration signatures, such as increased high-frequency vibrations or changes in their spectral content, can signal the early stages of bearing wear, rotor imbalance, or even blade damage. By learning the normal operating profiles of each turbine and comparing them against real-time sensor readings, AI can flag a specific bearing for inspection weeks or even months before it would likely fail, allowing for planned maintenance during scheduled downtime, thereby preventing catastrophic failure, reducing repair costs, and avoiding extended outages. Similarly, temperature monitoring of generator windings can reveal overheating issues caused by insulation degradation or poor cooling, which AI can detect and alert operators to, preventing irreversible damage and ensuring continued operation.

The intricate web of transmission and distribution lines, which carry electricity from generation sites to consumers, also stands to benefit immensely from AI-driven predictive maintenance. The health of these lines is influenced by environmental factors, physical stress, and aging components. AI can analyze data from sensors installed on transmission towers and power lines, such as strain gauges, weather monitoring stations, and even drone-based visual inspections. For instance, AI can correlate increased wind speeds and structural vibrations with data from optical sensors that detect minor damage to insulators or conductor sag.

By analyzing historical data on weather patterns and their impact on line performance, AI can predict when specific sections of the transmission network might be at higher risk of failure due to fatigue or environmental stressors. This enables utilities to prioritize inspections and repairs in vulnerable areas, thereby enhancing grid resilience and preventing widespread blackouts caused by line failures. Furthermore, analyzing the electrical signatures of transformers along the distribution network can reveal subtle signs of aging insulation or internal arcing, which AI can detect and flag for proactive intervention.

In the realm of renewable energy, the application of AI for predictive maintenance is equally impactful. Wind turbines, despite their clean energy credentials, are subject to harsh environmental conditions and continuous mechanical stress. AI algorithms can analyze data from accelerometers, anemometers, and pitch sensors on wind turbine blades. Patterns of increased vibration, unusual pitch adjustments, or anomalous power output can indicate issues such as gearbox wear, bearing fatigue, or blade delamination. Machine learning models can be trained on vast datasets of operational data from thousands of turbines, learning to recognize the unique fault signatures associated with specific component failures. This allows for highly accurate predictions of when a component is likely to fail, enabling technicians to replace it before it causes a significant downtime event. For solar photovoltaic (PV) installations, AI can analyze data from irradiance sensors, temperature sensors, and inverter performance monitoring. Anomalies in the energy output of specific solar panels or strings, or deviations in inverter performance, can indicate issues such as panel degradation, soiling, micro-cracks, or inverter malfunction. AI can help pinpoint the exact panels or inverters requiring attention, optimizing maintenance efforts and maximizing the energy yield from solar farms. For example, by analyzing the performance of individual solar panels over time and correlating it with weather data and historical maintenance records, AI can predict the likelihood of a panel failing prematurely due to manufacturing defects or accelerated degradation, allowing for timely replacement under warranty.

The predictive maintenance paradigm is not solely about individual components; it extends to the health of entire systems. For example, AI can analyze the collective performance data of a fleet of substations, looking for systemic issues or emerging trends that might indicate a broader problem. This could involve identifying common failure modes across similar equipment, optimizing spare parts inventory based on predicted needs, or even informing the design of future infrastructure to mitigate known failure points. The ability to understand the health of the entire grid infrastructure, from the largest power plant to the smallest distribution transformer, allows for a holistic approach to asset management.

A key enabler for AI in predictive maintenance is the increasing availability of sophisticated sensors and the proliferation of the Internet of Things (IoT). Modern infrastructure is equipped with a growing number of interconnected sensors that continuously stream data. This data, often referred to as "condition monitoring data," provides a granular and real-time view of the equipment's operational status. AI algorithms can ingest this high-velocity, high-volume data and process it efficiently. Techniques such as supervised learning, where models are trained on labeled data of past failures and their precursors, are widely used. However, unsupervised learning techniques are also gaining prominence, allowing AI to identify novel or previously unobserved failure patterns without explicit training data for every conceivable fault. Clustering algorithms, for instance, can group similar operational states, and deviations from these clusters can signal anomalies.

The process typically begins with data acquisition, where sensors collect operational and environmental data. This is followed by data preprocessing, which involves cleaning, filtering, and formatting the raw data to make it suitable for AI model consumption. Feature engineering might be employed to create new, more informative variables from the raw data that better capture the underlying condition of the equipment. The core of the predictive maintenance system lies in the AI model itself. Various machine learning algorithms are utilized, including:

Regression models: Used to predict the Remaining Useful Life (RUL) of a component. By analyzing historical degradation patterns, these models can estimate how much longer a component is expected to function before failure.
Classification models: Employed to categorize the current health state of equipment (e.g., healthy, warning, critical) or to predict the probability of a specific type of failure occurring within a given timeframe. Algorithms like Support Vector Machines (SVMs), Random Forests, and Gradient Boosting Machines are common in this domain.
Anomaly detection algorithms: These models identify data points or patterns that deviate significantly from normal behavior, serving as early indicators of potential issues that may not have been previously encountered. Techniques like Isolation Forests or Autoencoders are effective here.
Deep learning models: Particularly Convolutional Neural Networks (CNNs) and Recurrent Neural Networks (RNNs), are proving powerful for analyzing complex data such as acoustic signals, images from visual inspections, or time-series sensor data. CNNs can identify spatial patterns in images, while RNNs are adept at capturing temporal dependencies in sequential data.

The output of these AI models is not just a raw prediction; it is actionable intelligence. Alerts are generated when the probability of failure exceeds a predefined threshold, providing maintenance teams with advance notice. These alerts are often accompanied by diagnostic information, explaining why the alert was triggered and recommending specific inspection or maintenance actions. This allows for the creation of optimized maintenance schedules, ensuring that resources are allocated efficiently, and interventions are performed only when necessary.

The economic benefits of implementing AI for predictive maintenance are substantial. By preventing unexpected outages, utilities can avoid significant revenue losses and penalties associated with service disruptions. Extending the operational life of expensive assets through proactive maintenance reduces the need for premature replacement, leading to considerable capital expenditure savings. Furthermore, by optimizing maintenance schedules and reducing the number of emergency repairs, operational costs can be significantly lowered. The improved reliability of the energy supply also translates into greater economic stability and public trust.

Consider a real-world scenario with a large transformer in a critical substation. Traditionally, its maintenance might be based on a fixed schedule or visual inspections. However, with AI-powered predictive maintenance, sensors monitoring the transformer's oil temperature, dissolved gas content, and insulation resistance would feed data into an AI system. If the AI detects a subtle increase in specific gases within the oil – indicative of incipient internal arcing or insulation breakdown – and this pattern has been correlated with past failures, it can issue an alert. The utility can then schedule a detailed inspection and potentially replace a small, inexpensive component before it leads to a catastrophic failure of the entire transformer, an event that could cost millions to rectify and result in days or weeks of power outages for thousands of customers. The AI effectively provides a "crystal ball" into the transformer's future, enabling preemptive action.

Another critical area is the monitoring of high-voltage transmission lines. These are exposed to the elements and can be subject to various stresses. AI can analyze data from sensors that detect corona discharge (partial electrical breakdown of insulation), conductor sag, and tower integrity. By correlating this data with weather forecasts and historical performance, AI can predict which sections of the line are most likely to experience issues during an upcoming storm. This allows grid operators to take preventative measures, such as temporarily rerouting power, reducing load on vulnerable lines, or dispatching crews to perform rapid inspections before the storm hits. This proactive approach is far more effective than reacting to a line failure after it has occurred.

The adoption of AI in predictive maintenance also plays a crucial role in the integration of renewable energy sources. Wind turbines and solar farms often operate in remote locations and are subject to challenging environmental conditions. AI-driven maintenance strategies can optimize the deployment of maintenance crews, minimizing travel time and maximizing the effectiveness of their interventions. By predicting which turbines or solar arrays are most likely to require attention, utilities can schedule maintenance during periods of low wind or solar production, thereby minimizing the impact on overall energy generation. This ensures that these vital clean energy assets operate at peak performance and contribute reliably to the grid. For instance, AI can analyze acoustic data from wind turbine gearboxes, identifying specific sounds that correlate with impending bearing failure. This allows for targeted maintenance, preventing costly damage and ensuring the turbine remains operational during periods of high wind.

The implementation of AI for predictive maintenance is not without its challenges. These include the need for robust data infrastructure to handle the sheer volume and velocity of sensor data, ensuring data quality

and integrity, and developing cybersecurity protocols to protect this sensitive operational data from malicious actors. Furthermore, the development of explainable AI (XAI) is crucial to build trust among human operators and maintenance personnel. Technicians need to understand not just that a failure is predicted, but
why it is predicted, to effectively implement the recommended actions. The integration of AI-powered predictive maintenance systems into existing operational technology (OT) environments also requires careful planning and execution to ensure seamless operation and avoid disruption.

Despite these challenges, the trajectory is clear. AI is rapidly becoming an indispensable tool for managing the health and reliability of energy infrastructure. By transforming maintenance from a reactive or schedule-based activity to a data-driven, intelligent, and predictive discipline, AI is not only reducing costs and improving efficiency but also fundamentally enhancing the safety and resilience of the energy systems that power our modern world. This proactive approach ensures that the lights stay on, even as our energy landscape becomes increasingly complex and dynamic.

The increasing penetration of electric vehicles (EVs) and the widespread deployment of battery energy storage systems (BESS) represent a paradigm shift in how energy is consumed and managed. These technologies, while offering significant environmental and economic benefits, also introduce new complexities into grid operations. Artificial intelligence (AI) is emerging as a critical enabler for seamlessly integrating these distributed resources, transforming them from potential burdens into valuable assets for grid stability and efficiency. AI algorithms are at the forefront of optimizing the charging behaviors of millions of EVs, ensuring that their energy demands do not overwhelm local distribution networks or the broader power grid. Furthermore, AI is unlocking the potential of EVs to participate actively in grid services through vehicle-to-grid (V2G) technology, effectively turning parked vehicles into a vast, distributed network of mobile energy storage.

The sheer volume of EVs on the road, each requiring periodic recharging, poses a significant challenge to existing grid infrastructure. Without intelligent management, widespread, uncoordinated charging could lead to localized overloads, voltage sags, and increased stress on transformers and distribution lines, especially during peak demand hours. AI-powered charging management systems address this by analyzing real-time grid conditions, electricity prices, and user preferences to schedule EV charging intelligently. Machine learning models can predict charging demand based on historical data, traffic patterns, and weather forecasts, allowing for proactive adjustments to charging schedules. For instance, an AI system can detect an impending overload on a specific feeder in a residential area and automatically defer or slow down the charging of connected EVs until the demand subsides or until a less congested period. This is often achieved through smart charging protocols that communicate with EV chargers, adjusting the rate or timing of power delivery without compromising the user's required state of charge for their next journey. By orchestrating charging across a fleet of vehicles, AI can flatten the charging load profile, smoothing out peaks and valleys and reducing the need for costly grid upgrades.

Beyond simply managing charging, AI is pivotal in harnessing the bidirectional energy flow capabilities of EVs through V2G technology. When an EV is plugged in and parked, its battery represents a substantial energy reserve. AI algorithms can orchestrate the discharge of this stored energy back into the grid during times of high demand or grid stress, providing valuable ancillary services. This capability is particularly transformative for renewable energy integration. For example, during periods of low solar or wind generation, or conversely, when renewable generation is abundant and exceeding demand, AI can direct EVs to discharge stored energy. This helps to stabilize grid frequency, manage voltage fluctuations, and reduce reliance on fossil fuel-based peaker plants. The AI system continuously monitors grid signals, such as frequency deviations or price spikes, and dispatches charging or discharging commands to aggregations of EVs. The economic incentives for EV owners to participate in V2G are significant, as they can be compensated for providing grid services, effectively earning money while their vehicles are parked. AI optimizes these transactions, ensuring that EV batteries are not overly discharged, which could impact their lifespan or the owner's mobility needs, by considering factors like predicted travel needs and battery health.

Complementing the distributed storage offered by EVs, large-scale battery energy storage systems (BESS) are increasingly being deployed by utilities and grid operators to enhance grid flexibility and reliability. These stationary battery installations, ranging from megawatt-scale facilities at substations to smaller, behind-the-meter systems at commercial and industrial sites, are crucial for managing the intermittency of renewable energy sources. AI plays a central role in optimizing the operation of these BESS. For utility-scale systems, AI algorithms analyze a wealth of data, including forecasted renewable generation, predicted electricity demand, real-time grid conditions, and market price signals, to make optimal decisions about when to charge and discharge the batteries.

One of the primary functions of AI-managed BESS is energy arbitrage. By charging batteries when electricity prices are low (typically during periods of high renewable generation or low demand) and discharging them when prices are high (during peak demand), grid operators can capture economic benefits and reduce the overall cost of electricity supply. AI models can accurately forecast price fluctuations and optimize charging and discharging strategies to maximize profit or minimize cost for the system operator. This sophisticated forecasting is crucial, as it requires analyzing complex interactions between weather patterns, fuel prices, grid load, and market dynamics.

Furthermore, BESS managed by AI are indispensable for ensuring grid stability. They can provide rapid response services, such as frequency regulation, which helps to maintain the grid's operational frequency within tight tolerances. When the grid frequency deviates from its set point (e.g., 60 Hz), AI systems can instantaneously instruct the BESS to either absorb excess energy (if frequency is too high) or inject energy (if frequency is too low), acting as a virtual power plant that can respond much faster than traditional generators. This capability is vital for maintaining the reliability of a grid increasingly dominated by variable renewable sources. AI algorithms analyze real-time frequency measurements and make millisecond-level decisions to adjust the BESS output, ensuring seamless grid operation.

Another critical role for AI-managed BESS is in managing the intermittency of renewable energy sources like solar and wind. During periods of high renewable generation, when supply might exceed demand, AI can direct the BESS to store this surplus energy. This stored energy can then be released back into the grid during periods of low renewable generation or high demand, effectively smoothing out the variability of renewables and enabling higher penetration levels without compromising grid stability. AI models predict periods of surplus generation and optimal storage capacity utilization, ensuring that the BESS acts as a buffer, absorbing excess power and releasing it when needed. This process is akin to a large-scale energy buffer, managed intelligently to maximize the utilization of clean energy.

AI also facilitates the use of BESS for peak shaving and load shifting. By strategically discharging the batteries during peak demand hours, BESS can reduce the overall peak load on the grid, thereby deferring the need for expensive infrastructure upgrades and reducing wear and tear on grid assets. This also helps to avoid the use of less efficient and more polluting "peaker plants" that are typically brought online to meet peak demand. AI algorithms can identify the most strategic times for peak shaving based on grid load profiles, electricity tariffs, and operational constraints.

The integration of EVs and BESS, orchestrated by AI, creates a more dynamic, flexible, and resilient energy infrastructure. AI acts as the intelligent conductor, harmonizing the operations of these distributed resources to provide a range of grid services. This includes not only energy arbitrage and frequency regulation but also voltage support, black start capabilities (restoring power after a major outage), and congestion management. By treating EVs and BESS as integral components of the grid, rather than simply loads or isolated storage units, AI enables a transition towards a decentralized energy system where consumers are also active participants in grid management.

Consider a scenario where a utility deploys thousands of smart EV chargers in a new residential development. Without AI, the cumulative charging demand could strain the local transformer. However, with an AI-driven charging management system, the chargers communicate with a central AI platform. This platform analyzes the total demand on the transformer in real-time, along with the charging needs of each EV owner (e.g., "needs 80% charge by 7 AM"). The AI then intelligently allocates charging power, potentially staggering charging start times, adjusting charging rates, or even initiating a small discharge from some EVs if they are overcharged and the grid critically needs support during a very short-lived, localized peak. This sophisticated coordination ensures that the grid remains stable and reliable, even with a high concentration of EVs.

Similarly, a fleet operator managing a depot of electric buses can leverage AI for optimal charging and V2G services. The AI system would consider the bus routes, charging schedules, battery health, and overall grid conditions. It could schedule overnight charging when electricity is cheapest, ensure buses are fully charged by their departure times, and, during the day when buses are parked at the depot, utilize their large battery capacity to provide grid services. If the grid experiences a sudden frequency drop, the AI can dispatch energy from a portion of the bus fleet to stabilize the grid, earning revenue for the fleet operator while the buses are idle. The AI system would precisely manage the state of charge, ensuring that no bus is discharged to a level that compromises its operational readiness.

For large-scale BESS installations, AI's role extends to optimizing their long-term health and performance. By analyzing charging and discharging cycles, temperature variations, and battery chemistry data, AI can predict the degradation rate of the batteries and adjust operational strategies to maximize their lifespan. This might involve limiting the depth of discharge during certain operations or prioritizing less stressful cycling patterns when grid conditions permit. This proactive battery health management is crucial for ensuring the economic viability of BESS investments. Furthermore, AI can manage the optimal placement and sizing of BESS throughout the grid, identifying locations where they can provide the most value in terms of congestion relief, voltage support, or renewable energy integration based on detailed grid modeling and simulation.

The development and deployment of these AI-driven integration strategies for EVs and BESS are crucial for achieving ambitious decarbonization goals. By facilitating the efficient use of renewable energy, reducing reliance on fossil fuels, and enhancing grid stability, AI empowers the transition to a cleaner and more sustainable energy future. The ability to leverage millions of distributed energy resources—from individual EV batteries to large grid-scale storage systems—as active grid assets is a testament to the transformative power of AI in modern energy systems. As these technologies continue to mature and their adoption accelerates, AI will remain at the core of orchestrating their complex interactions, ensuring a reliable, affordable, and environmentally responsible energy supply for all. The future grid will be a symphony of distributed intelligence, with AI ensuring each EV and BESS plays its part harmoniously.

Chapter 11: AI in Transportation Systems

The landscape of modern transportation is undeniably complex, presenting a confluence of persistent and emergent challenges that strain existing systems and necessitate innovative solutions. At the forefront of these difficulties is the pervasive issue of traffic congestion, a phenomenon that plagues urban centers and major arterial routes worldwide. The sheer volume of vehicles vying for limited road space leads to protracted journey times, increased fuel consumption, and a significant reduction in overall economic productivity. Hours are lost daily by commuters and commercial vehicles alike, resulting in missed appointments, delayed deliveries, and a palpable sense of frustration. Beyond the economic and temporal costs, congestion exacerbates another critical challenge: air pollution. The idling and slow-moving traffic associated with gridlock means that vehicles spend more time operating inefficiently, spewing pollutants into the atmosphere. This contributes directly to adverse health outcomes, including respiratory illnesses, and has a detrimental impact on the environment, fueling climate change.

Furthermore, safety remains a paramount concern within transportation networks. Despite advancements in vehicle technology and road design, accidents continue to occur with alarming frequency. Human error, driver distraction, fatigue, and the inherent unpredictability of interacting with other road users all contribute to the risks associated with travel. The aftermath of accidents often includes not only tragic loss of life and serious injuries but also significant disruptions to traffic flow, further compounding congestion. The complex interplay of different road users – from private cars and commercial trucks to cyclists and pedestrians – in mixed-traffic environments presents a continuous challenge for ensuring safety for all.

Compounding these issues is the often-overlooked problem of aging infrastructure. Many road networks, bridges, and public transit systems were built decades ago and are struggling to cope with the demands of modern traffic volumes and vehicle types. Deterioration of road surfaces, structural weaknesses in bridges, and outdated signaling systems can all lead to inefficiencies, increased maintenance costs, and safety hazards. The continuous need for repairs and upgrades places a significant financial burden on governments and transportation authorities, often requiring difficult decisions about resource allocation and prioritization. Maintaining and modernizing this vast physical framework to meet current and future needs is a monumental undertaking.

The demand for efficient and sustainable mobility is also escalating. As populations grow and urbanization intensifies, the need for seamless, reliable, and environmentally responsible transportation options becomes ever more critical. Individuals and businesses alike expect to be able to move themselves and their goods quickly and affordably. This increasing demand places immense pressure on existing networks, often leading to capacity constraints and a struggle to keep pace with evolving user expectations. The desire for personalized, on-demand transportation services, while offering convenience, can also contribute to increased vehicle miles traveled and further strain on road infrastructure if not managed effectively.

Addressing these multifaceted challenges requires a holistic approach that moves beyond incremental improvements. The inherent limitations of traditional, human-driven systems in managing such complexity are becoming increasingly apparent. Optimizing traffic flow in real-time, instantaneously responding to safety incidents, dynamically managing infrastructure capacity, and fostering truly sustainable mobility paradigms demand capabilities that extend beyond conventional methods. This is precisely where the integration of artificial intelligence (AI) into transportation systems offers a transformative potential. AI promises to provide the intelligent tools necessary to analyze vast amounts of data, predict future conditions, and make proactive, optimized decisions across the entire transportation ecosystem, from individual vehicles to city-wide traffic management. The following sections will delve into how AI is being leveraged to tackle these pressing issues and usher in a new era of intelligent transportation.

The pervasive issue of traffic congestion stands as one of the most visible and impactful challenges facing modern transportation networks. In dense urban environments, the daily commute often transforms into a slow, frustrating crawl, consuming valuable time and resources. This congestion is not merely an inconvenience; it represents a significant economic drain. According to various studies, the economic cost of congestion, measured in lost productivity and wasted fuel, can amount to billions of dollars annually for major metropolitan areas. Vehicles stuck in traffic burn fuel inefficiently, leading to increased operating costs for individuals and businesses, particularly for the logistics and delivery sectors. This wasted fuel also directly contributes to air pollution, compounding environmental concerns. The sheer volume of vehicles, often exceeding the designed capacity of road infrastructure, creates a complex web of interactions where small disruptions can propagate and amplify, leading to widespread delays. Factors contributing to this include inadequate road capacity, poorly timed traffic signals, a lack of efficient public transportation alternatives, and a growing reliance on single-occupancy vehicles. The challenge is amplified by the dynamic nature of traffic, with patterns constantly shifting due to time of day, special events, weather conditions, and unforeseen incidents like accidents or breakdowns. Traditional traffic management systems, often reliant on fixed-time signal cycles or limited sensor data, struggle to adapt to these rapid changes, leading to suboptimal flow and persistent bottlenecks.

Closely intertwined with congestion is the critical issue of air pollution. The transportation sector is a major contributor to greenhouse gas emissions and urban air pollutants, impacting both climate change and public health. Vehicles emitting particulate matter, nitrogen oxides, and volatile organic compounds contribute to smog, acid rain, and respiratory problems such as asthma. In many cities, traffic is the primary source of these pollutants, creating unhealthy living environments and placing a significant burden on healthcare systems. The problem is exacerbated by the fact that older vehicles and those operating inefficiently, often due to congestion, tend to produce higher levels of emissions. Moreover, the reliance on fossil fuels as the primary energy source for most vehicles means that the transportation sector is a major driver of global carbon emissions, directly contributing to the climate crisis. The need for cleaner transportation options is therefore not just an environmental imperative but also a public health necessity. Transitioning to more sustainable fuel sources and improving the efficiency of vehicle operation are key to mitigating this challenge.

Safety remains an unwavering priority within transportation systems, yet accidents continue to pose a significant threat to life and well-being. Despite remarkable advancements in automotive safety features, such as airbags, anti-lock braking systems, and electronic stability control, the human element remains a critical factor. Distracted driving, whether due to mobile devices, infotainment systems, or simply a wandering mind, is a leading cause of collisions. Driver fatigue, impaired driving, and aggressive driving behaviors also contribute to a substantial proportion of accidents. The complexity of modern road environments, with an increasing diversity of road users including pedestrians, cyclists, and an ever-growing number of connected vehicles, introduces new layers of risk. Ensuring the safety of all road users requires constant vigilance, robust infrastructure, and effective enforcement, but the sheer scale of interaction and the potential for error present an ongoing challenge. Beyond the immediate human cost, accidents result in significant economic losses due to medical expenses, property damage, and the disruption of economic activity caused by road closures and delays.

The physical backbone of our transportation networks – the roads, bridges, tunnels, and public transit systems – often faces the silent challenge of aging infrastructure. Many of these vital assets were constructed during periods of rapid development and are now reaching or have surpassed their intended design life. The constant stress of heavy traffic loads, exposure to harsh weather conditions, and the passage of time lead to wear and tear, requiring substantial and ongoing investment in maintenance, repair, and replacement. Deteriorated road surfaces can lead to vehicle damage and accidents, while structural weaknesses in bridges and tunnels pose a direct safety risk. Outdated public transit systems may suffer from reliability issues, longer travel times, and lower passenger comfort, deterring potential users. The funding required for comprehensive infrastructure renewal is immense, often leading to difficult political and economic decisions about where to allocate limited resources. Furthermore, simply repairing existing infrastructure may not be sufficient; often, upgrades are needed to accommodate modern traffic demands, new vehicle technologies (like electric vehicle charging infrastructure), and enhanced safety features, adding to the complexity and cost of these endeavors.

In addition to these persistent issues, there is a growing demand for more efficient and sustainable mobility solutions. As global populations continue to urbanize, the pressure on transportation systems intensifies. People expect to be able to move around their cities and between them quickly, affordably, and with minimal environmental impact. This has fueled a demand for diverse and integrated transportation options, including efficient public transit, ride-sharing services, micro-mobility solutions (like e-scooters and bikes), and improved pedestrian and cycling infrastructure. The challenge lies in integrating these diverse modes into a cohesive and efficient network. Furthermore, the expectation for seamless travel, with real-time information and easy transfers between modes, places a demand on data management and communication systems. The need to reduce the environmental footprint of transportation also drives the demand for greener alternatives, such as electric vehicles and improved fuel efficiency, which in turn necessitates significant changes in infrastructure and energy supply.

The sheer scale and interconnectedness of these challenges – congestion, pollution, safety, aging infrastructure, and escalating demand for sustainable mobility – highlight the limitations of traditional, fragmented approaches to transportation management. Reacting to problems as they arise is no longer sufficient. A proactive, integrated, and intelligent approach is required to navigate the complexities of modern transportation. This necessitates a fundamental shift towards leveraging advanced technologies that can process vast amounts of data, identify patterns, predict future scenarios, and enable real-time, optimized decision-making across the entire system. This is the domain where artificial intelligence emerges as a critical enabler, promising to revolutionize how we design, operate, and experience transportation networks.

The intricate dance of vehicles on our roadways, a constant ebb and flow, presents one of the most enduring and complex challenges in transportation. Optimizing this flow, ensuring smooth journeys, and minimizing delays are objectives that have long driven innovation in traffic management. Traditionally, this has involved a combination of physical infrastructure design, static traffic control devices like fixed-time traffic signals, and human operators monitoring conditions through limited observation points. However, the inherent dynamism of traffic – influenced by time of day, weather, special events, and the ever-present possibility of unforeseen incidents – often renders these conventional methods insufficient. The limitations become starkly apparent during peak hours, when a surge in demand overwhelms existing capacity, leading to the familiar spectacle of gridlock. Even seemingly minor disruptions, such as a fender bender or a temporary road closure, can cascade through the network, creating extensive delays and frustration. The reactive nature of traditional systems means that by the time an issue is identified and addressed, significant congestion may have already materialized, exacerbating the problem and leading to suboptimal travel times and increased emissions. This is where the power of artificial intelligence (AI) steps in, offering a paradigm shift from reactive management to proactive prediction and intelligent control of traffic flow.

At the heart of AI's transformative potential in traffic flow management lies its unparalleled ability to process and interpret vast quantities of real-time data. Modern transportation networks are increasingly equipped with a rich tapestry of data sources. Traffic sensors embedded in roadways, cameras strategically positioned at intersections and along highways, and the ubiquitous GPS devices within our vehicles and smartphones all contribute to a continuous stream of information about traffic volume, speed, density, and travel patterns. However, the sheer volume and velocity of this data can overwhelm human analysts and traditional computational methods. AI, particularly through the application of machine learning (ML) algorithms, excels at discerning meaningful patterns within this data deluge. These algorithms are trained on historical traffic data, learning to identify the complex relationships between various factors – such as time of day, day of the week, local events, weather conditions, and incident occurrences – and their impact on traffic flow.

The predictive capabilities of AI are a cornerstone of intelligent traffic management. Machine learning models, ranging from sophisticated deep learning neural networks to more traditional regression and classification algorithms, are employed to forecast future traffic conditions. By analyzing current traffic speeds, densities, and historical trends, these models can predict the likelihood and severity of congestion, identify potential bottlenecks before they fully form, and estimate travel times with a remarkable degree of accuracy. For instance, an AI system can observe a gradual increase in vehicle speed reduction on a particular highway segment during the morning commute and, by cross-referencing this with historical data and real-time weather forecasts indicating a potential downpour, predict a high probability of significant congestion developing within the next 30 minutes. This predictive insight is crucial; it allows traffic management centers to move from simply reacting to existing problems to preemptively implementing strategies to mitigate them. This proactive approach is fundamental to optimizing traffic flow, reducing the duration and extent of congestion, and enhancing the overall efficiency of the transportation network.

One of the most direct applications of AI in traffic flow management is through the dynamic control of traffic signals. Traditional traffic signal systems often operate on fixed-time schedules, which are predetermined and do not adapt to real-time traffic demand. This can lead to unnecessary waiting times at intersections, even when there is no opposing traffic, and can exacerbate congestion when demand patterns deviate from the programmed schedule. AI-powered adaptive traffic signal control systems, however, revolutionize this by continuously monitoring traffic conditions at intersections and along corridors. Using data from sensors and cameras, these systems can analyze the number of vehicles waiting in each direction, predict arrival rates, and then dynamically adjust signal timings in real-time to optimize traffic flow. In a busy urban intersection, an adaptive system might detect a prolonged queue forming on a side street due to heavy incoming traffic on the main road. It can then extend the green light phase for the main road while minimizing the red light duration for the side street, or even temporarily reallocate green time from an adjacent, less busy intersection, to clear the backlog more efficiently. This intelligent adjustment helps to minimize vehicle queues, reduce unnecessary idling, and improve the overall throughput of the intersection, preventing localized congestion from spreading. Furthermore, these systems can coordinate across multiple intersections along a corridor, creating "green waves" that allow vehicles to travel through a series of signals without stopping, significantly reducing travel times and fuel consumption. The benefits extend beyond just efficiency; by reducing stop-and-go traffic, these systems also contribute to lower emissions and a more pleasant driving experience.

Beyond signal control, AI plays a pivotal role in guiding drivers through the network via intelligent routing and navigation systems. While GPS-based navigation apps have been around for some time, the integration of advanced AI significantly enhances their capabilities. These AI-powered navigation systems not only rely on real-time traffic data but also leverage predictive models to forecast traffic conditions along potential routes. When a user requests directions, the AI system doesn't just consider the current shortest or fastest route; it analyzes predicted congestion, potential incidents, and historical travel times to suggest routes that are likely to remain optimal throughout the journey. For example, if the AI predicts that a major sporting event will cause significant congestion on a primary arterial route in an hour, it might proactively reroute drivers away from that path even if it currently appears to be the fastest option. This distributed form of traffic management empowers individual drivers to make informed decisions, collectively contributing to a more balanced and efficient distribution of traffic across the network. The ability of these systems to learn from user behavior and traffic patterns further refines their recommendations over time, making them increasingly accurate and valuable for daily commuting and long-distance travel alike. These systems can also integrate information about public transit availability, suggesting multi-modal journeys that might be more efficient or environmentally friendly.

AI also offers powerful tools for managing traffic flow proactively through the implementation of variable speed limits (VSL). In traditional highway systems, speed limits are static and apply equally regardless of current traffic conditions. However, this can be problematic. During periods of heavy congestion or when visibility is reduced due to fog or heavy rain, maintaining a high, constant speed limit can increase the risk of accidents. Conversely, during periods of light traffic, a lower-than-necessary speed limit might unnecessarily impede flow. AI-powered VSL systems address this by dynamically adjusting the speed limits displayed on electronic signs based on real-time traffic data and predictive models. For instance, if an AI system detects the formation of shockwaves – spontaneous, localized congestion that can propagate backward through traffic – it can progressively reduce the speed limit upstream of the congestion point. This "smoothing" effect helps to prevent sudden braking and merging, which are common causes of accidents in congested conditions, and allows traffic to flow more smoothly at a reduced, safer speed. Similarly, in response to adverse weather conditions, speed limits can be lowered to enhance safety. The AI system analyzes sensor data from weather stations and traffic cameras to assess visibility and road surface conditions, then adjusts speed limits accordingly. This proactive management of speed not only improves safety but also helps to reduce the frequency and severity of traffic jams, leading to more predictable travel times and reduced fuel consumption. The integration of VSL with other AI-driven traffic management strategies, such as ramp metering and dynamic lane management, creates a comprehensive and intelligent approach to optimizing highway operations.

The implementation of AI in traffic flow prediction and management is not a futuristic concept; it is actively being deployed and refined in cities around the world. Consider the intricate intersections of a bustling metropolis, where numerous vehicles converge from multiple directions. Without intelligent management, these nodes often become choke points, leading to extensive queues and delays that ripple through the surrounding road network. AI-driven adaptive traffic signal control systems are specifically designed to tackle these challenges. In downtown areas, for example, these systems monitor traffic flow in real-time using inductive loop detectors buried in the pavement, radar sensors, and video analytics from strategically placed cameras. When a significant volume of traffic is detected approaching an intersection from one direction, while another direction has minimal demand, the AI algorithm will dynamically extend the green phase for the high-demand approach and shorten it for the low-demand one. This is far more nuanced than traditional pre-timed signals. The AI can even predict when a queue is likely to spill back and block an upstream intersection, proactively adjusting signal timings further back in the network to prevent such a cascade. Some advanced systems also incorporate predictive modeling, learning typical traffic patterns for different times of day and days of the week, and even factoring in data from special events like concerts or sporting matches that are known to impact traffic volumes. This allows the system to anticipate demand and adjust timings proactively rather than reactively.

Beyond intersection control, AI's predictive power is being harnessed for network-wide traffic flow optimization. Imagine a major urban highway experiencing a sudden surge in traffic volume due to an unexpected event, such as a major accident or a large public gathering. Traditionally, traffic management operators might only become aware of this congestion once it has formed and started to impact travel times significantly. However, AI systems can detect the early precursors of such congestion. By analyzing data from a network of sensors, including vehicle speeds, densities, and even the rate at which vehicles are braking, an AI can identify the subtle signs of an impending bottleneck or shockwave. Based on this analysis and its learned models of how traffic behaves under various conditions, the AI can then initiate a series of preemptive actions. This might involve dynamically adjusting the speed limits displayed on overhead electronic signs, gradually reducing speeds in advance of the developing congestion to prevent abrupt stops and reduce the likelihood of secondary accidents. Simultaneously, the AI could communicate with ramp metering systems at highway entrances, temporarily restricting the rate at which vehicles are allowed onto the highway to prevent overloading the already strained capacity. Furthermore, the AI can provide real-time updates and alternative route suggestions to navigation applications used by drivers, helping to distribute traffic more evenly across the network and avoid funneling more vehicles into the congested area. This integrated, multi-faceted approach, orchestrated by AI, aims to smooth out traffic flow, minimize delays, and enhance safety by managing the network proactively rather than reactively.

The effectiveness of AI in traffic flow prediction and management is heavily reliant on the quality and comprehensiveness of the data it receives. A robust network of interconnected sensors is therefore paramount. These sensors provide the raw input for the AI algorithms, enabling them to build an accurate picture of current traffic conditions. Inductive loop detectors, embedded beneath the road surface, have been a staple for decades, detecting the presence and passage of vehicles by sensing changes in inductance caused by the metal in their frames. More recently, advancements in sensor technology have led to the widespread deployment of radar and lidar sensors, which can provide more detailed information such as vehicle speed, classification (e.g., car, truck, motorcycle), and even occupancy of specific lanes. Traffic cameras, equipped with sophisticated computer vision capabilities, are another critical data source. AI algorithms can process the video feeds from these cameras to count vehicles, estimate their speeds, detect traffic incidents like stalled vehicles or debris on the road, and even monitor pedestrian and cyclist activity at intersections. The integration of data from connected vehicles, which transmit information about their speed, location, and braking behavior, further enriches the dataset. Smartphone GPS data, aggregated and anonymized, also provides valuable insights into travel times and route choices across the wider network. The challenge then becomes fusing these diverse data streams into a coherent, real-time model of the traffic system. AI plays a crucial role here too, not only in analyzing the data but also in filtering out noise, identifying anomalies, and ensuring data consistency across different sources. For example, if a sensor temporarily fails, the AI can use data from adjacent sensors and its historical knowledge to estimate the missing information, maintaining a continuous operational picture.

The deployment of AI for traffic signal optimization, often referred to as adaptive traffic signal control (ATSC), is a prime example of how these technologies are transforming urban mobility. Consider an intersection with four approaches. Without ATSC, fixed-time signals might allocate green light time based on a pre-determined schedule, perhaps assuming equal traffic volumes throughout the day. This leads to inefficiency; during off-peak hours, vehicles may spend unnecessary time waiting at red lights, while during peak hours, the fixed timing might be insufficient to clear the approaching queues, leading to gridlock. An ATSC system, powered by AI, continuously monitors the queues forming on each approach using sensors such as video analytics or induction loops. It measures the length of queues and the arrival rate of vehicles. The AI algorithm then dynamically adjusts the signal phasing – the sequence and duration of green, yellow, and red lights – to minimize overall delay across all approaches. For instance, if the AI detects a growing queue on the north-south approaches while the east-west approaches have very few vehicles, it will extend the green light duration for north-south traffic and shorten it for east-west traffic, or even skip a phase for the east-west direction if the queue is negligible. The AI can also coordinate with adjacent intersections to create "green waves," allowing a platoon of vehicles to travel through a series of intersections without stopping. This not only reduces travel times but also decreases fuel consumption and emissions from prolonged idling. Real-world implementations of ATSC systems in cities globally have demonstrated significant reductions in travel times, decreases in vehicle stops, and notable improvements in traffic flow, particularly in complex urban environments with a high density of intersections. The continuous learning capability of AI allows these systems to adapt to changing traffic patterns over time, ensuring sustained optimal performance.

Variable speed limits (VSL) represent another frontier where AI is enhancing traffic flow management, particularly on high-speed roadways like highways and freeways. The traditional approach of a single, static speed limit has limitations. During periods of heavy congestion, maintaining a high speed limit can lead to a phenomenon known as "phantom jams" or shockwaves – spontaneous slowdowns that propagate backward through traffic, often caused by a single driver braking unnecessarily. These shockwaves can create ripple effects, causing significant delays and increasing the risk of rear-end collisions. AI-powered VSL systems address this by dynamically adjusting the posted speed limits based on real-time traffic conditions and predictive analysis. Using data from sensors that measure vehicle speeds, densities, and headways (the distance between vehicles), the AI can detect the formation of these shockwaves or significant slowdowns. It can then progressively reduce the speed limits on electronic signs located upstream of the congestion. This gradual reduction in speed encourages drivers to slow down smoothly, preventing abrupt braking and helping to dissipate the shockwave before it intensifies. This proactive measure helps to maintain a smoother, more consistent flow of traffic, reducing the severity and duration of congestion. Furthermore, VSL systems can be integrated with weather data. In conditions of reduced visibility due to fog, heavy rain, or snow, the AI can automatically lower the speed limits to enhance safety, giving drivers more time to react to hazards. The system continuously monitors conditions, adjusting speed limits as the weather or traffic situation evolves. This intelligent management of speed not only improves safety but also contributes to more predictable travel times and can lead to a reduction in fuel consumption by promoting more efficient driving speeds.

The integration of AI into traffic management systems is also leading to sophisticated incident detection and response strategies. When an accident, breakdown, or other obstruction occurs on a roadway, timely detection and clearance are crucial to minimizing secondary congestion and ensuring safety. AI algorithms can analyze data from a variety of sources to identify incidents much faster than traditional manual methods. For instance, by monitoring traffic camera feeds, AI can detect unusual patterns such as vehicles stopped in travel lanes, sudden braking by multiple vehicles, or the presence of debris on the road. Similarly, analyzing aggregated GPS data, AI can identify significant deviations from expected travel times or unusual traffic patterns that might indicate an incident. Once an incident is detected, AI can assist in optimizing the response. It can automatically alert traffic management authorities, provide precise location information, and suggest the most efficient response routes for emergency vehicles. Furthermore, based on the predicted impact of the incident on traffic flow, the AI can recommend or automatically implement traffic control measures, such as dynamic speed limit reductions, diversion routing through navigation apps, and adjustments to traffic signal timings at nearby intersections to manage the altered traffic patterns. This rapid and intelligent response minimizes the disruption caused by incidents, reducing the overall impact on the transportation network and improving safety for all road users. The ability of AI to process vast amounts of real-time data and learn from past incidents allows for increasingly effective and timely incident management, a critical component of maintaining smooth and safe traffic flow.

The advent of autonomous vehicles (AVs) represents a profound evolution in personal and commercial transportation, driven fundamentally by advancements in Artificial Intelligence (AI). These self-driving machines are not merely sophisticated cruise control systems; they are complex AI-powered entities capable of perceiving their surroundings, making intricate decisions in real-time, and executing precise control actions to navigate the dynamic and often unpredictable environments of our roads. The journey towards widespread AV adoption hinges on AI's ability to replicate and, in many cases, surpass human capabilities in driving.

At the core of an autonomous vehicle's operation lies its **perception system**. This is the digital equivalent of a human driver's senses, tasked with gathering an exhaustive understanding of the vehicle's immediate environment. This system typically relies on a suite of sophisticated sensors, each with its strengths and limitations. Cameras, employing advanced computer vision algorithms, serve as the primary visual input. These systems can identify lane markings, traffic signs, traffic lights, pedestrians, cyclists, and other vehicles. Sophisticated deep learning models, trained on massive datasets of diverse road conditions, enable these cameras to interpret complex visual scenes, even in challenging lighting or weather. However, cameras can be hampered by glare, fog, heavy rain, or low light. To overcome these limitations, AVs integrate other sensor modalities. LiDAR (Light Detection and Ranging) systems emit laser pulses and measure the time it takes for them to return after reflecting off objects, creating a precise 3D map of the surroundings. This allows for accurate distance measurement and object detection, irrespective of lighting conditions. Radar sensors, which emit radio waves, are particularly effective at detecting the speed and distance of objects, and can penetrate fog, rain, and snow better than cameras or LiDAR, making them invaluable for long-range detection and adverse weather conditions. Ultrasonic sensors are typically used for short-range detection, crucial for tasks like parking and maneuvering in tight spaces. The real magic, however, happens through **sensor fusion**. AI algorithms are employed to intelligently combine the data streams from all these disparate sensors. This process creates a robust, multi-layered understanding of the environment, where the strengths of one sensor can compensate for the weaknesses of another. For example, if a camera struggles to discern an object in heavy fog, LiDAR and radar data can confirm its presence, distance, and velocity, allowing the AI to accurately track it. This fusion process generates a dynamic, high-fidelity digital representation of the world around the AV, crucial for safe navigation.

Beyond merely perceiving the environment, AVs must be able to

make decisions. This is where AI's computational and learning capabilities truly shine. Once the perception system has built a comprehensive understanding of the scene, sophisticated AI algorithms, often employing techniques like reinforcement learning and probabilistic reasoning, analyze this information to determine the optimal course of action. This involves predicting the behavior of other road users – a notoriously complex task given the inherent variability of human drivers, pedestrians, and cyclists. AI models trained on vast amounts of driving data learn to anticipate potential actions, such as a pedestrian stepping into the road, a car suddenly changing lanes, or a cyclist weaving through traffic. Based on these predictions and the current state of the environment, the AI must decide on actions such as accelerating, braking, steering, or changing lanes. The decision-making process must also consider the rules of the road, navigation goals, and safety constraints. For instance, an AV approaching an intersection might detect a pedestrian near the crosswalk. The AI will assess the pedestrian's proximity, direction of movement, and the AV's own speed and trajectory. If the AI predicts a high probability of the pedestrian entering the crosswalk, it will initiate braking to yield, even if the pedestrian has not yet fully committed. In more complex scenarios, such as navigating a busy roundabout, the AI must not only detect other vehicles but also predict their intended exit points and adjust its speed and position accordingly to merge safely and efficiently. The algorithms must also be able to handle edge cases – rare and unexpected situations that are difficult to train for explicitly. This requires a level of reasoning and generalization that AI research is continuously striving to improve.

Once a decision is made, the AI's **control system** translates it into physical actions. This involves precise manipulation of the vehicle's actuators – the steering wheel, accelerator, and brakes. This requires sophisticated control algorithms, often based on concepts like PID (Proportional-Integral-Derivative) control or model predictive control, which are tuned to ensure smooth, accurate, and responsive execution of the AI's commands. The control system must account for the vehicle's dynamics, road surface conditions, and external factors like wind resistance to ensure that the vehicle maneuvers as intended. For example, when the AI decides to execute a lane change, the control system calculates the precise steering angle, acceleration, and duration required to move the vehicle smoothly and safely into the adjacent lane, while maintaining appropriate spacing from other vehicles. The responsiveness of the control system is paramount. A fraction of a second's delay in braking can have critical consequences. Therefore, AV control systems are designed for extremely low latency, ensuring that decisions are translated into actions with minimal delay. Furthermore, these systems must be robust, capable of handling unexpected disturbances such as sudden road surface changes or evasive maneuvers required by the decision-making AI. The seamless integration between perception, decision-making, and control is what ultimately enables an AV to navigate its environment.

The widespread deployment of autonomous vehicles promises to reshape our transportation systems in profound ways, impacting **traffic flow, infrastructure requirements, and urban planning**. One of the most anticipated benefits is the potential for significantly improved traffic flow. AVs, by communicating with each other and with infrastructure (Vehicle-to-Vehicle, or V2V, and Vehicle-to-Infrastructure, or V2I, communication), can form platoons – tightly packed groups of vehicles traveling at consistent speeds with minimal spacing. This reduces aerodynamic drag and increases road capacity. Moreover, AVs can optimize their speed and acceleration more efficiently than human drivers, leading to smoother traffic flow and reducing the formation of shockwaves that cause congestion. Without the inherent variability of human driving – such as inconsistent braking, sudden lane changes, and distraction – roads could accommodate more vehicles, leading to reduced travel times and fewer traffic jams.

However, this optimistic outlook also necessitates a re-evaluation of our existing

infrastructure. Roads designed for human drivers may need modifications to better support AVs. Clearer lane markings, improved signage, and the deployment of V2I communication systems will be crucial. Smart traffic signals that can communicate with AVs, for instance, could allow for more efficient intersection management, optimizing traffic flow based on the real-time needs of connected vehicles. Charging infrastructure for electric AVs will also become increasingly important. Furthermore, the reduced need for human parking, as AVs can drop off passengers and find remote parking or return to a charging station, could free up valuable urban space.

The implications for
urban planning are equally transformative. With the potential for more efficient and potentially fewer privately owned vehicles (due to shared AV fleets), cities could see a reduction in parking lots and a redesign of urban landscapes. Public transportation could be integrated more seamlessly with AV services, offering first-mile/last-mile solutions. The concept of car ownership might shift towards mobility-as-a-service (MaaS), where users access transportation on demand. This could lead to denser, more walkable urban cores, with less space dedicated to roads and parking, and more space for green areas, housing, and commercial development.

Despite the immense potential, several
challenges remain significant hurdles to the widespread adoption of autonomous vehicles. **Safety** is, of course, paramount. While AI can surpass human reaction times and eliminate human error, it is not infallible. Proving that AVs are statistically safer than human-driven vehicles, especially in a wide range of unpredictable scenarios, is a monumental task. Testing and validation must be rigorous and exhaustive. The ethical dilemmas faced by AVs in unavoidable accident scenarios – the so-called "trolley problem" – are still subjects of intense debate and require clear, universally accepted programming guidelines.

Regulation and standardization are also critical. Governments and international bodies must establish clear legal frameworks for AV operation, including liability in the event of an accident, insurance requirements, and operational guidelines. Standardization across different manufacturers and systems is essential to ensure interoperability and safety. Without harmonized regulations, the widespread deployment of AVs across different regions could be severely hampered.

Finally,
public acceptance and trust are vital. Many people are understandably hesitant to cede control of their vehicles to machines. Building public confidence requires transparency in how AV systems work, clear communication about their safety capabilities, and successful real-world demonstrations. Education campaigns and gradual integration into society, perhaps starting with controlled environments or specific use cases like trucking or shuttle services, will be necessary to foster trust and overcome ingrained skepticism. The journey of autonomous vehicles is thus not just a technological one, but also a societal and regulatory one, all underpinned by the transformative power of artificial intelligence.
The transformative potential of Artificial Intelligence extends far beyond the realm of individual autonomous vehicles, offering a paradigm shift in how we approach and manage public transportation systems. The inherent complexities of moving large numbers of people efficiently, equitably, and sustainably have long presented significant challenges for urban planners and transit authorities. AI, with its unparalleled ability to process vast datasets, identify intricate patterns, and make predictive and adaptive decisions, is poised to address these challenges head-on, ushering in an era of smarter, more responsive, and user-centric public transit.

One of the most immediate and impactful applications of AI in public transportation lies in the optimization of

route planning and scheduling. Traditional public transit networks have often been designed based on historical data and static demand models, leading to inefficiencies such as underutilized routes during off-peak hours or overcrowded services during peak times. AI algorithms, however, can move beyond these static approaches by continuously analyzing a multitude of real-time data streams. This includes passenger count data from sensors on vehicles, ticketing and fare card usage patterns, real-time traffic conditions obtained from GPS data and traffic management systems, and even external factors like weather forecasts and local event schedules. By integrating and processing this dynamic information, AI can create optimized schedules that more closely align with actual passenger demand. For instance, an AI system can identify that a particular bus route consistently experiences a surge in ridership on weekday evenings heading towards a residential area, or that a subway line sees a significant drop-off in passengers after a certain station. Armed with this insight, the AI can recommend dynamic adjustments to service frequencies, adding more buses or train cars to high-demand routes during specific times or rerouting services to better serve emerging population centers. This not only maximizes resource utilization, reducing operational costs for transit agencies, but also significantly improves the passenger experience by minimizing wait times and overcrowding.

Furthermore, AI-powered
predictive modeling plays a crucial role in proactive service management. Instead of reacting to existing demand, transit authorities can leverage AI to forecast future ridership with greater accuracy. These predictive models can learn from historical trends, seasonal variations, demographic shifts, and even the impact of special events or economic changes to anticipate where and when demand will be highest. For example, an AI might predict an increased demand for a specific commuter train line due to a new large employer opening in a nearby district or a significant increase in concert attendance at a venue served by a particular bus route. This foresight allows transit operators to

preemptively adjust service levels. They can deploy additional vehicles, adjust crew schedules, or even implement temporary route modifications before the demand fully materializes, thereby preventing service disruptions and ensuring that capacity matches anticipated needs. This predictive capability transforms public transportation from a reactive service into a proactive one, capable of anticipating and meeting the evolving mobility needs of a city.

The enhancement of the
passenger experience is another area where AI is making significant strides. Gone are the days of static timetables and limited information. AI is enabling the development of sophisticated real-time information systems that provide passengers with accurate and up-to-the-minute updates on their journeys. This includes real-time vehicle tracking, estimated arrival times that account for current traffic and delays, and instant alerts about service disruptions or alternative routes. Mobile applications powered by AI can go even further, offering personalized journey planning. By learning a user's travel patterns, preferences, and even their typical departure and arrival times, these AI-driven systems can suggest the most efficient and convenient routes, combining different modes of transport – buses, trains, trams, and even ride-sharing or bike-sharing services – to create a seamless end-to-end travel experience. This level of personalization makes public transport more accessible and appealing, especially to individuals who may have previously found it daunting or inconvenient.

Beyond static services, AI is also a driving force behind the burgeoning field of
dynamic dispatching of on-demand transit services. This concept, often referred to as microtransit, utilizes AI to provide flexible, door-to-door or near-door-to-door transportation within a defined service area, often acting as a first-mile/last-mile solution to connect passengers to major transit hubs or serve areas with lower population density that cannot support traditional fixed-route services. AI algorithms are at the

heart of these systems, efficiently grouping passengers with similar travel requests, optimizing vehicle routes in real-time to minimize detours and travel times, and dynamically assigning vehicles to serve these evolving demands. When a passenger requests a ride through a mobile app, the AI analyzes their origin and destination, considers other active requests, and calculates the most efficient way to pick them up and drop them off, often in conjunction with other passengers. This not only offers a level of convenience akin to ride-sharing services but does so with the efficiency and sustainability benefits of shared transit. The AI continuously reroutes and reassigns vehicles based on new requests and changing traffic conditions, ensuring that the service remains fluid and responsive. This flexibility is particularly valuable in suburban areas, less densely populated regions, or during off-peak hours when traditional fixed routes may be infrequent or nonexistent.

The integration of AI into public transportation networks also has profound implications for operational efficiency and resource management. For instance, AI can be used for
predictive maintenance of vehicles. By analyzing sensor data from buses, trains, and subway cars – such as engine performance, brake wear, battery health (for electric fleets), and operational hours – AI algorithms can predict when a component is likely to fail. This allows maintenance teams to schedule repairs proactively, before a breakdown occurs, thus preventing costly service disruptions and extending the lifespan of the fleet. This shift from reactive maintenance to predictive maintenance not only saves money but also significantly improves the reliability of public transport services, a critical factor in passenger satisfaction.

Furthermore, AI can optimize
energy consumption in public transit. For electric buses and trains, AI can manage charging schedules to take advantage of lower off-peak electricity rates and optimize regenerative braking systems to recapture the maximum amount of energy during deceleration. For all types of vehicles, AI can refine driving patterns to promote smoother acceleration

and braking, reducing fuel or electricity consumption. By analyzing real-time traffic data and route topography, AI can also suggest optimal speeds and routes that minimize energy expenditure. This focus on energy efficiency aligns with broader sustainability goals and contributes to lower operational costs.

The role of AI in enhancing
accessibility within public transportation is also noteworthy. AI-powered navigation aids can assist visually impaired passengers in navigating complex transit stations, providing auditory cues and real-time guidance. For passengers with mobility issues, AI can help identify the most accessible routes and vehicles, ensuring that they can board and alight safely and comfortably. Personalized journey planning can also be tailored to specific accessibility needs, making public transport a more inclusive option for everyone.

Beyond the operational and passenger-facing aspects, AI also contributes to better
urban planning and integration. By analyzing ridership data, origin-destination patterns, and the impact of transit services on urban mobility, AI can provide valuable insights to city planners. This data can inform decisions about where to expand transit networks, how to redesign urban spaces to better accommodate public transport, and how to integrate different modes of transportation more effectively. For example, AI analysis might reveal that a new housing development is poorly served by existing transit, prompting the planning of a new bus route or a microtransit zone. Similarly, data on pedestrian flows around transit stations can help in designing safer and more efficient pedestrian access points. The ability of AI to model the complex interplay between transportation, land use, and population density provides a powerful tool for creating more livable and sustainable cities.

The successful implementation of AI in public transportation hinges on several factors, including the availability of robust data infrastructure, the development of sophisticated algorithms, and the establishment of clear ethical guidelines and regulatory frameworks. As AI technologies continue to advance and become more integrated into our daily lives, their role in revolutionizing public transportation will only grow, promising a future where cities are more connected, sustainable, and accessible for all their residents. The transition towards AI-enhanced public transit represents not just an upgrade in technology, but a fundamental reimagining of urban mobility, prioritizing efficiency, convenience, and passenger well-being.

The resilience and efficiency of any transportation network are intrinsically tied to the integrity of its underlying physical infrastructure. Roads, bridges, tunnels, and railway tracks are not merely static conduits; they are dynamic assets subject to constant wear and tear from environmental factors, traffic loads, and the passage of time. Historically, the maintenance of this critical infrastructure has often been a reactive process, relying on scheduled inspections and responses to visible signs of degradation. However, this approach can lead to unforeseen failures, costly emergency repairs, and significant disruptions to the flow of people and goods. Artificial Intelligence is now emerging as a powerful tool to revolutionize infrastructure maintenance, shifting the paradigm from reactive repair to proactive, predictive management.

At the forefront of this transformation is the application of AI-powered **predictive maintenance**. This approach leverages a sophisticated array of technologies to continuously monitor the condition of infrastructure assets, analyzing vast amounts of data to anticipate potential issues before they escalate into critical failures. The fundamental principle is to move beyond simply detecting damage to predicting the *likelihood* and *timing* of future degradation. This allows for maintenance to be scheduled strategically, optimizing resource allocation, minimizing downtime, and enhancing overall safety and longevity.

One of the most pervasive elements of transportation infrastructure is the road network. Roads are constantly exposed to the elements – freeze-thaw cycles, heavy rainfall, and intense sunlight – all of which contribute to material fatigue. Furthermore, the sheer volume and weight of vehicular traffic, particularly heavy goods vehicles, induce stresses that can lead to the formation of potholes, cracks, and rutting. AI is making significant inroads into monitoring and predicting the deterioration of roadways. Advanced sensor technologies, including embedded pavement sensors that measure strain, temperature, and moisture, can provide real-time data on the internal state of the road surface. This data, when fed into AI algorithms, can reveal patterns of stress and degradation that might not be immediately apparent through visual inspection.

Complementing embedded sensors, **imagery analysis** has become an indispensable tool. Drones equipped with high-resolution cameras, LiDAR (Light Detection and Ranging), and thermal imaging capabilities can systematically survey vast stretches of road networks. AI algorithms, trained on extensive datasets of road defects, are adept at automatically identifying and classifying various forms of damage from this imagery. This includes the precise detection and quantification of pavement cracks, from hairline fractures to larger spalls, the identification of potholes, and the assessment of surface texture and uniformity. Beyond simple detection, AI can analyze the *rate* of crack propagation or pothole formation over time, providing crucial data for predictive models. For instance, an AI might analyze sequential drone imagery of a particular highway section and observe that a specific type of crack is widening at an accelerated pace, indicating an underlying issue that requires urgent attention. Similarly, thermal imaging can reveal subsurface delaminations or moisture build-up that can predispose the road to future failure, especially during temperature fluctuations.

The integration of this data allows for the creation of **digital twins** of road networks. A digital twin is a virtual replica of a physical asset, continuously updated with real-time data. In the context of road maintenance, a digital twin of a road segment can simulate its structural behavior under various conditions, allowing engineers to test the impact of different maintenance strategies virtually before implementing them in the real world. AI algorithms can analyze the performance of the digital twin under simulated traffic loads and environmental stresses, predicting the remaining useful life of different road sections and prioritizing areas for maintenance based on risk and criticality. This sophisticated level of analysis moves beyond simple condition assessment to robust life-cycle management.

Bridges, often the most critical and costly components of a transportation network, also benefit immensely from AI-driven predictive maintenance. The structural integrity of a bridge is paramount, and failure can have catastrophic consequences. Traditional bridge inspections involve visual assessments by engineers, often requiring specialized equipment and sometimes leading to temporary closures or traffic restrictions. AI is enhancing this process significantly.

Embedded sensors are increasingly being deployed within bridge structures, including strain gauges, accelerometers, acoustic emission sensors, and fiber optic sensors. These sensors continuously monitor parameters such as structural vibration, deformation, stress distribution, and temperature fluctuations.

AI algorithms process the massive streams of data generated by these sensors. By learning the "normal" operational signature of a healthy bridge, AI can identify subtle deviations that might indicate the onset of structural issues. For example, an AI system might detect a slight but persistent increase in vibration amplitude at a specific point on a bridge deck under normal traffic loads. This could be an early indicator of a loose connection, a developing crack in a load-bearing element, or a sign of fatigue in the material. Acoustic emission sensors can detect the high-frequency stress waves released when materials fracture, allowing AI to pinpoint the location and severity of crack initiation or propagation with remarkable precision. Furthermore, AI can analyze the dynamic response of a bridge to various traffic conditions, identifying resonant frequencies that might indicate structural weaknesses.

Beyond embedded sensors,
drones and robotic inspection systems equipped with advanced imaging and sensing technologies are also playing a vital role. LiDAR can create highly accurate 3D models of bridge structures, allowing for precise measurements of geometry and deformation. Photogrammetry, combined with AI, can detect even minute changes in surface features over time, highlighting areas of potential corrosion, spalling, or crack development. Thermal imaging can identify moisture ingress beneath coatings or within concrete, which can lead to freeze-thaw damage and reinforcement corrosion. The AI's ability to correlate data from multiple sensor types provides a more comprehensive and reliable assessment of a bridge's health, enabling engineers to make informed decisions about repair or reinforcement strategies. For instance, if AI identifies a correlation between increased moisture levels detected by thermal imaging and micro-cracking observed via photogrammetry in a specific support column, it strongly suggests an imminent risk of corrosion-induced structural damage, prompting immediate investigation and intervention.

Tunnels, whether for road or rail traffic, present unique challenges for inspection and maintenance due to their often confined and inaccessible nature. AI is revolutionizing how these vital underground arteries are monitored.
Robotic inspection vehicles equipped with cameras, LiDAR, and other sensors can navigate tunnel environments, collecting data autonomously. AI algorithms analyze the imagery and sensor data to detect defects such as concrete spalling, water ingress, lining damage, and structural deformations.

Image processing and machine learning are critical here. AI models can be trained to recognize the specific patterns of degradation common in tunnel linings, which can be influenced by factors like soil pressure, groundwater ingress, and seismic activity. For instance, AI can differentiate between minor surface efflorescence (salt deposits left by evaporating water) and active water leakage, which requires more immediate attention. Furthermore, AI can analyze acoustic data from microphones placed within the tunnel to detect sounds indicative of structural distress, such as dripping water, creaking, or the movement of debris. By correlating these audio cues with visual data, AI can provide a more robust assessment of a tunnel's structural integrity. The predictive aspect comes into play by analyzing the rate of change of detected defects. If AI observes a consistent increase in the area of concrete spalling or the volume of water ingress along a particular section, it can forecast when these issues might compromise the tunnel's structural stability or operational safety, allowing for proactive repair work during planned maintenance windows.

Railway tracks, the backbone of freight and passenger rail transport, are another area where AI-driven predictive maintenance is making a substantial impact. The dynamic forces exerted by passing trains place immense stress on rails, sleepers, ballast, and fastenings. **Automated inspection trains** equipped with various sensors, including track geometry measurement systems, ultrasonic rail flaw detectors, and video cameras, collect vast amounts of data. AI algorithms process this data to identify anomalies and predict potential failures.

AI is particularly effective in analyzing ultrasonic inspection data to detect internal flaws within rails, such as cracks or inclusions, which can lead to catastrophic derailments if left unaddressed. By learning the acoustic signatures of different types of rail defects, AI can classify them with high accuracy and estimate their severity. Similarly, AI can analyze **track geometry data** – including gauge (distance between rails), cross-level (difference in height between the two rails), and alignment – to identify deviations from optimal conditions. By tracking the rate of change in these geometric parameters, AI can predict when track sections will fall outside acceptable tolerances, necessitating maintenance such as tamping (realigning the ballast) or grinding (reshaping the rail surface).

Furthermore, AI can analyze
ballast condition data, often obtained through visual inspection or ground-penetrating radar, to assess its drainage properties and stability. Poor ballast condition can lead to track instability, particularly under adverse weather conditions. By integrating data from all these sources, AI can provide a holistic view of track health, predicting which sections are most at risk of failure and prioritizing maintenance activities to ensure the safe and efficient operation of the railway network. This proactive approach reduces the likelihood of track-related incidents, minimizes unplanned service disruptions, and ultimately contributes to the economic viability of rail transportation.

The benefits of AI-driven predictive maintenance for transportation infrastructure are manifold. Firstly, it significantly enhances
safety. By identifying and rectifying potential structural weaknesses before they become critical, AI helps prevent failures that could endanger lives and cause widespread disruption. Secondly, it leads to substantial **cost savings**. Proactive maintenance is generally less expensive than emergency repairs, and by optimizing maintenance schedules, resources can be allocated more effectively, reducing operational expenditures. Thirdly, it improves **reliability and availability** of transportation networks. Reduced unplanned downtime means that roads, bridges, tunnels, and railways are available for use more consistently, facilitating smoother and more predictable movement of people and goods. Fourthly, it extends the **lifespan of assets**. By addressing degradation at its earliest stages, the structural integrity and operational life of critical infrastructure can be prolonged, deferring costly replacement cycles.

However, the successful implementation of AI in infrastructure maintenance is not without its challenges. It requires significant investment in sensor technology, data infrastructure, and skilled personnel. The quality and volume of data are crucial; AI models are only as good as the data they are trained on. Ensuring data security and privacy is also a paramount concern, especially when dealing with sensitive infrastructure information. Furthermore, establishing trust in AI-driven predictions among engineers and decision-makers requires rigorous validation and transparent algorithmic processes. The legal and regulatory frameworks also need to adapt to accommodate AI-assisted decision-making in critical infrastructure management.

Despite these hurdles, the trajectory is clear. AI is transforming the way we maintain the arteries of our transportation systems, ushering in an era of smarter, safer, and more resilient infrastructure. As AI capabilities continue to advance, and as more data becomes available, its role in safeguarding and optimizing the physical foundations of our mobility will only continue to grow, ensuring that our transportation networks can meet the demands of the future.

Chapter 12: AI in Building and Structural Health Monitoring

The built environment, encompassing everything from our homes and workplaces to vast commercial complexes and critical public infrastructure, is undergoing a profound transformation, driven by the integration of intelligent technologies. No longer are buildings merely static shells designed to provide shelter; they are evolving into dynamic, responsive ecosystems capable of optimizing their performance, enhancing occupant comfort, and drastically improving energy efficiency. At the heart of this evolution lies the concept of the **smart building**, a paradigm shift from passive structures to active participants in their own management and operation. This transformation is not solely about the adoption of novel gadgets; it is fundamentally enabled by the sophisticated capabilities of Artificial Intelligence (AI). AI acts as the central nervous system, processing vast amounts of data from a myriad of sensors and devices to orchestrate a building's various functions with unprecedented intelligence and efficiency.

The foundation of a smart building's intelligence is its **Building Management System (BMS)**, often referred to as a Building Automation System (BAS). Traditionally, BMS have focused on centralized control of key building services such as heating, ventilation, and air conditioning (HVAC), lighting, and security. However, these traditional systems often operate on pre-programmed schedules and simple feedback loops, lacking the adaptive intelligence to truly optimize performance in real-time. The advent of AI has revolutionized the BMS, transforming it from a mere control interface into an intelligent engine for building operations. AI algorithms can now analyze complex patterns and predict future needs, allowing for proactive and highly optimized control of these essential systems. For instance, instead of simply maintaining a set temperature based on a thermostat reading, an AI-powered BMS can consider numerous variables simultaneously: the current outdoor temperature and humidity, the forecast for the next several hours, the occupancy levels in different zones, the heat generated by equipment and people, and even the energy pricing tariffs. By integrating these diverse data streams, the AI can make sophisticated decisions to pre-cool or pre-heat spaces efficiently, minimize energy consumption during peak demand hours, and ensure optimal comfort levels without waste.

One of the most significant impacts of AI in smart buildings is its role in achieving
sustainable design and operation. As global awareness of climate change intensifies and regulations surrounding energy consumption become more stringent, the imperative to reduce the environmental footprint of buildings has never been greater. Buildings are significant consumers of energy, contributing a substantial portion of global greenhouse gas emissions. AI offers a powerful toolkit to address this challenge by enabling buildings to operate with significantly reduced energy demands. This is achieved through intelligent automation of HVAC and lighting systems, which are typically the largest energy consumers in any building. AI algorithms can learn occupancy patterns and user preferences, dynamically adjusting lighting levels and temperature setpoints in real-time. For example, AI can detect when a room is unoccupied through motion sensors or even by analyzing network activity, and subsequently dim the lights or adjust the thermostat. This is far more granular and responsive than traditional motion-activated or time-based systems. Furthermore, AI can predict the thermal load of a building based on historical data and external weather forecasts, allowing for anticipatory adjustments to HVAC systems. This might involve slightly pre-cooling a building during off-peak hours when electricity is cheaper and cleaner, thereby reducing the need for energy-intensive cooling during the hottest parts of the day. The ability of AI to perform these complex, multi-variable optimizations leads to substantial energy savings, often reducing a building's energy consumption by 15-30% or more, a critical step towards achieving sustainability goals.

Beyond energy efficiency, AI contributes to sustainable design by facilitating smarter resource management throughout a building's lifecycle. For example, in the design phase, AI can be used for

generative design, exploring thousands of design permutations to identify optimal building orientations, material selections, and window placements that maximize natural light and passive solar heating while minimizing heat gain in warmer months. AI can analyze environmental data for a specific site, simulating the building's performance under various conditions to ensure it meets stringent energy performance targets before construction even begins. During operation, AI can monitor water usage, detect leaks through anomalies in flow rates, and optimize irrigation systems based on soil moisture levels and weather forecasts, further reducing the building's environmental impact. The integration of renewable energy sources, such as solar panels, can also be managed more effectively by AI. The BMS can learn to predict energy generation from these sources and optimize their integration with the grid, maximizing self-consumption and minimizing reliance on fossil-fuel-based electricity. This creates a more resilient and sustainable energy ecosystem within the building.

The concept of occupant well-being is also intrinsically linked to the smart building paradigm, and AI plays a crucial role in enhancing it. A building that is responsive to the needs and comfort of its occupants fosters a more productive, healthier, and enjoyable environment. AI-powered systems can go beyond simply maintaining temperature and lighting to actively manage indoor air quality (IAQ). By monitoring levels of carbon dioxide (CO2), volatile organic compounds (VOCs), and particulate matter through a network of sensors, AI can dynamically adjust ventilation rates to ensure a constant supply of fresh air, preventing the build-up of pollutants that can lead to occupant discomfort, reduced cognitive function, and long-term health issues. This proactive approach to IAQ management is a significant improvement over traditional systems that often rely on fixed ventilation schedules, which may be insufficient during periods of high occupancy or when indoor pollutants are generated.

Personalized comfort is another area where AI is making a tangible difference. AI can learn individual occupant preferences over time, potentially through user feedback via smartphone apps or by analyzing historical settings. This allows for micro-adjustments to temperature, lighting, and even blinds in individual workspaces or zones, creating a more personalized and satisfying environment. For example, if AI notices that a particular desk area consistently has its thermostat adjusted lower by its occupant, it can learn this preference and make subtle adjustments to maintain that individual's comfort without negatively impacting others in the broader zone. This level of personalized control, orchestrated intelligently by AI, moves beyond a one-size-fits-all approach to building management.

Security and safety are also enhanced through AI in smart buildings. Integrated AI systems can analyze data from security cameras, access control systems, and even environmental sensors to provide a comprehensive overview of a building's security posture. AI algorithms can detect anomalous activities, such as unauthorized access attempts or unusual crowd movements, and alert security personnel in real-time. Furthermore, in the event of an emergency, such as a fire or an earthquake, AI can play a critical role in ensuring occupant safety. It can automatically unlock emergency exits, guide occupants to safety routes based on the real-time location of hazards, and communicate critical information to emergency responders. The ability of AI to process and correlate information from disparate security and safety systems allows for a much more rapid and effective response to critical incidents, potentially saving lives and minimizing damage.

The integration of AI into Building Management Systems is a continuous process of learning and adaptation. The more data the AI systems collect, the more sophisticated their analysis becomes, leading to increasingly refined control strategies. This creates a virtuous cycle where buildings become progressively smarter and more efficient over time. This data-driven approach also has significant implications for **operational cost reduction**. By optimizing energy consumption, AI directly reduces utility bills. Furthermore, predictive maintenance, a concept heavily reliant on AI and sensor data, can identify potential equipment failures *before* they occur. For instance, AI monitoring the vibration patterns of an HVAC fan motor might detect subtle anomalies that indicate a bearing is starting to wear out. Instead of waiting for the motor to fail, potentially causing an entire system to shut down and leading to costly emergency repairs and downtime, the BMS can schedule maintenance during off-peak hours to replace the worn component. This proactive approach minimizes unexpected breakdowns, reduces the need for expensive emergency services, and extends the operational life of critical building systems, all contributing to significant long-term cost savings for building owners and operators.

The sheer volume of data generated by modern smart buildings – from temperature and humidity sensors, occupancy detectors, light sensors, CO2 monitors, smart meters, security cameras, and more – is immense. Without AI, processing and deriving meaningful insights from this data would be an overwhelming, if not impossible, task. AI algorithms are uniquely equipped to handle this deluge of information, identifying correlations, detecting anomalies, and forecasting trends that would be invisible to human operators. This capability allows building managers to move from reactive troubleshooting to proactive, data-informed decision-making. They can access dashboards and reports that not only show the current status of building systems but also predict future performance and identify areas for improvement. This shift in operational philosophy transforms building management from a set of routine tasks into a strategic, data-driven discipline.

Consider the example of lighting control. A traditional system might use simple timers or occupancy sensors. An AI-enhanced system, however, can learn the patterns of natural light availability throughout the day and across different seasons for specific zones. It can then orchestrate artificial lighting to supplement natural light precisely where and when it is needed, maintaining a consistent and optimal illuminance level while minimizing energy use. If the AI detects that a particular area is consistently underutilized, it might suggest adjusting cleaning schedules or reconfiguring the space to improve its functionality and energy efficiency. This level of granular, data-driven optimization is a hallmark of smart building intelligence.

The implementation of AI in smart buildings also necessitates a robust and secure data infrastructure. As buildings become more connected, the potential attack surface for cyber threats increases. Therefore, cybersecurity becomes an integral part of smart building design and operation. AI itself can be used to enhance cybersecurity by detecting unusual network traffic patterns that might indicate a breach. Furthermore, the ethical implications of data collection and usage must be carefully considered. Transparency with occupants about what data is being collected and how it is being used is crucial for building trust and ensuring responsible implementation of these advanced technologies.

In essence, AI is transforming buildings from passive structures into intelligent, adaptive environments. It empowers them to optimize their performance, minimize their environmental impact, enhance the comfort and safety of their occupants, and reduce operational costs. This evolution represents a fundamental redefinition of what a building can be – not just a place to exist, but a dynamic partner in achieving efficiency, sustainability, and well-being. As AI technology continues to mature and become more accessible, its integration into the built environment will only deepen, paving the way for truly intelligent and responsive spaces that meet the complex demands of the 21st century and beyond. The journey from static construction to dynamic, AI-driven architecture is well underway, promising a future where our buildings are not just smart, but actively contribute to a more sustainable and livable world.

In the context of intelligent buildings and infrastructure, the advancement of Structural Health Monitoring (SHM) stands as a critical frontier, complementing the operational intelligence discussed previously. While smart building systems focus on optimizing daily functions like energy consumption and occupant comfort, SHM addresses the fundamental integrity and safety of the physical structure itself. The principle of SHM is rooted in the proactive and continuous assessment of a structure's condition, aiming to detect, localize, and quantify damage over its lifespan. This contrasts sharply with traditional methods of inspection, which are often periodic, subjective, and may only identify damage after it has become significant and potentially compromised safety.

The core tenet of SHM is the implementation of a system that can provide real-time or near real-time information about the state of a structure. This is achieved through the strategic deployment of various types of sensors directly integrated into the building or bridge during its construction, or sometimes retrofitted onto existing structures. These sensors act as the "eyes and ears" of the SHM system, constantly gathering data on parameters that can indicate the structural integrity and operational performance. Common sensor types include strain gauges, which measure the deformation of materials under load; accelerometers, which detect vibrations and dynamic responses; displacement sensors, which monitor movements; temperature sensors, which can reveal thermal stress and material degradation; and fiber optic sensors, which offer distributed sensing capabilities over long lengths, capable of measuring strain, temperature, and even acoustic emissions. The selection and placement of these sensors are crucial and depend heavily on the type of structure, the anticipated loading conditions, the materials used, and the specific damage mechanisms that are of concern. For instance, in a tall building, accelerometers might be strategically placed to monitor sway and seismic response, while strain gauges on critical load-bearing elements like beams and columns would track stress distribution under various load scenarios, including wind and live loads.

The continuous stream of data generated by these sensors is then transmitted to a central processing unit or a distributed network for analysis. This is where the intelligence of the SHM system truly comes into play. The raw sensor data, often voluminous and complex, is processed to extract meaningful information about the structure's behavior. This processing typically involves filtering out noise, correlating data from multiple sensors, and comparing current responses to baseline data collected when the structure was in a known healthy state. The goal is to identify deviations from this baseline that could signify the onset of damage. These deviations might manifest as changes in stiffness, altered vibration frequencies, increased displacement under load, or localized stress concentrations. Algorithms are employed to interpret these changes, ranging from simple statistical analysis to sophisticated machine learning models. The development of these algorithms is a key area of research in SHM, aiming to improve the accuracy, reliability, and sensitivity of damage detection.

A fundamental principle in SHM is the concept of a "damage indicator." This is a measurable parameter derived from the sensor data that correlates directly with the presence, extent, or severity of damage within the structure. For example, a decrease in the natural vibration frequencies of a bridge might indicate a reduction in its stiffness, which could be caused by cracking or yielding of structural members. Similarly, a sudden increase in strain readings under a constant load could point to localized stress redistribution due to material degradation or the formation of new cracks. The effectiveness of an SHM system hinges on the ability to identify and track reliable damage indicators. This often requires extensive experimental testing and finite element modeling to understand how different types of damage affect the structural response in a quantifiable manner. The research community has explored numerous potential damage indicators, including changes in modal properties (frequencies, mode shapes, damping ratios), load-deflection behavior, acoustic emission patterns, strain energy distribution, and even visual changes captured by embedded cameras.

The ultimate objective of SHM is to ensure the safety and extend the service life of critical infrastructure. By continuously monitoring the condition of a structure, SHM enables a shift from a reactive maintenance paradigm to a proactive and predictive one. Instead of waiting for visible signs of distress or relying on scheduled inspections that may miss developing issues, SHM systems can alert engineers to potential problems at their earliest stages. This early detection is paramount. Minor damage, if identified and repaired promptly, can often be fixed with minimal cost and disruption, preventing it from escalating into a catastrophic failure. This is particularly important for structures that are subjected to harsh environmental conditions, such as bridges exposed to de-icing salts and freeze-thaw cycles, or offshore platforms subjected to corrosive marine environments. The proactive approach offered by SHM can thus lead to significant cost savings in the long run by reducing the need for expensive emergency repairs, minimizing structural downtime, and preventing the loss of life or property that can result from structural collapse.

The process of establishing and maintaining an effective SHM system typically involves several key stages. The first stage is **design and installation**, where the SHM strategy is developed, sensors are selected and strategically placed, and data acquisition hardware and software are implemented. This stage requires a deep understanding of the structure's behavior, potential failure modes, and the capabilities of various sensing technologies. The second stage is **data acquisition and processing**, where data is continuously collected from the sensors and subjected to rigorous analysis to extract meaningful information. This is an ongoing process throughout the structure's operational life. The third stage is **data interpretation and damage assessment**, where the processed data is analyzed to identify any anomalies or trends that may indicate damage. This often involves comparing current structural behavior to a baseline or to expected performance under given loads. Expert judgment and sophisticated algorithms are crucial in this stage to accurately assess the severity and implications of any detected changes. Finally, the **decision-making and maintenance** stage involves using the insights gained from the SHM system to inform maintenance schedules, repair strategies, and even operational decisions, such as load restrictions or closure of the structure if immediate risks are identified.

One of the significant advantages of SHM is its ability to provide a continuous and objective assessment of structural performance under real-world operational conditions. Structures are not static entities; they are dynamic systems that experience varying loads from traffic, wind, seismic activity, and environmental factors over their entire service life. Traditional inspections, often conducted visually or with non-destructive testing methods, provide only snapshots in time and can be influenced by the inspector's experience and judgment. SHM, by contrast, offers a continuous, data-driven record of the structure's response, allowing for a more accurate understanding of its cumulative fatigue, the impact of extreme events, and the effectiveness of any implemented repairs. This historical data can also be invaluable for future design standards and for understanding the long-term degradation mechanisms of different materials and structural types.

The data collected through SHM is not merely for detecting damage; it also plays a crucial role in validating and refining predictive models used in structural engineering. Finite element models (FEMs) are widely used to simulate the behavior of structures under various loading conditions. However, these models are often based on idealized assumptions and material properties that may not perfectly reflect the complexities of a real-world structure. By comparing the predictions of the FEM with the actual measurements obtained from the SHM system, engineers can identify discrepancies, calibrate their models, and improve their predictive capabilities. This iterative process of modeling, monitoring, and refining leads to more accurate simulations and, consequently, better-informed decisions regarding structural design, maintenance, and remaining service life assessment. This feedback loop between monitoring and modeling is a cornerstone of advanced structural engineering practice.

Furthermore, SHM systems can be designed to provide crucial information during and immediately after extreme events, such as earthquakes or severe storms. In such scenarios, an SHM system can quickly assess the extent of damage and provide critical information to emergency responders and structural engineers about the structure's safety and usability. This allows for a more informed and rapid decision-making process regarding evacuation, access, and necessary repairs. For critical infrastructure like bridges or power plants, this rapid post-event assessment can be vital for restoring essential services and mitigating secondary impacts. The ability to swiftly and reliably determine the integrity of a structure after a disaster can literally save lives and significantly speed up recovery efforts.

The integration of SHM with the broader concept of smart infrastructure, as discussed in the context of smart buildings, represents a powerful synergy. Just as AI enhances the operational efficiency and occupant experience of a building, SHM provides the crucial layer of structural integrity assurance. Data from SHM sensors can be fed into a larger smart infrastructure management platform, which can then correlate structural conditions with operational data, environmental factors, and predicted usage patterns. For example, a smart city platform could use SHM data from a bridge to inform traffic management systems, perhaps diverting heavy vehicles if the bridge's structural capacity is found to be compromised. Conversely, operational data, such as traffic volume, could be used to provide more context for interpreting SHM sensor readings. This holistic approach, where operational intelligence and structural health monitoring work hand-in-hand, promises a future where our infrastructure is not only efficient and responsive but also fundamentally safe and resilient.

The development and widespread adoption of SHM technologies are also driven by economic and regulatory factors. As infrastructure ages, the cost of maintenance and repair increases significantly. SHM offers a cost-effective solution by enabling condition-based maintenance, prioritizing repairs based on actual need rather than arbitrary schedules. Furthermore, increasing public awareness of safety and the potential for catastrophic failures has led to stricter regulations and performance requirements for critical infrastructure, making robust monitoring systems like SHM a necessity. The long-term economic benefits of preventing failures, extending service life, and optimizing maintenance far outweigh the initial investment in SHM systems, making it a sound economic decision for asset owners and operators.

The principles of SHM are thus not merely about placing sensors on a structure. They encompass a comprehensive approach to understanding, assessing, and managing the long-term health of the built environment. It involves a deep understanding of mechanics, materials science, sensor technology, data science, and engineering judgment. By continuously observing and analyzing the physical state of our buildings and bridges, SHM empowers us to ensure their safety, reliability, and longevity, forming an indispensable component of the modern, intelligent infrastructure landscape. The evolution of SHM, particularly with the integration of advanced data analytics and AI, promises even more sophisticated capabilities in the future, further enhancing our ability to safeguard the structures that underpin our society.

The continuous influx of data generated by structural health monitoring (SHM) systems presents a formidable challenge and, concurrently, a golden opportunity for the application of artificial intelligence (AI). While traditional SHM relied on statistical methods and manual interpretation of sensor readings, the sheer volume, velocity, and variety of data now generated demand more sophisticated analytical tools. AI, particularly machine learning (ML) and deep learning (DL) techniques, has emerged as a transformative force in this domain, enabling the automated and intelligent detection of structural anomalies and damage. These algorithms are capable of sifting through complex, multi-dimensional sensor data, identifying subtle deviations from normal operational behavior that might otherwise go unnoticed by human inspectors or simpler analytical methods. This capability is crucial for early detection, which, as previously discussed, is key to preventing minor issues from escalating into major structural failures.

The core of AI's contribution to SHM lies in its ability to learn patterns of "normal" structural behavior and then flag any significant deviations. This learning process typically begins with a phase of training, where the AI model is fed a large dataset representing the structure's response under a wide range of expected conditions – varying environmental loads (wind, temperature fluctuations), operational loads (traffic, occupancy), and even baseline responses when the structure is in a known healthy state. During this training, the AI algorithm essentially builds a comprehensive understanding of how the structure *should* behave. Once trained, the model can then continuously analyze real-time sensor data. When the incoming data consistently deviates from the learned normal patterns, the AI flags it as an anomaly. These anomalies can arise from a multitude of sources, including cumulative material degradation (such as fatigue cracking or corrosion), sudden impacts, settlement of foundations, or the effects of extreme environmental events like seismic activity or high winds.

One of the most powerful AI techniques being applied to anomaly detection in SHM is
unsupervised learning. In this paradigm, the AI model learns the underlying structure of the data without explicit labels indicating "damage" or "no damage." Instead, it focuses on identifying clusters of normal data points and highlighting anything that falls outside these clusters. Algorithms like **K-Means clustering** or **Principal Component Analysis (PCA)** can be employed to group sensor readings into distinct operational states. Any new data that does not conform to these established clusters is then flagged as a potential anomaly. This approach is particularly valuable because obtaining labeled data for all possible damage scenarios can be exceedingly difficult and time-consuming.

However, for more nuanced and precise damage assessment, **supervised learning** techniques often come into play, especially when historical data with known damage incidents is available. In supervised learning, the AI model is trained on data that has been explicitly labeled with the type and severity of damage. For instance, datasets might include sensor readings from a bridge during normal operation, during the onset of a specific type of crack, or after a simulated impact. Algorithms such as **Support Vector Machines (SVMs)** or **Random Forests** can then be trained to classify new sensor data into these predefined damage categories. This allows for not only the detection of an anomaly but also its classification into a specific type of fault, such as a crack in a beam, a loose connection, or delamination in a concrete slab.

The real breakthrough in AI for SHM, however, has arguably come with the advent of
deep learning. Deep learning models, characterized by their multi-layered neural network architectures, are exceptionally adept at automatically learning hierarchical representations of data. This means

they can progressively extract more complex and abstract features from raw sensor signals, enabling them to capture intricate relationships that might be missed by traditional ML algorithms or human analysis.

Among the deep learning architectures,
Autoencoders have proven particularly effective for anomaly detection in SHM. An autoencoder is a type of artificial neural network trained to reconstruct its input. It consists of two main parts: an encoder that compresses the input data into a lower-dimensional latent space, and a decoder that attempts to reconstruct the original input from this compressed representation. When an autoencoder is trained on data representing normal structural behavior, it becomes very good at reconstructing these normal patterns. Consequently, when presented with data from a damaged state, which deviates from the normal patterns it was trained on, the autoencoder will struggle to reconstruct it accurately. The difference between the original input and the reconstructed output, known as the **reconstruction error**, serves as a powerful indicator of an anomaly. A high reconstruction error signifies that the input data is significantly different from what the autoencoder has learned as "normal," thus pointing to potential damage. Furthermore, the magnitude of the reconstruction error can sometimes be correlated with the severity of the damage.

Beyond reconstruction error, other deep learning architectures are also being leveraged.
Convolutional Neural Networks (CNNs), traditionally known for their success in image recognition, are being adapted for analyzing time-series sensor data from SHM. By treating sensor readings as "channels" or by converting time-series data into visual representations (e.g., spectrograms), CNNs can identify spatial and temporal patterns indicative of structural issues. For instance, a CNN could be trained to recognize the characteristic vibration signatures of a bridge under specific load conditions, and then detect subtle changes in these signatures that might signal the formation of cracks or loosening of components.

Recurrent Neural Networks (RNNs), and their more advanced variants like **Long Short-Term Memory (LSTM) networks**, are particularly well-suited for analyzing sequential data, such as the continuous stream of readings from accelerometers or strain gauges. These networks have internal memory mechanisms that allow them to capture temporal dependencies and long-term patterns in the data. This is invaluable for SHM, where the history of a structure's response can provide critical clues about its evolving health. For example, an LSTM network could learn the typical dynamic response of a building to wind gusts and identify subtle changes in this response over time that might indicate developing structural weaknesses. The ability of LSTMs to model temporal sequences makes them ideal for predicting future structural behavior based on past trends, thereby enhancing the predictive maintenance capabilities of SHM systems.

The application of these AI techniques moves beyond simple anomaly flagging to provide more sophisticated **damage assessment**, including **localization** and **quantification**. Localization refers to identifying *where* the damage has occurred within the structure. By analyzing the spatial distribution of anomalies across different sensors, AI models can pinpoint the affected areas. For instance, if strain gauges on a particular beam consistently show abnormal readings, while others on adjacent beams do not, the AI can infer that the damage is localized to that specific beam. Some advanced AI models can even perform multi-modal fusion, integrating data from different sensor types (e.g., strain, vibration, and visual data from cameras) to achieve more robust and precise localization.

Quantification, on the other hand, aims to determine the *extent* or *severity* of the identified damage. This is often a more challenging task. While the reconstruction error from an autoencoder or the prediction error from other models can sometimes be correlated with damage severity, precise quantification often requires a deeper understanding of the physics of damage. AI models can be trained to map specific patterns of sensor readings or reconstruction errors to known levels of damage severity (e.g., minor crack, moderate crack, severe crack). This might involve correlating AI outputs with results from physical tests on damaged specimens or with outputs from detailed finite element models that simulate different damage scenarios. For example, an AI model might learn to associate a specific pattern of vibration frequency shifts with a particular crack width in a bridge girder.

The process of employing AI for SHM typically involves several key steps. First,
data collection and preprocessing are paramount. This involves gathering data from various sensors, cleaning it to remove noise and outliers, and normalizing it to ensure consistency. Feature engineering, where relevant characteristics are extracted from the raw sensor data, can also be crucial for improving AI model performance. Second, **model selection and training** involve choosing the most appropriate AI algorithm for the specific SHM task and training it on a representative dataset. This is an iterative process, often requiring hyperparameter tuning and validation using separate datasets. Third, **deployment and monitoring** involve integrating the trained AI model into the SHM system for real-time analysis of incoming sensor data. Finally, **interpretation and action** involve engineers reviewing the AI-generated alerts and assessments, making informed decisions about maintenance, repairs, or further investigation.

Consider a large-scale infrastructure project like a complex bridge. Thousands of sensors – strain gauges, accelerometers, displacement sensors, fiber optics – are embedded within its structure. The data streams from these sensors generate terabytes of information daily. A traditional approach to analyzing this data would involve engineers manually sifting through reports, looking for significant deviations. This is often a reactive and time-consuming process, prone to human error and the possibility of missing subtle warning signs.

Introducing an AI-powered SHM system transforms this paradigm. An autoencoder model, trained on the bridge's healthy operational data, continuously processes the incoming sensor readings. When a series of strain gauges on a particular support pier start exhibiting readings that the autoencoder consistently fails to reconstruct accurately, a high reconstruction error is generated. This alert is immediately flagged. The AI system can then, based on its training or further analysis, attempt to localize this anomaly to a specific section of the pier. If the AI has been trained to correlate reconstruction error patterns with specific types of damage, it might suggest with a high probability that this indicates early-stage concrete cracking or rebar corrosion in that localized area.

This automated anomaly detection and initial assessment allows maintenance teams to be dispatched proactively to the specific pier section

before any visible signs of distress appear. Further inspections, guided by the AI's alert, can then be targeted to confirm the presence and extent of the damage. This prevents a minor issue from propagating, potentially averting a much larger, more costly, and dangerous structural failure. The AI doesn't replace the engineer; rather, it augments their capabilities, enabling them to focus on higher-level decision-making and intervention based on highly reliable, data-driven insights.

Furthermore, AI can significantly enhance the reliability of SHM systems by learning to distinguish between genuine structural anomalies and transient environmental noise or operational variations. For instance, an accelerometer might register a spike in vibration due to a particularly heavy truck crossing the bridge or a strong gust of wind. A naive system might flag this as an anomaly. However, an AI model trained on historical data would understand that such spikes are normal under specific load conditions. It could learn to correlate the vibration event with other sensor data – such as traffic sensors or wind speed sensors – and classify the event as a normal operational variation rather than a structural anomaly. This ability to contextualize sensor readings and reduce false alarms is crucial for building trust and confidence in AI-driven SHM systems.

The development of sophisticated damage classification and quantification models also opens avenues for predictive maintenance that is far more precise than what was previously possible. Instead of scheduling maintenance based on time intervals or generic condition indicators, AI-powered SHM can predict the remaining useful life (RUL) of structural components with greater accuracy. By tracking the progression of damage indicators identified by AI, engineers can forecast when a component is likely to reach a critical state, allowing for maintenance to be scheduled optimally, just before it is needed. This minimizes unnecessary maintenance, reduces costs, and ensures that structural integrity is maintained throughout the asset's lifespan.

The integration of AI in SHM is not without its challenges. The quality and quantity of training data are paramount; insufficient or biased data can lead to poorly performing models. Ensuring the interpretability of AI decisions, often referred to as the "black box" problem, is crucial for engineers to trust and act upon the AI's outputs, especially in safety-critical applications. Moreover, the computational resources required for training and deploying complex deep learning models can be substantial. However, ongoing advancements in AI algorithms, hardware, and data management techniques are steadily addressing these challenges, paving the way for more widespread and effective adoption of AI in structural health monitoring. The promise is clear: AI empowers us to move from a reactive approach to structural maintenance to a truly proactive, intelligent, and predictive one, safeguarding our critical infrastructure for generations to come.

The transition from reactive maintenance to proactive intervention in structural engineering hinges critically on the ability to forecast future performance and degradation. Artificial intelligence offers a powerful suite of tools to achieve this, moving beyond mere detection of current anomalies to actively predicting the trajectory of structural health. This predictive capability is fundamentally about understanding the complex interplay of factors that contribute to a structure's decline over time. By analyzing historical data, real-time sensor readings, and prevailing environmental conditions, AI models can learn the intricate pathways of degradation, thereby estimating the remaining useful life (RUL) of structural components and anticipating future maintenance needs. This foresight is invaluable for ensuring the long-term safety and operational efficiency of critical infrastructure.

At the heart of predictive modeling for structural degradation lies the concept of learning from experience. Structures are not static entities; they are dynamic systems that evolve under the constant influence of various loads and environmental stressors. These include operational loads such as traffic on bridges, occupancy in buildings, and the dynamic forces generated by machinery. Equally significant are environmental factors like temperature fluctuations, humidity, exposure to corrosive agents (e.g., de-icing salts, industrial pollutants), and seismic activity. Over time, these cumulative effects lead to material fatigue, corrosion, creep, and other forms of degradation. AI models, particularly those employing machine learning and deep learning, are exceptionally adept at capturing the complex, often non-linear, relationships between these influencing factors and the resulting structural deterioration.

The process typically begins with the aggregation of diverse datasets. This includes historical records of structural performance, maintenance interventions, and documented damage events, if available. Crucially, it also involves continuous streams of data from existing structural health monitoring (SHM) systems – sensors measuring strain, displacement, vibration, temperature, humidity, and even visual data from cameras or drone inspections. The inclusion of meteorological data, traffic volume records, and seismic event logs further enriches the dataset, providing a comprehensive picture of the external factors impacting the structure.

Once this data is collected and meticulously preprocessed – a crucial step involving cleaning, normalization, and feature extraction – it is fed into predictive AI models. Several algorithmic approaches are particularly suited for this task. One prominent category involves **regression-based models**. These models aim to predict a continuous numerical value, such as the remaining useful life or the rate of crack propagation. Techniques like **Linear Regression**, **Polynomial Regression**, and more sophisticated **Support Vector Regression (SVR)** can be employed. For instance, an SVR model could be trained to predict the future corrosion rate of steel reinforcement in concrete based on historical corrosion data, chloride ingress data, and environmental humidity levels. The model learns the function that maps these input variables to the predicted corrosion rate, allowing engineers to estimate how much longer the reinforcement will remain structurally sound.

Time-series forecasting models are also indispensable in predictive SHM. These models are designed to analyze data points collected over time and predict future values based on past trends and seasonality. **ARIMA (AutoRegressive Integrated Moving Average)** models and their more advanced variants, such as **SARIMA (Seasonal ARIMA)**, are well-established in this domain. However, for the complex, non-linear patterns often observed in structural degradation, **Recurrent Neural Networks (RNNs)**, particularly **Long Short-Term Memory (LSTM)** networks and **Gated Recurrent Units (GRUs)**, have shown exceptional promise. LSTMs can effectively capture long-term dependencies in sequential data, making them ideal for predicting the evolution of structural responses over extended periods. For example, an LSTM network could be trained on the vibration data of a bridge under varying traffic loads and wind conditions. By learning the temporal evolution of these vibration patterns, the model can predict how these patterns might change in the future due to accumulating fatigue, thus indicating an increased risk of failure.

Another powerful approach is the application of **prognostic models**, which focus on estimating the Remaining Useful Life (RUL). These models often integrate physics-based degradation models with data-driven AI techniques. A common strategy is to use AI to calibrate or update parameters within a physics-based degradation model. For instance, a model describing concrete carbonation might have parameters that are difficult to measure directly. An AI algorithm can learn to infer these parameters by analyzing sensor data (e.g., surface electrical resistivity, humidity within the concrete) and correlating them with predicted future degradation. By continuously updating the model's parameters with new sensor data, the RUL estimation becomes increasingly accurate.

Machine learning survival analysis models, inspired by medical prognostics, are also gaining traction. These models are designed to predict the probability of an event (e.g., structural failure, exceeding a serviceability limit) occurring within a specific timeframe. Algorithms like **Cox Proportional Hazards models** and **Random Survival Forests** can incorporate a multitude of features, including material properties, environmental exposure, and load history, to predict the survival function of a structural component. This allows engineers to quantify the risk of failure at any given point in time.

Consider the example of a high-rise building. Its façade is subjected to daily cycles of heating and cooling, expansion and contraction, and the relentless forces of wind. Over years, these cycles can lead to micro-cracks in façade materials or loosening of anchor points. An AI-powered predictive model could integrate data from embedded temperature sensors, strain gauges on façade panels, anemometer readings, and historical maintenance records. The model, perhaps an LSTM network trained on this data, could learn the typical thermal expansion and contraction patterns and how they interact with wind loads. If the model detects a gradual increase in the strain range experienced by certain façade panels during extreme temperature events, even if these strains are currently within acceptable limits, it could predict that these panels are on a trajectory towards fatigue failure within, say, the next five years. This prediction would trigger a proactive inspection and potential repair or replacement of those specific façade elements, preventing water ingress and more extensive damage down the line.

The predictive modeling approach extends to assessing the health of bridges. A steel bridge, for instance, is vulnerable to fatigue cracking, especially at welded joints and connection points, due to repetitive traffic loads. Accelerometers placed strategically on the bridge can capture its dynamic response. AI models, such as deep neural networks or Gaussian Process models, can learn the signature vibration patterns of the bridge in a healthy state. When fatigue cracks begin to form, even at a microscopic level, they alter the structural stiffness and damping characteristics, leading to subtle changes in these vibration signatures. Predictive models can be trained to detect these subtle deviations and forecast the rate at which these cracks might grow under continued traffic loading. This allows bridge engineers to prioritize inspections and maintenance activities on critical sections
before the cracks reach a stage where they compromise the bridge's load-bearing capacity, significantly enhancing safety and optimizing maintenance budgets.

Furthermore, predictive modeling can be used to estimate the long-term impact of extreme events. A structure might withstand a major earthquake or hurricane without immediate collapse, but the event could initiate or accelerate underlying degradation processes. AI models can be trained to assess the "hidden" damage caused by such events. By analyzing sensor data collected immediately after the event, and comparing it with pre-event baseline data and established degradation models, AI can predict the long-term consequences. For instance, it might predict an accelerated rate of corrosion in reinforced concrete structures due to the ingress of water and salts facilitated by earthquake-induced cracking. This prediction enables targeted inspections and preventative measures to mitigate the long-term risks.

The integration of predictive capabilities into SHM systems transforms them from passive monitoring tools into active management systems. Instead of merely reporting that a component is currently damaged, the system can forecast its future condition. This enables a shift from scheduled maintenance to condition-based and predictive maintenance. Maintenance teams can be dispatched precisely when and where they are needed, based on data-driven forecasts of component degradation. This not only minimizes costly and disruptive interventions but also maximizes the lifespan of structural assets. For critical infrastructure like power plants, dams, or transportation networks, this proactive approach is paramount for ensuring resilience and public safety.

The accuracy and reliability of these predictive models are heavily dependent on several factors. Firstly, the quality and comprehensiveness of the training data are paramount. A model trained on incomplete or unrepresentative data will inevitably produce unreliable predictions. Secondly, the choice of AI algorithm and its specific configuration (hyperparameters) must be appropriate for the complexity of the degradation process being modeled. Thirdly, continuous validation and recalibration of the models are essential. As structures age and environmental conditions change, the predictive models must be updated to reflect these evolving realities. Techniques like online learning and transfer learning can be employed to ensure that the models remain relevant and accurate over the structure's entire service life.

The ultimate goal of predictive modeling in structural health monitoring is to move towards a state of
prescriptive maintenance, where AI not only predicts when a component will fail but also recommends the optimal course of action to prevent failure or mitigate its consequences. This could involve suggesting specific repair strategies, optimal timing for interventions, or even recommending design modifications for future structures to enhance their durability. This advanced level of intelligence allows for unprecedented levels of control and optimization in the management of our built environment, ensuring its safety, sustainability, and longevity. The continuous evolution of AI techniques, coupled with the ever-increasing availability of sensor data, promises to further enhance our ability to predict and manage structural degradation, safeguarding critical infrastructure for future generations.
The practical implementation of Artificial Intelligence in Structural Health Monitoring (SHM) finds a compelling illustration in the comprehensive monitoring of bridge infrastructure. Bridges, as critical arteries of transportation networks, are constantly subjected to dynamic loads from traffic, environmental weathering, and the occasional impact of seismic events. Ensuring their continued integrity is paramount for public safety and economic stability. AI, in conjunction with advanced sensing technologies, offers a sophisticated approach to proactively manage bridge health, moving beyond traditional visual inspections and scheduled maintenance to a more intelligent, data-driven paradigm.

A typical AI-enhanced bridge monitoring system begins with the strategic deployment of a diverse array of sensors. These can include accelerometers to capture dynamic responses under traffic and wind loading, strain gauges to measure structural deformations, displacement sensors to track movements, and corrosion sensors embedded within concrete or attached to steel elements. Furthermore, cameras, potentially mounted on drones or fixed points, provide visual data for crack detection and general visual integrity checks. Acoustic emission sensors can also be integrated to detect the formation and propagation of micro-cracks through sound waves. For a comprehensive case study, let us consider a hypothetical, yet representative, scenario involving a major steel-concrete composite bridge spanning a river. This bridge, due to its age and the increasing volume of heavy vehicular traffic it supports, has been identified as a candidate for an advanced SHM system incorporating AI.

The sensor network is meticulously installed across critical locations of the bridge. For instance, accelerometers are placed at mid-span and at the bridge deck ends to capture distinct vibrational modes. Strain gauges are affixed to key structural elements such as girders, deck connections, and suspension cables (if applicable), especially in areas known to be prone to fatigue. Corrosion sensors are strategically positioned within the concrete deck and at exposed steel members in the splash zone of the river. A high-definition camera system, periodically surveying the entire structure, is also part of the deployment. This dense network generates a continuous stream of data, painting a detailed picture of the bridge's real-time condition.

The data acquisition process is a critical first step. Raw data from the sensors is collected by a centralized data logger and transmitted, often wirelessly, to a central processing unit. This unit can be located on-site or in a remote data center, depending on the scale and security requirements. The raw sensor data, in its native format, is a complex and voluminous entity. For example, accelerometer data consists of time-series measurements of acceleration in multiple axes, often sampled at frequencies of several hundred Hertz. Strain gauge data represents minute changes in electrical resistance, directly correlating to applied stress. Corrosion sensor data might be in the form of current or potential measurements indicating electrochemical activity.

Before this data can be effectively utilized by AI algorithms, it undergoes a rigorous preprocessing phase. This involves several key operations. Firstly, data cleaning is essential to remove erroneous readings caused by sensor malfunctions, electrical noise, or communication dropouts. Techniques like outlier detection and interpolation are employed here. Secondly, data normalization is performed to bring data from different sensors and units onto a common scale, ensuring that one sensor's readings do not disproportionately influence the AI model due to its inherently larger numerical range. Thirdly, feature extraction is a crucial step where meaningful information is derived from the raw data. For example, from acceleration time series, features such as peak amplitudes, root mean square (RMS) values, and spectral characteristics (e.g., dominant frequencies) can be extracted. For strain data, features might include maximum strain values, strain ranges, and trends over time. For visual data from cameras, image processing techniques are used to identify and quantify features like crack width, length, and density.

Once the data is cleaned, normalized, and relevant features are extracted, it is fed into various AI and machine learning algorithms for analysis. One of the primary applications in this case study is anomaly detection. Anomalies can manifest in numerous ways, such as sudden, unexpected increases in vibration levels, unusual strain patterns, or the detection of new cracks. Consider the scenario following a moderate earthquake. While the bridge might not exhibit visible macroscopic damage, the seismic event could have induced transient stresses and deformations, potentially initiating or exacerbating micro-cracks or loosening connections. An AI model, trained on the "healthy" operational data of the bridge under normal traffic and environmental conditions, can compare the post-earthquake sensor readings against this baseline.

Specifically, a deep learning model, such as a Convolutional Neural Network (CNN) or a Recurrent Neural Network (RNN) with Long Short-Term Memory (LSTM) units, could be employed. For instance, an LSTM network is particularly adept at processing sequential data like time-series vibration readings. The model would have learned the typical vibrational signatures of the bridge under various load conditions. After the earthquake, if the accelerometers register a subtle but persistent shift in the bridge's natural frequencies or a marked increase in damping, the LSTM model can flag this as an anomaly. This anomaly might not be immediately apparent to a human inspector without detailed analysis of the sensor data. The AI system would generate a real-time alert to the bridge engineers, indicating that the structure has experienced an event and that its dynamic characteristics have potentially changed.

Beyond detecting anomalies, AI algorithms can also be used to diagnose potential causes and assess the severity of issues. For example, if corrosion sensors indicate elevated levels of electrical activity in a specific section of the bridge deck, and this is correlated with visual data showing minor surface spalling, an AI model can help quantify the extent of the corrosion and predict its likely progression rate. Machine learning models, such as Support Vector Machines (SVMs) or Random Forests, can be trained on historical data of corrosion progression under different environmental conditions (e.g., humidity, de-icing salt exposure) and material types. Given the current sensor readings and environmental data, these models can predict the remaining useful life of the affected concrete or steel components, or estimate the time until the corrosion reaches a critical threshold that compromises structural integrity.

The AI system's output is designed to be actionable for bridge engineers. Instead of presenting raw data, it provides clear diagnostic information. For the earthquake scenario, the alert might state: "Anomaly detected post-seismic event. Vibration analysis indicates a potential shift in natural frequencies (e.g., decrease by 2%). Recommend immediate visual inspection of critical connection points and mid-span deck elements." For the corrosion issue, the alert could be: "Elevated corrosion activity detected in Sector 3B of the deck. Predicted progression rate suggests potential for significant rebar degradation within 3-5 years if left unaddressed. Recommend targeted ultrasonic testing and concrete core sampling for precise assessment." This diagnostic information allows engineers to prioritize their inspections and allocate resources effectively. Instead of a general visual survey of the entire bridge, they can focus their attention on the areas flagged by the AI as most likely to be affected.

The AI system's ability to detect early signs of corrosion is particularly valuable. Corrosion of steel reinforcement within concrete is a pervasive problem that can lead to significant structural degradation and costly repairs. Traditional methods of detecting corrosion often rely on visual inspection for surface defects (like rust stains or spalling) or covermeter surveys to estimate the depth of concrete cover over the rebar. However, corrosion can be occurring internally, beneath the surface, long before visible signs appear. AI-powered monitoring systems can provide a much earlier warning. By analyzing data from electrochemical sensors, humidity sensors, and even acoustic sensors that can detect the subtle sounds of cracking induced by rust expansion, AI can identify the onset of corrosion at a much earlier stage. For instance, an AI model might learn that a combination of high humidity within the concrete, fluctuating temperatures, and specific chloride ion concentrations detected by sensors is a precursor to accelerated corrosion. By monitoring these parameters, the system can alert engineers to potential corrosion long before it becomes visually apparent, allowing for less invasive and more cost-effective interventions, such as applying protective coatings or cathodic protection systems.

Furthermore, the AI system contributes to predictive maintenance by forecasting future structural performance. By continuously collecting data and updating its models, the AI can track the rate of degradation of various bridge components over time. This allows for a shift from time-based maintenance schedules to condition-based and predictive maintenance. Instead of inspecting a component every five years, engineers will be alerted to inspect it when the AI predicts that its condition is likely to have deteriorated to a point requiring attention. For example, if strain gauge data shows a consistent upward trend in fatigue loading cycles at a specific welded joint, and this trend, when extrapolated by the AI model, indicates that the fatigue life of that joint is approaching its limit within the next two years, then a focused inspection and potential reinforcement of that joint can be scheduled proactively. This predictive capability is crucial for optimizing maintenance budgets, minimizing disruptions to traffic, and ensuring the long-term safety and reliability of the bridge.

The tangible benefits of such an AI-enhanced system are manifold. Firstly, it significantly enhances safety. By detecting anomalies and degradation early, often before they become visible or critical, the system provides crucial lead time for repairs, preventing potential catastrophic failures. Secondly, it optimizes maintenance costs. Proactive interventions are typically less expensive than emergency repairs. By identifying specific problem areas, resources can be directed efficiently, avoiding unnecessary work on unaffected parts of the bridge. Thirdly, it extends the lifespan of the bridge. By addressing degradation issues promptly and effectively, the overall service life of the structure can be prolonged, maximizing the return on the initial investment. Fourthly, it provides invaluable data for future design. The continuous stream of performance data, analyzed by AI, offers insights into how bridges of similar design and materials perform under real-world conditions, which can inform the design of new structures and retrofitting strategies for existing ones.

The success of this AI application relies on continuous learning and adaptation. The AI models are not static; they are continuously updated with new data collected from the bridge. This allows them to adapt to changing conditions, such as variations in traffic patterns, new environmental stressors, or the effects of previous repair interventions. Techniques like online learning can be employed, where the model is updated in near real-time as new data arrives, ensuring that its predictions remain accurate and relevant throughout the bridge's operational life. Moreover, if the bridge undergoes significant repairs or retrofits, the AI models can be retrained or fine-tuned to reflect the modified structural characteristics, ensuring that the monitoring system remains effective. This dynamic and adaptive nature of AI is what sets it apart from traditional, static monitoring methods.

In conclusion, this case study exemplifies how AI, when integrated with a comprehensive sensor network and robust data processing capabilities, transforms bridge health monitoring from a reactive or scheduled activity into a proactive, intelligent, and predictive process. By enabling early anomaly detection, facilitating accurate diagnostics, and forecasting future degradation, AI-powered SHM systems are instrumental in ensuring the safety, reliability, and longevity of critical bridge infrastructure, ultimately benefiting public safety and economic efficiency. The continuous advancement of AI algorithms and sensor technologies promises to further enhance these capabilities, paving the way for even more sophisticated and resilient built environments.

Chapter 13: AI for Environmental Impact Assessment and Mitigation

The relentless march of human development, while often driving economic progress and improving quality of life, invariably leaves an indelible mark on the natural world. Infrastructure projects – the very arteries and organs of modern civilization, encompassing everything from sprawling urban developments and intricate transportation networks to vital energy grids and water management systems – are at the forefront of this interaction. These monumental undertakings, essential for connecting communities, facilitating commerce, and providing fundamental services, are inherently disruptive. Their construction and subsequent operation can initiate a cascade of environmental consequences, often complex and far-reaching. Understanding these impacts is not merely an academic exercise; it is a critical prerequisite for responsible planning, sustainable development, and the preservation of ecological balance.

The environmental footprint of infrastructure is multifaceted, manifesting in a variety of forms that can profoundly alter natural systems. Perhaps the most immediate and visible impact is **habitat destruction and fragmentation**. The clearing of land for roads, buildings, dams, and pipelines necessitates the removal of existing vegetation and natural landscapes. This process directly displaces countless species of flora and fauna, leading to loss of biodiversity. Forests are felled, wetlands are drained, grasslands are paved over, and natural watercourses are channelized or dammed. Beyond outright destruction, infrastructure often dissects and isolates previously contiguous habitats. A highway cutting through a forest, for instance, creates barriers that impede wildlife migration, gene flow, and access to essential resources like food and water. This fragmentation can lead to the isolation of populations, making them more vulnerable to local extinction, especially for species with limited mobility or specific habitat requirements. The cumulative effect of such fragmentation across a landscape can lead to a significant decline in overall ecological resilience. For example, the construction of a new railway line through a sensitive ecological corridor can divide breeding grounds, disrupt foraging patterns for animals like deer or wild boar, and increase the risk of roadkill for smaller creatures. The loss of mature trees in a previously undisturbed forest not only removes habitat for arboreal species but also impacts the understory ecosystem that relies on the shade and leaf litter provided by the canopy.

Hand-in-hand with habitat destruction is the pervasive issue of **soil erosion and degradation**. The excavation, grading, and earthmoving activities inherent in infrastructure construction expose soil to the elements. Without the protective cover of vegetation, topsoil becomes highly susceptible to erosion by wind and rain. This runoff carries precious topsoil into nearby waterways, leading to sedimentation. Soil erosion diminishes land fertility, rendering it unsuitable for agriculture or natural regeneration. The increased sediment load in rivers and streams can smother aquatic habitats, harm fish populations by clogging gills and burying spawning grounds, and reduce water clarity, impacting the photosynthetic capabilities of aquatic plants. Furthermore, the compaction of soil by heavy machinery can impede water infiltration, leading to increased surface runoff and a greater risk of localized flooding, while also hindering root growth for any future vegetation attempting to re-establish itself. Consider the construction of a large-scale residential development on a hillside; the extensive excavation and removal of trees can lead to significant soil loss during rainfall events, potentially causing landslides and depositing large amounts of sediment into adjacent streams, disrupting the aquatic ecosystem. The long-term consequences can include reduced agricultural productivity in the surrounding areas and the degradation of the aesthetic and recreational value of water bodies.

The impacts on water resources are equally significant, encompassing both
water pollution and alterations to hydrological regimes. Construction sites are often sources of pollutants such as sediment, oil, grease,

chemicals from construction materials, and waste. Runoff from these sites can carry these contaminants into rivers, lakes, and groundwater. During the operational phase, infrastructure continues to impact water quality. Roads, for instance, are significant sources of pollutants from vehicle emissions, tire wear, and de-icing salts, which are washed into storm drains and eventually into receiving waters. Oil spills from transportation accidents or leaks from pipelines can have catastrophic effects on aquatic life and ecosystems. Beyond pollution, infrastructure can drastically alter the natural flow of water. Dams built for hydroelectric power or water supply create reservoirs, inundating land, altering downstream flow patterns, and disrupting fish migration. Urbanization, with its extensive networks of impervious surfaces like roads and buildings, dramatically increases surface runoff, overwhelming natural drainage systems and leading to more frequent and severe flooding. This altered hydrological cycle can lead to reduced groundwater recharge, changes in wetland ecosystems, and increased erosion downstream. A classic example is the construction of a major highway that bisects a wetland; this can disrupt the natural water table, reduce the inflow of fresh water, and lead to the desiccation of parts of the wetland, impacting its biodiversity. The subsequent runoff from the highway surface, laden with pollutants, further degrades water quality in any remaining water bodies.

The issue of
air quality degradation is another critical environmental consequence of infrastructure. During the construction phase, dust generated from earthmoving, demolition, and material transport can significantly reduce local air quality, posing risks to construction workers and nearby communities. The operation of construction machinery and vehicles also releases exhaust fumes, contributing to local air pollution. Once operational, infrastructure, particularly transportation networks, becomes a major source of air pollutants. Vehicles emit nitrogen oxides (NOx), volatile organic compounds (VOCs), particulate matter (PM2.5 and PM10), carbon monoxide (CO), and sulfur dioxide (SO2). These pollutants contribute to smog formation, acid rain, and respiratory health problems.

Industrial facilities and energy generation plants, often connected by infrastructure like pipelines and transmission lines, are also significant sources of air pollution, releasing pollutants into the atmosphere that can travel long distances, impacting regional and even global air quality. For instance, a new industrial complex built alongside a major highway will contribute to increased levels of particulate matter and ground-level ozone in the surrounding area, impacting public health and potentially damaging vegetation.

A significant and growing concern associated with infrastructure is its contribution to
greenhouse gas emissions (GHGs). The construction phase itself is energy-intensive, relying heavily on fossil fuels for machinery and the production of materials like cement and steel, which have a substantial carbon footprint. Cement production, for example, is a major global source of CO2 emissions. During the operational phase, transportation infrastructure is a primary driver of GHG emissions, particularly carbon dioxide (CO2) from the combustion of fossil fuels in vehicles. Energy infrastructure, such as power plants, also contributes significantly, especially those burning coal or natural gas. Even the production and maintenance of infrastructure materials, from asphalt to concrete, require energy and often release GHGs. The long-term operational emissions from a vast network of roads, airports, and railways, coupled with the embedded carbon in their construction, make them substantial contributors to climate change. Consider a new, extensive highway network designed to connect several cities; the initial carbon emissions from its construction are considerable, and its operational phase will lock in decades of CO2 emissions from increased vehicle traffic.

Finally,
noise pollution is an often-overlooked but impactful environmental consequence of infrastructure. Construction activities, with their heavy machinery, drilling, and blasting, can generate extreme noise levels, disrupting wildlife behavior, causing stress to nearby human populations,

and impacting sleep patterns. Once operational, transportation infrastructure, especially roads and airports, becomes a constant source of noise. The sound of traffic – engines, tires on pavement, horns – can significantly degrade the quality of life for residents living near these facilities. This persistent noise pollution can have detrimental effects on human health, including increased stress levels, hypertension, and sleep disturbances. It can also disrupt wildlife, affecting communication, foraging, and predator-avoidance behaviors. The construction of a new international airport, for example, will not only lead to significant construction noise but will also create a persistent and widespread noise footprint from aircraft operations that will affect a large surrounding area, impacting both human communities and local wildlife.

Recognizing the potential for these diverse and significant environmental impacts, the practice of
Environmental Impact Assessment (EIA) has become a cornerstone of responsible infrastructure development worldwide. An EIA is a systematic process designed to identify, predict, evaluate, and mitigate the potential environmental consequences of a proposed project before decisions are made about its approval and implementation. It is a proactive tool, aiming to ensure that potential negative effects are understood and addressed early in the planning stages, rather than being dealt with reactively after damage has occurred. The EIA process typically involves several key stages: screening (determining if an EIA is required), scoping (identifying the key issues and impacts to be studied), impact analysis (predicting the nature and magnitude of impacts), mitigation (proposing measures to reduce or offset adverse effects), reporting (documenting the findings in an Environmental Impact Statement or Report), and review (evaluating the adequacy of the EIA by regulatory agencies and the public). The goal is to integrate environmental considerations into the project design and decision-making process, promoting more sustainable and environmentally sound development.

The findings of an EIA are crucial for informing the development of

mitigation strategies. These strategies are designed to avoid, minimize, or compensate for the adverse environmental effects identified. Mitigation can take many forms. **Avoidance** might involve altering the project's location or design to bypass sensitive areas, such as rerouting a road to avoid a wildlife corridor or a pristine wetland. **Minimization** strategies aim to reduce the severity of impacts that cannot be avoided, such as implementing strict erosion control measures during construction, using noise barriers along highways, or employing advanced wastewater treatment technologies. **Compensation or offset** measures are employed when significant residual impacts remain after avoidance and minimization efforts. This could involve creating or restoring habitats elsewhere to compensate for habitat lost, or contributing to conservation funds. For example, if a new housing development will result in the loss of a small area of woodland, a mitigation strategy might involve planting a larger area of new woodland in a nearby location or restoring a degraded habitat to enhance biodiversity. Effective mitigation requires careful planning, ongoing monitoring, and a commitment to implementing proposed measures throughout the project's lifecycle.

In an era of increasing global environmental awareness and the undeniable reality of climate change, the imperative to conduct thorough EIAs and implement robust mitigation strategies for all infrastructure projects has never been greater. The cumulative impact of unchecked development can lead to irreversible ecological damage, threatening biodiversity, natural resources, and the very systems that sustain human life. AI is increasingly being recognized as a powerful tool to enhance and revolutionize both the assessment and mitigation phases of this crucial environmental management process.

The application of Artificial Intelligence (AI) within the domain of environmental data analysis and modeling is rapidly transforming our capacity to understand, monitor, and predict ecological processes. As the scale and complexity of environmental challenges escalate, traditional methods of data processing and analysis often struggle to keep pace. AI, particularly through its subfields like machine learning (ML) and deep learning (DL), offers powerful capabilities to sift through massive, heterogeneous datasets, uncover intricate patterns, and generate predictive insights that were previously unattainable. This computational prowess is not merely an incremental improvement; it represents a paradigm shift in how we approach environmental science and impact assessment.

One of the most significant contributions of AI lies in its ability to process and interpret vast quantities of diverse environmental data. Consider the deluge of information generated by Earth observation systems. Satellite imagery, captured at various resolutions and frequencies, provides a global perspective on land cover change, vegetation health, water bodies, and atmospheric conditions. However, manually analyzing these terabytes of data to detect subtle changes, such as early signs of deforestation, the expansion of invasive species, or the spectral signatures of pollutants, is an arduous and often impractical task. AI algorithms, especially convolutional neural networks (CNNs) which excel at image recognition, can automate this process with remarkable efficiency and accuracy. These models can be trained to identify specific land cover types, quantify changes over time, and even detect anomalies indicative of environmental stress or degradation. For example, ML models can be deployed to analyze time-series satellite data to accurately map the extent and rate of deforestation in the Amazon rainforest, identify illegal logging activities by detecting patterns of forest clearing, or monitor the health of coral reefs by analyzing changes in their spectral reflectance that indicate bleaching events.

Beyond imagery, AI is instrumental in analyzing data from extensive sensor networks. Ground-based sensors, deployed across terrestrial, aquatic, and atmospheric environments, collect real-time data on parameters like air and water quality, temperature, humidity, seismic activity, and pollutant concentrations. The sheer volume and velocity of this sensor data necessitate intelligent processing. AI, particularly through techniques like recurrent neural networks (RNNs) and long short-term memory (LSTM) networks, is adept at handling time-series data. These algorithms can learn temporal dependencies and patterns, enabling them to predict future sensor readings, detect unusual spikes or dips that signal an environmental event (e.g., an industrial leak, a harmful algal bloom), and identify the source of pollution by triangulating data from multiple sensors. For instance, AI can analyze data from a network of air quality monitors to pinpoint the specific industrial facilities or traffic corridors contributing most significantly to localized smog, or it can process data from underwater sensors to predict the trajectory and potential impact of an oil spill.

The integration of AI with climate models represents another frontier in environmental analysis. Climate models are complex simulations that project future climate scenarios based on various anthropogenic and natural forcures. However, these models generate immense datasets that are computationally intensive to run and analyze. AI can assist in several ways: accelerating the processing of model outputs, identifying key drivers of climate change within the model, and improving the accuracy and resolution of predictions. Techniques such as surrogate modeling, where simpler AI models are trained to emulate the behavior of complex climate models, can significantly speed up scenario analysis. Furthermore, ML algorithms can be used to downscale global climate model outputs to provide more localized and actionable predictions of temperature changes, precipitation patterns, and the frequency of extreme weather events. This enhanced predictive capability is crucial for infrastructure planning, allowing engineers and policymakers to design resilient systems that can withstand future climate conditions. For example, AI can help refine projections of sea-level rise for specific coastal regions, informing the design of seawalls and urban drainage systems to account for increased flood risk.

AI's predictive capabilities extend to forecasting the spread of environmental hazards. This is particularly critical for events like wildfires, floods, and the dispersal of airborne pollutants. By analyzing historical data, real-time meteorological information, topographical features, and even social media data that might indicate early sightings, AI models can predict the path and intensity of these events with greater accuracy. For instance, AI-powered wildfire prediction systems can analyze fuel loads, wind patterns, and lightning strike data to forecast areas at high risk of ignition and the likely spread of an ongoing fire, enabling more effective resource allocation for firefighting and evacuation planning. Similarly, AI can model the dispersion of pollutants released from industrial accidents or volcanic eruptions, predicting the areas that will be affected and the potential health risks, thereby facilitating timely public health advisories and emergency responses.

The ability of AI to simulate the effects of different infrastructure designs and mitigation strategies is a game-changer for environmental impact assessment. Before any physical construction begins, AI models can be used to create virtual simulations that predict the environmental consequences of various design choices. For example, an AI model could simulate the impact of different road alignments on wildlife migration patterns, identifying routes that minimize habitat fragmentation or the risk of animal-vehicle collisions. It could also model the hydrological effects of a proposed dam, predicting changes in downstream water flow, sediment transport, and the potential for flooding or drought under different operational scenarios. This "digital twin" approach allows for the testing of multiple alternatives and the optimization of designs to minimize negative environmental footprints.

Furthermore, AI can be employed to evaluate the efficacy of proposed mitigation measures. For instance, if a project involves the construction of a new industrial facility, AI could simulate the dispersion of potential air or water pollutants under different emission control scenarios, helping to determine the most effective abatement technologies. Similarly, for a large-scale development project, AI could model the long-term ecological benefits of proposed habitat restoration or creation efforts, comparing the projected biodiversity outcomes of different restoration techniques. This allows for evidence-based decision-making, ensuring that mitigation strategies are not only proposed but are also likely to be effective in achieving their intended environmental protection goals.

The insights generated by AI-driven analysis and modeling are invaluable for informing critical decisions in environmental impact assessment and mitigation. By providing a more nuanced, predictive, and comprehensive understanding of potential environmental consequences, AI empowers stakeholders to make more informed choices, leading to more sustainable infrastructure development and effective environmental stewardship. The integration of these advanced computational tools is not a matter of future speculation; it is an ongoing revolution that is fundamentally reshaping our ability to address the complex environmental challenges of our time. This enhanced analytical capacity is crucial for ensuring that the infrastructure essential for human progress is developed in a manner that respects and preserves the ecological systems upon which all life depends.

The sophisticated analytical capabilities of AI are proving indispensable in precisely identifying and quantifying various forms of environmental degradation. For instance, in the realm of pollution detection, AI algorithms, particularly those utilizing supervised learning techniques, can be trained on vast datasets of spectral signatures associated with specific pollutants. This enables them to analyze multispectral or hyperspectral satellite imagery to pinpoint the sources and spatial extent of contaminants in water bodies, such as algal blooms caused by nutrient runoff from agricultural or urban areas, or plumes of industrial discharge. Similarly, airborne sensor data, processed by AI, can identify atmospheric pollutants like sulfur dioxide (SO2) and nitrogen oxides (NOx) emanating from power plants or transportation hubs, even differentiating between emissions from different sources based on their unique spectral fingerprints and dispersal patterns. This granular level of detection facilitates targeted regulatory action and the implementation of localized abatement strategies.

Tracking deforestation and land-use change, a critical aspect of monitoring environmental impact, is another area where AI excels. Beyond basic land cover classification, deep learning models can analyze high-resolution satellite imagery to detect subtle changes indicative of illegal logging or unsanctioned agricultural expansion. They can identify individual tree removal events, distinguish between selective logging and clear-cutting, and even estimate the volume of timber extracted. Furthermore, by integrating data from multiple sources, including radar imagery (which can penetrate cloud cover), AI can provide continuous monitoring, even in remote or perpetually overcast regions, ensuring that deforestation activities are identified and reported in near real-time. This capability is crucial for enforcing forest protection policies and for accurately assessing the carbon sequestration losses associated with deforestation.

The monitoring of biodiversity, a cornerstone of ecological health, is being revolutionized by AI. Traditionally, biodiversity assessments relied on manual field surveys, which are labor-intensive, costly, and often provide only snapshots of ecological conditions. AI is enabling more comprehensive and efficient monitoring. Acoustic sensors deployed in forests and oceans can capture a vast array of animal vocalizations. ML algorithms can be trained to identify specific species by their calls, enabling researchers to estimate species abundance, distribution, and even detect the presence of rare or elusive animals without direct observation. Similarly, AI can analyze camera trap imagery to identify individual animals and track their movements and behaviors. In aquatic environments, AI is used to analyze underwater video footage from remotely operated vehicles (ROVs) or autonomous underwater vehicles (AUVs) to identify fish species, count populations, and assess the health of marine ecosystems. For instance, AI models trained on the distinct patterns of whale songs can monitor the migration routes and population dynamics of these marine mammals, providing crucial data for conservation efforts.

Predicting the spread and impact of environmental hazards is a complex but vital application of AI. Wildfire prediction systems, for example, leverage ML to integrate data on vegetation type and moisture content, topography, historical fire occurrences, and real-time weather patterns (wind speed and direction, humidity, temperature). These models can generate high-resolution risk maps, identifying areas most susceptible to ignition and predicting the rate and direction of fire spread. This predictive power allows for proactive measures, such as pre-positioning firefighting resources, implementing targeted fuel management strategies, and issuing timely evacuation orders for at-risk communities.

Similarly, AI is enhancing flood forecasting capabilities. By analyzing hydrological data from rainfall, river flow sensors, soil moisture levels, and topographical data, AI models can predict the likelihood and severity of flooding in specific areas. This includes not only riverine floods but also flash floods and coastal inundation events driven by storm surges. These predictions are critical for infrastructure management, enabling authorities to implement temporary flood defenses, reroute traffic, and warn vulnerable populations. The integration of AI with climate projections further enhances long-term flood risk assessments, informing the design of flood-resilient infrastructure in areas projected to experience increased precipitation or sea-level rise.

The application of AI in modeling the environmental effects of infrastructure is equally transformative. AI-powered simulation tools can create detailed virtual representations of ecosystems and the potential impacts of proposed projects. For a new transportation corridor, for example, AI models can simulate the effects of noise pollution on wildlife behavior, predicting how increased sound levels might disrupt breeding patterns or foraging activities of sensitive species. They can also model the fragmentation effects of roads on wildlife movement, identifying critical pinch points where wildlife crossings or underpasses would be most effective in maintaining ecological connectivity.

In the context of urban development, AI can simulate the impact of new buildings and paved surfaces on local microclimates and stormwater runoff. Models can predict how increased imperviousness will alter drainage patterns, leading to higher peak flows and increased pollutant loads in receiving waters. By testing different green infrastructure solutions—such as permeable pavements, green roofs, or bioswales—within the simulation environment, planners can identify the most effective strategies for managing stormwater and mitigating urban heat island effects. This allows for the proactive integration of sustainable urban drainage systems (SuDS) into project designs, rather than as an afterthought.

Furthermore, AI can be used to model the complex interactions within ecosystems, predicting how a proposed infrastructure project might trigger cascading effects. For instance, the construction of a dam might not only alter downstream flow but also impact sediment transport, which in turn could affect the fertility of riparian floodplains and the health of downstream aquatic ecosystems. AI models, by considering these interconnected relationships, can provide a more holistic understanding of potential environmental consequences, enabling more comprehensive impact assessments.

The use of AI to evaluate the effectiveness of mitigation strategies offers a powerful feedback loop for environmental management. For a proposed wind farm, for instance, AI could analyze data from bird and bat monitoring programs, alongside turbine operational data, to assess the actual risk of avian mortality and to identify specific turbine locations or operational adjustments that minimize this risk. This data-driven assessment allows for adaptive management, where mitigation measures are refined based on real-world performance.

In essence, AI is providing environmental scientists, engineers, and policymakers with unprecedented tools for data analysis and predictive modeling. This enhanced understanding of environmental processes and the potential impacts of human activities is foundational to effective environmental impact assessment and the development of robust mitigation strategies. By leveraging AI's capacity to process complex data, identify subtle patterns, and simulate future scenarios, we can move towards a more informed, proactive, and ultimately more sustainable approach to infrastructure development and environmental protection. The ongoing advancement of AI promises even more sophisticated applications, further deepening our understanding of the intricate environmental systems we seek to protect and manage responsibly.

The proactive identification and subsequent management of environmental risks associated with infrastructure development and operation represent a critical frontier where Artificial Intelligence (AI) is demonstrating profound value. Beyond its capabilities in monitoring and assessment, AI is increasingly being leveraged to anticipate the occurrence of specific pollution events and to devise strategies for their mitigation before they escalate into significant environmental crises. This predictive and prescriptive capacity is particularly relevant for infrastructure projects that inherently carry a risk of contaminant release, whether through routine operation, accidental spills, or natural degradation processes.

One of the most tangible applications of AI in this domain lies in the realm of air quality forecasting, especially in proximity to major transportation networks and industrial complexes. Highways, with their constant flow of vehicles emitting particulate matter, nitrogen oxides (NOx), and volatile organic compounds (VOCs), can significantly degrade local air quality. Similarly, industrial sites, depending on their processes, can release a variety of airborne pollutants. AI models, trained on historical air quality data, meteorological patterns (wind speed and direction, atmospheric stability), traffic volumes, and emissions inventories from these sources, can predict localized air quality degradation with remarkable accuracy. For instance, a system could forecast a spike in fine particulate matter (PM2.5) concentrations downwind of a busy highway interchange during a period of stagnant air and high traffic density. Such predictions allow for the timely implementation of mitigation measures. These might include dynamic traffic management systems that reroute heavy vehicles away from sensitive areas during predicted high-pollution periods, or advisory systems that alert vulnerable populations to reduce outdoor activities. Furthermore, for industrial facilities, AI can analyze real-time process data and emission monitoring to predict potential exceedances of regulatory limits. If the AI detects a trend indicating an impending exceedance, it can automatically recommend adjustments to operational parameters, such as reducing the output of a specific production line or increasing the efficiency of pollution control equipment, thereby preventing an actual violation and minimizing environmental impact.

The potential for accidental spills from infrastructure carrying hazardous materials is another area where AI is revolutionizing prediction and mitigation. Oil pipelines, for example, are vital arteries for energy transport, but they also pose a significant risk of leaks or ruptures due to corrosion, ground movement, or external damage. AI can analyze a multitude of data streams to predict the likelihood of such an event. This includes data from internal pipeline sensors (pressure, flow rates, acoustic emissions that might indicate leaks), external sensor networks monitoring ground conditions (seismic activity, soil moisture), satellite imagery detecting subtle ground deformations, and even historical maintenance records. By identifying anomalies and patterns that precede known failure modes, AI can flag sections of the pipeline that require immediate inspection or maintenance, thus preventing a spill. Beyond pipelines, maritime transport, which relies heavily on oil tankers and cargo ships, also presents spill risks. AI can analyze shipping traffic data, weather forecasts, and vessel condition reports to predict high-risk voyages or areas where collisions or grounding are more probable. If a high-risk scenario is identified, AI can recommend adjustments to shipping routes to avoid hazardous conditions or alert vessels to exercise greater caution. In the event of a spill, AI can play a crucial role in predicting its trajectory and impact. Models can integrate oceanographic data (currents, tides, wave patterns), meteorological data, and the properties of the spilled substance to forecast the spread of oil slicks or the dispersal of chemical pollutants. This predictive capability is essential for effective response, enabling authorities to strategically deploy containment booms, absorbent materials, and cleanup crews to the areas most likely to be affected, thereby minimizing the ecological damage to sensitive coastlines, marine life, and water resources.

Water pollution from infrastructure is also a significant concern, and AI offers advanced tools for both prediction and mitigation. Runoff from urban areas, industrial sites, and agricultural lands, often channeled through engineered drainage systems, can carry a cocktail of pollutants, including heavy metals, nutrients, and microplastics, into rivers, lakes, and coastal waters. AI models can analyze rainfall data, land use patterns, soil types, and the condition of drainage infrastructure to predict the likelihood and magnitude of pollutant loads entering water bodies. For instance, an AI system can forecast that a heavy rainfall event following a dry period in an urban area with extensive impervious surfaces will likely result in a significant surge of pollutants into the local river. Based on such predictions, proactive measures can be implemented. This could involve activating advanced treatment systems at wastewater outfalls to remove a higher percentage of contaminants during anticipated high-runoff events, or temporarily restricting certain industrial discharges. In coastal environments, AI can be used to model the dispersion of pollutants entering estuaries and bays. By integrating data on tidal flows, riverine input, and wind-driven surface currents, AI can predict how pollutants will spread and where they are likely to accumulate. This is crucial for managing water quality for recreational uses, protecting fisheries, and safeguarding sensitive habitats like coral reefs or seagrass beds. For example, if AI predicts that nutrient-rich runoff from agricultural areas will concentrate in a particular bay, it can inform local authorities to issue advisories against swimming or shellfish harvesting in that area and guide the deployment of targeted remediation efforts, such as the use of floating wetlands or bioremediation agents to absorb excess nutrients.

The concept of "digital twins" powered by AI is particularly potent for simulating the environmental impacts of complex infrastructure and for testing mitigation strategies in a virtual environment. A digital twin of a power plant, for instance, could integrate real-time sensor data with AI algorithms to monitor and predict the quality of its wastewater discharge under various operational loads and environmental conditions. If the AI predicts that a particular operational shift will lead to an increase in thermal pollution or the discharge of specific chemicals, it can automatically trigger alarms and suggest adjustments to cooling systems or effluent treatment processes. Similarly, a digital twin of a port facility could use AI to model the dispersion of potential fuel spills from berthed vessels or during bunkering operations. By simulating different spill scenarios and the deployment of various containment and recovery technologies, port authorities can optimize their emergency response plans and pre-position resources effectively. This allows for a "what-if" analysis of mitigation effectiveness without real-world risk, leading to more robust and efficient environmental protection protocols.

Furthermore, AI's ability to process vast datasets from distributed sensor networks allows for the continuous monitoring and adaptive management of environmental conditions around infrastructure. For a large-scale mining operation, AI can analyze data from groundwater monitoring wells, surface water quality sensors, and air quality monitors to detect early signs of contamination migrating from the site. If the AI identifies a pattern indicative of plume movement, it can alert operators and recommend adjustments to water management practices, such as increasing water recirculation to reduce discharge or modifying the placement of active tailings impoundments to contain potential seepage. This real-time, data-driven approach moves beyond traditional, periodic environmental monitoring, enabling swift and targeted interventions that can prevent minor issues from escalating into major environmental incidents. The integration of AI with predictive analytics for pollution events not only enhances regulatory compliance but also fosters a more proactive and responsible approach to infrastructure development and operation, ultimately contributing to better environmental stewardship.

The application of Artificial Intelligence extends beyond the direct mitigation of pollution events and environmental risks, delving into the fundamental aspects of resource efficiency and waste management within infrastructure development and operational lifecycles. These areas are intrinsically linked to environmental impact, as inefficient resource use and excessive waste generation contribute significantly to carbon emissions, habitat destruction, and the depletion of finite natural resources. AI offers sophisticated solutions to optimize these processes, paving the way for more sustainable infrastructure practices and fostering a move towards a circular economy.

In the realm of construction, a sector notoriously prone to material waste, AI is revolutionizing how projects are planned and executed. Traditional construction planning often involves estimations based on historical data and experience, which can lead to over-ordering of materials to account for potential unforeseen issues or inefficiencies. AI-powered predictive analytics can significantly enhance the accuracy of material quantity estimation. By analyzing detailed project blueprints, historical construction data from similar projects, and even real-time site conditions through drone imagery and sensor networks, AI algorithms can generate highly precise material take-offs. This reduces the likelihood of ordering excessive amounts of concrete, steel, timber, and other building components. Furthermore, AI can optimize construction scheduling and sequencing. Complex building projects involve numerous interdependent tasks. AI can analyze these dependencies, project durations, and resource availability to create optimal construction schedules that minimize idle time for machinery and labor, thereby reducing the overall project duration and associated resource consumption. For instance, an AI system could identify that a specific pouring sequence for concrete will allow for faster curing and earlier access to subsequent construction phases, thereby accelerating the project and potentially reducing the need for temporary climate control measures that consume energy. The optimization of logistics is another critical area. AI can manage the just-in-time delivery of materials to construction sites, reducing the need for on-site storage which can lead to material degradation or damage, and also minimizing the carbon footprint associated with numerous delivery trips. By predicting the exact moment materials are needed, AI ensures they arrive with minimal delay and without surplus stockpiling. Beyond material management, AI can also optimize the use of heavy machinery on construction sites. By analyzing task requirements and machine capabilities, AI can assign the most appropriate equipment for each job, ensuring optimal fuel efficiency and reducing wear and tear. It can also schedule machine usage to avoid operational conflicts and minimize downtime, further enhancing overall resource utilization. This proactive approach to material and resource management at the construction phase directly translates into a reduced environmental footprint by minimizing virgin material extraction, energy consumption in manufacturing and transport, and the generation of construction and demolition waste.

The operational phase of infrastructure, particularly in the built environment, presents significant opportunities for AI-driven energy efficiency improvements. Buildings are major consumers of energy for heating, ventilation, and air conditioning (HVAC), lighting, and powering various systems. AI-powered Building Management Systems (BMS) are transforming how these systems are controlled. Traditional BMS often operate on pre-set schedules and simple sensor inputs, leading to inefficient energy use when occupancy or external conditions change unexpectedly. Advanced AI-driven BMS can learn the unique thermal characteristics of a building, predict occupancy patterns based on historical data, external factors like weather forecasts, and even real-time sensor data (e.g., CO2 levels indicating occupancy), and dynamically adjust HVAC and lighting systems to meet demand precisely. For example, an AI system can predict that a particular zone of an office building will be unoccupied during a specific period and proactively reduce the heating or cooling output for that zone, leading to substantial energy savings without compromising occupant comfort. Similarly, AI can optimize lighting levels by integrating data from occupancy sensors, natural light sensors, and the building's energy tariff, ensuring lights are only on when and where they are needed, and at the appropriate brightness. Beyond HVAC and lighting, AI can also optimize the energy consumption of other building systems, such as elevators, pumps, and escalators, by predicting usage patterns and adjusting operational cycles accordingly. For large commercial or industrial facilities, AI can analyze energy consumption patterns across different equipment and processes, identifying anomalies that might indicate inefficiencies or impending equipment failures that lead to increased energy use. This predictive maintenance capability not only prevents costly breakdowns but also ensures that energy-consuming equipment operates at peak efficiency. Furthermore, AI can integrate with smart grids, enabling buildings to optimize their energy consumption based on real-time electricity prices and grid demand, shifting non-critical energy use to off-peak hours and thereby supporting grid stability and reducing reliance on peak generation, which is often more carbon-intensive. This intelligent energy management contributes significantly to reducing the operational carbon footprint of infrastructure.

Water resource management is another critical area where AI is making substantial contributions to efficiency. Infrastructure projects, from urban developments to industrial facilities and agricultural operations, all have significant water demands. AI can optimize water usage by analyzing real-time consumption data, weather forecasts, and operational requirements to manage water distribution and treatment more effectively. In urban water networks, AI can predict water demand at different times and locations, allowing water utilities to optimize pumping schedules and reduce energy consumption associated with water transport. It can also identify leaks in the distribution network by analyzing pressure and flow rate data, enabling rapid response and minimizing water loss. For industrial processes that rely heavily on water, AI can optimize water recycling and reuse systems. By monitoring water quality in real-time and predicting the effectiveness of different treatment methods, AI can ensure that recycled water meets the required quality standards for various applications, significantly reducing the demand for fresh water. In agriculture, which is a major water consumer, AI-powered irrigation systems can analyze soil moisture levels, weather forecasts, and crop-specific water needs to deliver water precisely when and where it is required, minimizing waste and maximizing crop yield. This precision agriculture approach drastically reduces water consumption compared to traditional irrigation methods. Furthermore, AI can be employed in the management of wastewater treatment plants. By analyzing influent characteristics and operational parameters, AI can optimize treatment processes to ensure efficient removal of pollutants while minimizing energy and chemical consumption. This not only conserves water resources but also reduces the environmental impact of wastewater discharge. The integration of AI in water management is therefore crucial for ensuring the sustainability of infrastructure projects in water-scarce regions and for minimizing the environmental burden associated with water use and wastewater generation.

The critical role of AI in waste management, particularly in the context of infrastructure and urban environments, is multifaceted and transformative. At the forefront is the enhancement of recycling processes through intelligent sorting. Traditional Material Recovery Facilities (MRFs) often rely on manual labor and basic mechanical separation, which can be inefficient and lead to contamination of recyclable materials. AI, combined with advanced robotics and computer vision, is revolutionizing this sector. High-resolution cameras and sensors can analyze waste streams in real-time, identifying different types of materials (plastics, paper, metals, glass) based on their visual characteristics, density, and spectral properties. AI algorithms then direct robotic arms to precisely pick and sort these materials with speed and accuracy far exceeding human capabilities. This leads to higher purity rates of recycled commodities, making them more valuable and increasing the overall efficiency of the recycling process. For instance, AI can distinguish between different types of plastics (PET, HDPE, PVC), which are often difficult to separate manually but crucial for effective recycling. This enhanced sorting capability directly contributes to a more robust circular economy by diverting more materials from landfills and reducing the need for virgin resource extraction.

Beyond sorting, AI is optimizing waste collection logistics, a significant operational aspect for municipal services and large infrastructure complexes. Traditional waste collection routes are often pre-determined and may not account for real-time variations in waste generation or traffic conditions. AI-powered route optimization algorithms can analyze data from smart bins equipped with fill-level sensors, historical collection data, and real-time traffic information to dynamically generate the most efficient collection routes. This means collection trucks only visit bins that are full or nearing capacity, and routes are adjusted on the fly to avoid traffic congestion. The benefits are substantial: reduced fuel consumption for collection vehicles, lower emissions, decreased operational costs, and a more timely and responsive waste collection service. For large infrastructure projects or sprawling urban areas, this optimization can lead to significant environmental gains by reducing the mileage covered by heavy vehicles.

Furthermore, AI plays a crucial role in predicting landfill capacity and managing landfill operations more effectively. As landfills are a common end-point for non-recyclable waste, understanding their remaining capacity is vital for urban planning and waste management strategies. AI models can analyze historical waste disposal data, current waste generation trends, and the physical characteristics of existing landfills to predict their lifespan with greater accuracy. This foresight allows municipalities and infrastructure operators to plan for future waste management solutions, such as investing in advanced waste-to-energy technologies or establishing new, more sustainably designed landfills. In existing landfills, AI can also monitor environmental parameters such as methane gas generation and leachate production. By analyzing sensor data and operational records, AI can predict potential issues and optimize landfill management practices to minimize environmental risks, such as gas leaks or the contamination of groundwater. This predictive and data-driven approach to landfill management is essential for minimizing the long-term environmental footprint of waste disposal.

The integration of AI across these domains—resource efficiency in construction and operations, optimized water management, and advanced waste management—collectively contributes to a more sustainable infrastructure ecosystem. By enabling precise estimation, reducing waste, optimizing energy and water use, and enhancing recycling and waste collection, AI empowers stakeholders to significantly lower the environmental impact of infrastructure projects throughout their entire lifecycle, from conception to decommissioning. This shift towards intelligent, data-driven decision-making is fundamental to achieving environmental goals and fostering a truly circular economy.

The pervasive integration of Artificial Intelligence into environmental management systems is profoundly transforming the landscape of monitoring and reporting. Moving beyond the complex predictive and optimization tasks previously discussed, AI's capacity to process vast datasets and discern intricate patterns offers unparalleled efficiency and accuracy in understanding and documenting an infrastructure project's environmental footprint. This subsection delves into how AI automates the collection, analysis, and dissemination of environmental data, thereby enhancing compliance, facilitating proactive management, and fostering greater transparency.

One of the most significant contributions of AI in this domain is the automation of environmental data analysis. Infrastructure projects, by their very nature, are subject to a myriad of environmental regulations and require continuous monitoring of various parameters. These can range from air and water quality indicators, noise levels, and soil erosion, to the presence and impact on biodiversity. Traditionally, this data collection and subsequent analysis have been a laborious, time-consuming, and often manual process. Field sensors, sampling devices, and visual inspections generate an enormous volume of raw data that must be meticulously reviewed, cataloged, and interpreted. AI algorithms, particularly those employing machine learning and deep learning techniques, are adept at processing these large, heterogeneous datasets at speeds and scales unattainable by human analysts. For instance, AI can be trained to identify subtle anomalies in sensor readings that might indicate an emerging environmental issue, such as a gradual increase in a specific pollutant in a water discharge or a shift in air quality readings that deviates from expected patterns. This proactive detection allows for early intervention, potentially averting more significant environmental damage and costly remediation efforts. Beyond mere anomaly detection, AI excels at identifying complex trends and correlations within the data. It can correlate environmental parameters with specific project activities, weather patterns, or operational changes, providing a nuanced understanding of the causal relationships that impact the environment. This deep analytical capability moves beyond simple compliance checks to a more sophisticated environmental performance assessment.

Furthermore, AI significantly streamlines the generation of compliance reports, a critical and often burdensome requirement for regulatory bodies. Environmental impact assessments and ongoing operational monitoring necessitate regular reporting that adheres to strict formats and content requirements. Manual report generation is not only time-intensive but also prone to human error, which can lead to inaccuracies and potential penalties. AI-powered reporting tools can automate much of this process. By integrating with data acquisition systems and employing natural language generation (NLG) capabilities, AI can automatically compile data, populate predefined report templates, and even generate narrative descriptions of environmental performance. For example, an AI system can analyze data from continuous emissions monitoring systems (CEMS) on a power plant, compare the results against permitted emission limits, and automatically generate a report detailing compliance status, identifying any exceedances, and noting the contributing factors as inferred from other sensor data. This not only drastically reduces the time and resources dedicated to reporting but also enhances the accuracy and consistency of the information provided. The ability to quickly generate accurate reports also ensures that organizations remain compliant with evolving regulatory frameworks, which is crucial in sectors with dynamic environmental legislation. This automation frees up environmental professionals to focus on higher-level strategic tasks, such as developing mitigation plans or conducting deeper investigations into environmental performance, rather than being bogged down by routine data entry and formatting.

The advent of AI also enables the creation of real-time environmental performance dashboards, providing unprecedented visibility and enabling continuous improvement. In the past, environmental performance was often assessed retrospectively through periodic reports. This lagged approach meant that issues might have persisted for extended periods before being identified. AI facilitates a paradigm shift towards real-time monitoring and dynamic management. By aggregating data from a network of sensors, drones, satellite imagery, and operational systems, AI can feed into dynamic dashboards that offer an up-to-the-minute view of an infrastructure project's environmental status. These dashboards can be customized to display key performance indicators (KPIs) relevant to different stakeholders, from site managers and environmental officers to corporate executives and external regulatory bodies. For instance, a construction site might have a dashboard showing real-time dust levels, noise pollution readings, and the status of erosion control measures. If any of these parameters approach predefined thresholds, the system can trigger immediate alerts, allowing for prompt corrective actions, such as adjusting construction activities, deploying additional dust suppression equipment, or reinforcing containment measures. This continuous feedback loop fosters a culture of proactive environmental stewardship, enabling teams to identify and address potential problems before they escalate.

This real-time visibility also enhances transparency and facilitates communication with stakeholders and the public. Environmental performance data, when presented in an accessible and understandable format, can build trust and demonstrate an organization's commitment to sustainability. Interactive dashboards powered by AI can allow the public to view, for example, the air quality around a new development or the water quality of a nearby river system that is being monitored for impact. This open communication can help to mitigate public concerns, foster community engagement, and build a positive reputation. For large-scale projects, such as renewable energy farms or major transportation networks, demonstrating transparent environmental performance is crucial for maintaining social license to operate. AI-driven reporting and visualization tools make this level of transparency achievable by transforming raw data into meaningful insights that can be readily shared. The ability to provide evidence-based accounts of environmental performance, supported by real-time data and automated analysis, solidifies an organization's commitment to responsible development.

Moreover, AI's analytical capabilities extend to the prediction of environmental impacts, enabling preemptive mitigation strategies. While previous discussions focused on optimizing operations to reduce environmental burdens, AI can also forecast potential future environmental scenarios based on current data and projected operational changes. For example, by analyzing historical rainfall data, topographical information, and planned construction activities, an AI model could predict areas at high risk of soil erosion during a particular phase of a project. This foresight allows project managers to implement targeted erosion control measures in advance, rather than reacting to problems after they have occurred. Similarly, in the context of biodiversity monitoring, AI can analyze patterns in wildlife movement data, combined with habitat mapping and projected land-use changes, to identify areas where species are likely to be most impacted. This enables the implementation of specific conservation measures, such as wildlife corridors or habitat restoration efforts, in a proactive and strategic manner. The integration of AI in environmental monitoring and reporting thus represents a significant leap forward, moving from reactive compliance to proactive environmental management and informed decision-making, ultimately contributing to more sustainable infrastructure development and operation. The automation of data processing and reporting frees up valuable human capital, while real-time analytics and predictive capabilities empower stakeholders with the insights needed to minimize environmental footprints and foster genuine ecological responsibility throughout the lifecycle of any project. The potential for AI to refine our understanding of complex environmental systems and to translate that understanding into actionable, transparent, and compliant reporting is a cornerstone of its transformative power in the field of environmental impact assessment and mitigation.

Chapter 14: Socio-Technical Systems and Stakeholder Engagement Infrastructure, at its core, is far more than a collection of physical assets and the technologies that govern them. To truly understand its functioning, evolution, and impact, we must conceptualize it as a deeply intertwined **socio-technical system**. This framing acknowledges that any piece of infrastructure – be it a transportation network, a power grid, a communication system, or a water supply facility – is simultaneously a product of technological design and engineering ingenuity, and a product of human actions, societal structures, economic forces, and political will. The technical components, such as bridges, turbines, fiber optic cables, and pumps, are undeniably critical. However, their effectiveness, their very purpose, and their ultimate success are inextricably linked to the human and social dimensions that surround them.

The performance of infrastructure is not solely dictated by its engineering specifications or its operational efficiency in a vacuum. Instead, it is profoundly influenced by
user behavior. Consider a newly constructed public transit system. While the trains might be state-of-the-art and the tracks perfectly laid, the system's viability hinges on whether people choose to use it. This choice is influenced by a complex web of factors: convenience, cost, habit, cultural norms, perceived safety, and even aesthetic appeal. A user might opt for a private vehicle despite the availability of public transport due to a lack of understanding of the system, concerns about overcrowding, or a preference for the privacy and flexibility of personal travel. Similarly, the adoption of smart grid technologies, designed to optimize energy distribution, depends on homeowners embracing smart meters and potentially altering their energy consumption patterns based on real-time pricing signals. Without active and often adaptive engagement from its users, even the most technologically advanced infrastructure can fall short of its intended goals.

Beyond individual user behavior,

policy and regulatory frameworks play a pivotal role in shaping infrastructure. Government policies dictate where infrastructure can be built, what standards it must adhere to, how it is funded, and who operates it. For instance, the rollout of broadband internet infrastructure in rural areas is often driven by government subsidies and mandates aimed at bridging the digital divide. Environmental regulations influence the design and construction of power plants, while safety standards dictate the design of bridges and tunnels. Furthermore, policies related to urban planning, land use, and transportation modes directly impact the demand and necessity for specific types of infrastructure. The political landscape, including lobbying efforts, public opinion, and inter-governmental relations, can either accelerate or impede infrastructure development and adaptation. The decision to invest in a high-speed rail network, for example, is not purely an economic or technical one; it involves extensive political negotiation, public consultation, and alignment with national development strategies.

Public perception and social acceptance are equally crucial, especially for large-scale or controversial projects. The "NIMBY" (Not In My Backyard) phenomenon, where communities oppose infrastructure projects near their homes, highlights the powerful influence of local concerns, environmental anxieties, and a desire to maintain the status quo. Infrastructure projects, particularly those involving significant land acquisition, environmental disruption, or novel technologies, often face public scrutiny. Building trust and achieving social license to operate requires open communication, genuine engagement with affected communities, and a clear demonstration of how the project will benefit society while mitigating negative impacts. The successful implementation of wind farms, for instance, often depends not just on the technical feasibility of harnessing wind energy, but on addressing concerns about visual impact, noise, and potential effects on wildlife, and on building local support through shared benefits or community ownership models.

The **organizational structures and governance models** under which infrastructure is developed and managed are also integral to its socio-technical nature. Whether an infrastructure system is owned and operated by a public entity, a private corporation, or a public-private partnership, the organizational culture, decision-making processes, and accountability mechanisms significantly influence its performance and responsiveness. Bureaucratic structures, for example, might lead to slower decision-making and adaptation, while highly competitive private models might prioritize short-term profit over long-term sustainability or public good. The way maintenance is scheduled, how emergencies are handled, how innovation is fostered, and how stakeholders are integrated into governance are all organizational choices with profound socio-technical consequences. For a complex system like a national electricity grid, its resilience and reliability are not just about the physical assets but also about the coordinated efforts of numerous entities – generation companies, transmission operators, distribution networks, and regulatory bodies – all working within a defined governance framework.

Therefore, understanding infrastructure as a socio-technical system compels us to move beyond a purely engineering-centric view. It requires us to consider the human element not as a secondary factor or an external constraint, but as an intrinsic and active component of the system itself. This holistic perspective is not merely an academic exercise; it is essential for effective planning, design, implementation, operation, and evolution of infrastructure in the real world. It recognizes that technology and society are not separate entities that interact, but are co-evolving and mutually shaping forces. The challenges and opportunities in infrastructure development and management arise from this dynamic interplay, and successful outcomes depend on our ability to understand and navigate this complex socio-technical landscape.

The very definition of what constitutes "performance" for infrastructure is broadened when viewed through a socio-technical lens. It is no longer just about technical efficiency or output capacity. Performance also encompasses factors like equity of access, affordability, resilience to disruptions (both technical and social), environmental sustainability, and contribution to social well-being. For example, a road network that is technically well-maintained but inaccessible to low-income communities or exacerbates air pollution in residential areas would not be considered high-performing from a socio-technical perspective. Similarly, a water distribution system that provides reliable water delivery but at exorbitant costs, leading to public health crises due to unaffordability, demonstrates a failure in its socio-technical integration.

The adoption and evolution of infrastructure are characterized by a continuous feedback loop between the technical and the social. A new technology, such as autonomous vehicles, does not simply appear and function independently. Its development is shaped by societal needs, regulatory approvals, and public acceptance. Once introduced, its use patterns are influenced by existing road infrastructure, traffic laws, ethical considerations, and consumer trust. This, in turn, influences how road infrastructure itself might need to adapt, perhaps requiring new signage, sensing capabilities, or dedicated lanes. This co-evolutionary process highlights that infrastructure is not static; it is a living system that adapts to and is adapted by the society it serves.

Furthermore, the socio-technical perspective is crucial for identifying and addressing unintended consequences. A new dam might provide significant hydroelectric power and water for irrigation (technical benefits), but it can also displace communities, alter river ecosystems, and impact downstream agricultural practices (social and environmental consequences). The failure to adequately consider these socio-technical dimensions during the planning and implementation phases can lead to significant social unrest, environmental damage, and economic losses, undermining the intended benefits of the infrastructure project. Proactive stakeholder engagement, grounded in an understanding of these interconnected elements, becomes paramount. This means engaging not just with engineers and policymakers, but also with end-users, community representatives, environmental advocacy groups, and affected populations from the earliest stages of a project.

The concept of
resilience in infrastructure is also deeply rooted in its socio-technical nature. While technical resilience focuses on the ability of physical components and systems to withstand shocks and stresses (e.g., seismic resistance of a bridge, redundancy in a power grid), socio-technical resilience considers the capacity of the entire system, including its human actors and organizational structures, to adapt and recover from disruptions. A severe storm might damage physical power lines, but the speed and effectiveness of restoration depend on the coordination between utility companies, emergency services, government agencies, and even the willingness of the public to conserve energy and assist in recovery efforts. Social cohesion, trust in institutions, and robust communication channels are as critical to resilience as the strength of the physical infrastructure.

When examining the implementation of digital infrastructure, such as the expansion of 5G networks or the deployment of smart city technologies, the socio-technical lens is indispensable. The technical capabilities of these systems – higher bandwidth, lower latency, greater connectivity – are undeniable. However, their societal impact hinges on issues of digital equity, data privacy, cybersecurity, algorithmic bias, and the potential for job displacement or the creation of new forms of social stratification. The governance of these digital infrastructures, who controls the data, and how decisions are made about their use, are all critical socio-technical considerations that will determine whether they ultimately serve the broader public interest or exacerbate existing societal divides.

The influence of
economic structures and market forces also weaves through the socio-technical fabric of infrastructure. The decision to invest in certain types of infrastructure is often driven by economic imperatives, such as improving supply chain efficiency, attracting foreign investment, or creating jobs. However, economic models can sometimes incentivize infrastructure development that prioritizes profit over broader societal or environmental goals. For instance, a privatized utility might underinvest in maintenance to boost short-term profits, or a transportation project might be driven by the interests of construction firms rather than the long-term needs of the populace. Understanding these economic drivers and their interplay with social and technical factors is key to shaping infrastructure development that aligns with sustainable and equitable outcomes. This involves examining funding mechanisms, market regulations, and the allocation of risks and rewards among different stakeholders.

In essence, every piece of infrastructure exists within a complex ecosystem where technology, people, policies, economics, and culture are constantly interacting and influencing one another. Recognizing infrastructure as a socio-technical system means acknowledging that:

Technology is socially shaped: The design, development, and deployment of technologies are influenced by human values, social needs, and political priorities.
Society is technologically shaped: The technologies we create and adopt, in turn, alter social structures, behaviors, norms, and opportunities.

Performance is multi-dimensional: Infrastructure performance must be evaluated not only on technical metrics but also on social, economic, and environmental criteria, including equity, accessibility, and sustainability.
Implementation is a socio-political process: The success of infrastructure projects relies heavily on stakeholder engagement, negotiation, consensus-building, and navigating complex political landscapes.
Evolution is co-dependent: Infrastructure and society evolve together, in a continuous process of adaptation and mutual influence.

This holistic understanding moves us beyond simplistic views of infrastructure as mere physical objects or abstract technological systems. It emphasizes the critical importance of the human element – the users, operators, regulators, affected communities, and the broader societal context – in determining the true value, effectiveness, and sustainability of any infrastructure endeavor. It underscores that effective infrastructure development and management are not just engineering challenges, but profoundly social and political ones that require interdisciplinary approaches and a deep commitment to engaging with all stakeholders.

The integration of Artificial Intelligence (AI) into the realm of stakeholder analysis and communication presents a transformative opportunity for managing complex socio-technical systems. As our understanding of infrastructure deepens to recognize it as an intricate web of human and technical interactions, the challenge of effectively identifying, understanding, and engaging with the diverse array of stakeholders becomes increasingly significant. Traditional methods of stakeholder analysis, while valuable, often struggle to cope with the sheer volume, velocity, and variety of information generated in modern projects. This is where AI, particularly through its capabilities in natural language processing (NLP) and machine learning, offers powerful new tools to augment and, in some cases, revolutionize how we approach stakeholder engagement.

One of the most profound contributions of AI lies in its ability to sift through and make sense of vast quantities of unstructured data. Consider the public consultation phase for a major infrastructure project, such as a new transportation corridor or a renewable energy facility. During this phase, feedback can flood in from numerous sources: online comment portals, emails, transcribed public meetings, social media discussions, and formal survey responses. Manually reviewing and categorizing this information is a monumental task, prone to human bias, oversight, and significant time delays. AI-powered tools, however, can process this deluge of text data with remarkable speed and scale. By employing NLP techniques, AI can automatically identify key themes, extract sentiment, and categorize stakeholder concerns. For instance, an NLP algorithm can be trained to recognize keywords and phrases associated with environmental impact, economic benefits, noise pollution, or disruption to local communities. It can then assign a sentiment score (positive, negative, or neutral) to each piece of feedback, providing a rapid overview of how different groups feel about specific aspects of the project.

This automated sentiment analysis goes beyond simply counting positive or negative comments. More sophisticated AI models can delve deeper, identifying the nuances of stakeholder opinions and uncovering underlying motivations. For example, an AI could distinguish between a stakeholder expressing general dissatisfaction with a project's timeline and another articulating specific concerns about the impact on their property value or local ecosystem. By identifying patterns and commonalities across thousands of individual comments, AI can help project managers pinpoint critical areas of concern that might otherwise be lost in the noise. This allows for a more proactive and targeted approach to stakeholder engagement, enabling teams to address potential issues before they escalate into significant opposition or conflict. The ability to rapidly identify emerging trends in public discourse is invaluable, allowing for timely adjustments to project plans or communication strategies.

Furthermore, AI can significantly enhance the summarization and categorization of stakeholder feedback. Imagine a project team needing to present a concise overview of public opinion to senior management or regulatory bodies. Instead of manually synthesizing lengthy reports, AI can generate intelligent summaries that highlight the most salient points, the prevalence of specific issues, and the overall sentiment spectrum. This not only saves considerable time and resources but also ensures a more objective and comprehensive representation of stakeholder perspectives. Categorization can be performed based on various criteria, such as stakeholder type (e.g., residents, businesses, environmental groups), geographic location, or the specific issue being discussed. This granular level of organization allows project leaders to understand the diverse needs and priorities of different stakeholder groups, fostering more tailored and effective engagement strategies.

The proactive identification of potential conflicts is another critical area where AI excels. By analyzing the sentiment and stated positions of various stakeholder groups, AI can flag instances where interests are likely to clash. For example, if an AI identifies a strong negative sentiment from a community group regarding a proposed construction site and simultaneously detects positive sentiment from a business association advocating for the project's economic benefits, it can alert the project team to a potential conflict zone. This early warning system allows for the initiation of dialogue and mediation efforts before positions harden and opposition becomes entrenched. AI can help map out stakeholder relationships and potential alliances or points of friction, providing a strategic overview that informs communication and negotiation efforts.

AI's utility extends to improving the efficiency and effectiveness of direct communication channels. Chatbots powered by AI can handle a large volume of routine inquiries from stakeholders, providing instant answers to frequently asked questions about project timelines, environmental impact assessments, or contact information. This frees up human communication teams to focus on more complex issues requiring personalized attention and relationship building. Moreover, AI can assist in drafting communication materials, such as press releases, website updates, or social media posts, by analyzing past successful communications and ensuring consistency in messaging and tone. AI can also help in identifying the most effective channels and times to reach specific stakeholder groups, optimizing the delivery of information and increasing engagement rates.

Consider the iterative nature of stakeholder engagement. As a project progresses, new information emerges, plans evolve, and stakeholder concerns may shift. AI tools can continuously monitor public discourse and stakeholder feedback, identifying changes in sentiment or the emergence of new issues. This allows for an adaptive and responsive engagement process. For example, if an AI detects a sudden surge in negative comments related to a specific aspect of a project, it can trigger an immediate review and response from the project team, demonstrating responsiveness and a commitment to addressing concerns. This continuous feedback loop is essential for maintaining trust and fostering positive relationships throughout the project lifecycle.

The application of AI in stakeholder analysis is not without its challenges. Ensuring the accuracy and fairness of AI algorithms is paramount. Bias can creep into AI models if the data used for training is not representative or if the algorithms are not carefully designed. For instance, an AI trained primarily on data from a specific demographic might misinterpret or overlook the concerns of other groups. Therefore, rigorous testing, validation, and ongoing monitoring of AI systems are essential to mitigate bias and ensure equitable representation of all stakeholder perspectives. Furthermore, transparency in how AI is used for stakeholder analysis and communication is crucial. Stakeholders should be aware that AI tools are being employed, and there should be clear avenues for recourse if individuals believe their input has been misrepresented or unfairly categorized.

Despite these challenges, the potential benefits of AI in stakeholder analysis and communication are immense. It offers the prospect of moving from reactive, often overwhelming, engagement processes to proactive, data-driven, and highly targeted interactions. By leveraging AI, project managers can gain a deeper, more nuanced understanding of their stakeholder landscape, anticipate potential challenges, and build stronger, more trusting relationships. This ultimately contributes to the successful development and operation of socio-technical systems that are not only technically sound but also socially accepted, equitable, and sustainable. The ability to process and interpret vast, complex datasets related to human sentiment and opinion represents a significant leap forward in our capacity to manage the human dimensions of infrastructure development. This intelligent augmentation of human capacity allows for more informed decision-making, more effective resource allocation for engagement activities, and a greater likelihood of achieving project goals while simultaneously fostering positive societal outcomes. It transforms stakeholder engagement from an art to a more robust, evidence-based discipline, powered by the insights derived from sophisticated analytical tools.

Moreover, AI can facilitate longitudinal analysis of stakeholder sentiment and engagement over the entire lifecycle of an infrastructure project. By tracking changes in opinions, concerns, and levels of engagement over time, project teams can gain valuable insights into the long-term impact of their efforts. For instance, an AI could identify that initial concerns about a project's environmental impact, once addressed through specific mitigation measures, gradually fade, replaced by concerns about ongoing operational noise. This temporal understanding allows for strategic planning and resource allocation, ensuring that engagement efforts remain relevant and effective throughout the project's duration and into its operational phase. This continuous monitoring and analysis are critical for maintaining adaptive management strategies in complex socio-technical environments.

The integration of AI also has the potential to democratize access to information and participation for a broader range of stakeholders. While complex reports and technical documents can be intimidating, AI-powered summarization tools can render key information more accessible. Plain language summaries of environmental impact assessments, for example, can be automatically generated, allowing individuals without specialized technical backgrounds to better understand the implications of a project. This enhanced accessibility can empower more diverse voices to participate in the decision-making process, fostering greater inclusivity and equity in stakeholder engagement. AI can also identify stakeholders who may be less vocal or have historically been marginalized, prompting project teams to proactively reach out and ensure their perspectives are heard. This is crucial for building truly representative and robust stakeholder engagement frameworks.

Furthermore, AI can play a role in evaluating the effectiveness of communication strategies themselves. By analyzing engagement metrics, such as website traffic, social media interaction rates, attendance at public meetings, and the sentiment of feedback received following specific communication campaigns, AI can help identify what is working and what is not. This data-driven approach allows for the continuous refinement of communication plans, ensuring that messages are reaching the intended audiences, are being understood, and are eliciting the desired responses. For example, if an AI identifies that a particular communication channel is generating low engagement or negative sentiment, the project team can reallocate resources or adjust their messaging accordingly. This iterative process of communication, analysis, and adaptation is fundamental to successful stakeholder management in complex socio-technical projects. The continuous loop of deployment, feedback, analysis, and refinement, powered by AI, ensures that communication efforts are not static but dynamically evolve to meet the changing needs of both the project and its stakeholders.

The advent of sophisticated AI tools for stakeholder analysis and communication marks a pivotal moment in the management of socio-technical systems. It moves us beyond the limitations of manual processes, enabling a more comprehensive, nuanced, and responsive approach to understanding and engaging with the diverse human elements that shape infrastructure. By harnessing the power of AI, we can foster greater transparency, build stronger trust, anticipate and mitigate conflicts, and ultimately ensure that infrastructure projects are designed, built, and operated in ways that are truly aligned with societal needs and values. This is not about replacing human judgment or empathy, but about augmenting it with powerful analytical capabilities, allowing for more informed decisions and more effective stewardship of our vital infrastructure.

The intricate dance between human beings and the infrastructure that underpins their lives is a complex phenomenon, one that has long been a subject of study and speculation. Traditionally, understanding this interaction relied heavily on observation, surveys, and statistical analysis of past usage patterns. However, the advent of Artificial Intelligence (AI) has ushered in a new era of possibility, enabling the creation of sophisticated models that can not only describe but also predict human behavior in relation to infrastructure. This capability is transformative, moving us from reactive adaptation to proactive design and management.

Consider the realm of transportation. How do individuals choose their mode of travel? What factors influence their decisions to adopt new forms of mobility, such as ride-sharing services or electric vehicles? AI algorithms, particularly those leveraging machine learning, can sift through vast datasets encompassing travel logs, demographic information, traffic patterns, and even social media sentiment to identify subtle yet powerful correlations. For instance, an AI model might discover that while proximity to public transport is a primary driver for urban dwellers, the perceived safety and availability of parking are more significant for suburban commuters. By analyzing historical data on route choices, congestion levels, and public transit ridership, AI can predict how a proposed new bus route or a change in traffic light timing might alter travel behavior, leading to optimized traffic flow and reduced congestion. This predictive power allows urban planners to simulate the impact of infrastructure changes before they are implemented, averting costly and ineffective interventions.

Furthermore, AI's ability to analyze individual choices at scale provides invaluable insights into the adoption rates of new infrastructure technologies. The rollout of smart meters in electricity grids is a prime example. While the technical benefits of smart meters are clear, their successful integration hinges on consumer acceptance and utilization. AI models can analyze data from early adopters, correlating factors such as socioeconomic status, environmental consciousness, educational background, and even the specific communication strategies employed by utility companies, to predict broader adoption trends. Such models can identify potential barriers to adoption, such as concerns about data privacy or perceived complexity, allowing for targeted educational campaigns and tailored incentive programs. If a model indicates that a particular demographic is hesitant due to privacy concerns, proactive communication emphasizing data anonymization and security protocols can be deployed, thereby smoothing the path for widespread adoption and maximizing the benefits of the new technology, such as more efficient energy distribution and reduced waste.

The impact of policy changes on human behavior is another area where AI modeling offers profound advantages. Imagine a government introducing a congestion charge in a city center or offering subsidies for installing solar panels. Predicting the precise behavioral response to such policies can be challenging using traditional methods. AI, however, can learn from pilot programs or similar initiatives in other regions. By analyzing data on purchasing decisions, travel patterns, and energy consumption before and after a policy is introduced, AI can build models that forecast how different segments of the population will react. For example, an AI might predict that a congestion charge will disproportionately affect low-income individuals who rely on private vehicles for work, prompting policymakers to consider alternative solutions like enhanced public transport or targeted exemptions. Similarly, AI can model the uptake of electric vehicle charging infrastructure based on factors like electricity prices, government incentives, and the availability of charging stations, guiding investment decisions to areas where demand is likely to be highest.

The water sector also stands to benefit immensely from AI-driven behavioral modeling. Understanding how households and industries consume water is crucial for effective resource management, especially in water-scarce regions. AI can analyze historical water usage data, factoring in weather patterns, seasonal variations, and demographic changes, to predict future demand. More importantly, it can model behavioral responses to water conservation policies. If a utility company implements a tiered pricing structure where higher consumption incurs significantly higher costs, AI can predict how households are likely to adjust their water usage, perhaps by taking shorter showers, watering gardens less frequently, or investing in water-efficient appliances. This predictive capability allows water authorities to set realistic conservation targets and design more effective strategies to meet them, ensuring the sustainability of this vital resource. The insights derived from such models can also inform the design of public awareness campaigns, tailoring messages to resonate with specific behavioral patterns and motivations observed within different communities.

Beyond macro-level predictions, AI can also delve into the granular patterns of human interaction with specific infrastructure components. In the context of smart grids, for instance, AI can analyze data from smart appliances and home energy management systems to understand how people adjust their energy consumption in response to dynamic pricing signals or grid load management requests. This level of detail is critical for developing demand-response programs that effectively balance energy supply and demand without compromising user comfort or convenience. By identifying patterns in when and how individuals respond to such signals, AI can help optimize the scheduling of energy-intensive tasks like charging electric vehicles or running dishwashers, leading to significant cost savings for consumers and enhanced grid stability for utilities.

The adoption of smart city technologies, from intelligent traffic management systems to smart waste collection, is another domain ripe for AI-powered behavioral modeling. Understanding how citizens interact with these new systems is paramount for their success. For example, AI can analyze data from public transit apps to understand user preferences for real-time information, route planning, and payment methods. This can inform the design of more user-friendly and efficient public transportation networks. In waste management, AI can analyze data from smart bins to predict fill rates and optimize collection routes, but it can also model citizen behavior related to waste segregation and recycling, identifying areas where public education or altered bin placement might lead to improved diversion rates. This holistic approach ensures that technological advancements are complemented by an understanding of the human element, fostering genuine adoption and behavioral change.

The predictive power of AI extends to understanding the emergent behaviors that arise from the interconnectedness of socio-technical systems. As different infrastructure systems become more integrated – for example, the interplay between the energy grid and electric vehicle charging infrastructure, or the connection between smart water meters and building management systems – predicting the combined impact of human behavior on these linked systems becomes more complex. AI models, capable of handling multivariate analysis and identifying complex interdependencies, are uniquely suited to this challenge. They can help anticipate how changes in one system might ripple through others, driven by human responses. For instance, a widespread shift towards electric vehicles, while improving air quality, will place additional demands on the electricity grid. AI can model the cumulative behavioral response to charging needs at different times of day and forecast the potential strain on the grid, informing proactive investments in grid upgrades and smart charging solutions.

Moreover, AI can be instrumental in understanding resistance to infrastructure change. Not all behavioral responses are positive or adaptive. Resistance, whether active or passive, is a common feature of infrastructure development and deployment. AI can analyze patterns in public discourse, survey responses, and historical project data to identify factors that contribute to resistance, such as perceived loss of control, equity concerns, or a lack of trust in authorities. By understanding the root causes of resistance, policymakers and project managers can develop more effective strategies for engagement, communication, and mitigation, thereby increasing the likelihood of successful project outcomes. This includes identifying early warning signs of potential opposition and understanding the specific concerns driving that opposition.

The ethical implications of AI-driven behavioral modeling in infrastructure use are also a critical consideration. As these models become more sophisticated, there is a risk of unintended consequences, such as reinforcing existing inequalities or creating new forms of discrimination. For example, if an AI model predicts lower adoption rates for a new public service in a low-income neighborhood based on historical data, it could inadvertently lead to reduced investment and service provision in that area, creating a self-fulfilling prophecy. Therefore, it is imperative that AI models are developed and deployed with a strong ethical framework, emphasizing fairness, transparency, and accountability. Regular audits and impact assessments are necessary to ensure that these technologies are used to promote equitable access to infrastructure and enhance societal well-being, rather than to exacerbate existing disparities. The goal must always be to leverage AI to better serve all members of society, ensuring that infrastructure development contributes to inclusive and sustainable communities. This requires a continuous dialogue between AI developers, infrastructure planners, policymakers, and the communities they serve, fostering a collaborative approach to the design and deployment of these powerful predictive tools.

The increasing complexity of socio-technical systems, particularly in the context of large-scale infrastructure development and policy implementation, often leads to diverse and sometimes conflicting stakeholder interests. Navigating these divergent perspectives to achieve consensus and resolve disputes is a formidable challenge. Traditional methods of conflict resolution and consensus building, while valuable, can be time-consuming, resource-intensive, and may struggle to adequately represent the multifaceted nature of stakeholder concerns. This is where the analytical power of Artificial Intelligence (AI) presents a compelling opportunity to augment and enhance these critical processes. AI's capacity for data processing, pattern recognition, and predictive modeling can illuminate pathways towards common ground, facilitate understanding of complex trade-offs, and ultimately support more robust and equitable decision-making.

One of the primary ways AI can contribute to conflict resolution is by identifying areas of shared interest and potential collaboration among seemingly disparate groups. Stakeholders often approach a project or policy with a specific set of priorities, which can appear at odds with those of others. For instance, in the planning of a new public transportation network, residents in one area might prioritize increased frequency of service, while businesses in another might focus on improved accessibility for customers and employees, and environmental advocates might push for electrification and reduced carbon emissions. AI algorithms can analyze extensive datasets related to these stakeholders' stated preferences, historical engagement patterns, demographic profiles, and even sentiment expressed in public forums. By processing this information, AI can identify underlying commonalities that might not be immediately apparent through conventional dialogue. For example, an AI might reveal that while the specific demands differ, both residents and businesses share a common interest in reducing commute times and improving the economic vitality of the region, and that environmental sustainability is a shared value across many groups. This identification of common ground can serve as a crucial starting point for de-escalation and constructive engagement, shifting the focus from what divides to what unites.

Furthermore, AI excels at dissecting complex trade-offs inherent in any decision-making process involving multiple stakeholders. Infrastructure projects, policy changes, or resource allocation decisions rarely offer a win-win scenario for everyone. There are almost always compromises to be made, with benefits and drawbacks distributed unevenly. AI can systematically model these trade-offs, providing an objective and data-driven assessment of the consequences of various choices for different stakeholder groups. Consider the development of a new urban water management strategy. This might involve decisions about water pricing, conservation mandates, or investment in new infrastructure like desalination plants or advanced recycling facilities. Each of these options carries different implications for residential users, industrial consumers, agricultural entities, and environmental protection agencies. An AI model, fed with data on consumption patterns, economic impacts, environmental flows, and public health considerations, can simulate the outcomes of different policy combinations. It could quantify, for instance, how a particular pricing structure might impact household budgets in low-income areas versus high-income areas, or the economic effect of water restrictions on different agricultural sectors. This transparent and quantifiable depiction of trade-offs allows stakeholders to move beyond emotional appeals and engage in a more pragmatic discussion about acceptable levels of compromise. It helps to answer the critical question: "What are the tangible implications of this decision for *my* group, and what are the implications for others?" By presenting these impacts clearly, AI can foster a more informed and potentially less adversarial negotiation process.

The ability of AI to simulate and forecast the outcomes of different policy or design choices is another powerful tool for consensus building. When stakeholders have a clearer understanding of the potential future consequences of proposed solutions, they are often more willing to negotiate and find common ground. This predictive capability can be particularly useful in addressing concerns about uncertainty and risk, which are common sources of conflict. For instance, when planning a major renewable energy project, such as a wind farm, concerns might arise from local communities regarding visual impact, noise pollution, or potential effects on wildlife. Environmental groups might focus on habitat preservation, while energy providers prioritize grid stability and cost-effectiveness. An AI model could simulate various scenarios: the visual impact of different turbine placements, the noise levels at varying distances under different wind conditions, the predicted impact on specific bird or bat populations based on migratory patterns and habitat suitability, and the economic benefits in terms of jobs and tax revenue for the local area. By visualizing these outcomes, perhaps through augmented reality overlays or detailed statistical reports tailored to each stakeholder group's concerns, AI can provide a shared, objective basis for discussion. This allows stakeholders to collectively evaluate the potential positive and negative impacts and collaboratively adjust the project design or mitigation strategies to achieve a more broadly acceptable outcome. It moves the discussion from abstract fears to concrete, analyzable scenarios.

Moreover, AI can contribute to building trust and transparency in negotiation processes, which are essential for resolving deep-seated conflicts. Often, disagreements stem from a lack of faith in the fairness of the process or the impartiality of the information being used. AI, when deployed ethically and with transparency about its algorithms and data sources, can act as an objective arbiter. Instead of relying on data filtered through individual interests or potentially biased human analysis, AI can process information uniformly. For example, in land use disputes or zoning changes, where historical data on property values, environmental assessments, and community feedback might be contentious, an AI could be tasked with analyzing all available data impartially. The AI's methodology, if made accessible and understandable, can demonstrate that decisions are being informed by a comprehensive and unbiased review of relevant factors. This can help to level the playing field and reduce suspicion, allowing stakeholders to focus on the substance of the issues rather than questioning the integrity of the process. The transparency of AI's decision-making process, even if complex, can foster a sense of equity, ensuring that all parties feel their concerns are being considered based on the same set of facts and analytical rigor.

The application of AI in conflict resolution is not limited to large-scale infrastructure projects. It can also be instrumental in mediating disputes within organizations, communities, or even between different governmental agencies. For instance, consider a scenario where different departments within a large corporation have conflicting priorities for resource allocation, leading to interdepartmental friction. An AI could be used to analyze project proposals, budget requests, and strategic objectives from each department. By modeling the potential return on investment, the alignment with overall corporate strategy, and the synergistic effects of interdepartmental collaboration, the AI can provide an objective basis for prioritizing initiatives. This can help resolve disputes by demonstrating which projects offer the greatest overall benefit to the organization, thereby depersonalizing decisions and reducing the likelihood of protracted disagreements rooted in departmental rivalries. The AI's output can serve as a neutral recommendation, which leadership can then use as a foundation for making decisions that are perceived as fair and strategically sound.

In the context of public policy, AI can be employed to analyze public sentiment and identify emerging areas of concern or opposition to proposed legislation or regulations. Social media, online forums, and public comment portals generate vast amounts of unstructured text data reflecting the views of citizens. AI, particularly through natural language processing (NLP) techniques, can analyze this data to identify key themes, common concerns, and the intensity of public opinion on various aspects of a policy. This information can then be used to proactively address potential conflicts before they escalate. For example, if an AI detects a surge in public concern about the potential impact of a new trade agreement on local employment, policymakers can initiate targeted consultations with affected communities, provide clearer explanations of mitigation measures, or even adjust the terms of the agreement to address those specific worries. This anticipatory approach, powered by AI's ability to process and understand large volumes of public discourse, can prevent conflicts from festering and becoming intractable, leading to smoother policy implementation and greater public acceptance.

Furthermore, AI can assist in the development of communication strategies aimed at fostering consensus. Once areas of common ground and potential trade-offs are identified, AI can help tailor messages to resonate with different stakeholder groups. By analyzing the communication styles, values, and specific concerns of various stakeholders, AI can suggest language, framing, and communication channels that are most likely to be persuasive and build bridges. For example, when communicating the benefits of a new public health initiative, messages emphasizing individual well-being might be most effective for certain demographics, while messages highlighting community resilience or economic benefits might appeal to others. AI can analyze the effectiveness of past communication campaigns and identify patterns in engagement, thereby informing the design of future outreach efforts. This data-driven approach to communication ensures that efforts to build consensus are not based on guesswork but on a nuanced understanding of the target audiences, leading to more effective dialogue and stronger buy-in.

The integration of AI into conflict resolution and consensus-building processes also necessitates careful consideration of ethical implications and potential pitfalls. While AI offers immense potential for objectivity, it is crucial to acknowledge that AI systems are trained on data, and this data can reflect existing societal biases. If the data used to train an AI reflects historical discrimination or inequity, the AI's outputs could inadvertently perpetuate or even amplify these issues. For example, if an

AI is used to allocate resources for community development projects and the training data disproportionately favors certain neighborhoods over others due to historical funding patterns, the AI might recommend continued disinvestment in underserved areas, thereby exacerbating existing inequalities. Therefore, rigorous data auditing, bias detection, and mitigation strategies are paramount. Transparency about the data sources, the algorithms used, and the potential limitations of the AI is also essential. Stakeholders must understand how the AI is functioning and have mechanisms for challenging its outputs or assumptions if they believe it is leading to unfair or inequitable outcomes.

Moreover, over-reliance on AI without human oversight can diminish the vital role of empathy, nuanced understanding, and human negotiation skills in conflict resolution. While AI can identify patterns and quantify outcomes, it cannot replicate the human capacity for building rapport, understanding unspoken needs, or forging emotional connections that are often critical in resolving deeply entrenched disputes. Therefore, AI should be viewed as a powerful assistive tool, augmenting human capabilities rather than replacing them entirely. The insights generated by AI should inform and guide human negotiators, providing them with a more robust evidence base and a clearer picture of potential solutions, but the final decisions and the delicate art of persuasion and compromise must remain within the human domain. The goal is to create a synergy between AI's analytical prowess and human judgment, fostering more informed, efficient, and equitable outcomes in complex socio-technical systems.

The future of conflict resolution and consensus building in the context of socio-technical systems will undoubtedly involve a greater integration of AI. As AI technologies mature and become more sophisticated, their ability to analyze complex interdependencies, predict behavioral responses to different interventions, and identify optimal solutions across a wide range of stakeholder interests will continue to grow. The challenge lies in harnessing this potential responsibly, ensuring that AI is deployed in ways that enhance fairness, promote understanding, and ultimately lead to more sustainable and equitable outcomes for all involved. This requires a multidisciplinary approach, bringing together AI developers, social scientists, policymakers, and community leaders to co-design and co-implement these technologies, ensuring that they serve humanity's best interests in navigating the complexities of our increasingly interconnected world. The transformative power of AI in fostering agreement and resolving disputes in the realm of socio-technical systems is substantial, offering a pathway to more collaborative and effective decision-making in an era defined by intricate challenges and diverse human needs.

The increasing integration of Artificial Intelligence (AI) into the planning and management of socio-technical infrastructures presents a landscape ripe with opportunity, but also fraught with ethical complexities. As we delegate more analytical and predictive tasks to AI systems, a critical examination of their inherent biases and the implications for equitable outcomes becomes paramount. In the context of socio-technical infrastructure planning, where decisions profoundly impact communities and individuals, the deployment of AI demands a rigorous ethical framework to ensure that these powerful tools serve to augment human judgment and promote societal well-being, rather than inadvertently perpetuate or exacerbate existing inequalities.

One of the most significant ethical challenges lies in the potential for algorithmic bias. AI models learn from the data they are trained on, and if this data reflects historical societal inequities, discriminatory practices, or uneven resource distribution, the AI will inevitably internalize and propagate these biases. For instance, consider an AI system designed to optimize the allocation of resources for urban development and infrastructure upgrades. If the historical data fed into this AI predominantly showcases investment patterns that have historically favored affluent neighborhoods while neglecting marginalized communities, the AI might, through its optimization algorithms, recommend continued underinvestment in those underserved areas. This is not a malicious act by the AI, but a direct consequence of its training data. Such an outcome can lead to the deepening of existing socio-economic divides, creating a self-fulfilling prophecy of neglect and disparity. The AI, in its pursuit of "efficiency" based on skewed historical patterns, could systematically disadvantage certain demographic groups or geographic areas, leading to infrastructure deficits that further hinder their social and economic mobility. Therefore, it is imperative that AI systems used in socio-technical planning undergo thorough data auditing to identify and mitigate biases. This process involves not only scrutinizing the datasets for demographic disparities but also for proxies of discrimination that might not be immediately apparent. Techniques such as bias detection algorithms, fairness metrics, and adversarial debiasing can be employed to ensure that the AI's outputs are as equitable as possible, even when operating on imperfect real-world data.

Transparency in AI-driven decision-making is another cornerstone of ethical AI deployment in socio-technical infrastructure planning. When AI systems are used to inform or even make decisions regarding the allocation of public funds, the siting of essential services, or the design of public utilities, the rationale behind these decisions must be accessible and understandable to all stakeholders, including the public. Black-box AI models, where the internal workings are opaque and unexplainable, erode trust and can lead to suspicion and resistance. If a community is informed that a new utility project will be located in their neighborhood based on an AI's recommendation, they have a right to understand why. Is it based on proximity to existing infrastructure, cost-effectiveness, environmental impact assessments, or a combination of factors? Without transparency, stakeholders are left to speculate, potentially assuming unfair motives or hidden agendas. This lack of clarity can transform legitimate concerns into distrust and opposition, hindering collaboration.

To counter this, developers and deployers of AI systems in this domain should strive for explainable AI (XAI) techniques. XAI aims to make AI decisions understandable to humans, providing insights into how a particular outcome was reached. This could involve generating justifications for AI recommendations, visualizing the data that influenced a decision, or providing simplified models that approximate the behavior of more complex ones. When the decision-making process is transparent, stakeholders can engage more meaningfully, question assumptions, and contribute to refining the AI's outputs to better align with community needs and values. This fosters a sense of co-ownership and legitimacy for the decisions made.

The role of human oversight in AI-driven infrastructure planning cannot be overstated. While AI offers unparalleled analytical power and the ability to process vast amounts of data far beyond human capacity, it is crucial to recognize that AI is a tool, not a replacement for human judgment, empathy, and ethical reasoning. In complex socio-technical systems, decisions often involve nuanced considerations that go beyond quantifiable metrics. For example, an AI might optimize a transportation network based purely on traffic flow and travel time efficiency. However, a human planner, with a deeper understanding of community dynamics, accessibility needs for elderly or disabled populations, or the social fabric of neighborhoods, might advocate for route adjustments that, while marginally less efficient statistically, better serve the broader social good. Human oversight ensures that AI recommendations are critically evaluated against broader societal goals, ethical principles, and an understanding of human well-being. It allows for the integration of qualitative insights and the recognition of intangible values that AI might struggle to quantify. Furthermore, human oversight is essential for adapting to unforeseen circumstances and for ensuring that the AI's outputs remain aligned with evolving societal norms and ethical standards. Without this human element, there is a risk of creating systems that are technically optimized but socially detrimental, or that fail to account for the rich tapestry of human experience and needs. The goal is to create a symbiotic relationship where AI provides data-driven insights and predictive capabilities, empowering human decision-makers to make more informed, equitable, and ultimately, more humane choices.

Building and maintaining trust in AI as a tool for infrastructure planning is a continuous process that hinges on demonstrating its commitment to societal well-being and equitable outcomes. This means moving beyond mere technical implementation to actively engaging with stakeholders about the AI's purpose, limitations, and benefits. When communities understand that AI is being employed to help identify the most effective ways to deliver public services, to ensure that infrastructure development benefits all segments of society, and to minimize negative environmental impacts, they are more likely to embrace its use. This requires open communication channels, opportunities for feedback, and a commitment to acting on that feedback. For instance, if an AI identifies a potential disparity in internet access across different neighborhoods, a transparent approach would involve the AI's findings being shared with community leaders, followed by collaborative discussions on how to address the gap, potentially leading to new AI-informed deployment strategies for broadband infrastructure. The trust is built not just on the sophistication of the technology, but on its visible and tangible contribution to improving public welfare and promoting fairness. It means framing AI not as a system that dictates outcomes, but as a sophisticated assistant that enhances our collective capacity to design and manage infrastructures that are more resilient, sustainable, and equitable for generations to come. The ethical application of AI in socio-technical infrastructure planning is therefore not an afterthought, but an integral part of its design, deployment, and ongoing management, ensuring that technological advancement serves the broader public interest.

Chapter 15: Future Trends and Capstone Case Study: Resilient Water Grid

The trajectory of infrastructure development and management is intrinsically linked to the continuous evolution of artificial intelligence. As AI capabilities mature, a suite of emerging technologies is poised to revolutionize how we design, build, operate, and maintain critical infrastructure systems, including the vital water grid. These advancements are not merely incremental improvements; they represent paradigm shifts that promise to unlock unprecedented levels of efficiency, resilience, and sustainability, moving beyond the foundational ethical considerations discussed previously to address practical implementation and future potential.

One of the most impactful emerging trends is the proliferation of AI at the "edge." Edge computing refers to the practice of processing data closer to its source, rather than sending it to a centralized cloud server. In the context of infrastructure, this means AI algorithms will increasingly reside on devices themselves - sensors, actuators, local control units, and even smart meters within the water grid. This decentralized approach to AI offers several profound advantages. Firstly, it dramatically reduces latency. For real-time applications like leak detection or anomaly identification in water distribution networks, the ability to process data instantaneously on-site, rather than waiting for it to travel to and from a distant data center, can be the difference between a minor inconvenience and a catastrophic failure. Imagine a burst pipe; with edge AI, sensors can detect the pressure drop and flow anomaly immediately, triggering automated valve closures and alerting maintenance crews within seconds, thus minimizing water loss and potential damage. This contrasts sharply with traditional systems that might rely on manual monitoring or cloud-based analysis, which could introduce delays of minutes or even hours.

Secondly, edge AI significantly enhances data security and privacy. By processing sensitive operational data locally, the amount of information that needs to be transmitted over networks is reduced. This minimizes the attack surface for cyber threats and ensures that proprietary operational data or personally identifiable information related to water consumption remains within a secure local environment. For critical infrastructure like water systems, where security is paramount, this localized intelligence offers a robust defense mechanism. Furthermore, edge computing can improve operational continuity in the face of network disruptions. If a communication link to the cloud is lost, edge AI-enabled devices can continue to operate autonomously, performing essential functions and making critical decisions based on their local processing capabilities. This ensures that the water grid remains functional even when external connectivity is compromised, a crucial aspect of resilience. The development of more powerful, energy-efficient processors and specialized AI chips is accelerating the adoption of edge AI. This trend is already visible in advanced metering infrastructure (AMI), where smart meters are beginning to incorporate AI for real-time consumption analysis, fraud detection, and localized fault identification, moving beyond simple data collection to proactive operational intelligence.

Another transformative technology gaining traction is the concept of digital twins. A digital twin is a dynamic virtual replica of a physical asset, process, or system. In the realm of infrastructure, this means creating a comprehensive, real-time digital model of the entire water grid, from reservoirs and treatment plants to pumps, pipelines, and consumer connections. This digital replica is not static; it is continuously updated with data from a vast network of sensors, IoT devices, historical records, and operational logs, mirroring the state and behavior of its physical counterpart. AI plays a pivotal role in powering these digital twins. AI algorithms are used to ingest and analyze the massive volumes of data fed into the twin, to simulate various operational scenarios, predict future performance, and identify potential issues before they manifest in the physical world.

For the water grid, a digital twin offers unparalleled capabilities for planning, optimization, and resilience. Engineers and operators can use the digital twin to test the impact of different operational strategies, such as altering pumping schedules to optimize energy consumption or simulating the effects of a drought on water supply. They can virtually commission new infrastructure projects, evaluating their performance and integration into the existing network before any physical construction begins, thereby de-risking investment and accelerating deployment. Furthermore, the digital twin becomes an indispensable tool for predictive maintenance. By analyzing patterns and anomalies within the virtual model, AI can forecast the likelihood of component failure, such as a pump wearing out or a pipe developing a weakness, allowing for proactive maintenance interventions that prevent costly breakdowns and service disruptions. The ability to conduct "what-if" analyses within the digital twin also significantly enhances emergency response planning. Operators can simulate the impact of extreme weather events, contamination incidents, or large-scale infrastructure failures, and develop optimized response strategies based on these virtual exercises. The integration of AI with digital twins moves us from reactive problem-solving to proactive, predictive, and prescriptive management of infrastructure, offering a significant leap in operational intelligence and resource management.

The need for greater transparency and interpretability in AI systems, as highlighted in previous discussions, is directly addressed by the advancement of Explainable AI (XAI). While AI offers powerful predictive and analytical capabilities, the "black box" nature of some complex models can be a barrier to trust and adoption, particularly in critical infrastructure sectors where accountability is paramount. XAI techniques aim to make AI decision-making processes understandable to humans, providing insights into *why* a particular recommendation or prediction was made. For the water grid, this means that when an AI system flags a potential issue – for example, suggesting an adjustment in water pressure or recommending a specific maintenance task – operators can access an explanation for that decision. This might involve understanding which data points were most influential, what correlations the AI identified, or what patterns led to a specific conclusion.

XAI is crucial for building confidence among operators, regulators, and the public. If an AI recommends a costly infrastructure upgrade, stakeholders need to understand the justification behind that recommendation. XAI can provide this clarity, enabling informed decision-making and fostering trust. Techniques such as LIME (Local Interpretable Model-agnostic Explanations), SHAP (SHapley Additive exPlanations), and attention mechanisms in deep learning models are contributing to making AI more transparent. In the context of water management, XAI can help answer questions like: "Why is the AI predicting a surge in demand in this district?" or "What factors are contributing to the elevated risk of pipe corrosion in this segment of the network?" This level of understanding not only builds trust but also empowers human experts to validate, refine, or override AI suggestions based on their own domain knowledge and contextual understanding, ensuring a human-in-the-loop approach that leverages the strengths of both AI and human intelligence. As AI becomes more integrated into critical infrastructure operations, XAI will be instrumental in ensuring that these systems are not only effective but also accountable and trustworthy.

The synergy between AI, the Internet of Things (IoT), and blockchain technology represents another frontier in the evolution of infrastructure management, offering enhanced capabilities in data collection, operational control, and security. IoT devices – the sensors, meters, valves, and actuators deployed across the water grid – generate continuous streams of data. AI algorithms process this data to extract insights, detect anomalies, and optimize operations. Blockchain technology, on the other hand, provides a secure, decentralized, and immutable ledger for recording transactions and data.

The integration of these three technologies can create a highly robust and secure infrastructure ecosystem. For the water grid, IoT devices can collect real-time data on water quality, flow rates, pressure, energy consumption, and equipment status. AI then analyzes this data to identify patterns, predict failures, and optimize resource allocation. Blockchain can be employed to secure the data generated by IoT devices, ensuring its integrity and preventing tampering. Each data point collected by a sensor, for instance, can be cryptographically hashed and recorded on a blockchain, creating a verifiable audit trail of operational events. This is particularly valuable for ensuring compliance with regulatory standards, tracing the source of contamination events, or managing water rights and allocations.

Furthermore, the combination of AI, IoT, and blockchain can enable sophisticated automated transactions and smart contracts within the water system. For example, a smart contract could automatically trigger payments to energy providers when water pumping operations are scheduled during off-peak hours, as optimized by AI based on real-time grid conditions and energy prices. Similarly, in a context of water trading or resource sharing between different municipalities or agricultural users, blockchain-based smart contracts, informed by AI-driven demand and supply forecasts, could facilitate transparent and automated transactions. The enhanced security and data integrity offered by blockchain, coupled with the analytical power of AI and the pervasive sensing capabilities of IoT, create a foundation for truly intelligent and resilient infrastructure. This convergence promises to elevate efficiency, security, and transparency to new heights, enabling a more dynamic and responsive management of essential resources like water.

The application of these emerging AI technologies – edge computing, digital twins, explainable AI, and the convergence with IoT and blockchain – heralds a new era for infrastructure. For the water grid, this translates into the potential for a significantly more resilient, efficient, and sustainable system. It means anticipating problems before they occur, optimizing resource utilization in real-time, enhancing security against both physical and cyber threats, and fostering greater trust and accountability in operational decisions. As these technologies mature and become more integrated, they will fundamentally reshape our approach to managing the critical infrastructure that underpins modern society, moving towards a future where systems are not just functional, but intelligently adaptive and inherently trustworthy.

The escalating reality of climate change presents one of the most profound challenges to modern infrastructure. As global temperatures rise, the frequency and intensity of extreme weather events are increasing, placing unprecedented strain on systems designed for more stable climatic conditions. From prolonged droughts and heatwaves to torrential rainfall, coastal flooding, and more powerful storms, the physical and operational integrity of critical infrastructure, including water grids, is increasingly jeopardized. In this evolving landscape, Artificial Intelligence (AI) is emerging not merely as a tool for optimization and efficiency, but as an indispensable ally in the crucial endeavor of climate change adaptation. AI's capacity for rapid data analysis, pattern recognition, prediction, and simulation offers a powerful suite of capabilities to anticipate, respond to, and ultimately build resilience against the multifaceted impacts of a changing climate.

One of the most immediate and vital roles of AI in climate adaptation lies in enhancing our ability to predict and forecast extreme weather events.

Traditional meteorological models, while valuable, often struggle with the granularity and speed required to issue timely and actionable warnings for localized, high-impact events. AI, particularly through machine learning algorithms trained on vast historical weather data, satellite imagery, and real-time sensor networks, can significantly improve these predictive capabilities. These models can identify subtle precursor signals and complex atmospheric interactions that might elude conventional analysis, leading to earlier and more accurate predictions of phenomena such as flash floods, severe thunderstorms, heat domes, and even the intensification trajectories of tropical cyclones. For water utilities, this means having advanced notice of potential disruptions to water sources, increased demand during heatwaves, or the risk of damage to pumping stations and treatment facilities due to severe storms. The ability to anticipate such events allows for proactive measures, such as pre-positioning emergency resources, adjusting operational parameters to mitigate risks, or issuing targeted public advisories, thereby safeguarding both infrastructure and public safety.

Beyond prediction, AI is instrumental in optimizing disaster response and recovery efforts in the wake of climate-related extremes. When disaster strikes, the ability to quickly assess damage, allocate resources effectively, and coordinate response teams is paramount. AI-powered systems can analyze drone imagery, sensor data, and social media feeds to rapidly map affected areas, identify critical infrastructure failures (like pipeline breaks or power outages affecting water treatment), and prioritize repair efforts. For instance, in the aftermath of a major flood, AI algorithms can process satellite data to pinpoint submerged roads, identify buildings at risk of collapse, and help emergency managers understand the extent of contamination in water bodies. This allows for the efficient deployment of repair crews, the prioritization of essential services, and the more effective distribution of aid. Furthermore, AI can facilitate dynamic resource allocation, re-routing personnel and equipment to where they are most needed based on real-time situational assessments, ensuring a more agile and effective response.

A critical long-term strategy for climate adaptation involves the proactive design and construction of infrastructure that is inherently resilient to anticipated future climate conditions. AI plays a transformative role in this domain by enabling sophisticated simulations and vulnerability assessments. By feeding AI models with climate projection data, historical performance records, and detailed engineering specifications, researchers and planners can simulate how existing and proposed infrastructure will perform under various future climate scenarios. This includes modeling the impact of sea-level rise on coastal water treatment plants, assessing the stress of increased temperature fluctuations on pipeline materials, or evaluating the capacity of drainage systems to handle more intense rainfall events. These AI-driven simulations can identify weak points and predict potential failure modes long before they occur in the physical world.

This predictive power extends to informing the design of new, climate-resilient infrastructure. For example, AI can assist in optimizing the placement and design of flood defenses, such as levees and storm surge barriers, by analyzing topographical data, predicted storm surge levels, and historical flood patterns. It can help determine the optimal height and structural reinforcement needed for new bridges or roads to withstand more extreme weather. In the context of water management, AI can guide the design of water storage facilities to maximize capacity under drought conditions, or recommend specific materials and construction techniques for pipelines to resist thermal expansion and contraction cycles. The economic and safety benefits of this proactive, AI-informed design approach are substantial, preventing costly retrofits and avoiding catastrophic failures down the line.

Resource management under changing environmental conditions is another area where AI is proving indispensable for climate adaptation. Water resources, in particular, are becoming increasingly unpredictable due to shifting precipitation patterns, increased evaporation rates, and heightened demand during heatwaves. AI can analyze complex datasets encompassing rainfall, snowpack levels, river flows, groundwater recharge rates, and water consumption patterns to create highly accurate forecasts of water availability. This allows water utilities to optimize water allocation strategies, balancing the needs of different sectors (municipal, agricultural, industrial) and ensuring sufficient supply even during periods of scarcity. AI can also guide the efficient operation of water treatment and distribution systems. For instance, by predicting demand fluctuations, AI can optimize pumping schedules to reduce energy consumption and minimize stress on the system during peak periods, a crucial consideration as energy infrastructure itself faces climate-related challenges.

Furthermore, AI-driven insights can inform the strategic planning for water infrastructure investments. By assessing the long-term viability of current water sources under various climate scenarios and identifying regions most vulnerable to water stress, AI can help prioritize where new infrastructure, such as desalination plants, advanced water recycling facilities, or inter-basin water transfers, might be most needed. This data-driven approach ensures that limited resources are allocated to the most impactful adaptation measures, enhancing the overall resilience of water systems.

The vulnerability of existing water infrastructure to climate change is a significant concern. Many systems were built decades ago, under assumptions of climatic stability that no longer hold true. AI provides powerful tools to assess this vulnerability comprehensively. By integrating data from sensors monitoring pipe integrity, flow rates, pressure, water quality, and soil conditions with climate projection models, AI can generate detailed vulnerability maps of the entire water network. These maps can highlight specific sections of pipelines at increased risk of rupture due to soil desiccation and expansion, identify treatment facilities vulnerable to inundation from rising sea levels or extreme rainfall, and pinpoint areas where water supply reliability is most threatened by prolonged droughts.

Once vulnerabilities are identified, AI can then recommend specific adaptation measures and upgrades. This might include prioritizing the replacement of older, less resilient pipelines, strengthening flood defenses around critical facilities, implementing advanced leak detection systems to minimize losses during periods of scarcity, or diversifying water sources. AI can even optimize the phasing and sequencing of these upgrades to minimize disruption and cost, ensuring that the most critical vulnerabilities are addressed first. The ability of AI to perform these complex, multi-variable analyses and generate actionable recommendations is transforming how utilities approach infrastructure modernization in the face of climate change.

Moreover, AI's role in climate adaptation extends to managing the complex interplay between water systems and other critical infrastructures, such as energy and transportation. For example, AI can help predict how extreme heat might impact the efficiency of power generation or lead to increased demand for cooling, which in turn affects water consumption for both industrial processes and residential use. It can also identify how extreme weather events might disrupt fuel supply chains for water treatment plants or damage transportation networks essential for delivering water or repairing infrastructure. By modeling these interdependencies, AI can help create more robust and integrated adaptation strategies that consider the system-wide implications of climate impacts, moving beyond siloed approaches to a more holistic view of infrastructural resilience.

The development and deployment of AI for climate adaptation also necessitate careful consideration of ethical implications and equitable outcomes. As AI-driven decisions increasingly shape where and how adaptation resources are allocated, it is crucial to ensure that these systems do not perpetuate or exacerbate existing societal inequalities. For instance, if AI models prioritize upgrades in wealthier neighborhoods, communities that are often more vulnerable to climate impacts may be left behind. Therefore, the development of AI tools for climate adaptation must be guided by principles of fairness, transparency, and inclusivity. This involves ensuring that the data used to train these models is representative of all communities and that the outputs are interpretable and justifiable to all stakeholders. The goal is to leverage AI not only to build more resilient infrastructure but also to foster more equitable and just outcomes in the face of climate change. The ongoing evolution of AI in this domain promises to be a critical determinant of humanity's capacity to adapt and thrive in a rapidly changing world.

The complexities of ensuring a consistent and safe water supply in an era defined by climate change and burgeoning urban populations demand innovative, forward-thinking solutions. To illustrate the practical application of the AI-driven principles discussed throughout this book, we present a capstone case study: the design and implementation of a highly resilient urban water grid. This hypothetical scenario centers on a mid-sized city, let's call it "Veridia," which, like many urban centers globally, grapples with a confluence of challenges. These include an aging, often fragmented infrastructure network, a steadily increasing population placing greater demand on resources, and the intensifying unpredictability of water availability due to climate variability – characterized by more frequent and severe droughts interspersed with intense rainfall events. Veridia's situation serves as a microcosm for the critical need to transition from reactive water management to a proactive, AI-empowered paradigm that can guarantee reliable water delivery across a spectrum of diverse and challenging scenarios.

The core objective of Veridia's Resilient Water Grid Initiative is to leverage artificial intelligence to create a water system that is not only efficient but also exceptionally robust, capable of anticipating, adapting to, and mitigating disruptions. This initiative aims to integrate a suite of advanced AI capabilities, drawing upon the concepts previously explored, to form a cohesive and intelligent operational framework. At its heart, this system will rely on sophisticated AI-powered demand forecasting models. These models will go beyond historical consumption patterns, incorporating real-time data streams from smart meters, weather forecasts (including temperature, humidity, and precipitation), local event calendars, and even social media sentiment analysis to predict water needs with unprecedented accuracy. This granular understanding of demand is crucial, enabling Veridia's water authority to optimize water treatment and distribution, minimizing waste and ensuring that supply closely matches requirements, even during periods of unexpected surges or dips.

A critical component of any resilient water grid is the ability to swiftly identify and address water losses. In Veridia's case, this translates to an advanced AI-driven leak detection system. Traditional methods, such as acoustic sensors and manual surveys, are often time-consuming and can miss smaller leaks. The proposed AI solution employs a multi-layered approach. This includes analyzing minute pressure fluctuations across the network, identifying anomalies in flow meter readings that deviate from predicted patterns, and utilizing machine learning algorithms trained on data from historical leaks to recognize precursor indicators. Furthermore, the integration of data from an extensive sensor network embedded within the pipeline infrastructure will allow for real-time monitoring of pipe integrity, soil moisture around pipelines, and even acoustic signatures, enabling the AI to pinpoint potential leaks with remarkable speed and precision, often before they become significant problems. This proactive approach not only conserves precious water resources but also prevents costly damage to surrounding infrastructure and reduces the energy expenditure associated with pumping lost water.

Ensuring the potability and safety of the water supply is paramount, and here, AI plays a vital role in continuous water quality monitoring. Veridia's water grid will be equipped with a distributed network of sensors at key points within the distribution system, as well as at intake points and within treatment facilities. These sensors will continuously measure a range of parameters, including chlorine residual, pH, turbidity, temperature, and the presence of specific contaminants. AI algorithms will then process this torrent of data, not just to flag immediate deviations from acceptable thresholds, but to identify subtle trends and patterns that might indicate a developing issue, such as the slow ingress of contaminants or the gradual degradation of disinfectant efficacy. This predictive water quality monitoring allows for early intervention, such as adjusting treatment processes or isolating sections of the network, thereby preventing widespread contamination events and safeguarding public health.

The efficient operation of Veridia's water pumps is another area ripe for AI optimization. Pumping stations are significant energy consumers, and their operation needs to be finely tuned to meet demand while minimizing energy costs and wear and tear on equipment. The AI system will integrate real-time demand forecasts with pump performance data, electricity tariffs, and reservoir levels. By employing optimization algorithms, the AI can dynamically adjust pump speeds and operational schedules to draw water when energy is cheapest and most plentiful, and to maintain optimal pressure levels throughout the network without overworking the machinery. This smart pumping strategy not only leads to substantial energy savings, contributing to Veridia's sustainability goals, but also extends the lifespan of critical pumping infrastructure, reducing the need for premature replacements.

Predictive maintenance is perhaps one of the most impactful applications of AI in ensuring the resilience of the water grid. Instead of relying on scheduled maintenance or waiting for equipment to fail, the AI system will analyze data from sensors on pumps, valves, treatment machinery, and even sections of the pipeline itself. This data includes vibration patterns, operating temperatures, motor current, and acoustic emissions. By applying machine learning models that have been trained on extensive datasets of equipment performance and failure modes, the AI can predict when a component is likely to fail, often weeks or months in advance. This allows maintenance crews to schedule repairs or replacements during planned downtime, preventing unexpected outages that could disrupt water supply to large segments of the city. The AI can also recommend specific maintenance actions based on the predicted failure mode, ensuring that the correct repairs are made efficiently.

The hypothetical city of Veridia is envisioned to have distinct zones, each presenting unique challenges. For instance, the older downtown core might feature a labyrinthine network of cast-iron pipes, prone to corrosion and leakage, situated beneath densely packed streets where excavation for repairs is costly and disruptive. Conversely, newer suburban developments, while having more modern infrastructure, face the challenge of rapidly expanding demand and potential strain on existing treatment and distribution capacities. Furthermore, Veridia's geographical location exposes it to a specific climate variability pattern: prolonged dry spells punctuated by intense, short-duration rainfall events that can overwhelm storm drainage systems and potentially impact raw water sources through runoff pollution.

The AI-integrated resilient water grid designed for Veridia would encompass several interconnected subsystems. The **Demand Forecasting Module** would utilize advanced machine learning algorithms, such as Long Short-Term Memory (LSTM) networks and ensemble methods, to predict water demand at granular levels – down to individual neighborhoods or even large commercial complexes. This module would ingest real-time data from smart meters, integrated weather services (predicting temperature, humidity, cloud cover, and precipitation probabilities), calendar data for public holidays and major events (like sports matches or festivals), and anonymized social media trends to capture shifts in local water usage patterns. The accuracy of these forecasts is crucial for optimizing the operation of treatment plants and distribution networks, ensuring sufficient supply without overproduction, which leads to energy waste and potential quality degradation. For example, if the AI predicts a heatwave coinciding with a major city event, it can anticipate a surge in demand far exceeding typical peak hours and proactively adjust reservoir levels and pumping schedules days in advance.

Complementing demand forecasting is the **Leak Detection and Localization System**. This system would employ a combination of methods. Firstly, an AI-powered anomaly detection algorithm would continuously monitor flow rates and pressure readings from sensors strategically placed throughout the distribution network. Deviations from expected patterns, when demand is stable and no large withdrawals are occurring, would trigger an alert. Secondly, acoustic sensors, deployed at regular intervals along major pipelines, would feed data into a machine learning model trained to distinguish the sound of water escaping from background noise. The AI would not only detect leaks but also triangulate their approximate location by analyzing the sound propagation across different sensors. For areas with older infrastructure, like Veridia's downtown core, the system might also integrate data from ground-penetrating radar or fiber optic sensors embedded in the soil to detect moisture accumulation or subtle ground movements indicative of buried leaks. This significantly reduces the time and resources required for manual leak detection, minimizing water loss and preventing secondary damage.

The
Water Quality Monitoring and Control System would represent a paradigm shift from reactive to proactive quality management. A dense network of in-situ sensors would continuously measure key parameters such as pH, turbidity, residual chlorine, dissolved oxygen, and conductivity. AI algorithms would perform real-time analysis of this data, looking for subtle deviations from established baselines or unusual correlation patterns between different parameters that might indicate the onset of contamination. For instance, a slight increase in turbidity coupled with a drop in residual chlorine could signal the potential ingress of surface water into the system. The AI would then trigger an alert, suggesting specific sampling points for laboratory confirmation or even recommending automated adjustments to disinfectant dosing or the temporary isolation of affected pipeline sections. This prevents widespread contamination events and ensures public safety more effectively than traditional, less frequent sampling protocols.

The
Pump and Energy Optimization Module is designed to address the significant energy footprint of water utilities. By integrating real-time demand forecasts, reservoir levels, pump performance characteristics, and dynamic electricity pricing, the AI would orchestrate pump operations to minimize costs and energy consumption. This involves utilizing low-cost electricity periods for filling reservoirs, adjusting pump speeds to match demand precisely, and avoiding unnecessary starts and stops that can reduce pump lifespan. For example, if the AI identifies a period of low electricity prices and moderate demand overnight, it can optimize pumping to fill elevated storage tanks to capacity, providing a buffer for anticipated high demand during the following day's peak hours,

all while minimizing expenditure. The system could also incorporate renewable energy integration, prioritizing the use of solar or wind power when available to further reduce the carbon footprint of water delivery.

The
Predictive Maintenance Engine is arguably the cornerstone of long-term resilience. By analyzing operational data from pumps, valves, actuators, and other critical mechanical components – including vibration signatures, temperature trends, pressure variations, and motor current draw – the AI can identify patterns indicative of impending failure. Machine learning models, trained on historical failure data and manufacturer specifications, predict the Remaining Useful Life (RUL) of components. This allows Veridia's maintenance teams to proactively schedule repairs or replacements during planned maintenance windows, avoiding costly emergency call-outs and service disruptions. For instance, if the AI detects a subtle increase in vibration frequency in a specific pump motor, it can flag this as a potential bearing issue, allowing for timely replacement before a catastrophic motor failure occurs, which could leave an entire neighborhood without water.

To address the diverse infrastructural challenges within Veridia, the AI system would employ a tiered approach to asset management and intervention prioritization. For the older downtown district with its aging pipelines, the AI would analyze a confluence of data: the age and material of the pipes, historical leakage records, soil corrosivity data, and the detected acoustic signatures. This would generate a detailed risk map, identifying the most vulnerable sections most likely to fail. The AI could then recommend a phased replacement strategy, prioritizing pipes based on their assessed risk, the criticality of the service they provide, and the potential impact of a failure on surrounding infrastructure and the economy. In contrast, for newer suburban areas experiencing rapid growth, the AI would focus on capacity planning. By analyzing population growth projections, new development permits, and historical consumption patterns in these areas, the AI can predict future demand bottlenecks and recommend timely upgrades to mains, pumping capacity, or treatment plant expansion, ensuring that infrastructure keeps pace with community needs.

The climate variability aspect – the interplay of drought and intense rainfall – would be addressed through specialized AI modules. For drought conditions, the AI would integrate real-time reservoir levels, river flow data, groundwater monitoring well data, and long-range weather forecasts to provide optimized water allocation strategies. This might involve recommending temporary restrictions on non-essential water use, adjusting irrigation schedules for municipal parks, or even initiating dialogue with agricultural users about voluntary water conservation measures. Conversely, during periods of intense rainfall, the AI would work in conjunction with storm water management systems. It could predict localized flooding hotspots based on precipitation forecasts and real-time sensor data from storm drains and sewers. This information would enable the timely deployment of portable pumps, the diversion of excess water to designated retention basins, and the issuance of localized flood warnings to residents. Furthermore, the AI would monitor raw water quality at intake points, detecting potential increases in turbidity or pollutant loads due to surface runoff and recommending adjustments to the water treatment process accordingly.

The implementation of such a sophisticated AI-driven system requires robust data governance and cybersecurity measures. All data streams – from smart meters, sensors, weather services, and operational logs – must be securely collected, transmitted, and stored. The AI algorithms themselves must be protected against manipulation or unauthorized access. A key consideration is data privacy, ensuring that information collected from residential smart meters is anonymized and aggregated to protect individual consumption habits. Moreover, the system's decision-making processes, especially those leading to service restrictions or significant operational changes, must be transparent and auditable. This ensures accountability and builds public trust.

The human element remains indispensable in this AI-augmented future. The system is designed to augment, not replace, the expertise of water engineers, operators, and maintenance personnel. The AI provides them with enhanced situational awareness, predictive insights, and optimized recommendations, enabling them to make more informed and effective decisions. Training programs would be crucial to equip the workforce with the skills to interpret AI outputs, manage the integrated system, and oversee its continuous improvement. The role of the human operator shifts from routine monitoring and manual adjustments to strategic oversight, complex problem-solving, and ensuring the ethical and equitable application of AI-driven recommendations.

In essence, Veridia's resilient water grid initiative represents a holistic, intelligence-driven approach to water management. By weaving together advanced AI capabilities for demand forecasting, leak detection, water quality assurance, energy optimization, and predictive maintenance, and by tailoring these to the specific challenges of aging infrastructure, population growth, and climate variability, the city aims to create a water system that is not only reliable and efficient but also remarkably adaptable. This case study demonstrates that by embracing AI, urban water utilities can move beyond the limitations of traditional infrastructure management and build a sustainable, secure, and resilient water future for their communities, ensuring that this most vital resource remains available and safe for generations to come. The integration of these diverse AI functions creates a feedback loop: accurate demand forecasts inform pump optimization, which in turn influences energy consumption. Early leak detection reduces the volume of water that needs to be treated and pumped. Continuous water quality monitoring ensures that optimized treatment processes are effective. And predictive maintenance safeguards the operational integrity of all these interconnected components. This synergy is what truly elevates the system from a collection of smart technologies to a truly intelligent and resilient water grid.

The journey from conceptualizing AI-driven solutions for a resilient water grid, as envisioned for Veridia, to their actual deployment is fraught with practical obstacles. While the potential benefits are immense, realizing them requires navigating a complex landscape of technical, organizational, and financial challenges. Understanding these hurdles and adopting proven best practices is crucial for any utility aiming to harness the power of artificial intelligence.

One of the most pervasive challenges is the **availability and quality of data**. AI models, particularly those involving machine learning, are inherently data-hungry. For a water utility, this data can originate from a multitude of sources: sensors embedded in pipes, smart meters at customer premises, SCADA systems controlling pumps and valves, laboratory analyses of water quality, weather stations, and operational logs. However, this data is often siloed, stored in disparate formats, and may suffer from inconsistencies, missing values, or inaccuracies. Smart meters might have calibration issues, pressure sensors could drift over time, and historical records might be incomplete or poorly documented. Before AI can even begin to learn, significant effort must be invested in data collection infrastructure, standardization, cleaning, and validation. For instance, a leak detection algorithm relying on pressure differential might produce false positives if upstream pressure readings are intermittently lost or corrupted. Similarly, a demand forecasting model will be less accurate if smart meter data is not consistently transmitted or if it contains erroneous readings due to faulty devices. Utilities must develop robust data governance frameworks, implement data quality checks at every stage of ingestion, and consider investing in sensor calibration and maintenance programs. The initial investment in data infrastructure might seem substantial, but it forms the bedrock upon which all subsequent AI applications will be built. Without high-quality, reliable data, even the most sophisticated AI algorithms will falter, leading to suboptimal performance and erosion of trust in the technology.

The
integration of AI solutions with existing legacy systems presents another significant hurdle. Most water utilities operate with a patchwork of older technologies that were not designed with AI or advanced digital integration in mind. Supervisory Control and Data Acquisition (SCADA) systems, for example, are often proprietary and may not readily expose data in formats accessible to modern AI platforms. Older network infrastructure might lack the bandwidth or connectivity to support real-time data streaming from a vast network of sensors. Replacing these legacy systems entirely can be prohibitively expensive and disruptive. Therefore, effective integration often requires developing custom middleware, APIs (Application Programming Interfaces), or utilizing data brokers to act as intermediaries. This process demands close collaboration between AI developers, IT departments, and OT (Operational Technology) engineers who manage the physical infrastructure. For example, integrating a predictive maintenance engine with an aging SCADA system might involve building a bridge that pulls pump operational data at scheduled intervals, transforms it into a standardized format, and then feeds it into the AI platform for analysis. This can be a time-consuming and technically intricate process, requiring a deep understanding of both the legacy systems and the requirements of the AI application. The goal is often to achieve a phased integration, starting with less critical systems or data streams and gradually expanding as confidence and technical capabilities grow.

The
workforce's readiness and the need for training are paramount. The introduction of AI fundamentally alters the roles and responsibilities of utility personnel. While AI can automate many tasks and provide

advanced insights, it does not eliminate the need for human expertise. Instead, it requires a shift in focus from manual data entry and routine monitoring to data interpretation, strategic decision-making based on AI-generated recommendations, and oversight of the AI systems themselves. This necessitates comprehensive training programs that equip engineers, operators, technicians, and managers with the skills to understand how AI models work, interpret their outputs, identify potential biases or errors, and effectively leverage the insights provided. For instance, an operator who previously manually adjusted pump schedules based on experience might now need to understand how an AI system recommends optimal schedules based on complex variables like electricity prices and demand forecasts, and how to intervene if the AI's recommendation seems counterintuitive or based on faulty input. A cultural shift is also often required, fostering a mindset that embraces AI as a collaborative tool rather than a threat. This might involve cross-training between IT and OT teams, creating new roles such as data scientists or AI system managers, and promoting continuous learning. Ignoring the human element can lead to resistance, underutilization of AI investments, and a failure to achieve the desired operational efficiencies and resilience.

Regulatory hurdles and standardization can also impede AI implementation. The water sector is heavily regulated, with stringent standards for water quality, safety, and environmental protection. Introducing AI-driven systems, especially those that automate critical decisions or control operational processes, requires careful consideration of how these systems comply with existing regulations. Furthermore, a lack of industry-wide standards for AI in water utilities can create uncertainty. For example, how is the performance of an AI-based water quality monitoring system validated and approved by regulatory bodies? What are the acceptable levels of uncertainty or error for an AI-driven leak detection system that might trigger costly investigations? The development of clear guidelines, best practices, and potentially new regulatory frameworks specifically tailored to AI in critical infrastructure will be essential. Utilities often need to engage proactively with regulators to demonstrate the safety, reliability, and benefits of their AI solutions, and to contribute to the formation of future standards. This can involve pilot projects demonstrating compliance, extensive testing and validation protocols, and open communication about the system's capabilities and limitations.

Cybersecurity concerns are magnified with the increasing interconnectedness of water systems powered by AI. As more sensors, devices, and control systems are brought online and connected to networks, the attack surface for cyber threats expands significantly. AI systems themselves can be targets for malicious actors seeking to disrupt operations, manipulate data, or compromise sensitive information. A compromised AI demand forecasting model, for instance, could be manipulated to create artificial demand spikes, leading to over-pumping and unnecessary energy consumption, or conversely, to underestimate demand, causing supply shortages. Similarly, an AI system controlling water treatment could be targeted to reduce disinfectant levels, leading to public health risks. Robust cybersecurity measures are therefore non-negotiable. This includes implementing multi-layered security protocols, end-to-end encryption for data transmission, access controls, regular security audits and penetration testing, and developing comprehensive incident response plans. Training personnel on cybersecurity best practices is also critical, as human error remains a significant vulnerability. The principle of "security by design" must be embedded from the initial stages of AI system development and deployment.

The

cost of implementation is a significant factor for many water utilities, especially those with limited budgets. The initial investment in hardware (sensors, computing infrastructure), software (AI platforms, analytics tools), data integration, and skilled personnel can be substantial. Furthermore, ongoing costs for maintenance, software updates, cloud services, and continuous training need to be factored in. Utilities must develop robust business cases that clearly articulate the return on investment (ROI), not just in terms of cost savings (e.g., reduced energy consumption, minimized water loss, lower maintenance expenses), but also in terms of improved operational efficiency, enhanced service reliability, and increased resilience against disruptions. Exploring funding opportunities, such as government grants for infrastructure modernization or partnerships with technology providers, can help mitigate these costs. A phased implementation approach, starting with pilot projects that demonstrate tangible benefits and can then be scaled up, is often a practical strategy to manage upfront investments and build momentum.

To navigate these challenges successfully, adopting a set of **best practices for AI deployment** is essential. **Pilot projects and proof-of-concept studies** are invaluable. Instead of attempting to deploy a fully integrated AI system across the entire utility from day one, it is often wiser to start with a focused pilot project in a specific area, such as leak detection in a well-defined zone or demand forecasting for a particular district. This allows the utility to test the technology, gather real-world performance data, identify unforeseen issues, and build internal expertise with a manageable scope and risk. Success in a pilot project can build confidence, provide valuable lessons learned, and create a strong foundation for broader deployment.

Iterative development and agile methodologies are also highly recommended. AI development is not a linear process. It often involves cycles of data preparation, model training, evaluation, refinement, and re-training. Adopting an agile approach allows teams to be flexible, adapt to new insights gained during development, and deliver value incrementally. This means continuously collecting feedback, monitoring performance, and making adjustments to the AI models and their integration. For example, a demand forecasting model might initially be trained on historical data. After deployment, its predictions can be compared against actual demand, and the discrepancies analyzed to refine the model by incorporating new features or adjusting parameters.

Strong stakeholder engagement is critical for sustained success. This includes not only internal stakeholders like engineers, operators, IT, and management, but also external stakeholders such as regulators, customers, and technology partners. Engaging with end-users early and often helps ensure that the AI solutions being developed address real-world needs and operational realities. Customer engagement is particularly important if AI-driven initiatives involve changes that might affect service delivery or billing. Transparency about the goals and capabilities of AI systems, and how they are being used to improve service, can foster trust and acceptance. Collaborating closely with technology vendors and research institutions can provide access to cutting-edge expertise and ensure that the chosen solutions are robust and scalable.

Finally, establishing clear
performance metrics and continuous monitoring is vital. Before deploying an AI solution, it is essential to define what success looks like and how it will be measured. These metrics should be aligned with the utility's strategic objectives, such as reducing non-revenue water by a certain percentage, improving energy efficiency by a specific amount, or decreasing the number of unplanned service interruptions. Once deployed, the performance of AI systems must be continuously monitored against these metrics. This involves not only tracking the accuracy of predictions or the effectiveness of recommendations but also monitoring the underlying data quality and system health. Deviations from expected performance can indicate issues that require attention, such as data drift, model degradation, or emerging cybersecurity threats. This ongoing vigilance ensures that the AI systems continue to deliver value and contribute to the overall resilience and efficiency of the water grid.

By anticipating these challenges and embracing these best practices, water utilities can significantly increase their chances of successfully implementing AI solutions, transforming their operations, and building the resilient, sustainable water systems of the future. The path is not always smooth, but with careful planning, strategic investment, and a commitment to continuous learning and adaptation, the potential rewards are immense.

The landscape of engineering is undergoing a profound transformation, a seismic shift driven by the pervasive integration of artificial intelligence. As we stand at the precipice of this new era, it is imperative to re-evaluate the very essence of what it means to be an engineer. Far from rendering human intellect obsolete, AI is emerging as a powerful, indispensable collaborative partner. This partnership is not a simple delegation of tasks, but a dynamic symbiosis, where the analytical prowess and computational speed of AI augment the creativity, critical thinking, and ethical judgment of human engineers. The future engineer will not be a mere operator of sophisticated tools, but a conductor, orchestrating complex systems with AI as their virtuoso ensemble.

To thrive in this AI-augmented reality, engineers must cultivate a new suite of competencies. Foremost among these is a deep-seated understanding of AI's capabilities and limitations. This is not about becoming an AI developer from scratch, but about developing a robust conceptual grasp of how algorithms learn, how models are trained, and the inherent biases that can be encoded within them. An engineer working on a resilient water grid, for instance, needs to understand that a predictive maintenance algorithm for pumps, while incredibly powerful, is only as good as the data it has been fed. If historical data has disproportionately represented certain failure modes due to insufficient sensor coverage in specific zones, the AI might not accurately predict failures in those underrepresented areas. Therefore, the engineer must possess the insight to question AI outputs, to recognize potential blind spots, and to advocate for more comprehensive data collection or model recalibration when necessary. This involves moving beyond simply accepting AI-generated recommendations at face value and engaging in a critical dialogue with the technology.

Interpreting AI outputs is another crucial skill. AI systems often provide outputs that are nuanced, probabilistic, and can be presented in ways that are not immediately intuitive to those outside the field of data science. For example, an AI model predicting water demand might output a range of probabilities for different demand scenarios, or present its findings as confidence intervals. The engineer must be adept at translating these complex statistical outputs into actionable insights for operational decision-making. This might involve understanding how to adjust pump operations based on a probabilistic forecast of high demand, or how to allocate resources for pipe maintenance based on an AI's assessment of risk factors that combine age, material, soil conditions, and historical pressure data. The ability to discern patterns, identify anomalies, and extract meaningful conclusions from AI-generated reports, dashboards, and alerts will be paramount. It requires a bridge-building capacity, connecting the abstract realm of data science with the tangible world of infrastructure management.

Guiding AI systems to achieve optimal and ethical outcomes represents the pinnacle of this collaborative partnership. Engineers will be responsible for setting the objectives and constraints within which AI operates. This means defining what "optimal" truly means in a given context. For a resilient water grid, optimality might involve a complex balancing act between minimizing energy consumption, ensuring water quality, maintaining service continuity, and minimizing operational costs. An AI optimizing solely for energy efficiency might inadvertently compromise water pressure in certain areas during peak demand, leading to service disruptions. The engineer’s role is to imbue the AI with these multifaceted objectives, ensuring that the pursuit of one goal does not lead to the detriment of others.

Furthermore, ethical considerations are intrinsically linked to the deployment of AI in critical infrastructure. Engineers must be the custodians of ethical AI usage, ensuring that systems do not perpetuate or exacerbate existing societal inequalities. Consider an AI system used for prioritizing infrastructure repairs. If historical data reflects disparities in maintenance investment across different socioeconomic neighborhoods, an AI trained on this data might inadvertently continue this pattern, leading to inequitable distribution of resources. The future engineer must possess the foresight to identify such ethical pitfalls and to actively design AI systems that promote fairness and equity. This involves understanding concepts like algorithmic bias, fairness metrics, and the importance of human oversight in ensuring equitable outcomes. The engineer, in essence, becomes an ethical gatekeeper, ensuring that AI serves as a force for good, enhancing public well-being rather than undermining it.

The proactive embrace of AI is not merely a matter of professional development; it is an existential necessity for tackling the grand challenges that lie ahead. Climate change, population growth, aging infrastructure, and increasing water scarcity demand innovative solutions that extend beyond traditional engineering approaches. AI offers a powerful toolkit for developing these solutions. For instance, in the realm of water resource management, AI can analyze vast datasets from weather patterns, hydrological models, and satellite imagery to provide more accurate long-term forecasts of water availability, enabling proactive planning and more efficient allocation. It can optimize irrigation schedules for agriculture, significantly reducing water consumption while maintaining crop yields.

In the context of urban water systems, AI can revolutionize leak detection, moving beyond reactive repairs to predictive interventions. By analyzing real-time pressure, flow, and acoustic sensor data, AI algorithms can pinpoint the location and even estimate the severity of leaks with unprecedented accuracy, minimizing water loss – a critical concern in water-stressed regions. Similarly, AI-powered demand forecasting can enable utilities to optimize pumping and treatment operations, reducing energy consumption and associated greenhouse gas emissions. This not only contributes to environmental sustainability but also leads to significant cost savings, which can be reinvested in infrastructure upgrades and improved service delivery.

The development of truly resilient water grids, capable of withstanding extreme weather events, cyberattacks, and other disruptions, will also heavily rely on AI. AI can facilitate the creation of smart, self-healing networks that can automatically reroute water flow around damaged sections or isolate compromised areas. It can enhance cybersecurity by detecting anomalous patterns in network traffic that might indicate an impending attack. Moreover, AI can play a crucial role in optimizing the design and operation of decentralized water systems, promoting greater local autonomy and reducing reliance on vulnerable centralized infrastructure.

Beyond the technical capabilities, the collaborative spirit fostered by AI integration can lead to a more dynamic and innovative engineering profession. As engineers work more closely with data scientists, IT professionals, and even social scientists, interdisciplinary collaboration will become the norm. This cross-pollination of ideas and expertise will undoubtedly spark novel approaches to engineering challenges, leading to solutions that are not only technically sound but also socially responsible and environmentally sustainable. The engineer of the future will be a lifelong learner, constantly adapting to new AI advancements and integrating them into their practice. This commitment to continuous learning will ensure that they remain at the forefront of innovation, equipped to design and manage the complex, interconnected systems that will define our future.

The transition to an AI-integrated engineering practice requires a shift in mindset from the outset of an engineer's education. University curricula must evolve to incorporate foundational AI concepts, data analytics, and ethical AI principles alongside traditional engineering disciplines. Graduates entering the workforce will need to possess not only a strong theoretical understanding but also practical experience in working with AI tools and platforms. This might involve project-based learning where students tackle real-world problems using AI, fostering the development of critical thinking and problem-solving skills in an AI-augmented context. Mentorship programs that pair experienced engineers with emerging talent, focusing on the collaborative aspects of AI integration, will also be invaluable.

Ultimately, the future engineer, empowered by AI as a collaborative partner, will be the architect of a more sustainable, resilient, and equitable world. They will leverage the immense computational power of AI to design infrastructure that can adapt to the challenges of a changing planet, to manage precious resources with unparalleled efficiency, and to ensure that essential services like clean water are accessible to all. This is not a future to be feared, but one to be actively shaped. By embracing AI not as a replacement, but as a powerful ally, engineers can unlock unprecedented potential, building the robust, intelligent systems that will safeguard human well-being and prosperity for generations to come. The journey requires continuous learning, adaptation, and a steadfast commitment to ethical principles, ensuring that technology serves humanity's highest aspirations. The engineer's role remains as vital as ever, perhaps even more so, as they guide the application of these transformative technologies toward a brighter future.

Algorithm: A set of rules or instructions given to an AI, computer, or other machine to perform a task.

Algorithmic Bias: Systematic and repeatable errors in a computer system that create unfair outcomes, such as privileging one arbitrary group of users over others.

Artificial Intelligence (AI): The simulation of human intelligence processes by machines, especially computer systems. These processes include learning, reasoning, and self-correction.

Augmented Reality (AR): A technology that superimposes computer-generated images, sounds, or other data onto a user's view of the real world, thus providing a composite view.

Critical Infrastructure: Assets, systems, and networks, whether physical or virtual, so vital that their incapacitation or destruction would have a debilitating effect on security, national economic security, national public health or safety, or any combination thereof.

Data Analytics: The process of examining large and varied data sets to uncover hidden patterns, unknown correlations, market trends, customer preferences, and other useful information.

Deep Learning: A subset of machine learning in artificial intelligence that imitates the way humans gain certain types of knowledge. It uses multi-layered neural networks to analyze data.

Ethical AI: The development and deployment of artificial intelligence systems that are fair, transparent, accountable, and respect human rights and values.

Machine Learning (ML): A type of artificial intelligence that allows software applications to become more accurate at predicting outcomes without being explicitly programmed to do so.

Neural Network: A computing system inspired by the biological neural networks that constitute animal brains. Neural networks process information through the concept of interconnected nodes or artificial neurons.

Resilience: The ability of a system, community, or infrastructure to withstand, adapt to, and recover from disruptions, shocks, and stresses.

Symbiosis: A mutually beneficial relationship between two different organisms or entities. In this context, the collaborative relationship between humans and AI.

Virtual Reality (VR): A simulated experience that can be similar to or completely different from the real world, often experienced through sensory stimuli provided by technology.

www.ingramcontent.com/pod-product-compliance
Lightning Source LLC
LaVergne TN
LVHW052018200926
848481LV00005B/1524